Double Century: A History of the MCC

To celebrate its bicentenary in 1987 the MCC opened its archives to Tony Lewis, the former England and Glamorgan captain, now a well-known writer and television commentator on the game.

DOUBLE CENTURY is the result, the highly readable and absorbing story of how a club that had its origins in an aristocrats' club in Islington became the organising body for cricket around the world.

All lovers of the game will enjoy the book's historical insights and good stories, its knowledgeable accounts of controversies such as 'bodyline', its appreciation of a rich cast of characters, and its fascinating discussion of the prospects that now face cricket, and MCC in its third century.

D0774838

About the author

Tony Lewis made his debut in first-class cricket for Glamorgan in 1955; he obtained a double blue for rugby and cricket as a Freshman at Cambridge and captained Cambridge in 1962. The same year he played for the Gentlemen against the Players in the last match of that famous old fixture. He captained Glamorgan from 1967 to 1973, and he has represented the MCC on various tours abroad, notably to India, Pakistan and Ceylon in 1972–73, when he led England in eight Test matches.

Throughout his playing career he wrote as a freelance rugby football correspondent for the *Daily Telegraph* and the *Sunday Telegraph*. He became the latter's cricket correspondent in 1974, a position he still holds, and he is now also a member of BBC TV's Test match commentary team.

He has sat on various MCC committees, was a member of the Sports Council for Wales; and is currently Chairman of the Glamorgan County Cricket Club, and President of the Welsh Schools Cricket Association. He is married with two daughters and lives in the Vale of Glamorgan.

DOUBLE CENTURY

TONY LEWIS

CORONET BOOKS
Hodder and Stoughton

Copyright © 1987 by Tony Lewis and the Marylebone Cricket Club

First published in Great Britain in 1987 by Hodder and Stoughton Limited

Coronet edition 1989

British Library C.I.P.

Lewis, Tony
    Double century: a history of the MCC.
    1. London. Westminster (London Borough).
    Cricket. Clubs. Marylebone Cricket Club, to 1986
    I. Title
    796.35'8'06842132

    ISBN 0-340-49743-2

Printed and bound in Great Britain for Hodder and Stoughton Paperbacks, a division of Hodder and Stoughton Limited, Mill Road, Dunton Green, Sevenoaks, Kent TN13 2YA (Editorial Office: 47 Bedford Square, London WC1B 3DP) by Butler and Tanner Limited, Frome, Somerset. Photoset by Rowland Phototypesetting Limited, Bury St Edmunds, Suffolk.

Contents

Note on the Illustrations

The illustrations are distributed
in two broadly chronological sequences.
Those in black and white accompany the text
throughout the book; those in colour
are grouped in four sections of eight pages each:
these start respectively on page 49, 89, 193 and 329.
    The majority of the pictures has been
selected from MCC's own collection and
these are not specifically acknowledged.
The source of those pictures which come
from other collections or ownerships is given
in brackets after each caption.
The Marylebone Cricket Club, the author and
the publishers would like to acknowledge
gratefully their use.

Author's Preface

To begin with a few defensive strokes, I should explain that I have not written a formal history of MCC nor of cricket. That would require a longer time than I was given and many more pages in the book. *Double Century: The Story of MCC and Cricket* is much more an attempt to find continuous themes over two hundred years, to follow them, and to plait them into a narrative.

Nor is it an exposé of Lord's. Geoffrey Moorhouse in his book *Lord's*, published as recently as 1983, has opened up every corner of the ground and its administration in a splendidly graphic style, and helped me considerably in the process.

Also I must apologise and explain if some names of worthy contributors to the Marylebone Cricket Club are omitted from the text. However I felt that if I followed a list of individuals rather than the mainstream of the Club's progress, the story itself would falter. So I emphasise – there has been no special concentration to mention or not to mention any individual, player or otherwise.

The Marylebone Club is still considered by some to be haughty and autocratic; many believe that a privileged, public-school style of posture still runs the cricket world as it did up to the Second World War. Inevitably MCC has attracted criticism, even anger, because it controlled all aspects of cricket in the country and was the ultimate international authority as well. All complaints were directed its way.

It can be argued, of course, that an author who is a member of MCC is the least likely to be critical. I was elected in 1965, but arrived by the 'alternative' route of Welsh Grammar School and non-commissioned National Service, as well as of Cambridge University and Glamorgan CCC. I have sat on MCC sub-committees many times and if there is a strong point which only as an insider I would want to make, it is that the MCC, in my time, has always been a chamber of fair debate, seriously democratic, everything decided in what was believed to be the best interests of cricket and cricketers. Therefore, if there is a bold line taken in this story, it is to reflect the normality of proceedings there, not to pander to any public view of a menagerie of colourful old school ties with matching accents.

Of course the story of an institution could also become a catalogue of meetings and ground developments, but if I have escaped that from time to time much is due to the diligent and resourceful research of Joanne Watson and her excellent eye for the colourful note or anecdote. I would like also to add my thanks to David Lemmon for special research and information. Happily the Lewis word-processor at home in the Vale of Glamorgan has withstood the strains but that is thanks to the patience and skills of my assistant, Sally Kennedy.

However all this tale would not have taken such form without my editor, John Bright-Holmes, who not only has seasons of publishing endeavour behind him but loves cricket too; and he would join me in thanking the curator at Lord's, Stephen Green, for his willingness to help both with the printed word and with the appropriate illustration. Lastly, I am most grateful to Professor G. Derek West for compiling the index.

January 1987   TONY LEWIS

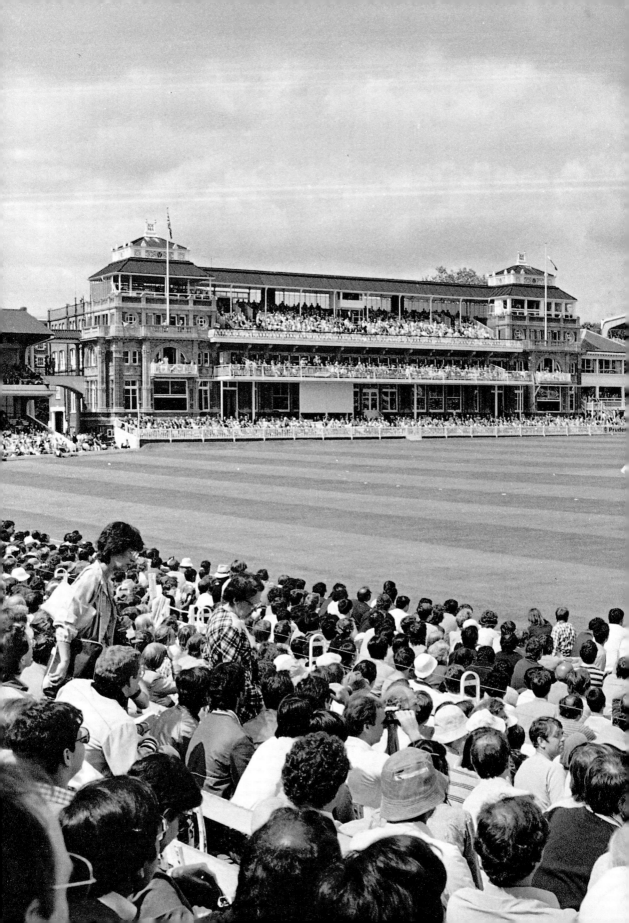

Concentration in the Long Room. *Previous page.* Lord's during Prudential World Cup match, England v. Pakistan, 13 June 1983. (*Patrick Eagar*)

1 Introduction – Lord's View

In December 1984, as the coach carrying the England team extricated itself from the ox-carts, auto-rickshaws, hooting cars, bicycles, and human pushers of overloaded wagons in Delhi, it passed under a freshly painted banner on the way down the rough road to the Feroz Kotla ground. The banner said, India v. MCC.

It seemed rude to tell the organisers, however, that the MCC had not organised an overseas Test tour for fifteen years, let alone that the last tour to bear the MCC prefix was in 1977. In the Indians' minds, as in everyone else's around the world, there has always been a confusion. To most, MCC *was* England; in Delhi at least it was unthinkable to have a Test which was not stamped with the MCC monogram, the hallmark of the genuine article.

The same misunderstanding was admitted by Sir Donald Bradman, when he was asked what his first memories were of the MCC. 'I have no first recollections of MCC,' he wrote in a letter to the secretary. 'In fact, I found some difficulty as a youth in differentiating between MCC and England. In subsidiary games in Australia the visiting team would be entitled MCC, but the same side in the Tests would be called England. No such distinctions were made for Australian teams visiting England.'

Nowadays, with the MCC two hundred years old, it is difficult for those who knew Lord's as the international headquarters of the game to understand that the MCC has transferred all powers, save only the custody of the Laws, to other councils and committees, like the Cricket Council, the Test and County Cricket Board, and the National Cricket Association. Yet if much of its public duty has gone, MCC is still a large private club, with a magnificent ground, the spiritual home of all cricket.

The image of Lord's was always of an autocratic seat, occupied by the privileged to dispense justice with an iron rod: but if the Marylebone Club was a pillar of the Empire, its reputation was also for fair play both on and off the field. The principle always applied was that decisions had to be taken in the interest of the game of cricket and of cricketers.

Because MCC accepted the responsibilities of running cricket at all levels it also attracted its iconoclasts. The Australians loved to rub some of the shine off the MCC's toffee nose. In 1948 their team raised many a glass, on the boat trip to England, to toast the apparent blindness of the MCC. Don Bradman, the captain, so report has it, kept rubbing his hands and laughing. There was England, with no fast bowlers and only one top-class medium-pacer in Alec Bedser, about to face Australia's speedsters Lindwall, Miller and Johnston, and the MCC had decided that a new ball could be taken every 55 overs. Doug Ring, the Victoria leg-spinner, was on that trip and he remembered how a role was planned for the other bowlers. 'Don told Ernie Toshack to bowl tight on leg stump and in the one Test I played at The Oval, he packed the off-side and told me to make 'em play every ball there. He just wanted us to shut up the game until the next new ball.' The figures confirm it – Ring 28–13–44–1. But if MCC thought that a quick succession of new balls would help cricket it was because they were thinking back to the shirt-front wickets and the timeless Tests of the 1930s, not to the more natural wickets of post-war England, let alone England's current lack of bowling.

West Indians also love to debunk the MCC with a story from the 1960s. At lunch on the third day of the Lord's Test of 1966 the West Indies were in serious trouble – 95 for 5 and only 9 runs ahead of England's first innings of 355. The secretary of MCC, S. C. Griffith, went to the West Indian dressing-room much concerned about the visit of Her Majesty the Queen which was scheduled for tea on the fourth day. 'Shall I see if the Queen can fulfil her visit today?' enquired Mr Griffith of the tour manager, Jeffrey Stollmeyer. The reply was, 'Can you delay that decision for an hour?' The not-out batsmen were G. S. Sobers and his young cousin, D. A. J. Holford; 274 runs later, with Sobers 163 not out and Holford 105 not out, they were able to meet Her Majesty at the appointed fourth-day teatime with their pads still on.

The MCC attracted stronger disrespect at a dinner in Pakistan in 1973, when Abdul Hafeez Kardar, formerly an Oxford University Blue who played for Warwickshire and went on to captain Pakistan, made a controversial speech in which he said it was time for the central control of world cricket to move away from Lord's. This was more than a questioning of MCC's role as the secretariat of the International Cricket Conference. Kardar believed that Pakistan was best placed geographically to replace the MCC and the old headquarters at Lord's. ICC meetings may well take place away from Lord's and England in the future, but all countries still acknowledge Lord's as the headquarters and centre of cricket.

Certain facts about Lord's are indisputable. For instance, the highest individual score there is by J. B. Hobbs, 316 not out in 1926 for Surrey against Middlesex. The best bowling analysis is by J. Southerton who, in 1875, took 16 wickets in the match for 52, all in one day. He was representing the South against the North.

The record crowd at Lord's was 33,800 to see England play Australia on June 25th, 1938; and the record match attendance 137,915, also for England v. Australia, in 1953.

Membership of the club is still prized by many and scorned by a few. There are 18,000 members and approximately 9,000 on the waiting list. Vacancies occur because of deaths, resignations or lapsed subscriptions. However, it would still take more than a decade for a non-cricketing member to get the little red membership card and the right to buy the orange and yellow colours. Back in 1939 the congestion was much worse: the wait was thirty years.

Yet there is a mystique too about Lord's. It is the great meeting place at Test match time for old friends, civilised traditions, picnicking on the lawns, chattering lunches in private boxes, bustling arbours, or gatherings around car boots; there is space and an old-world style about it. But the ground means different things to different people. Keith Miller, the Australian all-rounder, who began his association with Lord's in wartime matches for the Royal Australian Air Force, thought, when he first saw it, 'what a crummy little ground'. Nor could he believe how steep the slope was from one side to the other, a total drop in level of 6ft 6in. Yet nowadays he is able to write: 'Tradition, that's what it's called. Every time I walked up those sprig-scarred steps of the pavilion I knew I was in the very same footsteps as W. G. Grace. Every time I walk through the Grace Gates and head for the pavilion, I feel I'm home.'

To Sir Robert Menzies, Prime Minister of Australia, Lord's was 'the Cathedral of cricket'. Colin Cowdrey recalls: 'Even now I could take you to almost the exact spot among the free seats at Lord's where I was sitting that sunny wartime afternoon, just another small boy in a prep-school blazer. I was waiting impatiently for a wicket to fall because the next man in was Hammond . . . He came slowly down the pavilion steps, not a cricketer walking out to bat, but a god gracing the afternoon by his presence, and the effect on me was profound.'

Jeffrey Stollmeyer, who captained the West Indies and who is an honorary life member of the MCC, has a clear recollection of his early visits to Lord's:

I especially remember entering the Long Room in the pavilion through which one felt one ought to tiptoe. But I also recall the courtesy of the staff and dressing-room attendants and never forgetting the one and only Nancy in the lunch rooms. Jim Dunbar, such a sympathetic lover of cricket, was assigned to look after us. Any cricketer who walks on to the hallowed turf at Lord's for the first time and does not feel a special thrill, must be made of stone – not flesh and blood.

Everyone, of course, and for these very reasons, wants success at Lord's, but it takes a true sportsman, like Jackie McGlew, the former South African captain, to remind every cricket lover how the game can rarely be shaped to one's own needs.

In 1951 McGlew, 22 years old, scored 3 and 2 in the Lord's Test, falling to Tattersall twice on a difficult, rain-affected pitch. Alas, he was dropped from the remainder of the series, but he had already revealed his romantic view of Lord's, 'so heady I could almost touch, feel, taste the thousand intangibles for which Lord's and the MCC stand'.

In 1955, McGlew returned, mature and in excellent form. In the first Test he scored 68 and 51: indeed he had not scored less than a half-century for weeks before coming to Lord's for the second Test. On the morning of that match he received a tie from the talented Cambridge University player from Ceylon, the all-rounder Gamini Goonesena. Goonesena himself was to find Lord's accommodating because two years later, as Cambridge captain, he scored 211 against Oxford which still stands as the Light Blue individual record for the match. However, the tie he sent to McGlew was one which the South African had admired while playing at Fenner's and Goonesena insisted that it should never be worn until it had been earned; the qualification was a pair of ducks in a match. 'That was the crowning indignity,' recalls McGlew. 'I earned it in that very match: in a Test against England and at Lord's, with the figure of Father Time looking down upon me from the pavilion roof, no doubt in scorn.'

Jackie McGlew scored a century in each of the next two Tests both of which South Africa won by large margins, but none of his many fine Test innings came at Lord's. When he returned for a third tour, this time as captain in 1960, he scored 15 and 17 but he is as certain as anyone else that individual success is not the essence of cricket. 'To me and to hundreds of thousands of cricket lovers throughout the world, the striking red and gold of the MCC will never fail to quicken the heart-beats and arouse the sense of pride, almost elation, MCC has always stood for, fair play and total integrity.'

The present secretary of MCC is only the twelfth to hold the office since Benjamin Aislabie took it on, unpaid, in 1822. The secretary runs the club's business with the treasurer firmly at his side. There have only been fourteen treasurers since the post was created in 1826. It is an office of importance and continuity, and not surprisingly, the two commanding figures of Lord Harris and Lord Hawke alighted upon the treasurership, Harris from 1916–32 and Hawke, following, until 1938. In 1976, it was decided to split the treasurer's task and a chairman of finance took over the strictly money matters.

The president, on the other hand, changes every year, nominated by his predecessor. The change-over takes place on October 1st. The president was originally an aristocratic figurehead, a good name to have on the letter-head and in the chair at the anniversary dinner; however, the Bodyline and the D'Oliveira affairs are two of the consternations which have persuaded the club to nominate presidents with diplomatic skills as well as a love of cricket. Sir Alec Douglas-Home said there was as much paper work to review as President of the MCC, which he was in 1966, as he received as Prime Minister. Nowadays, the sort of men chosen are either those who were highly skilled in the game in their day and who have continued to help on committees, or men with high credentials in business and experience in the outside world. Only Prince Philip, the Duke of Edinburgh, has been president twice in this century, in 1949 and in 1974.

The bicentenary year president, Colin Cowdrey, captained Kent and England. He played 114 times for England and was one of the great batsmen, also an outstanding slip fielder. He scored 107 hundreds and for all his charm on social occasions he was inwardly a determined competitor, though perhaps as much riveted to the art of batsmanship as to the crunching of the opposition. Sir Donald Bradman, who responds to every challenge with the meat of the bat, still has some difficulty, however, in discerning the part the MCC has to perform: 'As for today I frankly am still somewhat confused myself over the role MCC does play, can play or should play in world cricket, and I think most overseas people share my view.' If that role is still uncertain, Colin Cowdrey's will be an authoritative voice in defining it; but should he look back into the Marylebone Cricket Club's history since 1787, he will find plenty of occasions both when its status lay in doubt and when, too, it emerged with fresh, renewed dominance and confidence.

The LAWS of CRICKET,

Revised at the STAR and GARTER PALL-MALL, *Feb.* 25th, 1784,

By a Committee of NOBLEMEN and GENTLEMEN

Of *Kent, Hampshire, Surry, Suffex, Middlesex,* and *London.*

The BALL

MUST weigh no less than five ounces and a half, nor more than five ounces and three quarters.

It cannot be changed during the game, but with consent of both parties.

The BAT

Must not exceed four inches and one quarter in the widest part.

The STUMPS

Must be twenty-two inches, the bail fix inches long.

The BOWLING-CREASE

Must be parallel with the stump, three feet in length, with a return creafe.

The POPPING-CREASE

Must be three feet ten inches from the wickets; and the wickets must be oppofite to each other, at the diftance of twenty-two yards.

The PARTY

Shall have the choice of the innings and the pitching of the wickets, which shall be pitched within thirty yards of a centre fixed by the adverfaries.

When the parties meet at a third place, the bowlers shall tofs up for the pitching of the first wicket, and the choice of going in.

The BOWLER

Must deliver the ball, with one foot behind the bowling-creafe, and within the return-creafe; and shall bowl fix balls before he changes wickets, which he shall do but once in the fame innings.

He may order the player at his wicket to stand on which fide of it he pleafes.

The STRIKER

Is out, if the ball is bowled, one ftump bowled out of the ground.

Or if the ball, from a ftroke over or under his bat, or upon his hands (but not wrifts) is held before it touches the ground, though it be hugged to the body of the catcher.

Or if, in ftriking, both his feet are over the popping creafe, and his wicket is put down, except his bat is grounded within it:

Or if he runs out of his ground to hinder a catch :

Or if a ball is ftruck up, and he wilfully ftrikes it again :

Or if, in running a notch, the wicket is ftruck down by a throw, or with the ball in hand, before his foot, hand, or bat, is grounded over the popping creafe; but if the bail is off, a ftump muft be ftruck out of the ground by the ball :

Or if the ftriker touches or takes up the ball before it has twice fill, unlefs at the requeft of the oppofite party :

Or if the ftriker puts his leg before the wicket with a defign to ftop the ball, and actually prevents the ball from hitting his wicket by it.

If the players have croffed each other, he that runs for the wicket that is put down, is out : if they are not croffed, he that has left the wicket that is struck down, is out.

When the ball has been in the bowler's or wicket-keeper's hands, the ftrikers need not keep within their ground 'till the umpire has called play; but if the player goes out of his ground with an intent to run, before the ball is delivered, the bowler may put him out.

When the ball is ftruck up in the running ground between the wickets, it is lawful for the ftrikers to hinder its being catched ; but they muft neither ftrike at, nor touch the ball with their hands.

If the ball is ftruck up, the ftriker may guard his wicket, either with his bat or with his body.

In fingle wicket matches, if the ftriker moves out of his ground to ftrike at the ball, he fhall be allowed no notch for fuch ftroke.

The WICKET-KEEPER

Shall ftand at a reafonable diftance behind the wicket, and fhall not move till the ball is out of the bowler's hand, and fhall not, by any ways incommode the ftriker, and if his hand, knee, foot, or head, be over or before the wicket, though the ball hit it, it fhall not be out.

The UMPIRES

Shall allow two minutes for each man to come in, and fifteen minutes between each innings : when the umpire shall call play, and the party refufing to play, fhall lofe the match.

When a ftriker is hurt, they are to allow another to come in, and the perfon hurt fhall have his hands in any part of that innings.

They are not to order a player out, unlefs appealed to by the adverfaries.

If the bowler's foot is not behind the bowling creafe, and within the return creafe, when he delivers the ball, umpire unafked, muft call No ball.

If the ftriker runs a fhort notch, the umpire muft call No notch.

BETTS

If the notches for one player are laid againft another, the bett depends on both innings, unlefs otherwise fpecified.

If one party beats the other in one innings, the notches in the first innings fhall determine the bett.

But if the other party goes in a fecond time, then the bett muft be determined by the numbers on the fcore.

RULES OF THE CRICKET CLUB.

ARTICLE I.

THAT each member .... and for the firft year, one guinea and a half, at the dinner, or at the tent.

II. That the club do meet to dine, at half paft five o'clock, at the Star, and Garter, on the laft Mondays in *April* and *May.* Members not attending at the dinner, (if in town) to forfeit half-a-guinea each time, which fhall go to the ftock-purfe of the club ;—if out of town, to fignify it in writing, to the mafter of the Star and Garter, two days before the dinners.—One guinea to be collected at the dinners, and the reft of the reckoning paid out of the ftock-purfe.—Members in town are particularly requefted to fend word to the Star and Garter, the day before the dinners, if they cannot dine, in order that dinner may be provided accordingly.

III. That all expences of hire of ground, umpires, bats, balls, &c. be paid out of the ftock-purfe.

IV. That the meat, &c. provided on the ground, be paid for by all the players. Members of the club going into the tent, to pay half-a-crown towards the reckoning. Any member introducing vifitors to pay 5s. and on particular matches, 5s. Players introducing ftrangers, 2s. 6d. befides their reckoning.

V. That a treafurer be elected, and a committee five, (the treafurer being one) to arrange and fettle all bufinefs relative to the club ; and to ferve one year ;—at the end of the year, the committee to name one of the fucceeding committee ; the five to chufe a treafurer from among them.

VI. That none but members of the club, are permitted to play, except when there are not fufficient members prefent to form a match ; in which cafe, any gentleman introduced by a member of the club, may play.

VII. None but gentlemen ever to play.

VIII. That gentlemen defirous of playing, are to write their names down themfelves, in the tent, as foon as they arrive upon the ground ; provided the number exceeds twenty-two, before half paft eleven, the twenty-two players to be decided by the perfons who tofs up to chufe.

IX. That any player being debarred out, and difputing the decifion of the umpires, or finding fault with them, during the match, fhall forfeit one guinea to the ftock-purfe of the club.

X. That the umpires, &c. be ready Tuefday, Thurfday, and Saturday morning, at eleven o'clock, from the firft day of *May,* to the laft day of *July.*

XI. No match began, to be interrupted by perfons who come too late.—The match to begin at half paft eleven.

XII. That at, and after the fecond meeting, no new member be admitted, but by ballot ;—a ballot may be held at the tent, twenty or more executing.

XIII. That no perfon whatever be permitted to enter the tent, unlefs introduced by a member of the club.

XIV. All matches made upon the ground, not to be played for more than half-a-crown each player, betts excepted.

XV. Any player leaving the ground without paying the reckoning of the day, to forfeit half-a-guinea to the ftock-purfe, befides his own reckoning.

XVI. All difputes relative to forfeits incurred to the club, to be referred to the committee, and their decifion to be without appeal.

XVII. All damage done in the tent, to be paid for by the perfon committing the offence.

XVIII. No horfes or carriages to be admitted on the cricket-ground.

XIX. That any member not paying his fubfcription and forfeits within the year, (if in England) be confidered as no longer of the club.

XX. That in cafe a match is not played out in one day, the players may play it out the next club-day, in preference to the reft of the club ; provided they are upon the ground, and begin playing by half paft eleven, after which time the ground to be at liberty for any other match.

COMMITTEE,

EARL of WINCHELSEA, TREASURER.
EARL of BERKELEY.
Honble. Capt. MONSON.
Honble. Mr. L. DAMER.
Sir PETER BURRELL.

LIST OF THE CRICKET CLUB.

Aylesford, Earl of	Crofbie, Mr.	Falconberg, Earl of	Ifted, Mr.	Monro, Mr.	Ruffell, Lord John	Talbot, Lieut. Col.
Archdall, Mr.	Cumberland, Mr.	Faur, Lieutenant Colonel	Ifted, Mr. George	Monfon, Mr. Charles	Rous, Sir John	Talbot, Mr.
Afton Mr.		Freemantle, Captain		Minfon, Mr. George	Rickets, Captain	Talbot, Mr. R.
		Farmer, Sir G.		Munday, Mr.	Kimbold, Captain	Thornode, Mr. T.
		Finch, Mr. S.			Rickets, Mr.	Trevrs, Mr.
	Dorfet, Duke of	Fitzroy, Mr. C.	St. John, Mr. Sr.			Tyfon, Mr.
Bedford, Duke of	Dare, Lord	Fazroy, Mr. G.	St. John, Mr. F.			
Berkeley, Earl of	Derby, Lord	Ford, Mr.	St. John, Mr. Charles	Narn, Mr.	Spencer, Earl of	
Bulkely, Lord	Davis, Sir John	Falkner, Mr. E.		Neve, Mr.	Spencer, Lord Robert	Velley, Mr.
Burrell, Sir Peter	D'Arcy, Sir N.	Frankland, Mr.		North, Mr. G.	Strathaven, Lord	
Baker, Mr. George	Damer, Mr. G.		Kingfcote, Mr.		Smith, Captain	
Barnet, Captain	Damer, Mr. L.				Smith, Mr.	
Barton, Mr.	Dampier, Mr.			Orchard, Mr.	Smith, Mr. T.	
Barton, Mr. Charles	Delany, Mr.	Graham, Marquis of			Sawbridge, Mr.	Winchelfea, Earl of
Bofanquet, Mr.	Defbrowe, Mr.	Gibbs, Mr.	Lewifham, Lord		Sheridan, Mr.	Webfter, Sir G.
	Dickens, Mr.	Gore, Mr. (of Langton)	Lake, Mr. W.		Singleton, Mr.	Watfon, Colonel
	Dooghty, Mr.	Gowland Mr.	Leicefter, Mr. O.		Smith, Mr. A.	Wells, Captain
Carlifle, Lord	Douglas Mr. J.	Grenville, Mr. T.	Lenox, Mr. C.	Payne, Captain	Smith, Mr. L.	Williams, Captain
Chewton, Lord	Drummond, Mr.	Grofvenor, Mr. T.	Lloy I.	Payne, Mr.	Snoyd, Mr.	Warren Mr.
Carpenter, Mr.	Dyke, Mr.		Lo..	Peachey, Mr.	Stville, Mr.	Watfon, Mr. L.
Cecil, Mr.				Peirfe, Mr.	Stepney, Mr. T.	Wilkinfon, Mr.
Churchill, Mr. W.		Hulfe, Colonel		Pelham, Mr. H.	Snell, Mr.	Wynward, Mr. H.
Clavering, M.	Eufton, Lord	Hardy, Mr.	May.. Lord	Pelham, Mr. T.	Snow, Mr.	Wyndham, Mr. Charles
Cooke, Mr.	Erfkine, Sir J.	Harvey, Mr.	Mo..	Pitt, Mr. George	Simons,.. Mr. J.	Wyndham, Mr. P.
Conway Mr. G.	Eaft, Mr.	Huffey, Mr.	Ma..	Philips, Mr.		Wyndham, Mr. W.
Conway, Mr. H.			Maure.. Mr.	Poole, Mr.		Wyndham, Mr. (of Norfolk)
Conyers, Mr.			M.ddox Mr.	Potts, Mr.		
			....	Poulter, Mr. Edmund	Tyrconnel, Ld.	
				Pratt, Mr.	Tarleton, Lieut. Col.	

Printed by H. REYNELL, No. ? ... ADILLY, near the HAY-MARKET.

2 White Conduit

The story of the Marylebone Cricket Club begins in the 1780s with a few aristocrats and noblemen, wealthy and game for a wager, who liked nothing so much as to take a coach-ride from their clubs in the fashionable and spreading West End of London, out along the New Road, just above Oxford Street, to the cricket at Islington. They played at the White Conduit Fields.

If now, 200 years later, you want to follow the clatter and rumble of their coach-wheels on a match day, you would have to start in Pall Mall at an office-block numbered 100, where most agree the Star and Garter inn once stood. This hostelry, popular with sportsmen, was a warren of private rooms for dining clubs. The Jockey Club (founded in 1751) held its meetings there, and cricketers went there, too. Back in 1755, the Laws of Cricket had been revised by 'Several cricket clubs, particularly that of the Star and Garter'.

Out of St James's, past Boodle's and Brooks's clubs, through Mayfair, past Portman Square and up Baker Street to the New Road, known today as Marylebone Road and Euston Road. It would be a bumpy trip on these northern limits of London. The roads were rough and rutted, and Edgware Road whenever it rained, for example, was deep sludge.

However, in those days it took a lot to separate the aristocracy from their pleasures. They were the men of property, affluent and glowing with the sharp rise of land prices. Some attached themselves to the new industrial surge, others to commerce. Almost all were conscious of fashion, looking to build a house in one of London's new squares – such as Portman Square (1764), Bedford Square (1769) and Portland Place (1778) – showing off the private ballroom in season, buying eye-catching 'fribble-frabbles of fashion' in one of Oxford Street's 153 shops, and reposing among the fine furniture of the day made by Chippendale, Sheraton, the Adam Brothers or Hepplewhite. Their silver glittered on the dumb-waiter, chinoiserie too, and tea was served from the new porcelain sets. Yet, more than anything else, our own particular heroes, the precursors of the Marylebone Cricket Club, were making a serious pursuit of leisure.

SIX PRINTS of MANLY RECREATION, as practised in PUBLIC PLACES in and about LONDON.

CRICKET, Played by the Gentlemen's Club, White Conduit Houfe, Islington.

'Representation of the Noble Game of Cricket Played by the Gentlemen's Club, in the celebrated Cricket Field near White Conduit House, Islington, 1787' – an etching. One of six prints of 'Manly Recreation'.

Shooting birds had become competitive; fox-hunting, with horses bred specially for pursuing and packs of hounds for the scent, began in this mid-eighteenth century. From the 1770s London gentlemen could race out to the country to join the Pytchley, the Belvoir, the Cottesmore or the Quorn; so a comparatively short if bumpy ride outside the small network of street lighting, beyond the police patrol, did not deter them. The White Conduit Fields (hard by the modern King's Cross station) were available for public hire. It was a rough ground, skirted only by a wooden rail-fence, but as soon as the bet was struck, the wickets pitched and a couple of scorers seated mid-wickets, with blades sharpened to notch the runs on a stout stick, battle would commence and the nobility and their friends were at peace with their world.

So if, *en route* to Islington, their clothes had been splashed by mud spun off the wheels, it would not have mattered. Cricket was played in ordinary everyday clothes. There was no change. At the field they just removed their tail-coats, some their hats, and went into action wearing whitish shirts, often frilly, waistcoats, mainly sleeveless for ease of arm movement, knee-breeches, silk stockings and buckled shoes. It is true that the Earl of Winchelsea's men also wore silver lacing around their tricorn hats, and that the Hambledon players, from that tiny Hampshire village club, had gold around theirs and also, off the field, sported sky-blue coats, black velvet collars and buttons engraved with the initials C.C. However, one of the appeals of cricket was its manliness. Outstanding players needed strength and a good eye, fitness to scamper the runs, skill and stamina to pitch the ball underarm fast and straight, and courage to stop a fast $5\frac{1}{2}$-oz ball with unprotected hand or shin-bone. Bumps and bruises showed through the stockings. So did blood. Trousers would have been an encumbrance both to a good sight of the ball and to a clear swing of the 4-lb curved bat.

Cricket was very much a betting game, too. England, indeed, suffered from gambling fever. Men bet on political events, or any future happenings. 'For a few pounds, challengers galloped against the clock, gulped down pints of gin, or ate live cats,' writes Roy Porter in *English Society in the Eighteenth Century*. 'A common wager was to take out insurance policies on other people's lives. When George II led his troops against the French in 1743 you could get four to one against his being killed.' Cards were described as 'the opium of the polite'. Gaming was the life-blood of London clubs like Almack's, White's and Boodle's. In 1751, when the Earl of Sandwich was still arranging some matches at Newmarket between 'Old Etonians' and 'England', a contemporary report said that 'near £20,000 is depending' on bets associated with these games. For the gambler, cricket's special piquancy was the second innings, where there was always a chance to recover a stake which looked lost. Our particular league of gentlemen, diners and drinkers at the Star and Garter, began to play regular games at Islington and became known as the White Conduit Cricket Club. There is some confusion exactly as to when: Lord Harris says 1782, H. S. Altham 1785. There was also some confusion over identity: in June 1786, the newspapers announced a match between Kent and the Star and Garter, but, in reporting it, headed it Kent v. White Conduit C.C.

White Conduit House and Fields were only prominent by chance. Conduits were watercourses which were being cut to take water from the Marylebone Basin, but, in 1750, the better patronised Lamb's Conduit Fields were requisitioned for the building of the Foundling Hospital. Many matches therefore needed to find a new home, and these came White Conduit's way. Then, in 1751, HRH Frederick, Prince of Wales, son of George II (1727–

60), died as a result of a blow from a cricket ball; an abscess formed which later burst. Possibly this accelerated the break-up of the London Club, of which he was the president, and the headquarters of which was the Artillery Ground in Finsbury, the scene for almost half a century of the matches that were advertised as 'great'. (The Artillery Ground had been presented to the Honourable Artillery Company in 1638.)

Not surprisingly, the lessee of the White Conduit hostelry, Robert Bartholomew, had given full vent to his entrepreneurial skills by buying space, for instance in the *Daily Advertiser* of August 10th, 1754.

> Hot loaves and butter every day, milk directly from the cows; coffee and tea and all manner of liquors in the greatest perfection; also a handsome Long Room from whence is the most copious prospect and envy situation of any now in vogue.
> Note: My cows eat no grains, neither any adulteration in the milk or cream. Bats and balls for cricket and a convenient field to play in.

Who were these gentlemen cricketers who now came to White Conduit? There was the Duke of Dorset, and the Earl of Tankerville. There was the Duke of Hamilton, who was at a cricket match in 1777 when he fell in love with his wife, Elizabeth Ann Burrell, because she made more notches than any other lady playing. There were the raisers of famous teams, the Earl of Sandwich, Sir Horatio Mann. There was Sir Peter Burrell, the Earl of Winchelsea, and Colonel Charles Lennox, the future (fourth) Duke of Richmond, names very familiar on the score-sheets of the day.

Most of them were the 'Great Patrons' who, for a long time, had kept an allegiance with Hambledon: no one can quite explain why a Hampshire village should have become the centre for some London gentlemen to gather more fine cricketers than had ever been together in one club. They were joined by Hambledon's own backers but theirs was a large share of the responsibility for the rise of cricket in the early 1770s. A nest of local players sprang up and the game's technique leaped forward. In 1772 Hambledon beat '12 of England' at Moulsey Hurst in Surrey and when they set off up to Dorking or across to Sevenoaks Vine, they were always the focus of attention.

However, it was when Sir Horatio Mann and the Duke of Dorset no longer found time for sponsoring that the best Hambledon cricket fell away, and when the money went the fine players drifted too. As they did so, around 1785, the White Conduit Club was flourishing.

London had magnetised 1 million people of a national population of 8 million. It was the centre of the aristocratic world. It

John Frederick
Sackville, 3rd Duke of
Dorset (1745–99)
pictured in 1769.
A friend of Joshua
Reynolds and a
pallbearer at his
funeral, he was
nevertheless
accounted 'not
distinguished for
mental vigour or
literary attainment'.
On the other hand,
'his raven locks and
milk white vest had
begun to allure a
crowd of feminine
spectators to the new
pastime'.

was spreading fast. There was a quickly increasing population, partly due to a significant drop in the death rate. Death from epidemic diseases had declined and would not peak again until the London and other industrial slums formed and cholera struck early in the next century. Nutrition was better; the environment was improved by such works as the drainage of stagnant waters, the paving of towns, the enclosing of sewers and the spread of piped water.

London's main artery was the River Thames. Life around it was hard. There was poverty and cruelty. Hogarth has left contemporary pictures of gin-swilling, of bony, lean faces and shrunken bodies, cramped in attics along long, gloomy streets. The rough, shambolic, poor East End spilled over into the new elegance of the West End, where the handsome squares were being built, all developed by speculative builders and by titled investors. The few were amazingly rich: the huge majority shatteringly poor.

Thus London life was brought into shocking focus. A nobleman might step out of his mansion to find himself in the middle of a herd of Welsh cattle which the drovers had brought from the West for sale at Smithfield Market. In the city the noblemen and the drovers would be castes apart; but if they had crossed paths in the countryside at cricket they might well have been at ease together discussing the merits of forward play on a bumpy pitch. It had been observed in the *British Champion* as long ago as September 9th, 1743, that 'noblemen, gentlemen and clergy' had made 'butchers, cobblers or tinkers their companions in the game'.

The Earl of Winchelsea, who encouraged Thomas Lord to find a new cricket ground nearer to the centre of London than Islington.
(*The Royal Institution*)

George, 9th Earl of Winchelsea K.G.

In the White Conduit Club there was no social mix, indeed the rules of the club stated, 'none but gentlemen ever to play'. It was natural that noblemen and gentlemen in London should spend their leisure with their own class. They were watched at play by ladies in flowing skirts and ostrich feather hats and when the day's play was over, they joked about repairing to the famous White Conduit tea-garden, a pretty lawn with a fishpond contained within a 7-ft fence to keep the noses of the general public out. It was quite the thing, so they said, for a gentleman cricketer to step on a lady's skirt, apologise profoundly and then, by way of making amends, suggest tea in an intimate arbour.

However, not everything at the White Conduit Fields was to the satisfaction of the noblemen. It was still too public; and in *The Times* of June 22nd, 1785, they were given open advice:

> It is recommended to the Lordling Cricketers who amuse themselves in White Conduit Fields, to procure an Act of Parliament for inclosing their play ground, which will not only prevent their being incommoded, but protect themselves from a repetition of severe rebuke which they justly merit, and received on Saturday evening from some spirited citizens whom they insulted and attempted *vi et armis* to drive from their footpath, pretending it was within their bounds.

It was only a matter of time before the instinct for privacy and exclusivity struck. Lord Winchelsea saw the good sense in having a ground enclosed as private property, and much nearer the West End, too. Travelling from St James's would be safer with less chance of being held up or pick-pocketed – to protect their one million dwellers London only had 1,000 constables. Winchelsea himself, unmarried, was educated at Eton and Oxford University. Although he had supported Hambledon he had not yet played for it. Indeed his first 'great' match was for the White Conduit Club against the Gentlemen of Kent in 1785 when he was 32. He had been a Lord of the Bedchamber since 1777 but spent most of his time at the family seat in Rutland, for he was extremely keen on agriculture. When the American War of Independence was being fought he is said to have volunteered himself and to have raised a regiment of infantry at a cost of £20,000.

However it was not the army which brought him into regular contact with Colonel Charles Lennox, but cricket. Lennox was a superb all-round athlete, a natural runner and jumper, a batsman and wicket-keeper of the highest class. In 1786 he and Winchelsea sounded out one of the men who acted as a ground bowler and general attendant at the White Conduit Club whether he would care to establish a private ground, assuring him, if he did, of their club's full support. The man's name was Thomas Lord.

3 Thomas Lord

Thomas Lord as a young man. (*Nina and Jimmy Thompson*)

'Thomas, son of William Lord, Labourer. Born November 23rd 1755. Baptized December 29th 1755' – a modest enough entry in the register of Thomas Lord's birthplace, Thirsk, in Yorkshire. In it there is the small indication by the description of his father's job, 'Labourer', that this was not a moneyed family. How was it, then, that Thomas Lord of Thirsk came to share the time of day with Lord Winchelsea or Charles Lennox, the future Duke of Richmond?

The Lord family had once been prosperous landowners, and it is possible to trace them back to the middle of the sixteenth century. Much of the land had been passed down to William Lord, Thomas's father, but theirs was a Catholic family. At a time when land tax was high and Roman Catholics were not only required to register their estates but were subject to penal laws, William Lord supported the Stuart cause and, in the 1745 Jacobite rebellion, raised a troop of 500 horse at his own expense to aid Bonnie Prince Charlie.

When the rising was put down, William Lord's property at Thirsk was sequestrated. To complete the humiliation, he was forced to work as a labourer on the very land he had once owned.

In time the family moved to Diss in Norfolk, where young Thomas learned his cricket.

Whatever else Thomas Lord may have acquired from his family background and upheavals, he certainly had an astonishing instinct for improving his lot, ambition and the courage to back it. After schooling in Diss he set off for London where he succeeded in becoming known both as a cricketer and as a seller of wine. He was durable and determined. He became the first Protestant in his family. Probably the cricket connections came first because he was only 21 when he first gained a job as an attendant with the White Conduit Club. He was a capable cricketer but no more, usually turning out for Middlesex. According to Haygarth's *Scores and Biographies*, 'in the field Lord generally stood at point, and his underhand bowling, for which he was noted, was slow'. On the other hand, in Sutton's *Nottingham Cricket Matches*, his bowling was described as 'extremely rapid', but that judgment may be related to the batting which was described as 'utterly inadequate'. Lord's own batting is described in *Lord's and the MCC*, by Lord Harris and F. S. Ashley-Cooper, as 'distinctly serviceable', which seems to suggest that he would be the sort of annoying 'night-watchman' who would hang on and make 25 runs the next morning.

Perhaps the White Conduit Club gave Thomas Lord his business inspiration too. From here on he certainly matched his financial enterprises to the requirements of the wealthy. Soon he would not only own the most fashionable cricket ground in the country, but he would be selling his wines from his rented office in Upper Gloucester Street to the king and to various noble houses.

Lord was 5ft 9in tall, weighed 12 stone, and was said to be a man of handsome presence as well as of charming personality. His great friend, Sir John Hall, Master of the Dock, once said to him after a formal evening in the presence of a couple of Russian grand dukes, 'Lord, you were the handsomest man present'.

Indeed, from the moment he arrived in London, the only grass which Thomas Lord allowed to grow under his feet was this cricket ground which Winchelsea and Lennox were trying to acquire. Lord seized the chance. He obtained the lease of his first ground on part of the Portman family's vast Marylebone estate and, in May 1787, it was ready for use and for members of the White Conduit Club to play there. Lord erected a high wooden fence around the ground and put up a hut to store the kit and accessories. The first certain and recorded encounter was on May 31st, 1787, a sort of county match. In Haygarth's records the teams are explained as 'Middlesex with Two of Berkshire and One of Kent, against Essex with Two given Men.' It was for 100 guineas a side.

MIDDLESEX

	FIRST INNINGS		SECOND INNINGS	
Stanhope, Esq	Run out	3	B by Butcher	1
T. Lord	B by Butcher	1	C by Newman	36
J. Boorman	B by Ditto	23	B by Butcher	37
White	B by Ditto	5	Run out	12
Z. Boult, Esq	P.O. by Clark	0	B by Butcher	18
W. Bedster	B by Martin	13	P.O. by Clark	14
G. Louch, Esq	B by Ditto	0	B by Butcher	14
G. Boult, Esq	B by Butcher	3	B by Martin	36
A. Boult, Esq	B by Martin	3	B by Butcher	0
Slater	B by Butcher	0	B by Martin	23
Oliver	Not out	0	Not out	1
Byes		7		11
Total		**58**		**203**

ESSEX

Newman, Esq	C by Louch	51	B by Boorman	5
Rimmington	Run out	28	C by G. Boult	0
Graham	B by Bedster	4	Run out	0
Clark	C by Louch	13	C by Boorman	1
Wyatt, Esq	B by Boorman	5	C by Louch	14
Butcher	C by Z. Boult	3	C by Slater	0
Jones	B by White	16	C by G. Boult	1
Davies	B by Boorman	1	B by Boorman	2
Dent	Not out	4	B by White	1
Martin	B by White	0	Not out	4
Barker	B by Boorman	2	B by Boorman	9
Byes		3		1
Total		**130**		**38**

Middlesex won, therefore, by 93 runs. It can be seen from the score-card that, when a batsman is caught out, the name of the bowler is not recorded. The word 'stumped' does not appear, but the letters 'P.O.' indicate that the batsman was 'put out' by the wicket-keeper. Wides could be bowled without penalty; leg-byes were not invented and would anyway have been quite painful for pads and gloves were not tolerated in this 'manly' game. The wickets were pitched, then as now, 22 yards apart and consisted of three stumps topped by a single bail. The old practice of having just two stumps had died out almost everywhere. The *Hampshire Chronicle* of September 7th, 1776, gives an account of a match played with three stumps, but John Nyren, the recorder of so many Hambledon tales, gives the date for the introduction of the third stump as 1779 or 1780.

The ball was only a little lighter in weight than that used today, 200 years later, but the bat was heavy – sometimes 4 lb – and

'Grand Cricket Match played in Lord's Ground, Mary-le-bone, on June 20th and the following day between the Earls of Winchelsea and Darnley for 1,000 Guineas.' Published in *The Sporting Magazine*, July 1st, 1793. One of the very few pictures of Thomas Lord's first ground.

The print, as Diana Rait Kerr points out in *The Game of Cricket* (1955), is 'unfortunately behind the times in showing a two-stump wicket. The three-stump wicket was first mooted about 1775, and was provided for in the 1785 edition of the Laws'.

a rather clumsy weapon of curved wood, in the shape of the old-fashioned dinner-knife, not unlike an extremely weighty hockey-stick.

Thomas Lord's field, which was on the site of the modern Dorset Square, became popular; and the White Conduit Club was soon being called the Marylebone Club. Although it was by that geographical description that the MCC came into being, there is no written proof that a Marylebone Cricket Club was officially founded because, as we shall read, fire destroyed all its records in 1825. However, the earliest words in the 1825 minute book refer to MCC being founded in 1787; also there is existing today a poster for a match in 1837 announcing the Marylebone Cricket Club's golden jubilee. As there would have been members in 1837 who had been alive fifty years earlier, it is reasonable to take their word for it. The Marylebone Cricket Club began in 1787.

The new club's first match on the new ground had, in fact, been against fellow members of the White Conduit Club and it was played on June 27th, 1788. Once Thomas Lord's ground was seen to be a good one, however, the White Conduit Cricket Club ceased to exist.

MARYLEBONE CLUB

	FIRST INNINGS		SECOND INNINGS	
Earl of Winchelsea	C by Price	2	B by W. le Gros	8
Lord Strathavon	C by W. le Gros	4	B by Nicholl	1
Sir Peter Burrell	Run out	14	C by Rutten	33
Hon H. Fitzroy	B by Weston	0	C by Sellers	0
Mr G. East	B by Nicholl	0	C by Rutten	16
Mr C. Drummond	B by W. le Gros	1	B by W. le Gros	4
Mr G. Louch	B by Weston	0	C by Rutten	12
Mr G. Talbot	Not out	20	B by Nicholl	31
Mr E. Hussey	B by W. le Gros	16	B by Nicholl	7
Mr Tyson	B by Weston	1	B by Nicholl	5
Mr Warren	B by Weston	0	Not out	5
Byes		4		2
Total		**62**		**124**

WHITE CONDUIT CLUB

	FIRST INNINGS		SECOND INNINGS	
Mr Everitt	B by Drummond	3	Run out	2
Mr W. le Gros	B by East	3	B by East	2
Mr Ogle	B by Drummond	0	B by East	2
Mr Sellers	B by East	0	B by East	0
Mr Rutten	B by East	0	C by Winchilsea	17
Mr Weston	B by East	3	B by Drummond	0
Mr Nicholl	B by Hussey	16	C by Hussey	2
Mr Chippendale	C by Tyson	0	B by Fitzroy	13
Mr C. Anguish	Run out	11	B by East	4
Mr J. le Gros	B by Drummond	0	Not out	10
Mr Price	Not out	0	B by East	0
Byes		6		9
Total		**42**		**61**

Recently discovered specimen of Thomas Lord's handwriting. (*North Yorkshire County Record Office*)

The Marylebone Club won by 83 runs.

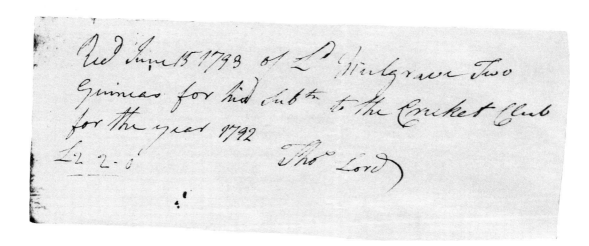

4 A New Club and a New Code

Even before they put bat to ball on Lord's ground, the members of the Marylebone Club wrote a new code of Laws for cricket: and from the start they presumed complete authority.

The first Laws had been settled in 1744, and there had been revisions in 1755, 1774 and in 1786. These had transformed cricket gradually from a folk-game with a multitude of local variations into a more standardised recreation. Some changes were introduced as the direct result of a tactic or piece of gamesmanship invented by a player, such as the bat used by 'Shock' White of Reigate which was as wide as the wicket. Nor could you now charge an opponent who was just about to catch you. But with money riding high on cricket, it was only to be expected that those who put up the money for the 'great' matches should frame the rules and regulations: they had the most to lose. This explains why the aristocrats who had drafted the 1774 code not only emphasised the gentlemanly qualities of fair play, but included regulations for the aspect of the game they had done most to encourage – gambling.

Indeed, the Laws derived their authority from the prestige of the men who made them. For example, the draftings of 1744 and 1774 were made by the London Club and 'committee of Noblemen and Gentlemen of Kent, Hampshire, Surrey, Sussex, Middlesex and London'.

Other revisions, such as that of 1755, had been made in the name of the Star and Garter Club. The gentlemen of this club had joined in the cricket at Islington of the White Conduit Club, and were now moving on to play at Marylebone. But they still made the Laws, which explains how the custom of law-making was handed on to the Marylebone Club.

The new Laws of 1788 describe a game which can be clearly recognised by cricket-lovers 200 years later. After this, only two main changes were to come: from underarm to round-arm and then to overarm bowling; and declarations.

THE LAWS OF CRICKET 1788

As revised by The Cricket Club at St Mary-le-bone

THE BALL
Must weigh not less than 5 ounces and a half, nor more than 5 ounces and three-quarters; it cannot be changed during the game but by the consent of both parties.

THE BAT
Must not exceed four inches and one quarter in the widest part.

THE STUMPS
Must be twenty-two inches out of the ground, the bails six inches in length.

THE WICKETS
Must be opposite each other at the distance of twenty-two yards.

THE PARTY
Which goes from home shall have the choice of innings and the pitching of the wickets, which shall be pitched within thirty yards of a centre fixed by the adversaries.

When the parties meet at a third place, the bowlers shall toss for the pitching of the wickets and the choice of going in.

It shall not be lawful for either party during a match, without the consent of the other, to alter the ground by rolling, watering, covering, mowing or beating. This rule is not meant to prevent a striker from beating the ground with his bat near where he stands, during the innings, or to prevent the bowler from filling up holes, watering his ground, or using sawdust, etc., when the ground is wet.

THE BOWLER
Shall deliver the ball with one foot behind the bowling crease, and within the return crease; and shall bowl four balls before he changes wickets, which he shall do but once in the same innings. He may order the striker at his wicket to stand on which side of it he pleases.

THE STRIKER
Is out if the bail is bowled off or the stump bowled out of the ground.

Or, if the ball, from a stroke over or under his bat, or upon his hand (but not his wrists), is held before it touches the ground, although it be hugged to the body of the catcher.

Or, if in striking, or at any time while the ball is in play, both his feet are over the popping-crease, and his wicket is put down, except his bat is grounded within it.

Or, if in striking at the ball, he hits down his wicket.

Or, if under pretence of running a notch or otherwise, either of the strikers prevents a ball from being caught, the striker of the ball is out.

Or, if the ball is struck up and he wilfully strikes it again.

Or, if in running a notch, the wicket is struck down by a throw, or with the ball in hand, before his foot, hand or bat is grounded over the popping-crease; but if the bail is off the stump must be struck out of the ground.

Or, if the striker touches or takes up the ball while in play, unless at the request of the opposite party.

Or, if with his foot or leg he stops the ball, which the bowler, in the opinion of the umpire at the bowler's wicket, shall have pitched in straight line to the wicket and would have hit it.

If the players have crossed each other, he that runs for the wicket which is put down is out; if they are not crossed, he that has left the wicket which is put down, is out.

When a ball is caught, no notch to be reckoned. When a striker is run out, the notch they were running for is not to be reckoned.

When the ball has been in the bowler's or wicket-keeper's hands, it is considered as no longer in play, and the strikers need not keep within the ground until the umpire has called PLAY; *but if the player goes out of ground with an intent to run before the ball is delivered, the bowler may put him out.*

If the ball is struck up the striker may guard his wicket either with his bat or his body.

In single wicket matches, if the striker moves out of his ground to strike at the ball, he shall be allowed no notch for such stroke.

THE WICKET-KEEPER
Shall stand at a reasonable distance behind the wicket, and shall not move until the ball is out of the bowler's hand, and shall not by any noise incommode the striker; and if his hands, knees, feet or head, be over or before the wicket, though the ball hit it, it shall not be out.

THE UMPIRES
Are the sole judges of fair and unfair play, and all disputes shall be determined by them; each at his own wicket. But in the case of a catch, which the umpire at the wicket cannot see sufficiently to decide upon, he may apply to the other umpire, whose opinion is conclusive.

They shall allow two minutes for each man to come in, and fifteen minutes between each innings; when the umpire shall call PLAY, *the party refusing to play shall lose the match.*

When a striker is hurt they are to permit another to come in, and the person hurt shall have his hands in any part of that innings.

They are not to order a player out unless appealed to by the adversaries.

But, if the bowler's foot is not behind the bowling-crease, when he delivers the ball, they must, unasked, call NO BALL.

If the strikers run a short notch the umpire must call NO NOTCH.

That the umpire at the bowler's wicket shall be first applied to, to decide on all catches.

BETS
If the notches of one player are laid against another, the bets depend on the first innings, unless otherwise specified.

If the bets are made on both innings, and one party beats the other in one innings, the notches in the first innings shall determine the bet.

But if the party goes in a second time, then the bet must be determined by the number of the score.

Sorting out the gambling was a priority, but almost impossible. Players were especially open to bribery when there was big money riding on the result. As Thomas Lord's ground became the centre for 'great' matches, the semi-professionals came to London for the summer. Those who could afford it put up at the Green Man and Still in Oxford Street, a jolly tavern but infested with 'legs'. 'Legs' were bookmakers' runners. They offered shady deals in dark corners and some players could not resist. The 'legs' would prey particularly on those who had been on a losing side, but who were still tucking into the good beef and best of wine at the Green Man. Everyone knew the playing fees. It was five guineas for a win and three for a loss if the player lived in London; it was six guineas for a win, four for a loss for someone who had to travel to London and take accommodation there. Inevitably there was many a young cricketer up from the country, struggling to keep his money in his pockets in the big city. The 'legs' would be at him with ready cash. Even in winter, when the cricketer had gone home, a knock on the door could mean a 'leg' down from London trying to fix a contest for the next season.

There is no shortage of examples of how cricket gambling was all the gossip. At Lord's ground in 1792, late in May, Marylebone were playing the Brighton Club. Marylebone scored 180 and 105 and the Brighton Club replied with 155 which left them 131 to win. It was 1 for 1 when the opener Marchant was out, bringing together P. Vallance and Borrer. Their partnership climbed and when they had put on 100, the spectators, wildly excited, struck bets on their winning the match without being separated. They actually bet the watches in their pockets and the rings on their fingers. There was more action off the field than on it because Vallance, 68 not out, and Borrer, 60 not out, eased home without any problem.

After a low-scoring match in 1793, in which Hornchurch scored 54 and 67, MCC 56 and 68, a revealing notice was published: 'The above game is remarked for the small number of runs on each side, which is fewer than was ever known for 4 innings together. The usual betting on a good eleven is that they do, or do not get 110.'

There were bets on individual innings, even on one stroke. In 1748 a London magistrate had ruled over a disputed wager at a cricket match that 'It is a manly game, and not bad in itself, but it is the ill-use that is made of it by betting above £10 that is bad and against the law, which ought to be constructed largely to prevent the great mischief of excessive gambling.' Despite this, there was a growing financial market for both single-wicket and double-wicket matches which gave the best professionals a chance to exploit their talents. In the double-wicket game the patron might go into the contest with his chosen man and the rivalries often became sharp.

By the turn of the century Lord's ground had established itself as a cricket centre without rival. The best players might be members of powerful counties like Kent or Hampshire, but they

Entrance to Thomas
Lord's first ground in
what is now Dorset
Square. (*Westminster
City Libraries*)

still liked to have their names on the Marylebone list. It had
become almost unthinkable that 'great' matches should be played
anywhere else.

On the field, the Marylebone Club had begun quietly. In 1790
they twice met Middlesex who were helped out by Thomas Lord.
Lord himself needed more business, so he set up unusual matches,
for example in 1790 between left-handed and right-handed men.
In 1791 the club began to keep a register at Lord's of matches
played.

The skills of the game were becoming more refined. For batsmen,
once the third stump was established in all 'great' matches from
1780, there was a much more urgent need for a sound defence:
whereas the ball used often to pass between the two stumps, now
there was more of a 'castle' to protect. William Beldham, known
as 'Silver Billy', one of the great characters of the Hambledon age
and a fine cricketer, recalled his young days about 1790 and said
that there was 'very little length bowling and very little straight
play and very little defence either'. A lot of batting had been done
from the position of the stance in the crease. However Beldham
used to run out to attack and Fennex was among the first to 'play
out at balls'. Bowlers began to try variety in their underarm style,
with break and swerve to go with their length. Thomas Brett was
very fast indeed.

Beldham could remember when all bowling was fast and along
the ground. David Harris was the extraordinary one who flipped
the ball down from just under armpit height and at great velocity.
Then Beldham saw Tom Walker, the lob bowler: 'When in 1792,
All-England played Kent, I did feel so ashamed of such baby

bowling: but, after all, he did more than even David Harris himself.' Two years after, in 1794 at Dartford Brent, Tom Walker, with his slow bowling, headed a side against David Harris, and beat him easily.

It was Tom Walker, in fact, who scored the first individual century at Lord's: 107 out of 193 for the Marylebone Club against Middlesex on May 7th, 1792, although 'Silver Billy' also made a century in the same match. Old Tom was amply described by John Nyren in *The Cricketers of My Time*:

> Never sure came . . . such an unaltered rustic . . . Tom's hard, ungain, scrag-of-mutton frame; wilted apple-john face (he always looked twenty years older than he really was), his long, spider legs, as thick at the ankles as at the hips, and perfectly straight all the way down . . . Tom was the driest and most rigid-limbed chap I ever knew; his skin was like the rind of an old oak, and as sapless. I have seen his knuckles handsomely knocked about from Harris's bowling; [David used to say he liked to 'rind 'em'] but never saw any blood upon his hands – you might just as well attempt to phlebotomize a mummy.

Walker was also a very slow runner:

> He moved like the rude machinery of a steam-engine in the infancy of construction, and when he ran, every member seemed ready to fly to the four winds. He toiled like a tar on horseback.

Noah Mann, when he batted with Walker, used to overtake him if they were going for four. Mann once tapped him on the back to say, 'Good name for you is Walker, for you never was a runner.' But whatever they said to mock him, Tom Walker's name was firmly in the history books.

Lord charged an admission fee of sixpence for the large crowds who watched the gentlemen of the Marylebone Club, splendidly sartorial now in their light blue club colours, and taking their games so seriously. On match days, Lord would hoist a flag on a pole to let passers-by know that cricket was in progress. The game was becoming popular, was beginning to settle into the affections of the country as a whole. It was local, firmly run by the noblemen, but widening rapidly in its appeal.

What was there to compete with it? Only racing and boxing, and they had quite different appeals. Cricket was the only team game. Soccer's national popularity did not come until the 1890s, over a hundred years after the founding of the Marylebone Club. And cricket's laws possessed an unusual fascination in that they were based on fair play and sportsmanship. Major Rowland Bowen, in his *Cricket: A History of its Growth and Development throughout the World* (1970), emphasises even more positive attractions:

> It possessed a fascinatingly complicated method of scoring – perhaps more complicated than any other team game even now. It provided the opportunity for displaying a great variety of different physical skills during actual play,

Sketches of cricketers in characteristic attitudes. Watercolour drawing by George Shepheard, sen., c.1790. Particularly notewothy for the only portraits in action of the Hambledon players – Walker, Harris, Beldham.

and it was and is the only game where you could 'come again': you could have a disastrous first innings but you could (if you could!) recover and even win in the second innings.

Marylebone's team did not have a programme of 'away' matches and that is why visits to Brighton and Nottingham were recorded in some detail, particularly the latter.

The first recorded trip north was in 1791. In *Nottingham Cricket Matches, 1771–1865*, A. K. Sutton reports that the Earl of Winchelsea, Lord William Bentinck, Colonel Lennox and the Hon. E. Bligh made the journey to Nottingham in their own carriages, and were attended by a convivial coterie and a retinue of servants. They put up at the White Lion and the Blackamoor's Head.

The invitation had come from Colonel the Hon. Charles Churchill, a member of the Marlborough family, who was with his regiment in Nottingham and was struck by the 'superior activity' of the Nottingham cricketers. The colonel sent a challenge to Marylebone and 'sundry lords and honourable gentlemen' responded.

Upper Meadow was chosen for the cricket. Booths were put

up, the weather was fine and 10,000 spectators came to watch. Marylebone scored 125. Nottingham got 63, went in again and made 62, leaving the club to make one run to win, which they did by running a bye. On the following day the Marylebone Club insisted on facing twenty-two of Nottingham whom they again beat, this time by 21 runs. Sutton wrote: 'All that men could do, animated by a strong desire to acquit themselves manfully in the presence of their assembled townsmen, was done: but the style of play of their aristocratic competitors was new and irresistible.'

Lord Winchelsea and his party remained in Nottingham for the entire week and spent every spare hour, so we are told, in 'cocking, milling, or some kind of gentlemanly amusement'. Yet, Sutton was anxious to point out, there was criticism.

The Duke of Dorset batting – a satirical print, 1784, from the *Rambler's Magazine*. The Duke had been appointed ambassador to the French Court in December 1783, and was even rumoured to be a lover of Marie Antoinette. (*British Library*)

From numerous well authenticated anecdotes, the following is illustrative of the fact that, whatever knowledge of cricket the 'eleven' may have imparted, they did NOT teach the provincials refined manners. One very wet afternoon, in returning from the old Riding School in Panniers' Close (the site of Clare-street, and that locality), they passed along Cow-lane (now known as Clumber-street). A deep channel or gutter ran down one side of the street and, by an accident, the cap of Colonel Lennox fell into the water which was the effect of a storm. He coolly picked it up, and dabbed it into Lord Winchilsea's face. His Lordship, incensed at the playful indignity, discharged his obligation to the Colonel in a similar manner; and the infectious example was imitated by the rest, who for some minutes, to the infinite amusement of the by-standers, paid off mutual attentions with usurious interest. The marks of defilement gave their white dimity clothes a chequered, but, as may readily be imagined, a by no means improved appearance.

The Grand Cricket Match

So these men of wealth and position put enough energy into the early days of the Marylebone Club to make certain it was active, that it lasted, and that a lot of others, jealous of the exclusive, aristocratic ambience would want to be members as well. They were the cornerstone personalities.

First among them was John Frederick Sackville, the third Duke of Dorset. He often wagered 500 or 1,000 guineas on a cricket match and his stable of professionals cost him £1,000 a year. He was a Member of Parliament in Kent in 1768 and from 1783 to 1789 was Ambassador Extraordinary and Plenipotentiary at the French Court. He brought from France the habit of taking tea in the afternoon. Does the modern cricketer therefore owe him a debt for instituting the tea interval? *Rambler's Magazine* of February 1st, 1784, attacked the duke in satirical print just after he had been appointed ambassador: he is depicted with bat poised, as one of the Frenchmen is saying: 'He no speak in de Senate but he be one bon Cricketer.'

He offered cricket influence and patronage. In 1769 the first century ever scored in cricket had been made by John Minshull for the duke's side against Wrotham. A few weeks later the duke engaged Minshull, at 8s. a week, to be his gardener at Knole, his home in Kent. He took on also the fine cricketers Miller and Bowra as gamekeepers. Then at Linton, Sir Horatio Mann employed two fine players, George and John Ring, as huntsman and whipper-in respectively. Incidentally Mann rather let the aristocratic side down by becoming bankrupt, but not before he had livened up the cricket scene with brilliant, generous occasions and many odd matches. He was always challenging a patron to cricket on horseback, for money of course, and providing the batsmen with extra-long bats. He once told Squire Osbaldeston, another early hero, that he was a better player on four legs than most men on two.

Then there was Lord Winchelsea (referred to as the eighth or ninth earl, but listed in *Burke's Peerage* as the ninth), described by Lord Frederick Beauclerk as 'urbane and loyal'. He never married, which his friends found surprising. His sister was known to wave a letter around in his defence, proving that he would have no trouble in finding a decent wife if he wanted one. It was from her lady friend in Lisbon in 1801: 'Why does not his Lordship marry? I cannot tell but it is a pity: he is so very agreeable and so formed to make others happy.' But Winchelsea apparently preferred his agriculture and took a lot of separating from his country home, Ravenstone at Burley-on-the-Hill in Rutland. And, as for his spare time in London, perhaps the jottings in his notebook supply the answer:

EXPENSES 1789

May 13	*Lost at cricket on Monday, for subscriptions, players etc.*	11 gns
May 9	*Won at cricket*	4 gns
May 21	*Lost at cricket*	15 gns
June 21	*to A. Smith for cricket*	£51.5s.6d.
June 23	*for cricket bets*	£26.5s.
July 16	*to cricket expenses at Hambledon*	£44
July 28	*gave at cricket ground*	£1.11s.6d.
July	*Rec'd balance of cricket match at Uxbridge*	£73.10s.
Aug 5	*Bal. of cricket match at Sevenoaks*	£69.16s.
	Rec'd balance of cricket match	£129.3s.
Sept 5	*Won at cards at Knole (Duke of Dorset)*	£25.4s.
25	*Balance of cricket match at Margate*	£8.8s.
Oct 12	*To Talbot cricket bet.*	2 gns

His Lordship's stakes appeared to get higher in the following year:

March 1	*Won at Hazard at Boodles*	£840
	but lost at Hazard at Whites on same day	£152.5s.
June 3	*Won at Hazard at Whites*	£315
May 1792	*Lost at Epsom*	£298.4s.

Colonel Charles Lennox was one of the first members of the Marylebone Club, and so was HRH Frederick, Duke of York, of nursery rhyme fame. Unfortunately, at the start of the third season's play they fell out over the appointment of Lennox to the command of a battalion of the Coldstream Guards. York was the Colonel of the Coldstreams and let drop some careless words about Lennox. On May 26th, 1789, they duelled on Wimbledon Common. Lennox fired and the story goes that his shot moved a curl on HRH's forehead. York did not return the fire but simply enquired if honour had been satisfied, saying that if it had not then Lennox could have another shot. Lennox did not. He turned to his second, Lord Winchilsea, York went to his, another cricketer, Lord Rawdon, and they parted.

A meeting of the officers of the Guards resolved that Lennox had 'behaved with courage, but, from the peculiarity of the circumstances, not with judgement'. Lennox was about to be posted to Scotland when he fought another duel, this time with Theophilus Swift, who had published a scurrilous pamphlet about his character. He wounded Swift in the body, but not fatally.

Lennox rejoined the 35th Regiment in Edinburgh. He took cricket there and indeed to wherever he served, including the Leeward Islands and Dublin, and he even played a game on the Heights of Abraham when he was Governor-General of British North America. He became the fourth Duke of Richmond in 1806, Lord Lieutenant of Ireland in 1807 and was seriously considered as Prime Minister in 1809.

As well as being alongside Wellington at Waterloo, this most lively Duke of Richmond had managed to fit into his already crowded life a marriage, with fourteen children. He died of rabies in 1819 after suffering a bite by a tame fox.

The fourth Earl of Sandwich was no longer an active player when the Marylebone Club began, but he was another of the original members. He was a prolific patron and maker of matches. Another original member was the Earl of Tankerville, said to be haughty but honourable: a misanthrope but very communicative when he liked his man. He was joint Postmaster-General and a Privy Councillor, and the patron who employed Lumpy Stevens as a gardener and William Bedster as a butler. No doubt he could command high-class practice at his home at Walton-on-Thames.

Why had the aristocracy taken to cricket and adopted it? It had been a village pastime and yet, by the middle of the eighteenth century, it involved landowners, the gentry, the noble people of the country. There is one simple answer: they recognised an excellent game, skilful and exciting, an individual art as well as a team pursuit. It was a game which fitted the desirable description of 'manly' and it also rewarded the player who made a study of technique and tactics. It had depth.

In his *English Cricket*, Christopher Brookes argues four strong social reasons for the attachment of the aristocrats to cricket. First, the game gave a landowner the chance to come into contact with a wide cross-section of those living on his estates, 'and by imposing his presence, increased his personal authority over them'.

Second, cricket matches enabled the gentry to renew old friendships or to make new associations with others of their class. For the landowner, matches between estates 'were a great way of keeping up-to-date with the latest gossip, scandal and intrigue'.

Another motivation suggested by Brookes was the competitive ingredient. Cricket contests with betting for high stakes was replacing duelling in the minds of gentlemen: maximum excitement, minimum of danger. A bloodless joust. The pain was in the money lost.

Lastly, cricket was a source of entertainment for those with the time and the money to indulge in it regularly, a natural for the leisured class.

Not at all in accord with this theme of the separation of society and the exploitation of cricket by nobles is the historian G. M. Trevelyan, in *English Social History*. He notes that when Kent scored 111 notches against All-England in 1744, Lord John Sackville was a member of the winning team of which his gardener at Knole was the captain. 'Squire, farmer, blacksmith and labourer, with their women and children came to see the fun, were at ease with each other and happy all the summer afternoon. If the French noblesse had been capable of playing cricket with their peasants, their chateaux would never have been burned.'

Who, then, were the gentry? The answer to this offers, perhaps a more straightforward reason why they took to cricket. They were a quickly expanding class because prosperous merchants taking advantage of the commercial times were able to buy land, and with land came position. They formed cricket teams in order to copy the manners and customs of the old landed classes.

Yet it was still the betting which was the lust. Accepting an expanding leisured class, a team game of unprecedented movement and the chance to keep in touch with sporting friends, it was still the cash game which brought the aristocracy out of their London clubs and up to Thomas Lord's field.

Within half a dozen years the Marylebone Club included in its membership the Earl of Dalkeith, Lord Strathavon, Lord Bentinck, Lord Mislington, Sir John Shelley, Sir Peter Burrell, Sir H. Marten. There are many references to cricket in the Tufton family. The Hon. John and Hon. Henry were good players and their brother, the Earl of Thanet, also played a few games at Lord's in 1791 and 1794. Thanet is probably the only member of MCC to have been imprisoned in the Tower of London. He was in his early thirties and a Whig sympathiser. In 1798 he attended the trial for treason of a man called Arthur O'Connor, who was found not guilty but who was not discharged because another warrant for his arrest was pending. Thanet and his friends, Richard Sheridan, the playwright, and Charles James Fox, put out the lights in court in the hope of smuggling O'Connor away. Subsequently, on June 10th, 1799, Thanet was charged, found guilty of causing a riot and assault, was fined and sent to the Tower for a year's imprisonment. Although it was public knowledge that Thanet was a scapegoat, it was too late for his uncle and guardian, the Duke of Dorset, to extricate him: the duke died in 1799, and for the last twenty months of his life was mad.

Right from the start there was a social scramble to obtain membership of the MCC. A London playwright, Frederick Reynolds, recalled deliriously the day his name first came up before the election committee.

> The day I was proposed as a member of the Marylebone Club, then in its highest fashion, I waited at the Portland Coffee House to hear from Tom Lord the result of the ballot with more anxiety than I experienced the month before, while expecting the decision of the audience on my new play. Being unanimously elected, I immediately assumed the sky-blue dress, the uniform of the club, and thoroughly entered into all the spirit of this new and gay scene.

5 Changing Times

For Thomas Lord, the cricket ground was only part of his great enterprise to repair the family fortune and restore it to its proper class.

He made a good marriage in 1793 to Amelia Smith (née Angell) who came from a well-known North London family and was the widow of a proctor. He was also now a property speculator. The records of the Middlesex Registry show Lord's many dealings as a buyer and seller of properties, taking leases and granting them, borrowing money on mortgage and lending it. In 1791 he took a lease of land in the western part of New Road, now the Marylebone Road, and mortgaged it. At the same time he had property in Gloucester Street and in New Street, in Orchard Street, Wardour Street and Dorset Place.

Lord's ground was still almost in the countryside, yet sometimes as many as 5,000 spectators came to watch. The entrance charge was still sixpence after 1800. The club worked out that every match cost about £70 to stage and so they appealed for financial support through subscriptions. There would be a subscription list for Surrey v. England or England v. Kent, or any big match, and also lists at Brooks's and other clubs.

But they were not all 'great' matches. Lord's ground was available for private wagers. Often they were single-wicket encounters as, for example, on a Friday in mid-October 1793, when Five Gentlemen of the Globe challenged Four Gentlemen of the MCC for 100 guineas. Thomas Lord played and besides making the highest score, took every wicket in both innings. The score was printed in *Sporting Magazine*.

FIVE OF THE GLOBE CLUB

Mr J. Beeston	*B by Lord*	1	*B by Lord*	1
Mr W. Beeston	*B by Lord*	0	*B by Lord*	0
Mr Hurnshaw, sen	*B by Lord*	0	*B by Lord*	0
Mr Booth	*B by Lord*	0	*B by Lord*	0
Mr Hurnshaw, jun	*B by Lord*	0	*B by Lord*	0
Total		**1**		**1**

FOUR OF THE MCC

Mr Ray	B by J. Beeston	I
Mr Sleeth	C by J. Beeston	0
Mr Wall	Run out	0
Mr Lord	C by J. Beeston	2
Total		**3**

In spite of the remarkable shortage of runs in that game, cricket was generally thought to be a game for batsmen, so in 1798 the MCC increased the size of the wickets from 22 inches high by 6 inches wide, to 24 by 7. Everyone gradually followed and the recorders were pleased to note that runs were much more difficult to come by in 1798.

Thomas Lord, however, could not make money solely from cricket. He would hire his ground out for anything. There were foot-races, pigeon-shooting contests and frequent hopping matches. Occasionally it was used by the St Mary-le-bone Volunteers, and more than once there was a consecration of colours presented by Lady Jane Dundas to various regiments of the Royal East India Volunteers.

In the 1780s there was a balloon craze, indeed in 1785 the first cross-Channel flight was achieved. Soon afterwards express coaches were nicknamed 'balloon coaches' because of their shape; and like everything else, ballooning was instantly commercialised, admission fees being charged for watching the preparation and take-off.

Lord was quickly into it. On Saturday July 3rd, 1802, the celebrated French balloonist Garnerin was to make his second ascent in England from Lord's cricket ground, accompanied by Mr E. H. Locker, in the presence of the Prince of Wales 'who was attended by several ladies of distinction and an immense number of the nobility'. There was such a crowd that Lord had to call out the police and the Horse Guards, but he soon had a furious horde on his hands. Because of high winds Garnerin had to postpone his act, but it was too late to stop the crush of hopefuls on foot or in carriages who jammed the streets leading to the New Road.

Just to make matters worse, it rained and when the crowd heard that the performance was off they got angry. Oxford Street was impassable; shopkeepers had to put up their shutters while the police tried to sort out the commotion.

Garnerin decided to have another go on the Monday. This time there were traffic jams for a mile and a half around Lord's ground.

The balloon was fastened on at the west end of the ground near the Long Room. Unfortunately one of the stands collapsed; a child died and many people were seriously injured.

At last Garnerin did go up. He was up at 4.50 and down in Chingford at 5.05, 17 miles away. Spectators who had charged along the New Road after him were met by a bullock produced, some said, by pick-pockets who wanted the crowd to panic and forget their purses. One person was gored and the bull ended up in the fields of Farmer Williams, who was not well pleased. He held some of the more eager equestrians for trespass and eventually released them but kept their horses. Sadly for Garnerin and Lord, Lord's ground was so overlooked that most of the crowd did not bother to pay. Garnerin ended up £400 out of pocket and a fund was opened to help him.

Cricket practice days for Marylebone members were Monday, Wednesday and Friday. There was also a Marylebone Thursday Club which had begun in 1794 and from which men of rank and title were debarred.

In 1805 a couple of schools, Eton and Harrow, booked the ground for a match: they still play at Lord's nearly two hundred seasons later. However they did not meet again until 1818 and this first match, won by Eton by an innings and 2 runs, is mainly recalled because Lord Byron was in the Harrow eleven. He batted with a runner because of his club foot and scored 7 and 2.

In 1806 the amateurs made a match against the professionals and called the match Gentlemen versus Players, because in MCC's accounts there were entries 'payment to players'. In 1806 the Players were a safe bet to win, but in this first match the Gentlemen were given W. Beldham and W. Lambert to balance the sides. In the match there were five cricketers from the old Hambledon Club which had disbanded in 1791. On the Gentlemen's side were Beldham and John Nyren and for the Players were T. Walker, J. Small and R. Robinson. In the end, the all-round play of Beldham and Lambert was crucial and the Gentlemen won by an innings and 14 runs.

There was more than a whisper at this time to say that Thomas Lord was not eager to part with money. He had always said, for example, that he would give £20 to anyone who hit a ball clean out of his ground in a match, and in 1808 he came face to face with Mr E. H. Budd, who claimed the reward. Budd was a magnificent hitter who used a three-pounder bat. While he was playing for England against Surrey he struck a mighty blow out of the ground and through the glass of a greenhouse. Lord pleaded that he had only been speaking figuratively when he had first

E. H. Budd, powerful hitter, in old age. He always wanted to win the game off a single hit, according to Lord Frederick Beauclerk.

mentioned the cash prize. He did not pay up. Everyone called him 'shabby'.

It may have been that blow of Budd's in 1808 which persuaded the Gentlemen of the club to alter the ground rules at the next general meeting. They stated that 'if LOST BALL is called, the striker shall be allowed four; but, if more than four are run before LOST BALL is called, then the striker shall have all they have run'.

A MCC 'B' Eleven was also started at Lord's. There was a match in 1805 when they beat England by 21 runs and another in 1810 when England were the winners. The 'B' side was a mixture of amateur club members and paid players, but not necessarily the best players or the first choice for 'great' matches.

The game itself was changing, too. In the early days of the Marylebone Club there were many terms used which have now become obsolete. Point was known as 'nips'; a ball that bounced twice before reaching the batsman was a 'didapper'; a yorker was a 'tice'; runs were 'notches'; an innings was often called a 'hand'; fieldsmen were 'watchers-out' or 'seekers-out'. You could always pick out long-stop – a vital man in the days of rough grounds and no gloves or pads – because he wrapped a handkerchief around his knee to protect it every time he went down to stop a ball.

Meanwhile Thomas Lord had his problems. The lease of the ground was expiring and, with London spreading and ripe for development of property, a much higher rent was requested by the Portman Estate. The Marylebone Club's aristocracy could not or would not help; Winchilsea no longer played cricket and Lennox, the Duke of Richmond, was out of the country. But as early as 1808 Thomas Lord was anticipating the problem and rented a couple of fields, the Brick Field and the Great Field, on the St John's Wood Estate, for a term of eighty years, free of land tax and tithe, at £54 per annum. The new ground was ready by 1809 and so for two seasons he had two venues on his hands. The new pitch was used by the St John's Wood Cricket Club.

In 1811 Lord's first ground at Dorset Square closed down. Thomas Lord took his hut, his hoardings, and much of his turf so that 'the noblemen and Gentlemen of the MCC' should be able 'to play on the same footing as before'. There was an atmosphere of real mourning at the main event of the club's year, the annual dinner of 1810. Then, strange to report, the new ground proved unpopular. The Marylebone Club did not play a single match there in 1811 or in 1812 and only three in the following year. Apparently the ground was far from habitation and lacked atmosphere.

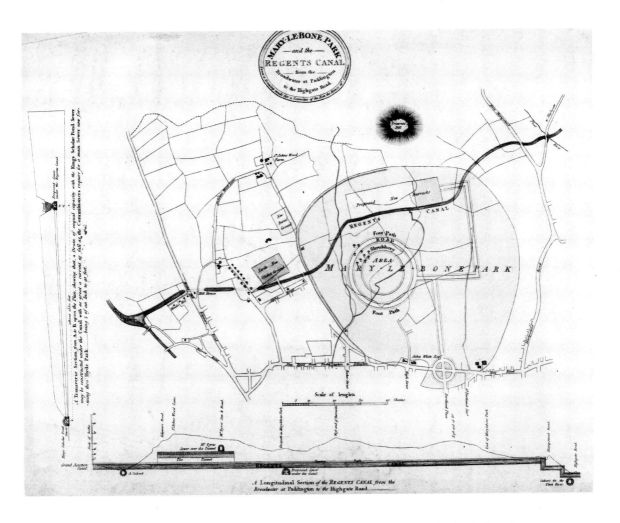

Map showing the planned course of the Regent's Canal which went through Lord's (unpopular) second ground.

Lord was in so many ways a man to be admired; but it was almost as if it took adversity to bring the best out of him. He proved that again in 1812 when Parliament informed him that they intended to cut the Regent Canal right through the middle of his cricket field. Lord made firm representations to the Eyre family who owned the land. They gave him £4,000 compensation and they found him another plot, this time in St John's Wood.

Lord dug up his turf again and paid up his first year's rent of £100. He was all ready to open at the new ground, just four days to go, when the public house there was rocked with a big explosion. As the press of the day records,

> The landlady of the house had occasion to use a small quantity of gunpowder and whilst in the act of taking the same from a paper, containing a pound weight, a spark from the fire caught it, and it went off with a great explosion. The landlady, her sister and four little girls were seriously burnt. The two former in a dangerous way.

45

For the stoical Thomas Lord, this was a mere hitch. Indeed he managed to purchase the ground lease which had almost eighty years to run and he became a very important person in the parish, a member of the Marylebone Vestry no less.

Of Lord's three grounds, the last had the smallest playing area – just 8 acres, rather inadequate for the 'great' matches. Yet his fence was in position, the new pavilion was up and the finest players were yet again in action on his turf. Mr Budd of the big hit, Mr Burgoyne, his patient if often bewildered solicitor, Mr Osbaldeston and Mr Ward, were all to go into the records as top players. There was one other, however, who already dominated all he touched. The Marylebone Club during its first quarter of a century had always been recognised as élite and aristocratic; the Rev. Lord Frederick Beauclerk was both of these, authoritarian as well, and one of the finest players of its early years.

Rev. Lord Frederick Beauclerk, D.D. (1773–1850), probably the finest player of his time. When he preached from his pulpit in St Albans, he sat on a saddle. A great gambler too.

'Squire' Osbaldeston, a notable all-round sportsman, who challenged Beauclerk. (*Roger Mann*)

6 Personification of MCC

Lord Frederick Beauclerk was an aristocrat and an amateur who played cricket like a professional. He was an autocrat who usually got his way, often bucolic on the field, arrogant enough to put a gold watch on his stumps in practice and, in the absence of a full-time secretary of the Marylebone Club, he pronounced to all on the Laws and their spirit.

The pursuit of the wager and the collection of side bets were his passions. He boasted that he could make a safe income of £600 a year from cricket, but he was not above bribing Bentley, the Marylebone scorer.

The ultimate contradiction was that Beauclerk was also the vicar of St Albans and he used to preach his sermons from a saddle which he had placed permanently in the pulpit to bring some reality to the hunt for Anglican souls. Yes, Lord Frederick Beauclerk was eccentric. Yet, the authors of *Lord's and the MCC*, F. S. Ashley-Cooper and Lord Harris, were able to write in their history, published in 1914, 'Lord Frederick Beauclerk is the greatest name in the history of the MCC.'

Lord Frederick was the fourth son of the fifth Duke of St Albans, who was a grandson of Charles II and Nell Gwyn. He was of solid, average build, 5ft 9in tall and between 11 and 12 stone. He was first discovered as slow bowler for Cambridge University by Lord Winchelsea. Winchelsea got him down to Lord's and he played his first game for the Marylebone Club in 1791. He continued to play for thirty-five seasons and completed sixty years as a MCC member before he died in 1850.

How good a cricketer was Beauclerk? The records show that his full career got going in 1796 when he was mainly a slow bowler. His style, underarm of course, was described by contemporaries as 'home and easy'; very slow, no speed on the ball to come on to the bat, but he did have the trick of making the ball hop up, to surprise the batsman.

However, the regular players began to work him out in spite of his many strategies. They recognised him as a captain with a deep understanding of batsmen which helped him to anticipate strokes, but no one in cricket had ever faced the new vogue of batsman who, following Fennex and Beldham, left the crease or 'gave her the rush'. Saunders, Beagley and Hammond were some who, as the Rev. John Mitford wrote, set the example of 'running in' at the slows. 'Hammond, on one occasion hit back a slow ball to Lord Frederick Beauclerk with such frightful force that it just skimmed his Lordship's unguarded head and he had scarcely the nerve to bowl after.'

Not that Beauclerk took this treatment well. John Nyren recalls his bowling to Tom Walker:

> Upon one occasion, on the Mary-le-bone grounds, I remember Tom going in first, and Lord Frederick Beauclerk giving him the first four balls, all of an excellent length. First four or last four made no difference to Tom – he was always the same cool, collected fellow. Every ball he dropped down just before his bat. Off went his Lordship's white hat – dash upon the ground (his constant action when disappointed) – calling Tom at the same time 'a confounded cold beast'.

Still, Beauclerk's bowling record is excellent, even though he took a lot of his wickets before anyone cared to note the bowler's name when a batsman was caught or stumped. Often he was the season's top wicket-taker. In 1797 he took 66 wickets (but the precise number of matches he played is not known), the seasonal record until 1831 when F. W. Lillywhite, with his round-arm action, exceeded it.

It was Beauclerk's batting that developed – to become scientific, elegant and prolific. His eight centuries were only beaten in his time by William Ward's nine. In aggregate only Fuller Pilch of the batsmen before W. G. Grace was higher, although it is fair to say that Pilch would have made even more runs if he had played against underarm bowling. Lord Frederick hit more half-centuries than anyone.

Imagine him coming out regally to bat, opening if it suited him, but lower in the order if there was an awkward bowler likely to be on first. He had one leg slightly shorter than the other, but it did not stop him racing for his runs to win his bets.

His friend Lord Charles Russell described him in his nankeen breeches and white silk stockings with another pair rolled over his instep, a scarlet sash around his waist, and a white beaver hat. John Nyren, trying to find someone to compare with the 'master', Silver Billy Beldham, first accuses Lord Frederick of getting out too often by trying to cut straight balls, then considering Beldham's style concludes, 'in this peculiar exhibition of elegance with vigour, the nearest approach to him, I think, was Lord Frederick Beauclerk.'

Lord Frederick was the most famous single-wicket or double-wicket player of his day. His most notorious match was against another superb sportsman, George Osbaldeston. Known as

'Cricket in Mary-le-bone Fields' by Francis Hayman (1744), shows that cricket was being played in the Regent's Park area before Thomas Lord bought his first ground in Dorset Fields, now Dorset Square. He opened it for members of the White Conduit Club in 1787, who wanted a ground nearer to the centre than Islington. He was encouraged to do this by support particularly from the Earl of Winchelsea and Colonel Charles Lennox, later the Fourth Duke of Richmond.

The LAWS) of the NOBLE) GAME) of CRIC

as Established at the Star and Garter Pall-Mall) by a Committee of Noblemen an

50

Cricket at White Conduit House c.1785,
illustrated on a silk handkerchief and surrounded by
the text of the Laws of Cricket.

A punch bowl, made in Jingdezhen c.1786,
which carries a reproduction of Francis Hayman's
'Cricket in Mary-le-bone Fields'.
No other piece of Chinese export porcelain
is known which portrays cricket.
   On the inside of the bowl is depicted a
Man-O'-War flying the Union flag of pre-1801.
On the poop is inscribed the name 'Thirks'.
This suggests that Thomas Lord himself
could have commissioned the piece,
for Thirsk was his birthplace.

A Game of Cricket *c*.1790. This painting has been variously described, but the period is clearly the last decade of the eighteenth century, which was when the top hat came into vogue. With the development of length bowling and the introduction of the three-stump wicket, bats ceased to be curved in the manner of a hockey stick, and had acquired instead a backwards arch, well illustrated here.

Fig. 72. ASCENT OF GARNERIN AND E. H. LOCKER FROM LORD'S CRICKET GROUND.
July 5, 1802.

Garnerin's ascent by balloon, July 5th, 1802.
There was a ballooning craze in the late eighteenth century.
Thomas Lord publicised Garnerin's planned ascent (in the company of E. H. Locker)
from Lord's ground 'in the presence of the Prince of Wales'.
The attempt was finally successful two days later,
when Garnerin flew 17 miles, as far as Chingford, but before
then there was difficulty in controlling the crowds.
Commercially the enterprise was a flop, because although the
crowds came to witness the event, most of the spectators were
able to do so without paying to enter the ground.
From *History of Aeronautics* (1932).
(*The British Library* and *J. Locker-Lampson*)

'Presentation of the Colours': a painting by Thomas Stothard.
The scene shows the presentation of Colours to the Bank of
England Volunteers on Thomas Lord's
cricket ground in 1805. In the early days, and even as late as the 1860s,
there was never enough cricket to make the ground pay.
(*Courtesy of the Governor and Company of the Bank of England*)

56

'Squire', Osbaldeston, of Eton and Oxford, was a brilliant rider to hounds, a superb shot – he once killed ninety-eight pheasants in a hundred shots – as well as being an expert fisherman. He was handy with his fists and promoted many a fight. He was only 5ft 6in, but muscular and fit: he was a charming man and a huge gambler. It was said that he lost £200,000 on the Turf and played cards for the highest stakes.

In 1831, at the age of 41, he made a wager for 1,000 guineas that he would ride 200 miles in ten hours. He won with an hour and eighteen minutes to spare, using a new horse every four miles.

In 1800 he won a bet of 200 guineas from another MCC member, Lord Bentinck who, on paying, let slip the words, 'This is robbery.' Osbaldeston responded with, 'This will not stop here,' and challenged Bentinck to a duel which took place at Wormwood Scrubs. One report says that Osbaldeston fired into the air, the other that a ball went through Bentinck's hat, missing his brain by 2 inches. Whatever the truth, there was a reconciliation.

As a captain, Beauclerk commanded respect because of his aristocratic birth, his outstanding play and his cricket intelligence, but when he attached his talents to the pursuit of money, as he frequently did, he became a cheat and a gamesman.

The Squire, a good hard-hitting batsman and even more menacing a fast bowler, was bound to be drawn into a challenge at some time or other with Beauclerk. It happened in July 1810 when Osbaldeston, with the paid player Lambert, challenged Lord Frederick with his man for 50 guineas. T. C. Howard was chosen.

Just before the match Osbaldeston was taken ill and suggested a postponement. 'No! Play or forfeit!' said Lord Frederick.

'I won't forfeit. Lambert shall play both of you,' was Osbaldeston's reply.

Lord Frederick complained that such a contest was ridiculous.

So, with great effort, Osbaldeston went out to play and made 1 run before retiring. Lambert then made 56 in the first innings and 24 in the second. He next dismissed Beauclerk and Howard for 24 and 42, to win by 15 runs. In fact Beauclerk looked like winning easily, but Lambert made him lose his temper by bowling wide after wide – there was no penalty for wide bowling at that time. The first straight ball then bowled him.

AT LORD'S 6TH AND 7TH JULY 1810

	BALLS	HITS		RUNS	BALLS	HITS		RUNS
W. Lambert	203	167	*b. Howard*	56	78	60	*b. Howard*	24
G. Osbaldeston	3	3	*retired ill*	1			*did not go in*	
				57				**24**

	BALLS	HITS		RUNS	BALLS	HITS		RUNS
Lord F. Beauclerk	52	27	*c.&b. Lambert*	21	60	40	*b. Lambert*	18
T. C. Howard	8	5	*b. Lambert*	3	106	77	*b. Lambert*	24
				24				**42**

Lambert (Osbaldeston) winning by 15 runs

William Lambert, professional cricketer. He helped Osbaldeston to win against Beauclerk who, however, had his revenge later.

Even more fascinating than the score-card is its omission from Bentley's book of scores because, it was said, a sum of money had been given to leave it out. There is no doubt that Lord Frederick took this badly which led to the Squire, in protest, striking his name from the list of MCC members. Some time later, when he came to live at 2 Grove End Road in St John's Wood, right next to the ground, he tried to rejoin. He had Ward and Budd, two of the most prominent men to support him, but he was prevented by the furious opposition of Lord Frederick. The autocrat was in full flow.

Lord Harris defends Beauclerk, allowing *autres temps, autres mœurs*, and that is fair. Betting was an integral part of the game, and perhaps victory alone accomplished only half of the objective. There had to be cash in hand on the carriage-ride back to St James's.

This is why the only change which Lord Frederick often made in the bowling was to switch himself to the other end. As for the batting, there is a famous account by Fred Gale, in his *Game of Cricket*, of a conversation he had with old John Bowyer after Bowyer had played a match for MCC 'B' against England at Lord's. There was a guinea lottery or sweep for the batsman who scored most runs. Lord Frederick, by chance, drew himself. Bowyer's name was drawn by Lord Ponsonby.

> Lord Ponsonby, who had drawn my name, promised me two guineas if I got most runs; but Lord [Frederick] went backwards and forwards to the scores to count his notches and mine and the end of it was that he got 64 and I got only 60. Though he did give me a guinea, Lord Ponsonby would have given me two, and I call that kind of thing which Lord [Frederick] did 'cheating' and nothing more or less.

Beauclerk's lust to win made him short-tempered, and the professionals would niggle him, like Lambert did, so that he would get furious. Not only did Lambert once 'put his Lordship out of temper', but Beldham, unseen by Beauclerk who was batting, stuck some wet sawdust to the side of the ball, and when it pitched, it broke sharply through his lordship's defence and bowled him out. But even though there were jokes and jibes against him all considered him a rare character. Hence a rhyme by Baxter in 1839.

My Lord he comes in next, and will make you all stare
With his little tricks, a long way from fair
Though his playing is fine, give the Devil his due,
There is very few like him at the Game take it through.

Yet of the few, there was one who would leave to posterity the strongest and most colourful writings on the habits of the Marylebone Club in those days. Mary Russell Mitford, author of *Our Village*, wrote of her loathing of the link between money and cricket in a letter to B. R. Haydon: it particularly concerned a match between Hampshire and England played at Bramshill in 1823.

> I anticipated great pleasure from so grand an exhibition, and thought, like a simpleton, the better the play the more the enjoyment. Oh! what a mistake! There they were – a set of ugly old men, white-headed and bald-headed (for half at Lord's were engaged in the combat, players and gentlemen, Mr Ward and Lord Frederick, the veterans of the green) dressed in tight white jackets (the Apollo Belvedere could not bear the hideous disguise of a cricketing jacket) with neck cloths primly tied around their throats, fine japanned shoes, silk stockings and gloves, and instead of our fine village lads, with the unbuttoned collars, their loose waistcoats and the large shirt-sleeves which give an air so picturesque and Italian to their glowing bounding youthfulness: there they stood, railed in by themselves, silent, solemn, slow – playing for money, making a business of the thing, grave as judges, taciturn as chess-players – a sort of dancers without music, instead of the glee, the fun, the shouts, the laughter, the glorious confusion of the country game. And there we were, the lookers-on in tents and marquees, fine and freezing, dull as the players, cold as this land, summer weather, shimmering and yawning and trying to seem pleased, the curse of gentility on all our doings, as stupid as we could have been in a ball-room. I never was so disappointed in my life. But everything is spoilt when money puts its nose in. To think of playing cricket for hard cash! Money and gentility would ruin any pastime under the sun. Much to my comfort (for the degrading my favourite sport into a 'science', as they were pleased to call it, had made me quite spiteful) the game ended unsatisfactorily to all parties, winners and losers. Old Lord Frederick, on some real or imaginary affront, took himself off in the middle of the second innings so that the two last men played without him, by which means his side lost, and the others could scarcely be said to win. So be it always when men make the noble game of cricket an affair of bettings and hedgings, and, maybe of cheatings.

So this was the Rev. Lord Frederick Beauclerk, DD, the vicar of St Albans, the verbal bully, the gamesman; but there must be something else? It was not for these qualities that he was elected President of MCC on May 11th, 1826.

Beauclerk was brave: he once broke a finger when fielding a throw from John Sherman at Nottingham. He gave Sherman a roasting, tied the finger with a handkerchief and finished the match.

During Lord Frederick's time the Marylebone Club became the accepted law-maker and the court of ultimate reference for

59

cricketers in all parts of the country. With its aristocratic core, it was the club of highest fashion and influence. London was the restless, expanding commercial capital which gave the club, and Lord's ground, a natural importance. In 1828, for the first time, the Laws of cricket required a full general meeting of the club before they could be changed.

At the same time, as emphasised by Christopher Brookes in *English Cricket*, there were no controlling fingers spreading out from Lord's through the country. 'In 1788, Leicester's victory led to a scene of bloodshed . . . scarcely to be credited in a country so entirely distinguished for the acts of humanity! In the following year, a return fixture "could not be played out" owing to a dispute between the players.' For with all the hardships of travel it is hard to see how such 'controlling figures' could have had a disciplinary hold over the mass of cricket being played in the country, at least until the coming of the railways.

Even so, in 1785, for instance, the Laws of Cricket were published in broadsheet for the first time, a sure sign of cricket's widening popularity. But much more likely than an already omnipotent MCC is an ad hoc committee, perhaps of one, Lord Frederick, who despite his penchant for betting at the guineas by the force of his personal presence, was a stickler for the Laws, a hounder of any man who tried to sell a match and, oddly, an upholder of the game's strict order to all others. The following report appeared in the *Leicester Journal* in July 1818.

> The rule of play in dispute between Oakham and Melton Mowbray Cricket Clubs, having been referred to the Marylebone Cricket Club, a decision was last week communicated by Lord F. Beauclerk that the Umpire at the bowler's end should have decided whether the striker were out or not without reference to the other Umpire, and consequently the Oakham striker was not out, and Oakham won the game.

A report in the *Norfolk Chronicle* of the same year indicated that disputes were sometimes referred directly to Lord Frederick without mention of MCC. In a match Downing v. Lynn, a batsman hitting at the ball lost his balance and fell on his wicket, and a dispute over this ended the match. A letter was sent to Lord Frederick Beauclerk requesting his opinion.

Thus it was that MCC developed as a powerful adjudicator, not in spite of the betting but because of it; because of the need for strict control when the stakes were high, a gentleman's code of conduct was imperative. So, by that strange equation, Lord Frederick Beauclerk became a personification of the Marylebone Club.

When he was not at the cricket or in the pulpit, or hunting or

The Laws, revised by
MCC and published by
John Wallis in 1809.

The LAWS of the NOBLE GAME of CRICKET
as revised by the Club at St Mary-le-bone.

winning running races at Lord's, he was shooting snipe in Belgravia. After his playing days he would still visit Lord's and sit just inside the entrance gate at the old pavilion smoking a cigar, 'attended by a little snapping white cur, which never bit anyone, but examined the calves of everyone who went in and out, and growled'. Beauclerk was the only man allowed in the ground with a dog. He would be seen seeking a corner out of the wind, on the arm of a friend. And, at the end of his days, his brougham would draw up quickly to Lord's and the autocrat, now just a ghostlike shadow, peered from a distance in the care of a lady nurse. He died on April 22nd, 1850.

7 Spreading Fast

Silhouettes of Thomas
Lord and his wife
Amelia, c.1820.

So, how was Thomas Lord faring at this time? Had his uphill trail through life levelled out into easier times? His third cricket ground was bought, the stabling was good, a tavern had gone up alongside and a wooden pavilion with several huts. All Lord needed in 1814 was the return of the Marylebone members.

The field itself, on the fringe of the great metropolis, was rough and uneven, still a rural site. There were two ponds where one of the ground-boys, Slatter, learned to swim by tying one end of a rope around his waist and the other to a tree. As soon as he got tired he hauled himself in. There was not a house to be seen on the north side of the ground until you came to Swiss Cottage. St John's Wood Church was being built at the same time; indeed, the first social occasion on the ground was the reception which followed the church's consecration.

Lord's crucial advertisement went into the *Morning Post* on Saturday May 7th, 1814:

> T. Lord respectfully informs the Noblemen and Gentlemen, Members of the Marylebone and St John's Wood Cricket Clubs that the New Ground is completely ready for Playing on: that the First Meeting of the Marylebone Club will be on Monday 9th May and continue every Monday, Wednesday and Friday during the season. The new Road leading to it is commodiously finished, the entrance to which is opposite Marylebone Workhouse or up Baker Street North, which is upwards of half-a-mile nearer than the old Road up Lisson Grove.

There was no doubt that Thomas Lord was in the right business at the appropriate time. Cricket was spreading fast. So were the reputations of the best players. Bowling was still underarm, mostly slow, batsmen were getting bigger scores, and those who were paid, not yet called professionals, were easily the best players. When Surrey beat England at Lord's in 1807, for example, there were only four amateurs in the game, all on England's side. Two of them did not bowl and they batted at numbers 10 and 11.

Thomas Lord would have known that the great drawing cards were still 'Silver Billy' Beldham, Tom Walker, that durable number one batsman known as 'Old Everlasting', and the young, outstanding all-rounder William Lambert, with his ferocious front-driving who stood with left foot a yard down the pitch, swaying his bat and body as if to get momentum and reaching forward almost to where the ball landed. Single- or double-wicket games were wonderful for betting, too, with their special rules. The bookmakers were as keen as ever to get their sites in front of the new pavilion.

It only remained for the men with the money, the aristocrats of the Marylebone Club, to renew their confidence in Thomas Lord's enterprise. This they did, almost immediately, and suddenly the ground became popular. Up went a couple of refreshment booths in the very first season, after an opening 'great' match was played between the Marylebone Club and Hertfordshire on June 22nd, 1814, which the club won easily by an innings and 27 runs.

MCC v. HERTFORDSHIRE

HERTFORDSHIRE

	FIRST INNINGS		SECOND INNINGS	
Mowbray	c Ward	4	b Beauclerk	1
H. Bentley	not out	33	run out	0
Bruton	b Budd	7	b Osbaldeston	17
S. Carter	b Budd	0	st Vigne	0
Sibley	b Beauclerk	6	c Budd	1
Taylor	c Beauclerk	6	run out	2
Denham	b Budd	10	st Vigne	21
T. Carter	b Budd	1	b Osbaldeston	0
J. Sibley	c Beauclerk	6	not out	3
Freeman	c Beauclerk	2	run out	5
Crew	b Beauclerk	0	st Vigne	0
Byes		4		5
Total		**79**		**55**

MCC

	FIRST INNINGS	
Mr A. Schabner	c J. Sibley	55
Hon. D. Kinnaird	b S. Carter	1
Mr C. Warren	b Taylor	25
Mr E. H. Budd	c T. Carter	36
Hon. E. Bligh	b Bentley	6
Mr T. Burgoyne	run out	0
Lord F. Beauclerk	b Taylor	3
Mr G. Osbaldeston	b Mowbray	18
Mr W. Ward	run out	10
Mr T. Vigne	b Bentley	2
Mr J. Poulet	not out	1
Byes		4
Total		**161**

MCC won by an innings and 27 runs.

There were also some interesting scratch games, single-wicket matches, and the St John's Wood Club met Cambridge University – all of these games getting the carriages rolling to Lord's ground once again and persuading others to book up for the next year. In 1815, Middlesex, Surrey and Epsom were all in action there.

In 1817 Epsom played in a match against Sussex at Lord's which went into the history books because Lambert, assisting the county, became the first man to score a century in each innings – 107 not out and 157. This was the same Lambert who earlier had helped Squire Osbaldeston against Lord Frederick Beauclerk, and who later in 1817 was warned off Lord's forever for 'selling' a match, justice being dispensed by Lord Frederick himself, that contradictory man who boasted that he played hard for money and yet described the game as 'unalloyed by love of lucre and mean jealousies'.

As soon as the MCC members were back, it was only natural that Lord's would be hired out to their sons. Eton and Harrow, who had played their first Lord's contest in 1805, played their second in 1818. When they came back again in 1822, it looked as if the idea of a regular match in London would catch on. Harrow certainly took it seriously because next season they hired their first professional coach from Lord's, Will Caldercourt.

The traditional letter of challenge between Eton and Harrow. This one is dated 1834.

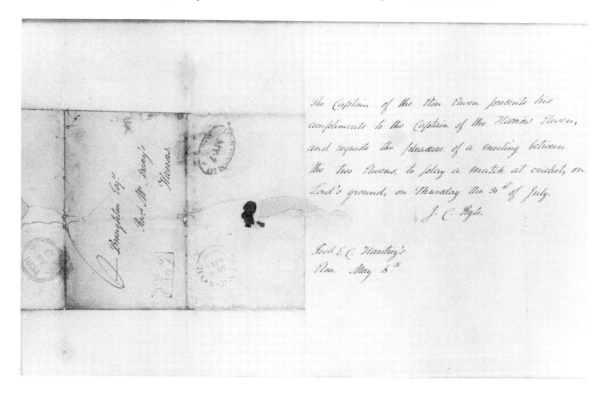

Most importantly for Lord, this game attracted its own following without his having to advertise and hope. The boys came up by coach or chaise: coach was cheaper but they preferred to save up the ten shillings a head for a chaise. Then they could all line up at the schools, give the word to charge and race, bump and rattle all the way to Lord's ground. There was a lot of overtaking, a lot of hurtling into ruts and crashing. It was a long day out: the matches began at ten o'clock and went through until eight o'clock with only a brief luncheon break, but it meant very few draws.

The third school involved with the straw-boatered boys of Eton and Harrow were the lads in the tall, white beaver hats from Winchester. Eton wore light blue, but as both Harrow and Winchester wanted dark blue, the right to wear that colour went to the school who had won the match the season before. Lord was delighted to see as many as 3,000 spectators at these school matches, especially as they were fixed to take place after the London season: the ground and pavilion were given over to the schools only when the noblemen had gone off to their country sports.

Another natural contest which came Lord's way was between the amateur cricketers and the paid players. There had been talk of a Gentlemen versus Commoners match in the 1790s, and the idea had crystallised into the first Gentlemen v. Players match in 1806. In 1819, the parties tried again but the amateurs were still not strong enough to give the professionals a decent game and so, to have a betting prospect, some of the professionals, as in 1806, had to play for the Gentlemen. In 1821 the Gentlemen batted first in a two-day match and were out for only 60. The Players batted for the rest of the match and scored 278 for 6 before the Gentlemen despaired of getting them out and 'gave up'. In this match W. C. Dyer, an amateur, was included on the Players' side, presumably because he had backed them and insisted on playing in the match. Nevertheless, within a decade of opening his new ground, Lord had seen the seeds of the 'great' matches take root, the Schools' Week and the Gentlemen v. Players.

The Marylebone Club itself could hardly claim to have set these glossy annual matches going. It was just that Lord's had become the élite venue and the boys were confirming parental connections; but whatever the accidents which created the MCC and made Lord's permanent, the forces of the nineteenth century swept both matches into a dominating position as the game spread quickly from the 1830s throughout England, Scotland and Ireland.

Although the Gentlemen could not give the Players a proper contest, there were still some good amateur cricketers. Indeed the MCC had the mighty hitter Mr E. H. Budd with his three-pound bat, Mr William Ward with his four-pounder, and 'Squire' Osbaldeston who needed two long-stops when he bowled fast. He was also a useful batsman who, in 1816, made 112 and 68 for MCC v. Middlesex at Lord's.

Budd's first match at Lord's had been for 22 of Middlesex against 22 of Surrey in 1802, when he was 17. He was an excellent catcher, an outstandingly quick stumper and he took many wickets with a high underarm action, whipping the hand through at hip-height.

Budd became involved in a famous challenge. At the annual dinner of 1820 he chided Mr Ward that he could beat anyone at a single-wicket match for 50 guineas, and challenged him to nominate an opponent. Ward was not to reveal the identity of his chosen man until the morning of the match. It so happened that Mr Ward hired Sussex's demon bowler, Brand. Budd, batting first, was battered through his silk stockings but had still scored 70 runs when he realised that he had to be at work at his War Office desk the next morning. If the match lasted more than a day, he would forfeit his money. So he hit his wicket on purpose. Brand went in and made 0. Budd batted a second time for 30, and hit his wicket down again before bowling Brand a second time for 0. 'One hundred to a duck's egg,' they all chorused, and Budd claimed, and received, his 50 guineas.

The entertainment was popular and lively. Yet, in 1825, Thomas Lord, now almost seventy, gave hints that he was not happy with the profits, or maybe he could not resist one more dabble in the property market. Whatever the case, he informed the Marylebone Club that he had permission from the Eyre Estate to develop seven pairs of houses on the ground, leaving only 150 square yards for cricket. There was not enough time for the shock to get around the whole of the MCC membership: William Ward promptly brought out his cheque-book and asked Lord how much he wanted. £5,000 rescued the ground from the builders and Thomas Lord, who had provided the Marylebone Club with a cricket ground for thirty-eight years, had retired.

He lived for a while in St John's Wood and then went to West Meon in Hampshire, only a few miles from Hambledon, where he died on January 13th, 1832, aged 76. Behind him he left the most unusual personal monument – a cricket ground, because William Ward never changed its name. It always was, and surely always will be, Lord's.

Thomas Lord.

William Ward, therefore, who played his cricket for MCC and Hampshire, is clearly one of the most important men in the MCC's early history. He was a director of the Bank of England and, later, MP for the City of London. Just five years before he bought Lord's he became known throughout the country for scoring 278 for MCC against Norfolk, the highest individual innings then made at Lord's. He was an outstanding banker, an athlete and a champion of cricket. Born in Islington in 1787, educated at Winchester, he learned his banking in Antwerp and then returned to the London Stock Exchange. He was only 30 in 1817 when he was elected a

William Ward took over the lease of Lord's from Thomas Lord and also helped to secure The Oval for cricket. A considerable cricketer in his own right, his 278 for MCC v. Norfolk stood as the highest score at Lord's for over a hundred years. His son, Rev. A. R. Ward, was a major influence in establishing cricket at Fenner's.

director of the Bank of England, specialising in foreign exchange. However, alongside him during this change of ground ownership was Benjamin Aislabie, a jovial, rotund man, who had been a member of the club since the early 1800s, but who accepted the post of Honorary Secretary in 1822. He was perfect for the job: he might even have invented it himself because he was the most diligent keeper of records and lists.

Aislabie was a bustling presence at Lord's, pursuing members with his Red Book, trapping them in odd corners of the pavilion or even in the shrubbery, asking for subscriptions, which was the way the Marylebone Club supported the game. Aislabie was also a clubbable man, mischievous in rhyme and song after dinner. Not even William Ward escaped him, nor Ward's habit as captain to bowl himself too long and to field well away in the safety of deep point.

Benjamin Aislabie, who figures in *Tom Brown's Schooldays*, was the first (unpaid) Secretary of MCC, and most assiduous in collecting subscriptions in his 'Red Book'.

With Marsden, Pilch and Cobbett too, I think it will be hard, oh!
If we don't rip the County up without the aid of Ward, oh!
'Aroint,' the Hampshire hero cried, 'Fell Aislabie, aroint, oh!
At least you will admit that I'm a deep one at point, oh!'

Aislabie, was the same gentleman as the one described in *Tom Brown's Schooldays* – 'old Mr Aislabie stood looking on in his white hat, leaning on his bat, in benevolent enjoyment'. He was a wine merchant, living part of his time in Lee Place, a fine old house in Kent which his friends used to call, because of his enormous bulk, the Elephant and Castle. He was generous. When the MCC books did not balance he was known to supply the extra cash himself. He and Ward were both genuine cricket-lovers and, although they had one big rift – there is reference in the club minutes to a mysterious letter prompting Ward to stand down from the committee and not play in 1841 when he was 54 – the two of them ensured that Lord's, after years of uncertainty when the site of the ground had been moved twice, looked safe again.

Not for long, however. In the early hours of July 29th, 1825, the Lord's pavilion, which Ward had just extended and decorated, burned to the ground. The following report appeared in *The Times* on July 30th, 1825:

> About half past one yesterday morning fire broke out in a large building called the Pavilion, erected in the cricket-ground near the school of the orphans of the clergy, on the St John's Wood Road. From the nature of the materials, which were chiefly of wood, although lately enlarged and beautified at a great expense, the fire in a very short time defied the power of the fire-engines and water, if there had been sufficient supply of the latter, which happened not to be the case. In about an hour and a half after the commencement of the fire, the whole Pavilion was reduced to a heap of ruins, saving only the foundation, which is about three feet high of brickwork. So strong was the fire, that the wooden rails round the building were partly destroyed. There was a very valuable wine-cellar well stocked in the Pavilion, belonging to the gentlemen of the various clubs who frequently play in the ground, which shared the same fate with the building. Happily no houses were near enough to the spot to be in the least danger, but some of the trees on the adjoining grounds were scorched. Yesterday a grand match of cricket was to have been played between the Young Gentlemen of Eton and Harrow Schools.

Arson was suspected because there was never any fire in the pavilion during the season, only a candle for cigar lighting. Yet nothing was proven. Within ten hours Eton and Harrow played their match. Thomas Lord would have approved how the show went on, but all the records of the Marylebone Club and its trophies were destroyed.

MARYLEBONE CRICKET CLUB – THE OLD PAVILION

When the Lord's pavilion burned down in 1825, members were surprised by the speed with which William Ward erected a new building for the 1826 season. See Colour pages, 92–3. This drawing was made in 1889 by the architect of the present building (1890), by which time the 'old' pavilion had been considerably altered. Two wings, a basement and a new frontage were added in the 1860s.

The 1825 pavilion, taken down in 1889, was rebuilt, with its wings and balcony, on the Ranfold estate in Slinfold, Sussex. It survived, used latterly as a rather grand gardening shed, into the early 1980s when it was pulled down to make way for property development.

8 Round-Arm

In William Ward, the new proprietor, Lord's was known to be in safe hands and the speed with which he carried out the pavilion improvements proved it: Thomas Lord's work would be energetically carried on, and the playing opportunities for members improved. This perhaps had much to do with the club's excellent practice bowler, 'Honest' Will Caldercourt. Caldercourt had been taken on as a ground-boy at the Brick Field when he was only six. Now, at 15, his bowling was so expert that he was given a man's wage. He could bat, too, and was soon to score six sixes off a six-ball over in a match between Watford and Hertfordshire, for which Mr Ward gave him two guineas.

Caldercourt's contemporaries among the playing servants were equally fine practice bowlers: John Bayley of Mitcham, devoted to the Marylebone Club, and John Sparks of the strange but effective pirouette bowling action in which he transferred all his weight on to the front leg and spun to face the batsman as he bowled the ball down. Also, in 1820, William Ward foretold great days for a 17-year-old who had made 0 and 2 for Norfolk v. MCC in his first Lord's match. His name, Fuller Pilch.

Tom Beagley was always in form for Hampshire, especially at long-stopping as described in an old poem.

> ... *Worthy Beagley, who is quite at the top*
> *With the bat he's first rate, a brick-wall at long-stop.*

Jordan of Chatham was the astonishing little man, often frail and unwell, with the thunderbolt hit. When he was cracking 94 for England against MCC 'B' at Lord's in 1822, he broke three bats and called to the pavilion for something heavier.

The public schools were now beginning to lead boys into the Marylebone circle, the best of newcomers being Herbert Jenner, later Jenner-Fust, who, by 1833 was president of the club.

> *Wicket-keeper or bowler or batter, in all*
> *He is good, but, perhaps shines most with the ball.*

In 1827 Oxford and Cambridge Universities met at Lord's for the first time. It is fair to say that Charles Wordsworth, later the

Rt Rev. Bishop of St Andrews, started the University match. Possibly the fact that his father was Master of Trinity College, Cambridge, made liaison easier, but it was still a feat to get the contest put on in London. Oxford's matches with 'the Marylebone' had not yet started and the travelling difficulties were considerable. James Pycroft in *The Cricket Field* says that much of the organisation was done by a Mr Cole and that, when stagecoaches from Oxford had no room, 'Private gentlemen' would convey undergraduates to Lord's in carriages and billet them among their friends.

Rain ruined that inaugural Lord's match when Cambridge were in a desperate position. Only two innings were completed: Oxford 258: Cambridge 92, and it is always known as Wordsworth's match, because Wordsworth arranged it; he was Oxford's captain, went in first, and bowled seven Cambridge men out for 25. Two years later Wordsworth organised the first University Boat Race, and rowed in that – Hambledon Lock to Henley Bridge – just two days after captaining Oxford in the second cricket match against Cambridge. In the first University match, six of the Oxford side were Wykehamists, and the Oxford number three was William Webb Ellis of Rugby School, whose name is recorded in Rugby Close as the boy who 'first picked up the ball and ran'. Also H. E. Knatchbull played, who later, as the Rev. H. E. Knatchbull, would hit so many balls down to the south side of the Lord's pavilion that it would be called 'Knatchbull's corner'!

Such was the ambience of amateur and employee enjoying their early connections with Lord's. But Lord's was not only a ground: its Committee was supposed to be the authority of the game of cricket, and yet there was a band of paid players getting more and more annoyed with the Marylebone Club and growing anxious to run games in their own way. The main battlefield was Rule 10 of the Laws of Cricket which defined fair bowling. The trouble, as far as the bowlers were concerned, was that the batsmen were on top. The most prolific run-getters were Beldham and Fennex, Lambert and Budd: centuries were beginning to become common-place. Batsmen no longer stayed inside their creases playing defensively; they advanced out of them and swung the bat as they went.

What had the Marylebone Club done, as the maker and cus-todian of the rules and regulations, to redress the balance between bat and ball? They had moved in a very reasonable way by increasing the size of the stumps to 24 by 7 inches in 1798, and in 1819, when the growth of runs became a glut, they added another 2 inches to the height. Runs still flowed, however, and bowlers moaned, so just four years later another inch was added each way, to make the wickets 27 inches high by 8 inches wide. (The present size is 28 by 9 inches.)

What could the bowlers, for their part, do about this? The answer was to scheme up to the very limit of the law. It always had been that way and always would be. How could they obtain more speed, more cut, more guile, more deceit? The old methods were not working, even though Lumpy Stevens, gardener to the Earl of Tankerville, had shown how to bowl 'the greatest number of length balls in succession' and David Harris, the finest of the Hambledon bowlers, 'would bring it from under the arm with a twist, nearly as high as his armpit, and with his action push it, as it were, from him.' Not even Nyren, that particular writer, could believe Harris's velocity.

But was it not Tom Walker of Hambledon who, back in the 1780s, had tried bowling with his arm out sideways? As Nyren put it, writing in 1833, 'he began the system of throwing instead of bowling, now so much the fashion. At that time it was esteemed foul play, so it was decided by a council of the Hambledon Club, which was called for the purpose.' True, Walker was warned not to do it again, but there was talk of another man in Kent, in Sutton Valence, who bowled what was called round-arm. His style was not popular: often he was jeered and booed.

The story of John Willes is a filigree of fact and fantasy. Some say he got the round-arm idea from his mother, who used to throw him practice balls in their barn at Fonford. Others say that his sister, Christina, was his model. Whichever it was, a lady was trying to bowl underarm while avoiding the hoops of her skirt: the arm was forced to prescribe a wide arc away from the body.

In 1807, on Penenden Heath, playing for Twenty-three of Kent against Thirteen of England, Willes bowled round-arm and the *Morning Herald* reported that this 'new' form of attack 'proved a great obstacle against getting runs in comparison to what might have been got by straightforward bowling'. Would the country's bowlers unite? There were only one or two volunteers, perhaps because they saw Willes battle against a raging unpopularity in many parts. Some games ended in uproar but, heroically, he would persevere 'till the ring closed on the players, the stumps were lawlessly pulled up, and all came to a stand-still'. Some did join him, like William Ashby, also from Sutton Valence, who used round-arm occasionally. At the Oval, Budd and Lambert claimed reasonable success with it, but a booming voice from Lord's denounced it – William Ward's. Some said it was because he could not play it!

Whether he could or not scarcely mattered. The only hope of

Silhouette of John Willes who was no-balled at Lord's in 1822 for his round-arm action and never played again in a first-class match.

order at this moment, when some players were trying to change the nature of the game, was to have a central authority, one body of law-makers. By some fluke the Marylebone Club had become that because they made the Laws. Not that players in rural areas ever felt they had to observe them. Willes's doggedness, however, and Ward's intransigence put the matter on the agenda when the Laws of Cricket were serviced by the MCC in 1816.

There appeared to be only a mild acceptance that the arm could fly out a little way from the body, but, 'The ball must be delivered underhand, not thrown or jerked, with the hand below the elbow at the time of delivering the ball. If the arm is extended straight from the body, or the back part of the hand be uppermost when the ball is delivered, or the hand horizontally extended, the umpire shall call no-ball.'

John Willes, playing mostly in Kent, out of sight of Lord's, with his arm straight out from the shoulder, was not put off. Nor did umpires stop him bowling nor opponents, apparently, complain. Clearly MCC did not have nationwide sway. However Willes saved his most determined protest for Lord's itself on July 15th, 1822. Opening the bowling for Kent against an MCC side which included Lord Frederick Beauclerk, Ward, Budd and Aislabie, Willes slung down a round-arm delivery and was immediately no-balled by Umpire Harry Bentley (though some say Noah Mann). Willes flung the ball down in disgust, walked off to his horse and rode away: the first bowler ever to be called for throwing. Sadly he never played in an important match again.

However his cricket demise only just preceded stirrings in Sussex. The county's cricket had risen suddenly; they were demanding matches with the best. Yet their prominence appeared to depend on two bowlers, William Lillywhite and Jem Broadbridge, who both used the round-arm style. The Marylebone Club called it 'throwing' yet the Sussex supporters dubbed it 'the march of the intellect system'.

Lillywhite was called the 'nonpareil' bowler. He was born near Goodwood in 1792, and his first recorded match was at the age of 30 in 1822. In the next five years he and Broadbridge raised the county to the position of the ultimate challenge, Sussex against All-England in the best of three matches. It was going to be fascinating to see how these questionable bowlers would be hit by the best batsmen, the idea coming from Mr Kingscote, the MCC President of that year, 1827.

The first of the three games, played at Sheffield, Sussex won by 7 wickets. Lillywhite and Broadbridge appear to have bowled right through both innings. The second match was at Lord's. This time

Sussex won by 3 wickets. The graceful underarm bowling method of the old school was looking unequal and outdated, so much so that a declaration was signed by nine of the England side who had been selected to go on to the third match at Brighton:

> We the undersigned do agree, that we will not play the third match between All England and Sussex, which is intended to be at Brighton, in July or August, unless the Sussex players bowl fair: that is, abstain from throwing.
> Signed: T. Marsden, W. Searle, W. Caldercourt, W. Ashby, J. Saunders, F. Pilch, W. Mathews, T. C. Howard, T. Beagley.

Nothing came of this protest and the third match was duly played, arousing more than usual interest. *The Times* of July 25th, 1827, reported:

> The grand match of cricket, between the county of Sussex and All England, commenced here yesterday. The interest which it had excited is unprecedented, and it is doubtful whether, within the memory of man, so many persons were ever before assembled at a cricket match. People have come, not only from all parts of Sussex, but from London and even distant parts of England; and the cricketing ground, which is very spacious and one of the finest in the kingdom, was literally thronged. The number of spectators present was variously estimated at from 3,000 to 6,000.

England won, but only because one of their players, Mr G. T. Knight, a powerful member of MCC, adopted what they were calling the 'liberal' method of bowling, or the 'intellect system'. He was nowhere as good as Lillywhite or Broadbridge, but he was effective and immediately established as the leading advocate to legalise the round-arm style. His opponent was a Mr. W. Denison. The battleground was the *Sporting Magazine*.

Mr Denison had the full support of the old brigade, William Ward, old Thomas Lord, and John Nyren. He argued against the new style because it was mostly inaccurate and was fatal to scientific play, put a premium on 'chance hits' and therefore made nonsense of thoughtful field-placing. Furthermore, he branded it as 'throwing, pure and simple', bound to lead to high speeds and physical danger.

Mr Knight, on the other hand, reaffirmed the current dominance of bat over ball. He complained that the Marylebone Club had made no attempt to regulate the new style reasonably by law, and insisted that, far from 'throwing', the straight arm was the very antithesis and, of course, with a straight arm it would be impossible to bowl fast and dangerously.

Lillywhite and Broadbridge continued round-arm as if nothing had been legislated and umpires refused to 'call' them. It was impossible for the MCC to sustain nationwide authority. They could be consultants and law-makers, but the day-to-day adjudication depended on the local conditions set down in wagers, and on how the umpires chose to perform their duties. Essentially, too, the professional players, an increasing body of men, could see themselves what was required to make cricket a suitably stern contest, but because the Marylebone Club itself did not possess great players there was bound to be a divergence of opinion. There was much to be said on the MCC's side. Mr William Bishop of New Bond Street wrote to *Bell's Life*: 'A gentleman, who is a member of Lord's, told me that once at practice one of these high bowlers asked whether he would like to take a few balls. "Oh, dear no!" was the answer. "If I have to meet you in the field, I must take my chance. That could be another matter entirely."'

However, even at Lord's, umpires found it impossible to apply Rule 10 because it was difficult to spot an illegal action quickly and shout 'no-ball'. In one match there in 1829, Lillywhite and Broadbridge were no-balled during the first innings but allowed to bowl uninterrupted in the second. So if Lord's could not sort the problem out, who else could or even cared to? In the *Bury and Norwich Post* of July 1831 it was noted that 'as throwing was tolerated at Lord's, the umpires, Bentley and Mathews, did not dare call "no-ball" in the county.'

Inevitably, the Marylebone Club was dragged along by the events. At last, in 1835, it was forced to accept round-arm bowling, at least up to the shoulder instead of the elbow and so Rule 10 was altered: 'The ball must be bowled, and if it be thrown or jerked, or if the hand be above the shoulder in the delivery, the umpire must call "No Ball".'

At this point it is right to consider one of the objections to round-arm bowling put up by Mr Denison and the MCC, that it would lead to extremely fast bowling and therefore to physical danger on uneven surfaces.

They could support their case by drawing attention to the first of the demon round-armers, the Nottinghamshire professional, Sam Redgate, and Alfred Mynn, the Kent amateur. Redgate had great speed and spin; Mynn, 6ft 1in and weighing between 18 and 20 stone, used to advance off half a dozen strides and whip a ramrod arm around his body faster than anyone had ever seen. The ball was said to fizz to a perfect length on leg stump and hit off. Redgate and Mynn themselves proved how ferocious such play could be. It was at Leicester in the first season of the North versus South matches, 1836. The North had won at Lord's and there was £500 a side on this return.

In practice before the match, Mynn was hit painfully on the shin. Remember that pads were rarely used in those days – but he was given medical treatment and played. However the leg was

Alfred Mynn.
Drawing of Mynn in
his prime by G. F.
Watts, showing the
characteristic action of
the round-arm bowler,
legalised in 1835.

so uncomfortable he bowled only briefly, but walked in staunchly at number five. 'The better I bowled,' said Redgate later, 'the harder he hit me away.' Mynn, batting with a runner, was many times struck by fast balls on the injured leg, but he followed his first innings of 21 not out with an heroic 125 not out in the second.

He was in agony. He called Lord Frederick Beauclerk to one of the marquees to show him the dreadfully bruised and bloodied leg. His Lordship insisted he return straight to London to see a doctor, but when the stagecoach arrived they could not fit his huge frame inside so they strapped him to the roof. Imagine the agony he experienced over the rough, rutted roads. He almost lost a leg: it was a last-minute decision not to amputate. Only slowly did he recover and he missed the whole of the 1837 season.

When he did return he was the fastest and the most accurate bowler in the land. He so confused the law-makers at MCC that, in 1845, they tried to insist that umpires call 'no-ball' if there was a split second of doubt as to whether the bowler had swung his arm around over the imaginary line of the shoulder. There was to be no benefit of the doubt. But how could an umpire be sure about an arm that flashed over so quickly?

MCC also tried to outlaw the doubtful bowlers from taking part in any match in which 'the Laws of Cricket' were in dispute. So there was a split between the old amateurs, who preferred their élite underarm games in private, and the progressives, led by G. T. Knight, who wanted professionals and amateurs to play together in a more highly skilled 'county' game. As late as 1860 Lord William Pitt Lennox remarked:

> If the present system of bowling is continued, we should strongly advise that suits of armour from the Tower of London be forwarded to all members at Lord's and other cricketing clubs. Indeed, the Household Brigade might turn out in jack-boots, gauntlets, cuirasses and helmets to contend with the Zingari in chain hauberks, steel head-pieces and iron armlets.

Eventually, in 1864, the Marylebone Club did move. It then legalised overarm bowling: the revolution that had begun in the early part of the century was complete.

The club's reputation, largely because of this question of delivery and 'fairness', could not then have been lower or less effective in its public role. Perhaps, many people were saying, the time had come to release it from its guiding role now that cricket matters were becoming more vital than the actual betting: perhaps rather than tugging an old, snorting bull by the ring on its nose into new fields, it should be released and allowed to graze quietly in its preferred pastures. Presumably, however, the members of MCC did not see it quite like that.

9 Half Century

What would it have been like to be a member of the Marylebone Club in the early days? The simple answer is – you would not have been one unless you were an aristocrat, a nobleman, or thus brilliantly connected. This did change. Benjamin Aislabie, the wine merchant, Ward, the banker, Reynolds, the playwright, were among the names and professions which widened the social scope. By 1832, the members' list included only one duke, two marquesses, eleven earls, eight baronets, twenty-three honourables and nearly 200 other gentlemen, so MCC could hardly be described as wholly aristocratic, but membership was certainly exclusive. In a national population of 13 million, a club of 245 members made the Laws of the spreading, increasingly popular game.

Gentlemen were elected as much for their social prowess as for their cricketing ability and once you had got to the rare and formal stage of a proposal for membership, it would not take long for you to get in. The Hon. F. Ponsonby, for example, was elected the day he was put up, while the Hon. Robert Grimston, whose name was brought forward on the last day of one season, was elected on the first day of the next. Only very occasionally did a candidate suffer the humiliation of a rejection at the late stage, but two blackballs out of a minimum quorum of nine could do it. It is possible to write a fond history of a glorious club with instant power, but this was not truly a body of cricket cognoscenti taking a hold on cricket wherever it was played, even though it eagerly took on the framing of the Laws. If you had asked the majority of members what was the main event of the year, they would not say a cricket match but the anniversary dinner. After all, exclusive clubs were mostly founded in the private dinner meetings. Take note of the large quantity of excellent wine lost in the pavilion fire of 1825.

The earliest dinners of the Marylebone gentlemen were at the Star and Garter in Pall Mall. After that they were put on at the cricket ground, apart from short stints at the Clarendon Hotel in Bond Street, Grillions in Albemarle Street and occasional venues in St James's. Early in the nineteenth century dinner began at 5.20 p.m., later it eased out to 7 or 7.30 p.m.

Membership did swell. By 1842 it was 381 and there were strong

J. H. Dark – from ground-boy to owner of Lord's where the grass was kept short by sheep. Dark proved an enterprising showman at a time when Lord's staged no more than 23 cricket matches a season.

words being scrawled in the complaints book about accommodation. The Committee duly resolved: 'That complaints having been made that the Pavilion is frequently too crowded, no Gentleman, who is not a Member, can be allowed to make use of it, unless actually engaged in a Match.'

The membership subscription at this time was raised by the consent of all. The method for major rule changes within a club which had no professional administration was for one member to take on a revision. The 1843 revision was done by Sir John Bayley, Bart., and approved at the general meeting before the anniversary dinner. Every new member had to pay £1 entrance to the stock purse as well as his first yearly subscription of £3. Of his subsequent £3 a year, half a sovereign went to the stock purse.

As for the members' cricket, there was always practice, even if no selection, for major games with perhaps Thomas Lord himself and 'Honest Will', Caldercourt's father, to bowl a few at the ground. Samuel Britcher was the scorer, but a ground staff as such did not exist until later. In 1826, when the club was in its fortieth year, there were still only four bowlers at Lord's and two boys for fielding, called scouts. There were four days a week for practice between four o'clock and six.

The lease of Lord's remained with William Ward for ten years but in 1835, because of a 'reverse of fortune', he transferred the lease with fifty-eight years left to Mr J. H. Dark, for £2,000 and an annuity of £425. Dark knew all of Lord's grounds. He had been born in the Edgware Road in 1795, the son of a saddler, and by the age of ten used to earn a little money as fielder for practices at the first Lord's, the Dorset Square site. He was now 39 and listed in the 1851 census as 'proprietor of houses'.

Dark was very much the entrepreneur and improver of Lord's ground. He took over a rural scene in which Lord's was like a village green with post-and-chain fencing and in the middle of the bumpy grassy field was a patch constantly rolled for the cricket. Generally, it was a ridge-and-furrow surface; you could easily wrench an ankle while fielding and the pitch itself was uneven and often stony. A scythe would have been useful, but it was not allowed and mowers were not yet invented.

The grass was kept low by sheep which were penned up on match days. As many as 400 sheep would be driven on to the pitch some Saturdays, to chew around before being ushered to Smithfield Market on Monday. They cleaned the herbage and then the boys went around after them to pick up the rough stalks.

In those days the creases on the actual pitch were cut with a knife. A lot of effort went into it, but Dark, and presumably his advisers, failed to realise, especially since faster round-arm bowling with its higher bounce was legalised in 1835, that the playing surface should be 'as flat as table beer' as the *Sporting Magazine* said. Instead, this Lord's was described as bumpy and dangerous by batsmen, but, by bowlers, full of life and spirit.

The ground was not exclusively held for the Marylebone members. On non-match days the public could hire an old pitch, stumps, bat and ball for one shilling. The man who looked after everything on the ground for Mr Dark was Stevey Slatter, and on a fine Saturday, when the MCC was not playing, he would fit in enough matches, side by side, to make as much as £20.

It was a struggle for Dark to make the cricket pay, however. Between 1830 and 1863 there were never more than twenty-three MCC matches at Lord's in a year and sometimes as few as nine. Most club members did not show a jot of interest in the daily running of the ground or even in the club's cricket.

Dark had arrived just in time for an historical year, 1837. It was the year of Queen Victoria's accession, of course, but it was also the golden jubilee of the Marylebone Club. The grand match to celebrate it was North v. South, but there was no great publicity because it took place two days after the funeral of William IV.

Mr Aislabie, always the man for celebration, whether in verse or song, or even in the club minutes, declared:

> The Marylebone Club having been established in the year 1787, it is resolved that a Jubilee Match shall take place at Lord's Ground on the second Monday in July 1837, for the benefit of the Players; twenty-two of whom shall be chosen to perform on that day. The Earl of Thanet and the Lord Frederick Beauclerk are requested to make the selection: and every Member of the Club is solicited for a subscription of One Pound towards the promotion of the sport on this interesting occasion.

South beat the North, who were given Box, the Sussex stumper, and Cobbett, the Surrey spinner, by five wickets. They were two superb days' cricket, swayed in the South's favour by William Lillywhite's fourteen wickets. In fact, the betting throughout had been on the South. Three thousand spectators attended on both days. There were social sightings of Lords Thanet, Chesterfield, Beauclerk, March, Portman, Craven, Verulam, Lyttelton, Aboyne and Suffield among what was described in the newspapers as 'a long list of fashionables'.

After the match, all those who played attended the jubilee dinner which 'was served up in Mr Dark's usual excellent style and consisted of every delicacy of the season'.

NORTH v. SOUTH

Played at Lord's, July 10th and 11th, 1837

THE NORTH, *with* BOX *and* COBBETT

W. Garrat	*run out*	5	*b Lillywhite*	25
H. Hall	*b Lillywhite*	14	*b Lillywhite*	0
T. Barker	*c Dorrington b Millyard*	1	*st Wenman b Lillywhite*	0
G. Jarvis	*c Dorrington b Lillywhite*	17	*c Wenman b Lillywhite*	0
J. Cobbett	*b Lillywhite*	0	*b Lillywhite*	15
E. Vincent	*b Lillywhite*	7	*b Lillywhite*	0
T. Marsden	*st Wenman b Millyard*	5	*c Lillywhite b Adams*	1
J. Dearman	*b Millyard*	8	*not out*	7
T. Box	*c Adams b Lillywhite*	4	*hit wkt b Lillywhite*	0
S. Redgate	*c Pilch b Lillywhite*	2	*c Pilch b Adams*	12
G. Rothera	*not out*	0	*b Lillywhite*	0
Extras	*Byes*	1		5
Total		**64**		**65**

THE SOUTH

T. Beagley	*b Redgate*	5		
J. Broadbridge	*st Box b Redgate*	0	*c Redgate b Cobbett*	8
W. Ward	*c Box b Redgate*	0	*not out*	0
E. G. Wenman	*b Cobbett*	4	*not out*	7
F. Pilch	*c Box b Redgate*	13		
J. Taylor	*b Cobbett*	14		
G. Millyard	*b Redgate*	5	*b Redgate*	23
T. Adams	*b Cobbett*	0	*b Redgate*	1
W. Clifford	*not out*	6	*b Redgate*	26
W. Dorrinton	*b Redgate*	0	*b Cobbett*	0
W. Lillywhite	*b Cobbett*	0		
Extras	*Byes* 12, *wides* 1	13	*Byes* 4, *wide* 1	5
Total		**60**	*Total* (5 wkts.)	**70**

The South won by five wickets

1837 Jubilee goblet.

Dark's enterprises were helped along by the regular playing at Lord's of the Gentlemen v. Players match, although in this same season, 1837, there was the ultimate proof that the series had become a farce. The professionals were far too strong. Every year the amateur sides had to poach the best professionals to create any sort of market for the odds: they had not won a level match since 1822. For example, when Dark took over Lord's, in the first Gentlemen v. Players match he staged in 1835, he saw one of the most brilliant professionals, Fuller Pilch, bowled out twice by the Gentlemen, without scoring; but that 'Gent' was in fact the ferocious round-armer, Redgate of Nottingham.

Next season, 1836, the Gentlemen put out a team of eighteen against the Players' eleven. Alongside the great amateurs, such as Mynn and Jenner-Fust, were three Winchester schoolboys, astonishing choices. In an earlier MCC match against Winchester, the members had been impressed by the performances of A. J. Lowth, N. Darnell and the Hon. W. L. Pakenham, particularly Lowth's left-arm bowling. As it turned out, Lowth took nine wickets, Alfred Mynn eight and the Gentlemen won by 35 runs. The score-card of the game was written up for the first time, as it is in modern days, with bowlers credited with catches and stumpings.

THE GENTLEMEN

	FIRST INNINGS		SECOND INNINGS	
A Mynn	run out	29	c Redgate b Cobbett	30
W. Mynn	c Cobbett b Redgate	20	b Bayley	10
C. G. Taylor	b Redgate	3	b Redgate	0
Hon. E. H. Grimston	b Redgate	3	b Redgate	1
Hon. F. Ponsonby	b Redgate	6	b Barker	0
A. Lowth	b Redgate	0	b Redgate	1
H. Jenner	b Bayley	1	b Redgate	6
Lord Grimston	run out	21	b Corbett	15
E. H. Pickering	b Bayley	3	run out	10
F. J. Pigou	run out	3	c Cobbett b Bayley	0
J. Strange	c Clifford b Barker	1	b Cobbett	7
H. Walker	b Redgate	2	b Redgate	1
A. Buller	b Barker	5	b Cobbett	0
C. Parnther	st E. G. Wenman b Redgate	1	b Redgate	0
Hon. W. L. Pakenham	c Pilch b Barker	0	st E. G. Wenman b Cobbett	0
W. Brown	b Barker	0	b Cobbett	0
C. Beacham	not out	0	not out	0
N. Darnell	absent	0	b Cobbett	0
Extras	Byes 11, wides 6	17	Byes 13, wides 1, no-ball 1	15
Total		**115**	*Total*	**96**

THE PLAYERS

T. Barker	b A. Mynn	8	b A. Mynn	13
R. Mills	b A. Mynn	2	b A. Mynn	2
J. G. Wenman	b Lowth	1	b Lowth	13
F. Pilch	b A. Mynn	5	c and b A. Mynn	5
J. Cobbett	b Lowth	4	b A. Mynn	3
E. G. Wenman	b Taylor	1	b Lowth	19

Contd.	FIRST INNINGS		SECOND INNINGS	
S. Redgate	*b A. Mynn*	9	*c Taylor b Darnell*	3
J. Bayley	*b Lowth*	8	*c Lord Grimston* *b Lowth*	2
G. Jarvis	*run out*	4	*b Lowth*	3
T. Beagley	*not out*	1	*b Lowth*	0
W. Clifford	*c Darnell b Lowth*	5	*not out*	0
Extras	*Byes* 16, *wides* 13	29	*Byes* 22, *wides* 12, *no-balls* 2	36
Total		**77**	*Total*	**99**

The sad postscript for young Lowth, later the Rev. Alfred J. Lowth, was that, while at Oxford, his sight failed and he bowled only once more for the Gentlemen after his sensational debut.

It was the perpetual weakness of the Gentlemen which led to a match played just before the jubilee game of 1837, to be called 'The Barn Door Match' or 'Ward's Folly'. William Ward arranged the game, an eleven-a-side level match, but in order that the Players should play under some penalty, he had them defending giant wickets – four stumps 36 inches high and 12 inches wide. The Gentlemen defended ordinary stumps, 27 inches by 8 inches, and had in their side well-known cricketers like Ward, Kynaston, Felix, the Hon. E. Grimston, C. G. Taylor, 'the most graceful of all', Knatchbull, aiming no doubt for his corner, G. T. Knight of the round-arm school and Robert W. Keate, nephew of the famous headmaster, Meyrick, Coote and Sir F. Bathurst. They lost by an innings and 10 runs!

Incensed, the Gentlemen immediately arranged a return match, just a fortnight later, after the jubilee celebrations. Equal wickets this time, but the Gentlemen fielded sixteen, including J. H. Kirwan, another Reverend to be, claimed to be the fastest of all bowlers. His credentials were Eton 1834–5, Cambridge 1839, and he did take three wickets, but the Players only batted once in a victory by an innings and 38 runs.

So what next for Mr Dark? His ground had been a focus of celebration, but, from a business point of view, what improvements could he make?

Within a year, the sporting newspaper of the time, *Bell's Life*, drew attention to the changes that were happening at Lord's.

The pavilion is lighted with gas. A new assembly-room has been built over the parlour of the Tavern, and the long room at the east end of the Tavern is now converted into a billiard room. At the west end, a piece of ground, which had long been in a neglected state, is now turned into an excellent bowling-green, the whole of which is railed in. Mr Dark has also taken a large portion of the nursery ground on the north side, which is intended for an archery ground.

Then in the same year, Dark boldly decided to spread the appeal of Lord's, and again, the information reads best in the stately prose of the day. The real tennis court is announced in Denison's *Sketches of the Players* as if it is a great liner being launched:

> In 1838 he [Dark] erected a capacious Tennis Court at an expense of upwards of £4,000, a proceeding which has tended very considerably to increase the memberhood of the Mary-le-bone Club, seeing that more than 150, amongst whom are the very first nobles of the land, have enrolled their names since the completion of the building.

By way of enticement Dark was offering '100 warm and 100 cold baths per diem with dressing rooms; couches provided after a heavy practice, and there are two of the best billiard tables that can be manufactured, the one by Thurston, the other by Burroughs.'

The fees set for tennis were '1/– a set for members and 1/6 for strangers: all fees to be paid by the loser. Gentlemen playing with markers were liable to 3d. extra, though markers could charge 1/– for a love set.'

The other notice on Dark's board was to explain that the hire of racket, shoes, flannels was 6d. for one, 9d. for two.

Dark next made a running track: a path around the field, 640ft long and 7ft 6in. wide, and if the conventional sort of race did not pull the crowds up to St John's Wood, perhaps he should reveal his true 'roll-up, roll-up' instincts of the showground?

It was May 8th, 1837: a stone-picking race. There were two contestants – Townsend, champion of the Pedestrians, and Drinkwater, a Lancastrian. The prize was 200 sovereigns. This was the condition – that they had to pick up 300 stones each placed a yard apart and return them to base, one by one, so that, in effect, the distance to be covered was 51 miles 540 yards. If that does not sound tough enough for the sort of sanguine spectator Dark was trying to attract, then the other condition of the wager would surely have them flocking to the large flag advertising his name, which he flew on the days of big events. Drinkwater could pick up the stones with his hands: Townsend, by way of handicap, to level the betting chances, had to pick them up in his mouth. Townsend may have ended up toothless, but, after 8 hours and 11 minutes, he won, Drinkwater having collapsed on his way back with the very last stone.

Lest anyone should say that Dark entirely ignored the aesthetics, he planted 400 trees. He also started pony-racing and, in August 1844, he had a touch of commercial luck when he allowed the Red Indians of the Iowa(y) tribe to encamp at Lord's. How the crowds loved their dancing and archery, and Dark, seeing how the jamboree

The Iowa Indians were a great attraction at Lord's in 1844. (*Roger Mann*)

atmosphere was infectious, persuaded businessmen to take marquees to exhibit their products at the shows, and, through the commercial tumult, the band played on for the benefit of the Shipwrecked Fishermen and Mariners Benevolent Fund.

Fairground people usually keep the business in the family. Thus, while James Henry Dark held the lease of Lord's, his brother Benjamin was a bat-merchant who kept his willows at the north-west end of the ground and he in turn was succeeded in the business by Benjamin Junior. Another of J.H.'s brothers, Robert, made leg-guards and balls at Lord's and also collected the admission money at the gate. Just to complete the family picture, on the death of J.H., Frank Dark purchased his interest in Lord's as well as the bat business from Mrs Matilda Dark. Sydney Dark, nephew of J.H., was assistant secretary and clerk to the MCC from 1862–71.

For MCC these were tricky days financially. Only a sixth of the income went into the stock purse; the rest went to pay the annual rent of the ground. For example, five matches in 1841 cost £209, but the club also had to pay the expenses of the away game. It was very much a Micawber situation, which was why Aislabie was so assiduous in squeezing subscriptions out of members into his Red Book.

Each year the club's anniversary dinner was fully reported in *The Times* and the forthcoming fixtures laid out.

16th May 1843
THE MARYLEBONE CRICKET CLUB

At the anniversary dinner of this distinguished and celebrated club, which took place at the Clarendon Hotel a few days since, the Earl of Ducie, the President, in the chair, 35 new members were balloted for and elected, amongst whom were the Earl of Munster, the Hon. Henry Neville, Sir John Shelley, Colonel Fane, the Hon. Captain Vivian, Viscount Glamis, the Hon. Charles Neville, the Hon. Captain Lindsay, the Hon. C. B. Lyon, Captain Newton. His late Royal Highness the Duke of Sussex was an honorary member and his Royal Highness Prince Albert has been graciously pleased to become patron of the club.

Matches to come off this season have been arranged with the undermentioned clubs as follows:

St John's Wood (to have come off yesterday), at Lord's; University of Cambridge, May 18, at Cambridge; Clapton Club, May 22, at Lord's; University of Oxford, May 25, at Oxford; Haileybury College, May 29, at Haileybury; County of Sussex, June 5, at Lord's; the Garrison of Chatham, June 8, at Chatham; University of Cambridge (return match), June 12, at Lord's; Northern Counties, June 19, at Lord's; Clapton Club (return match), June 22, at Clapton; Present Etonians, June 24, at Eton; Gentlemen of Hants, June 26, at Lord's; Rugby School, June 29, at Lord's; Present Harrovians, July 1, at Harrow; University of Oxford (return match), July 6, at Lord's; England, July 24, at Lord's; Garrison of Chatham (return match), July 27, at Lord's;

Augt 1844

Under Noble and Distinguished Patronage.

ENCAMPMENT

OF THE

Ioway Indians!

AT

LORD'S CRICKET GROUND,

St. John's Wood Road,

FOR ONE WEEK ONLY.

FIRST TIME IN EUROPE.

Indian Archery Fete & Festival!

Twenty-six Thousand Persons crossed the River from the city of New York to Hoboken, in one Day, to witness the Ball-Play and other Amusements of the Ioway Indians.—*NEW YORK HERALD.*

The celebrated party of IOWAY INDIANS, amounting to Fourteen persons, including the principal chiefs, " Braves" or Warriors, and the Great "Mystery" or "Medicine Man" of the Tribe, with their "Squaws," their Children, and a "Papoose" (or infant), who have been brought to this country at an enormous expense, and who lately arrived from New York,

WILL, ON MONDAY AUGUST the 26th, AND FIVE FOLLOWING DAYS,

BE ENCAMPED

AT LORD'S CRICKET GROUND,

when they will display their skill in shooting with Bows and Arrows, in a grand archery *fête*; also will give their extraordinary and amusing Ball-play; and exhibit several of their peculiar and characteristic Dances, the programme of which is subjoined.

The Editors of the public press (whose opinions are quoted on the other side) have universally pronounced the IOWAY INDIANS to be the finest specimens of the "Red Men," the denizens of the forest and lake, ever seen in England. The party are thus described:—

THE DELEGATION.

CHIEFS.

MEW-HU-SHE-KAW—(White Cloud) first Chief of the Nation.
NEU-MON-YA—(Walking Rain) third Chief.
SE-NON-TY-YAH—(Blister Feet) great Medicine Man.

WARRIORS AND BRAVES.

WASH-KA-MON-YA—(Fast Dancer).
NO-HO-MUN-YA—(One who gives no attention).
SHON-TA-YI-GA—(Little Wolf).
WA-TAN-YE—(One always foremost).

WA-TA-WE-BU-KA-NA—(Commanding-General). The Son of Walking Rain, 10 years old.
JEFFREY—(The Interpreter).

SQUAWS.

RUTON-YE-WE-MA—(Strutting Pigeon) White Cloud's wife.
RUTON-WE-ME—(Pigeon on the Wing).
OKE-WE-ME—(Female Bear that Walks on the back of another).
KOON-ZA-YA-ME—(Female War Eagle sailing).
TA-PA-TA-ME—(Sophia) Wisdom; White Cloud's daughter.
CORSAIR—(A Papoose).

This, it should be remembered, is the first time that ever a party of Indians have appeared encamped in an open plain in Europe: they will appear in their tents as in their native village, and will enable the public to form a correct idea of their peculiar habits, manners, and customs; exhibiting a perfect representation of Indian forest life, and will form a most romantic and beautiful scene.

[Turn over.

87

Nottingham, Trent-bridge Club, July 31, at Lord's; County of Sussex (return match), August 14, at Brighton; Northern Counties (return match), August 21, at Leicester; Nottingham, Trent-bridge (return match), August 24, at Nottingham; and Gentlemen of Hants (return match), August 28, at Southampton.

The following matches were also arranged at the anniversary dinner to come off at Lord's in the course of the season: Two select elevens of England, May 29; Oxford versus Cambridge, June 15; Gents of England versus Gents of Kent, July 3; Kent versus England, July 10; Gentlemen versus Players, July 17; and the usual matches between Harrow, Winchester and Eton, August 2, 3, 4 and 5.

The two following return matches have also been arranged by the club to be played at Canterbury: Kent versus England, Aug 7; and the Gents of England versus the Gents of Kent, August 10. A match will also be played in the County of Kent for the benefit of Wenman, on Thursday, the 17th of August. Altogether, the forthcoming season, with regard to the prospects of this distinguished and old-established club, is more promising than it has been during the last few years.

It is not surprising that the playing activity of the Marylebone Club was more active even though they kept electing many who joined in order to collect the social badge of membership. Cricket was spreading fast. A lot of members practised at Lord's in order to be in good form when they returned to the country. In 1838, the Trent Bridge Ground, Nottingham, was opened by William Clarke. In 1841 the Commander-in-Chief, Lord Hill, gave orders that a cricket ground should be built at every army barracks in the country. Since there were few towns of any size without a garrison at that time, many new cricket clubs must have been established and the troops either joined local teams or inspired them. The army was to be a huge propagator of the game.

Bell's Life reported that there were 130 matches in 1838. Five years later there were 230; five years after that there were 400, and then the figures moved rather more slowly to 500 in 1860. Of course the railways were spreading tentacles in all directions. Many more trips were possible, less arduous and less expensive than coach-travel.

'Kind and manly' Alfred Mynn; the portrait by Bromley which hangs in the Long Room at Lord's. Mynn was the fast round-arm bowler and powerful hitter who was 'Champion of England' from his single-wicket victories over Hills, Dearman, and his Kent colleague Felix.

Improved communications also meant that *Bell's Life* received more match details and they were even more pleased to receive them after 1840 by the Penny Post. It meant that postage on letters from London was prepaid, not cash on delivery.

Another indication of the spread of cricket can be gauged from Haygarth's *Scores and Biographies*, published in fifteen volumes and covering all cricket matches played and cricketers involved between 1744 and 1878. It is a monumental work. In the period between 1843 and 1853 the pages he gives to important matches rise in number from 53 to 76.

Single-wicket cricket was still popular and this was how the

Before the days of mowing machines, one of the most
effective ways of keeping the grass down was to use sheep.
On match days they were penned-up in a special enclosure.
Deer were also brought in at one time, but a comment in
The Sporting Magazine in 1838 said that 'sheep are the only
quadrupeds fit for cricket fields'.

This picture, showing Lord's in 1837, is taken from a woodcut
published in a periodical in 1860.

William Slatter, once a ground-boy at Lord's, relates how in 1861
a ball was driven so hard into the slats of the sheep-pen
that the batsmen ran 100 runs before the ball was extracted.
He also comments on how one of the ground-boy's duties was
to clear up the ground after the sheep.

Opposite: Lord's, a contemporary print of about 1835, after C. Atkinson;
and, below, a water colour painting by Felix, 1851.

The Lord's pavilion and MCC members, 1874.
This, the second pavilion, built for the 1826 season after the fire
the previous year, was expanded in the 1860s under R. A. FitzGerald,
and replaced in 1890 by the present pavilion.
Amongst the notable figures can be seen the 26-year-old
W. G. Grace in the centre foreground. (*Museum of London*)

94

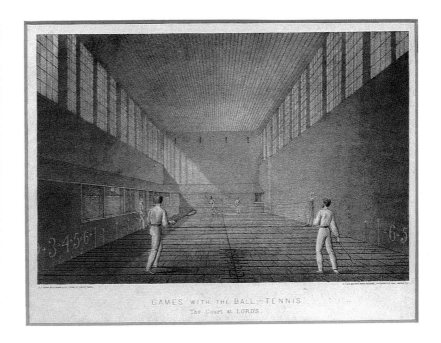

GAMES WITH THE BALL.—TENNIS.
The Court at LORD'S.

The Tennis Court, built 1838.

Lord's, 1837.
The 'Grand Jubilee Match' played on July 10th, 1837
between the North and the South of England to commemorate
the 50th anniversary of the Marylebone Club.

R. A. FitzGerald, Secretary of MCC, appointed 1863;
and W. G. Grace elected a member of MCC at the age of
18, in 1867. Grace was proposed by the Secretary and
seconded by the Treasurer. Both FitzGerald and Grace
are caricatured here in 1872. Between them, with
administrative reforms, and a transcendent ability on
the field, they helped to restore MCC's sunken prestige
in the 1860s.

One of the MCC 'pillbox' caps favoured by FitzGerald
but which were superseded by the more modern designs
such as that which Grace is wearing.

championship of England was decided. Alfred Mynn of Kent proved himself unbeatable. He had three main challengers in the country and beat them all twice: Thomas Hills in 1832; the Yorkshire champion, James Dearman, in 1838; and, the best documented of the games, against his Kent friend and fellow amateur, Nicholas Wanostrocht, known as 'Felix', in 1846.

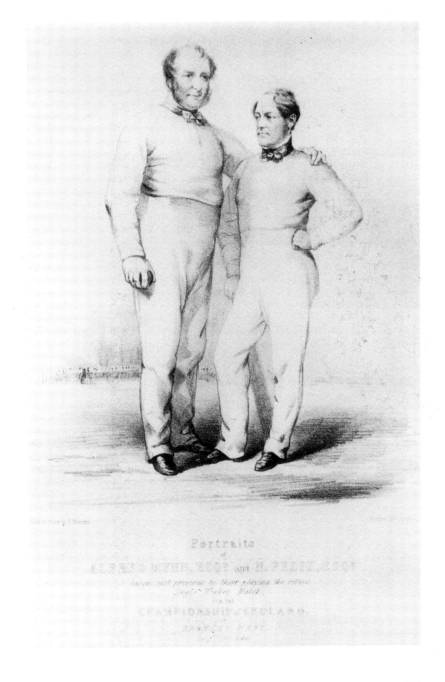

The Championship of England – the single-wicket contest between Mynn and Felix, 1846.

Mynn portrayed by his old friend and Kent colleague, Felix; and a self-portrait of Felix.

Mynn was the massive, lovable yeoman giant nourished on beef and beer, the fast and accurate round-arm bowler, the ungainly but hard-hitting batsman. Wanostrocht the schoolmaster, who wrote and played under the *nom de plume* of Felix, was a violinist, singer, linguist, artist, inventor and author. He had invented the catapulta, the first bowling-machine, some said in order to prepare to meet the fast round-arm bowlers, and also the tubular batting gloves. Felix was a brilliant left-handed batsman with fine off-hitting. He was also the author of the instructional book, full of drawings and puns and sensible advice, *Felix on the Bat*.

Each player had two fielders, who were there only to prevent runs. Hits scored runs only *in front of* the wicket when teams were five-a-side or less, and this was a one-a-side contest. Also, in single-wicket the batsman had to get to the non-striking end *and* back to earn one run.

Lord's was at its best on these great occasions. Three thousand people attended the first of the two matches. Felix was bowled out sixteenth ball by Mynn for nought. Mynn was also out to his sixteenth ball, but he had scored 5. Felix was then patient in the face of Mynn's speed and accuracy on (to him) the off-stump line. Off the 247 balls he received he made 175 hits with the bat but only 3 runs. Add to those a wide and his total reached 4. Thus Mynn won by an innings and rightfully kept his champion's title, strictly an individual honour.

Cricket publications were increasing. Dating from the 1830s was *Bat's Manual*, which had some seasonal averages, and Denison's *Cricketers' Companion*, quickly followed by Fred Lillywhite's *Guide*, often called *Fred's Guide*. In 1845 Felix brought out his *Felix on the Bat* which included the Laws as revised by the MCC in that year. In 1864 there were three annuals, *Wisden*, just beginning, *Bayly's Cricket Chronicle* (only one edition ever made) and *Fred's Guide*, soon to cease and be replaced by the 'Green Lillywhite'. Meanwhile *Bell's Life* grew fatter and fatter. Competition killed it in the end, but during its heyday in the middle of the nineteenth century, it carried a lot of authority. People often contacted *Bell's Life*, rather than the MCC, to solve knotty problems with the Laws.

In 1845 the first match was played on The Oval. Also in 1845, an amateur club, founded in friendship, benevolence and vintage port became the first and most famous wandering club in the world, I Zingari – the idea of J. L. Baldwin, Hon. Spencer Ponsonby-Fane and the Hon. F. Ponsonby, afterwards Lord Bessborough. The name I Zingari means 'the gypsies' in Italian. The club did a great service to amateur cricket by refusing to hire professionals to do their bowling, which was the usual practice at that time, so standards improved. Its colours of black, red and gold became famous, symbolising an ascent 'out of darkness, through fire, into light'. Perhaps this also symbolised how, in the mid-nineteenth century, the Laws of Cricket as well as the techniques of play were changing. From 1849 the pitch could be swept and rolled before each innings at the request of either side.

Dark's bats were sold by Sadd of Cambridge for 8s. 6d. but in 1853–4 cane-handled bats were invented by Nixon; the circumference of the ball was settled in 1838 to between 9 and 9¼in; leg-guards were becoming popular as the round-arm bowlers built up their speed, although the tubular gloves, produced by Daniel Day, were already protecting batsmen's hands and fingers. About 1850 wicket-keeping gauntlets were on the scene, again reflecting the changes in the manner of play. There were still between four and six balls to an over, depending on local agreements. In 1835 the follow-on had been made compulsory after a deficit of 100 runs.

Although in the eighteenth century the toss had given choice of pitch and innings, in the nineteenth century it was the umpires who chose the pitch and the toss gave only choice of innings. There was a lbw law against the striker who prevented the ball hitting the wicket if the ball was 'delivered straight'. Wides were recorded and, from 1844, would count one if no run was made, or else you could run as many as you could. Four years later leg-byes were recorded.

What were cricketers wearing in these times when both batting and bowling methods were changing? Following the example of I Zingari, colours suddenly blossomed, often as ribbon around white bowler hats which were replacing the straw hats of the previous two decades. Club caps dated from around 1850, but Eton was said to have sported its light blue caps as early as 1831, and Rugby certainly had them a few years later. The Winchester School XI wore blue caps in 1851 and Harrow striped ones in 1852. The Cambridge Blue appears to date from 1861 and Oxford Blue from 1863. Coloured shirts were fashionable as uniforms. The All-England XI, the touring circus started by William Clarke in 1846, wore white shirts with pink spots; the universities for many years wore dark and light blue shirts; and the Harlequins, founded in 1852, originally wore blue trousers. Blazers were becoming popular soon after this, while shoes slowly gave place to boots, either brown, or white with brown straps.

So the picture is an exciting one, composed of a more organised, more colourful game taking its hold on villages, towns and counties, offering shades of regional identity and, of course, reflecting the everyday changes which the whole country had undergone in the Industrial Revolution.

Britain still remained a predominantly rural population, but there had been a surge to urban life. The cotton and wool production in Yorkshire and Lancashire had led the way to heavier industries, iron, coal, and engineering. Railway lines had proliferated, and were taking over much of the traffic on the canals, and main roads were being remade by Thomas Telford and John McAdam.

There was a new relationship for the worker: patronage no longer applied in towns and cities but, instead, a labour contract between employer and employed. The new gentry of those who had made money bought country estates and, aping the manners of the old gentry, set up occasional cricket matches. Most of them concentrated too hard on confirming their position up the social ladder and they separated themselves by every artificial means possible. Inevitably snobbery increased. Membership of county cricket teams, for example Montgomeryshire in Wales, who first played in 1853, was open only to country gentlemen. Carmarthenshire in 1860 specifically excluded tradesmen. But nothing now could stop the spread of the game. The army, especially after Lord Hill's edict, was crucial to the planting of cricket. In Scotland the first known match had been played on September 3rd, 1785, on the estate of the Earl of Cathcart, Schaw Park, Alloa. In 1817 there is proof of cricket at the Old High School, Edinburgh, and soon the Edinburgh Academy was playing too.

The military, again, was the game's principal propagator in Ireland. When cricket first went to Phoenix Park in Dublin it was to confer the benefits of manly exercise on the officers of the garrison. The North of Ireland Cricket Club was founded in 1859.

From the 1840s cricket was being referred to as 'the national game'. When Prince Albert was chosen as patron of the MCC, the annual report of 1843 observed that his connection placed the club in an exalted position 'because the national and manly game of cricket cannot but still rise more in public estimation under such distinguished patronage'. Thus the Marylebone Club was lifted to prominence, both by its aristocratic content and because the game itself was soaring in popularity. James Pycroft, publishing his *The Cricket Field* in 1851, opened his preface – 'The following pages are devoted to the history and science of our National Game'. The one obvious question was, however, how long could a small corps of amateur cricketers understand and act for the aspirations of an increasing number of professional players and also for the mass of common people who were taking to the game?

Not surprisingly, perhaps, the Marylebone Club failed to see the warning streaks of lightning or hear the thunder rolling across their light blue heaven. They had given Lord's the atmosphere of a cosy West End club, oozing with the same comforts and conceits, while, in the mid-1840s in Nottingham, the professional cricketer William Clarke was putting his own All-England team together.

Gentlemen v. Players, 1847. The fixture survived and was popular even though the contest was often absurdly uneven, with the Players providing 'given' players or playing against odds.

10 MCC Under Fire

'Old Clarke', creator of the All-England XI in 1846.

The first sign that the Marylebone Club was not being accorded nationwide obeisance in cricket matters came, in fact, from Nottingham, not surprisingly because at this time this was the game's northern stronghold. Nor would it have been a shock to learn that the orchestrator of the northern mischief was a bricklayer, who had lost an eye before he was 30, who bowled unbelievably old-fashioned underarm but with such skill that he made the Nottinghamshire side at the age of 18 and stayed in it for twenty years. William Clark ('Old Clarke') was 48 in 1846 and only once, for North v. South in July 1836, had he played in one of the 'great' matches at Lord's. He decided to do more than organise 'great' matches of his own; he planned a grand tour of the United Kingdom, each season commandeering the finest cricket players in the country even if it meant depriving the MCC or other patrons of their services. Clarke was planning what he called the All-England Eleven, the first cricket 'circus'.

He was a publican. First he ran the Bell Inn and then, in 1838, he moved to the Trent Bridge Inn and laid out his cricket field alongside. The Nottingham folk did not like paying an admission charge, so much of his cricket was poorly supported, but by the time he left the inn, his mind was too full of money-making ideas to worry: All-England was on the road.

The name 'England' had been used before to describe teams recruited from several areas, but Clarke was seriously advertising the best. He probably did most of his recruiting at the match played at Nottingham in 1845 between the MCC and the North: so what happened off the field was a lot more important than what took place on it. William Clarke sold his idea to the famous players who would be essential to his outfit – Mynn, Felix and Pilch for example, even though the former two were amateurs. He offered the standard wage to professionals which was between £4 and £6 depending on how much travel was involved, but more to the amateurs. Although there was no formal network of competitive cricket throughout the country, the business of the professional player was advancing, a possible alternative to the lowly, often hard, jobs which most of them would otherwise have had to take.

A year later Clarke had a squad of fifteen men to play a benefit match for himself at Southwell in August and then, four days later at the beginning of September, the All-England Eleven took the field for the first time at Hyde Park in Sheffield. It played XX of Sheffield and lost.

What did the Marylebone Club do about Clarke? They offered him an engagement at Lord's for the first time. He went down to London to become a MCC practice bowler. In that same summer he played his first game for the Players against the Gentlemen at Lord's. Next year, 1847, he and Lillywhite took all twenty of the Gentlemen's wickets between them, eleven for Lillywhite, nine to Clarke.

Clarke was indeed a superb cricketer. His slow, lobbing under-arm was a complete throwback to the style of fifty years before, which he had learned from William Lambert of Surrey. His run to the wicket was short and then he turned sideways, just before delivering the ball, moving the hips well out of the way, so that the arm and wrist could flick through waist-high. H. S. Altham in *A History of Cricket* credits Clarke with 'a consistent spin from leg'. He was called 'the General' at Nottingham because he was very much the cunning old pro, 'a crafty and foxheaded one', Haygarth added. Before matches he would walk around the ground watching the opposition practising on the outfield and return with his battle plans for each of them. 'Felix,' he would announce, 'I have noted three or four pretty hitters among them when they understand the bowling, but they are as good as ready money to me.' Felix himself was so impressed by the tortuous complexities of Clarke's tantalising slowness and spin, and often the victim of it, that he wrote an amusing pamphlet called *How to Play Clarke*. Clarke also knew his market for professional players; there was a world of increasing opportunity.

The Marylebone Club had, of course, long kept a few professional bowlers employed at Lord's. They had taken on four – Caldercourt, Noah Mann, junior, Ashby, and Robinson, in 1825, as well as two young scouts for fielding. Later, by 1836, there were ten professional players at Lord's. Mostly they bowled at practice and so the pattern had emerged of amateurs batting and professionals bowling, which may in part have accounted for the Gentlemen always having to borrow professional bowlers to even up their annual match against the Players, just as it inspired I Zingari to correct it. While there was obviously disagreement between the club and paid players who insisted on bowling round-arm, overall the club was grateful to its loyal servants and expressed it often in the minutes.

'Labitur infelix.' Felix wrote 'How to play Clarke', but still fails to solve the mysteries of his slow underarm, a style from fifty years earlier.

Many professionals were itinerant. Fuller Pilch, for example, born in Norfolk in 1803, sold his skills in Sheffield, Bury St Edmunds and to Norwich Cricket Club where he kept a pub near the ground. Then, in the mid-1830s, he went to Town Malling in Kent and to the Beverley Club in Canterbury. In all he played for thirty-five seasons which included over a hundred matches at Lord's, in his style described by Lord Charles Russell as 'very commanding, extremely forward and he seemed to crush the best bowling by his long forward plunge before it had time to shoot, rise or do mischief by catches'.

Of course, there was not enough cricket for a professional to be full-time and, alas, Pilch, like others, was forced to dabble in another trade and got into financial trouble. He tried tailoring but left bankrupt. Alfred Mynn was a hop merchant, sometimes unable to pay his creditors and imprisoned. His friends were known to bail him out on the eve of a big match. William Clarke's touring side offered, therefore, the assurance of continuity of work.

For professionals playing at Lord's there were disciplines to obey. In 1840 the MCC decided 'that any paid player, umpire or scorer, failing to appear at his post one moment after play had been called, do forfeit two shillings and sixpence for such an offence. The Committee are earnestly desired to enforce the payment of the penalty.'

Far from being restrictive, this was just the sort of discipline which these freelance money-earners needed to shape what might become a responsible profession. An employer-employee contract, though unwritten, was established. Eight years later heavier penalties were imposed on late-comers for matches at Lord's. 'That all players engaged in every match at Lord's ground shall be in readiness to take their place at that hour (11 o'clock) or be excluded from playing in that match. (Or if belonging to the Lord's ground, pay for a substitute, if a substitute be allowed by the manager of the side.)'

The working arrangement was, of course, cemented by divisions of class which were becoming rock-hard as the Victorian era progressed. Clarke's All-England venture was not so much an effort to dynamite that as an entrepreneurial lust to make money for himself. In addition to a match fee, professionals playing at Lord's could also qualify for a bonus for outstanding performance. But then the MCC changed it to an award for good professional conduct. At a time when cricket was spreading rapidly and shapelessly, MCC was simply keeping its own house in order and insisting that, if these wandering players wanted to be considered professional, they should get to work on time and behave them-

Fuller Pilch,
by G. F. Watts.

THE BATSMAN!
PORTRAIT OF FULLER PILCH
Dedicated to the lovers of the noble game

selves. At the same time they proposed the setting up of a cricketers'
fund to enable donations to be made to luckless or ill old professionals.

So money and regular work were the lures. Remember, the
Lord's members in those days did not play into August, 'grouse
or fashion having long since led the gentlemen to relinquish their

The All-England XI, by Felix. From left to right – Guy, Parr, Martingell, A. Mynn Esq., W. Denison Esq., Dean, Clarke, Felix, O. C. Pell Esq., Hillyer, Lillywhite, Dorrinton, Pilch, Sewell.

bats eight or ten weeks before their more rustic brethren', as the *Sporting Magazine* put it.

Clarke's team was superb. Everyone wanted to play against them or watch. Between 1847 and 1853 he himself took 2,385 wickets for his All-England Eleven (they often played against odds), a seasonal average of 340 for something like twenty or twenty-five matches per season. His matches attracted large crowds and made plenty of money. Billposters went up in Scotland and Wales and throughout the country advertising the best – Pilch, Mynn, Felix and Parr, Guy, Hillyer, Martingell, Dean, John Wisden, the smallest of fast bowlers, Clarke himself, and Thomas Box keeping wicket.

Inevitably there came the clash of fixtures. In 1854 the All-England Eleven was hired to play XVIII of Maidstone on the same day as the Gentlemen versus Players match at Lord's. Julius Caesar and William Caffyn were two of Clarke's men chosen for the Players, but Clarke, apparently annoyed about his own omission from the match, even at the age of 55, refused to release them.

The All-England Eleven players often accepted invitations to turn out at Lord's. Richard Daft of Nottinghamshire, the most complete of professional players, reckoned to be playing or travelling for six days a week. The journeys, mostly overnight, were arduous, the pitches rough and the opposition often untutored.

The Marylebone Club never had an open battle with Clarke, nor did they need to because his 'circus' operation self-destructed. In 1852 he was accused by his own players of grabbing too much of the money. As one of the players, Tom Sherman, later told the historian, F. S. Ashley-Cooper:

> The cricketers went up to him one after the other for their money, and as I was the last in the row I was able to take in all that transpired. Clarke had a heap of gold and silver in front of him and during the pay-out process you would hear something like this: 'Four pounds for you,' the amounts vary according to each player's fame and what he had done in the match. When I approached him he looked up, saying 'Fifty shillings for you,' and then shovelling the balance into his trouser pocket, and giving the most satisfied smile, added, 'and thirty-seven pounds for me.'

Many of the players defected, and drew up a manifesto vowing 'not to play in any match, for or against, wherein William Clarke may have the management or control, in consequence of the treatment they have received from Clarke at Newmarket and elsewhere'. The southern professionals suspected a northern bias against them, so when the Sussex pair, John Wisden and James Dean, started up a rival group called the United England Eleven, most went with them.

The MCC embraced both Englands by giving Lord's every Whitsun Monday for a match between 'the Great Elevens' with the considerable profit going to the Cricketers' Fund Friendly Society. All went well for a decade before United England became disunited and a third group, the United South of England Eleven, was formed. The professionals in a very real way were running their own game, yet there was no peaceful fusion geographically. In fact the North was soon to go on strike over the choice of a touring captain.

In 1859 twelve professionals had crossed the Atlantic to play a series of matches in Canada and the United States. The venture was set up overseas by the old Eton and Cambridge cricketer, W. P. Pickering, and the Montreal Cricket Club and, at home, by Mr Edmund Wilder, president of the Cricketers' Fund. The captain was George Parr of Nottingham. After William Clarke's death in 1856, Parr had become the 'Lion of the North' and natural captain of the All-England Eleven. He was a crouching thumper of the ball even off the back foot, which was new, and also to leg, especially to 'Parr's tree' near the Trent Bridge Inn which was known as that because of the peppering he gave it. 'Where did

Professionals' tour to
Canada and USA,
1859.

that ball pitch?' asked one indignant bowler whom Parr had
hoicked to leg. 'In the hedge, I think,' he replied.

In 1861 another team was invited overseas, this time to Australia. The promoters, Messrs Spiers and Pond, had wanted to
attach their name to a lecture tour by Charles Dickens, but had
to settle for cricket instead. They offered £150 a man plus travel
expenses, but George Parr and the northern players turned that
down. So the leadership was offered to H. H. Stephenson at The
Oval. He accepted and a corps of Surrey men agreed to go with
him. The northerners responded by announcing their refusal to
play matches at The Oval or any southern matches at all. It even
affected the Marylebone Club some years later when they recorded
in the club's minutes, May 21st, 1866: 'Northern players secede
from Lord's on the day of the Two Elevens Match, played for the
benefit of Professionals, the ground being given to them for that
purpose – gratitude!'

Thus the MCC found themselves not only challenged openly
by the cricketers on the bowling law, but now found half of
them withdrawing their services. *The Times* blamed the rise of
professionalism:

The cause of this unfortunate position of things is to be found in the too prosperous conditions of the players. So long as they can earn more money by playing matches against twenty-twos than by appearing at Lord's – so long as they can be 'mistered' in public houses, and stared at at railway stations, they will care very little for being absent from the Metropolitan Ground, but they are wrong. They may be certain that the 'Gentlemen' will not give way in the struggle.

That last sentiment scarcely matched the reality. The cricketers may well have been increasing both their strength as a group of workers and their social presence, but the steady decline of the Marylebone Club towards the 1860s was mostly its own fault. To begin with, the ground itself was not good enough, despite fond memories to be read from Lord Harris (born 1851) who was a boy at the time:

Richard Daft and George Parr.

Dark's house was in the left-hand corner of the ground, going in, and the only other buildings were the Pavilion – a green-painted wooden building, with a kind of dressing room at the back – Tennis court and a rustic tavern with bow windows with a row of very leafy trees in front. On one side of the Pavilion stood a row of pollard trees, and behind them were the beautiful gardens, four acres in extent, belonging to Landseer, the great animal painter.

There had been small improvements, too. A telegraph was put up to show the score; a small room was built on the north side of the pavilion for professionals who, before that, had to walk out to bat around the back of the pavilion and in through the ground's main entrance gate. In 1848 score-cards were first printed at Lord's on a portable press and a scorers' perch was erected so that they would not be disturbed by spectators.

Long overdue, however, was the draining of the playing area which J. H. Dark did at his own expense. *Lillywhite's Guide* of 1850 said that the cost was £300: 'Four hundred loads of clay were taken out, and the same quantity of gravel laid on the pipes'. However, the mid-nineteenth-century scene can be imagined only as a small gathering of amateurs and members; low benches as the only public seating and pot-boys going around in loose white jackets and aprons, shouting, 'Give your orders, gents!' In truth, Lord's was an atrocious playing surface and not a comfortable place even for members to watch either. Dark's showground was tatty and deteriorating and again it was the professionals who were quick to let the MCC know.

John Lillywhite enjoyed bowling at Lord's, but conceded that it did not remotely resemble a billiard table 'except for the pockets'. Even at one of the 'great elevens' matches on a Whit Monday

The dangers of fast bowling, as caricatured by *Punch*, 1854. One of the worst 'offenders' was the Lord's pitch. (*Punch*)

there was an unholy scramble by officials, only twenty minutes before the start, to find a decent pitch because the one prepared had a large hole in it. When a wicket-keeper named Pooley had three teeth knocked out he was attended by Jem Mace, a useful cricketer as well as pugilist. Mace, hardly comforting, said that he would rather face up to any man in England for an hour than take Pooley's place behind the wicket.

Eventually *Bell's Life* published a damaging letter from a MCC member no less:

> What stranger would believe that this great club plays upon a ground which not only prevents good cricket, but renders the game absolutely unsafe to limb and also to life? And yet it does so: I do not exaggerate when I say that during the whole of last season no good wicket was to be found at Lord's. Away from the centre of the ground you would not know you were in a cricket field. The fieldsman who stands cover slip farthest from the Pavilion finds himself in the original ridge and furrow which existed when the late Mr Lord still had his habitation in Dorset Square.

The criticisms piled up: it was suggested that a new ground for 'great' matches be built in Brompton. Why no accommodation for ladies? Why no acceptable luncheon or dinner? The Lord's pavilion was called 'a wretched penthouse' and a 'cowshed' when compared with the excellent pavilion at The Oval, where there was much more informality. The wedge between sinking Lord's and soaring Oval was thrust in deeper by the continued friction over the bowling law. Surrey claimed to know the mood of the country at large and, indeed, in the annual report of 1864, its chairman begged the Marylebone Club, 'the only true cricket Club in England', to 'travel out of their ordinary routine' and get out among the massive cricket fraternity building up among all classes. Surrey wanted overarm bowling, and most players agreed with them.

In 1857, J. H. Dark had told the MCC that he wanted to sell Lord's, and hoped that the club would buy it. It was, after all, his fifty-second year of service to them. Incredibly, when the freehold came up for auction in 1860, the club did not even bid. It was bought by a Mr Isaac Moses for £7,000, according to Pelham Warner in *Lord's*. So the Marylebone Club entered the 1860s without professional players, without decent pitch or pavilion, comparing badly with Surrey and, at the same time, preserving round-arm bowling against the tide of opinion and failing to secure its own future by purchasing the ground. All it had were the glittering occasions of the University match, Eton v. Harrow, and Gentlemen v. Players. Other than that its cricket was a succession of scratch games by amateurs against the MCC. How long could it keep its authority?

Suddenly a torrid attack came, mercilessly orchestrated in column inch after column inch for two years by *Sporting Life*: the Marylebone Club should be ousted and a Cricket Parliament be elected immediately. The letters appeared under jovial *noms de plume* such as Mid-on, Watchman and Long-stop, but their messages were sanguine. The mildest of them recommended that the Marylebone Club should become the 'upper house' of the Cricket Parliament, but not the prime legislator. The most serious proof of MCC's inadequacy was its resistance over Law X, and many references were made to the recent commotion at The Oval in 1862 when the umpire, Lillywhite, 'honest and conscientious', had no-balled Edgar Willsher under Law X 'which has been practically ignored for years'.

The Cricket Parliament idea was easy to understand – practical businessmen elected from every part of the United Kingdom each voicing his constituency's thoughts. It was felt that only practising cricketers should stand, that there would be two meetings a year, and that fair play could be observed from a gallery by spectators who had been given a special entrance ticket by their home cricket clubs.

In December 1863 the Kent Club publicly threw its weight behind the Cricket Parliament, although Nottinghamshire re-affirmed its conviction that the members of the Marylebone Committee were the best men to run the game.

For month after month the MCC was depicted as amateur gentlemen locked in time, blindfolded, unable to see ahead, only existing on the crusty assertions of the likes of Beauclerk, who had thought leg-guards unfair to the bowler, or of Grimston who considered mowing machines new-fangled and unwelcome, or for that matter, of a committee which side-stepped a major problem by decreeing that 'the umpire was to be responsible for the state of the pitch'. The Marylebone Club was facing the most serious choice of its life – if only it could recognise it – to go out to find the real public it claimed to serve, or to sit in a crumbling pavilion, smoking cigars, babbling on about the cricket of a bygone age.

The Committee did not recognise a choice so much as a right, tempered by a feeling of duty to the game. They and the members wanted the MCC to have the same sort of authority as the Jockey Club. They did not want to see 'England Elevens' going around playing against 'Eighteens' and 'Twenty-twos' – 'cricket under such circumstances ceased to be what it could be when played by thorough professors of the art'. The MCC wished to be 'masters of the ground and the law-makers of the game, and that they should be enabled to use the power which their long existence gave them the right to claim and to wield.'

Nonetheless the Cricket Parliament concept was eventually put to the MCC itself in a private letter from the *Sporting Life*. The official reply from the MCC secretary came months later, dated April 20th, 1864, and addressed to W. M. Kelson Esq.

> I am desired to express the Committee's unanimous disapproval of any such scheme as may be entertained under the specious name of a Cricket Parliament. The laws that regulate the game of cricket are so excessively simple the questions that arise are so easily to be met by them and, in fact, they are and have long been acknowledged by the MCC to be quite sufficient authority – that, without dictating to the contrary or desiring anybody, if otherwise inclined, to follow blindly in their steps, the Committee do not see any reason to depart from the course which they have pursued in the spirit of cricket through all difficulties since the first year of their existence as a club in 1787.
>
> (signed) R. A. FitzGerald
> Honorary Secretary

That was that: but the story does not end there. A few months later the MCC changed Law X. Overarm bowling, 'but not jerked or thrown', was admitted. In the autumn the pavilion at Lord's was enlarged, a large area of ground, about 80 by 40 yards, was levelled and returfed; the rackets court was restored and the billiard tables, too. The first groundsman was appointed, Mr David Jordan, at 25s. a week.

The year 1864 had been that in which the MCC virtually died and was reborn. Mr R. A. FitzGerald, appointed secretary the year before, was the man for the future.

However, 1864 was also the year in which, on July 21st, a young batsman aged 16 years and 3 days, scored 50 for the South Wales Club against the MCC in his first match at Lord's. His name was William Gilbert Grace, and his ambition was to play cricket for the MCC.

11 W.G.

W. G. Grace, the large, bearded cricketer under the faded MCC cap, was a phenomenon: he is so well-known a figure even today that he sometimes seems like a totem pole, but his achievements were such that, having slipped on to the London cricket stage at the age of 16, he suddenly, within two seasons, had given the art of batsmanship a breathtaking new role. Before him were the Middle Ages of cricket. Now, as K. S. Ranjitsinhji put it in *The Jubilee Book of Cricket* (1897): 'There is one great landmark that separates the old batting from the new – the appearance of Dr W. G. Grace in the cricket world. In 1865 W.G. came fully before the public that has admired and loved him ever since. He revolutionised batting. He turned it from an accomplishment into a science.'

W. G. Grace's father, Henry Mills Grace, from the rural middle class, was a doctor who sometimes rode with the Duke of Beaufort's hounds. His mother's father was George Pocock, an eccentric schoolmaster. In his *W. G. Grace, His Life and Times*, Eric Midwinter observes that his parentage put W.G. between the upper and middle classes: there was room for ambivalence.

He was born at Downend, near Bristol, on July 18th, 1848, and claimed to have held a bat at the age of two. There were nine children, five boys and four girls. They all played non-stop cricket in the orchard alongside the house with serious tuition from their father and from 'Uncle Pocock', his mother's brother. Nor could they exclude Mother herself, because Martha Grace knew her cricket. She was a strong influence in W.G.'s life. To this day she has her own entry in the births and deaths pages of *Wisden*: 'Grace, Mrs H.M. (Mother of W.G., E.M. and G.F.)' all three of whom represented England; E.M. and G.F. once each, W.G. 22 times.

W.G.'s first sight of cricket, although he did not remember it, was a trip into Bristol to see William Clarke's All-England XI play the local team which had been collected together by his father. W.G. himself went to local schools and was always available for practices. His début in a proper match came when he was nine, on July 19th, 1857, going in last for West Gloucestershire against

The 24-year-old
W. G. Grace, 1872.

114

Bedminster. He scored 3 not out, a tiny innings recorded in *Bell's Life* on July 26th.

In 1864, when he was 16, he was on the annual tour of the South Wales Club. How Bristol came to be part of Wales, W.G. half explains in his autobiography *W.G., Cricketing Reminiscences and Personal Recollections* (1899), through the helpful pen of Arthur Porritt: 'I do not know what was my qualification for playing for South Wales, but we didn't trouble much about qualification in those days. Still, most of the players came from the West Country, and after all, my brother and I were only divided from Wales by the Severn.' This was when he first played against the MCC at Lord's and the innings was noted in *The Times* on July 22nd:

> At Lord's Ground yesterday this match was commenced, the attendance being very scanty. South Wales went in first, and Mr E. M. Grace made his first appearance since his arrival from Australia, but was not fortunate enough to score. Mr W. G. Grace made a fine innings of 50, but the 'leger' was taken by Captain R. Jones with 65, and the total of the whole was 211. Messrs. Teape, Hearne and Nixon bowled.

MCC and Ground made 186. The match was drawn.

He had advantages from the start. The first was physical. As a youngster he was described as having a lank, loose-limbed frame and was quite an athlete with a special skill at hurdling. Although already by his early twenties he weighed 15½ stone, he had the height, over 6 feet, and the extraordinary energy, to carry it rumbustiously day after day. Strangely, though, out of this large body squeaked a high falsetto voice, which surprised people, but he was talkative and easy in conversation, if abrupt and tense in speeches and rather brusque with the professionals. Overall, he was tireless and immensely strong. Writing in 1921, six years after Grace died, Colonel Philip Trevor described a stay with the Graces not long before W.G.'s death. Up with a gun to meet the dawn, pause for breakfast, and then more shooting; off to the cricket, with net practice after lunch; then a route march home and, after dinner, billiards until the small hours. Eric Midwinter writes of the 66-year-old W.G. taking the young Gilbert Jessop around Maidenhead golf club for forty-five holes in awful weather, then back to London for dinner and on to Prince's ice-skating club for curling until midnight.

To match his energy was a schoolboy enthusiasm for cricket. The key to him is his direct, simple, almost puerile mind. What could be more direct, for example, than his way of employing a groundsman: 'You'll be paid two pounds a week and do what you're told.'

After the family cricket, nothing ever shook W.G.'s resolution to play the great matches. This was a particularly understandable attitude in Victorian England. His ambitions were the embodiment of so many middle-class ethics which were being taught to drive young men outwards and upwards – hard work and single-mindedness within the team context. This reflected the new society within which there was ample room for the unstinting pursuit of the private ideal. Not surprisingly, then, this fostered a love of the heroic and acclaim for the man who set high sights and conquered. Cricket, too, was the perfect vehicle. It was still the manly game, but also the embodiment of decency and fair play.

So cricket and W.G. cemented as one, and grew into a solid pillar of all that was good. In addition W.G. was an amateur cricketer who loved the Marylebone connection. He supported the club's matches and showed off the colours: as his fame rose to a national level, so he revived the club's stock in the nation's eye. So too the Marylebone Club, hanging on to W.G.'s shirt-tails, found its authority seeping back: away from the professionals who had set up their itinerant teams, and back to the amateurs.

In 1865, as Ranji said, W.G. 'came fully before the public'. He alerted them of his presence with over 2,000 runs in all cricket and then, in 1866, at the age of 18, he played his first major innings, 224 for All-England against Surrey; yet during that match young Mr Grace was given time off to run a hurdle race at Crystal Palace, which he is said to have won in a time of 1min. 10secs. Already he seemed to be breaking the conventions, if not the rules.

Grace could never be part of the inner aristocratic core of cricket: he had no public school behind him. So what pulled him closer to Lord's? It is possible that the Marylebone Club made the first move. Financially, however, there was no way that a doctor's family could sustain three sons, E.M., W.G., and G.F., as amateurs. It is likely, therefore, that W.G. wavered between the amateur role and the professional. It suited MCC to keep him playing for the club, so it was essential that he was seen to be an amateur, too. Very quickly there were doubts about his status, especially his involvement with the itinerant South of England XI. Surrey, in the future, would be forced by criticism to publish a statement that they only ever paid W.G. £10 expenses to come to The Oval to play. The truth is, a lesser player than W. G. Grace would have been squashed in the social sandwich. But he was so brilliant a cricketer he could run with the amateurs and hunt with the professionals. He was a sensation. His presence trebled every attendance. People used to ask at the gate of a ground if he was playing, and if he was not, turn away.

In 1868 he played what he always thought was his finest innings,

134, all run, on a dreadful pitch, out of the Gentlemen's 201 at Lord's against the Players. He also took 10 wickets for 81 runs. He then provided the South with two centuries in a match against the North of the Thames at Canterbury, the first time such a feat had been achieved since William Lambert at Lord's in 1817.

The following year, proposed by T. Burgoyne, the Treasurer, the son of E. H. Budd's solicitor, and seconded by R. A. FitzGerald, the Secretary, Grace was elected a member of the MCC at the youthful age of 21. And he could hardly have had two more influential sponsors who undoubtedly saw Grace's potential as the MCC's standard bearer in the field. The colours had changed from light blue to yellow and orange, so similar to I Zingari's red, yellow and black that I Zingari protested. The cross-pollination of MCC and I Zingari members seems to be the only explanation available of how the yellow and orange was adopted.

When Grace went out to bat for his new club for the first time as a full member, he scored 117 against Oxford University at the Magdalen ground. Now actively helping to restore the sunken prestige of the MCC, he was launched on a brilliant decade. He completely reversed the most predictable result of the year. In the thirty-five years before his first appearance for the Gentlemen versus the Players, the Gentlemen had won only 7 times; of their next 50 matches, they won 31 and lost only 7. In that series only, he made 15 hundreds and took 271 wickets. It was feats such as these that made him known as 'The Champion'.

Grace's fame spread quickly for several reasons. First, Bristol, his home, was a large conurbation of 166,000 inhabitants by 1851 and although no longer second in size to London, as it had been before the spread of the Industrial Revolution, it was a focal point in the development of rail travel. In 1841 the Great Western Railway line reached there from London and by 1845 there were rail-links to the main towns of the West Country and to Birmingham.

In the second place, his long association with the travelling sides, particularly the United South of England, gave a great many cricket-lovers a sight of him in the flesh all over the country.

Third, after his MCC membership, his regular appearances in London and his outstanding performances there placed him at the centre of the national stage.

Soon he would be internationally famous too. In 1872 he went on a tour to Canada and the United States which was not officially labelled MCC, but all twelve of the Gentlemen were MCC members. Mr R. A. FitzGerald, the Secretary who played non-

The English Gentlemen Cricketers in America, 1872.

stop cricket, was the captain. Grace was hailed out there as 'the Champion Batsman of cricketdom and a monarch in his might'. Obviously they had not seen him wretchedly seasick on the ocean!

The following winter he raised a team to go to Australia at the invitation of the Melbourne Cricket Club. The professionals were paid £170 and second-class passage. W.G., just married to Agnes Day, went on a prolonged honeymoon, although he had to play in every match. It is said he was paid £1,500 as a fee which, translated into our currency a hundred years later, is approximately £18,000. There were huge crowds and Grace's side won twelve of the fifteen matches, all against odds.

In eight days of August 1876 W. G. Grace scored 839 runs, set off by a memorable second innings of 344 for the MCC against Kent at Canterbury. Lord Harris, on the Kent side, scored one of his own best centuries, 154. Kent were all out for 473 then, removing the MCC for 144, looked set for an innings win. W.G. batted for six hours and twenty minutes and as *Bell's Life* states: 'He scored those 344 runs without positively giving a chance.'

Lord Harris knew Grace's play at close quarters. W.G., he

believed, was different from all other batsmen because he could hit everywhere. 'He used every known stroke except the draw which had become all but obsolete.' He thought W.G. had invented a stroke, too, 'the push to leg with a straight bat off the straight ball, and his mastery of this stroke was so great that he could place the ball with great success clear of short leg and even of two short legs. It was not the glide which that distinguished cricketer Ranjitsinhji developed so successfully, or a hook, but a push and a perfectly orthodox stroke.'

Grace, of course, had learnt his cricket against round-arm bowling, and it is important to realise that overarm bowling was not taken up by everyone, all at once, even when it was made legal in 1864. Most of the bowling was still round-arm and around the wicket – otherwise the arm would hit the umpire. What W.G. was doing, by pushing for singles on the leg side towards mid-on, was playing, with complete straightness and orthodoxy, down the line of the ball's flight. Fuller Pilch's strength, on the other hand, had been much more to the off-side and stronger on the front foot than the back. He is described by H. S. Altham as 'a most forward player'. Grace could play a wide range of strokes whether back or forward.

He was always a correct batsman, playing with a straight bat which he kept very close to his pad. Indeed Harris observed how W.G. 'made great use of his legs in protecting his wicket, not, be it understood, by getting in front of the wicket and leaving the ball alone, for no batsman left fewer balls alone, but bat and legs were so close together that it was difficult for the ball to get past the combination'.

Appeals for lbw would rage, and Grace in his high-pitched but authoritative voice would retaliate even as the umpire was cogitating, 'Didn't pitch straight by half an inch'. Grace never slogged, never forced. He was committed hour after hour, day after day to 'the same watchful, untiring correct game'. He was fast between the wickets. As a bowler he was medium-fast at first and later slower with the ability to turn the ball from leg. He delivered the ball with a strong round-arm and then would dash away to off in his follow-through, creating an extra fielder on that side.

His fielding, when he was young, was agile. *Wisden* records a match between Gloucestershire and Surrey in 1874 which Gloucestershire won by an innings, although bowled out for 124. Surrey got 27 and 73 on what was described as a rotten turf. A local report quotes: 'The Doctor, standing resolutely close up at point, took the remaining batsmen one after the other almost off

Grace bowling, photographed by G. W. Beldam. Even though it is quite late in his career, he still has the almost round-arm action with which he had been brought up. (*Beldam Collection*)

their bats.' In his later days his physical bulk got the better of him.

Grace began his medical studies at the age of 19, in 1869, at the Bristol Medical School. By a protracted process of study, adulterated by cricket, he did not qualify for ten years; then he received the diploma installing him as Licentiate of the Royal College of Physicians of Edinburgh and a member of the Royal College of Surgeons.

The members of the Marylebone Club were so delighted with his glorious play in the 1870s and aware that he was now a qualified doctor but without a practice, that they awarded him a testimonial. In a fine ceremony at Lord's after a match between the Under-30s and the Over-30s in July 1879, he received a cheque for £1,458, a marble clock and a pair of bronze obelisks. Lord Charles Russell, the oldest MCC member, made a speech out in front of the pavilion and concluded,

If you want to see Mr Grace play cricket, I would ask you to look at him playing one ball. You all know the miserably tame effect of the ball hitting the bat instead of the bat hitting the ball, whether acting on the offensive or the defensive. In playing a ball, Mr Grace puts every muscle into it from the sole of his foot to the crown of his head.

Mixing the daily duties of a doctor with his extensive cricket programme was never easy; often he would have to pay a locum, and once, in 1883, he even missed a Gentlemen v. Players match. Gradually his playing performance dipped and he looked settled into general practice, slowing down, much more the family man – but then, in 1895, W.G. produced an amazing summer of cricket during which he reached his forty-seventh birthday.

That season in first-class cricket he scored 2,346 runs at an average of 51, becoming the first man ever to score a hundred first-class hundreds, and also the first to score 1,000 runs in May. In fact he made 1,389 runs in that month. He scored an innings of 118, his first century for the Gentlemen against the Players at Lord's since 1876, and 125 for MCC against Kent.

The *Daily Telegraph* launched a National Shilling Testimonial for the 'Old Man' which raised £4,000. Two other funds appeared, one a combination of the *Sportsman* and the MCC raised well over £3,000 and another, a Gloucestershire appeal headed by the Duke of Beaufort, raised £1,500.

In 1899, however, W.G. split with Gloucestershire. The County Committee had heard of W.G.'s offer of employment with the London County Club which was just being formed at Crystal Palace. They wrote to ask Grace what matches he intended to play for Gloucestershire. Grace was furious: he had played all of Gloucestershire's first-class matches of the season so far. He replied, sending in his resignation as captain and inviting them to choose teams for all future games. 'I shall not get them up,' wrote Grace. That same year he captained England in just the first Test against Australia at Trent Bridge, and, as expected, left Bristol to take up the London County job, where he spent eight more seasons playing in first-class cricket.

His last century at Lord's was in 1900, 126 for the South against the North. Happily there is a delightful eye-witness account of his last cricket, a London County match against Surrey, from a young lad who was to become a humorous novelist and playwright, Ben Travers:

I watched him make a century in partnership with Ranji, who also made one of his own. I was favoured by good fortune and so was W.G. because he looked to be out when he had made only about 20, caught at short leg by Brockwell, who was incidentally a top-class all-rounder, in and out of the England sides. Brockwell threw the ball up triumphantly, but W.G. made violent gestures intimating that he had hit a bump-ball and then advanced towards Brockwell, brandishing his bat as if to fell him. He looked very formidable but perhaps it was merely his good-natured way of indicating that he wished to go on batting. This, with the umpire remaining intimidated and mute, the great man proceeded to do with the result that I have ever since been able to boast that I saw him make one of his many hundreds.

It was not just the longevity which made W.G.'s career famous. His hundred centuries was more than twice the number anyone had scored before; in a first-class career which extended from 1865 to 1908, he scored, according to *Wisden*, but not all statisticians agree, 54,896 runs and took 2,876 wickets.

When he first began, calling major cricket matches 'first-class' was just beginning and so W.G.'s record should be amplified by other games in which he collected about 45,000 more runs, and 4,500 more wickets. Add them all up and you reach mammoth totals which had never occurred before, nearly 100,000 runs and well over 7,000 wickets.

He was the most famous man in the country. In spite of the amazing duality – which allowed him to receive payments for playing in matches, either by way of appearance money or an extra large travel allowance to compensate for the hiring of a medical locum in Bristol – there was a vogue to attach the great Victorian respectabilities to him. His fame had come single-handed; it was heroic. Thus it happened that, in 1895, both cricket and W. G. Grace were linked in censorious contrast to Oscar Wilde's trial which centred on Wilde's homosexuality. *Punch*, the weekly magazine, wrote:

> *Reaction's the reverse of retrograde,*
> *If we recede from dominant excesses,*
> *And beat retreat from novelists who trade*
> *On 'six' from artists whose chefs d'oeuvres are messes,*
> *'Tis time indeed such minor plagues are stayed.*
> *Then here's for cricket in this year of Grace,*
> *Fair play all round, straight hitting and straight dealing*
> *In letters, morals, arts and commonplace*
> *Reversion into type in deed and feeling*
> *A path of true reaction to retrace.*

Cricket and the Marylebone Club had come a long way since the 1860s and without Grace they might not have done so. As a cricketer, as Ranji described in an often quoted passage, 'he founded the modern theory of batting by making forward- and back-play of equal importance. He turned the old one-stringed instrument into a many-chorded lyre'. In terms of social history, as C. L. R. James wrote in *Beyond a Boundary*, Grace had lifted cricket from a casual pastime into a national institution: 'Like all truly great men, he bestrides two ages.'

12 FitzGerald and Expansion

However brilliantly W. G. Grace sported the Marylebone colours and drew large crowds to cricket at Lord's, the club itself still needed to stir within, if it cared to hang on at the heart of cricket. It had required a flat pitch to lead to a higher standard of play at Lord's, and a more cricket-conscious, vibrant membership with facilities to accommodate them. Someone, therefore, had had to give the administrative lead. On the Committee there was a solid, hard core of the loyal and concerned, who selected teams, initiated changes and answered criticism, but much depended on how forward-looking they were. They made their first constructive move in 1863 when Mr Kynaston proposed, and the Hon. F. Ponsonby seconded, that R. A. FitzGerald should succeed Alfred Baillie as honorary secretary.

FitzGerald was 29, energetic, witty and a non-stop, active cricketer. Among his many writings on the game he asserted that 'the greatest duffer at the game is the most enthusiastic'. He himself was a lot better than that. In 1866, for example, he played 48 matches, mainly for MCC and I Zingari, and scored 1,420 runs. He had been a member of the MCC for five years and had already expressed a keenness to see Lord's the great centre of cricket.

He inherited the secretaryship in difficult and controversial times when the various professional 'England Elevens' were commandeering the best players and when the columns of *Sporting Life* were calling for a Cricket Parliament. MCC's was mainly a reactionary committee set in its ways; no one more so than the Hon. Robert Grimston, who had scorned William Clarke's All-England venture:

> No. Let the men who want to choose their own elevens do so, and pay for them themselves, and go about the country on their own speculation; but don't let them dictate to committees of their grounds; and if they do, we must not allow those clubs to play here; it is our duty to keep cricket as a game and not as a gate-money business.

Robert Allan, or 'Bob', FitzGerald was born in Purley House, Berkshire, and was in the XI both at Harrow and at Cambridge University. He played for Middlesex, Buckinghamshire, Hert-

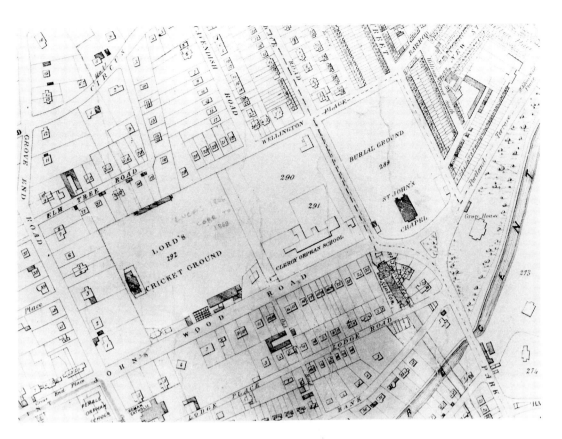

Lord's in 1856,
corrected to 1868.

fordshire, the Cambridge Quidnuncs, as well as the MCC and I Zingari. When he had a bat in his hand play was never dull: he hit the ball as hard as possible, gathering the reputation of a regular remover of the cricket ball from Lord's. He was especially famed for one blow which sent the ball over the tennis court and out into St John's Wood Road.

FitzGerald, as the new honorary secretary, acted promptly. He supervised the extending of the pavilion. Two wings were added, a room in the basement for players, accommodation on a flat roof for members and public; there was a new frontage, a committee room, a library, and a new, principal dressing-room.

He began scheming the election of young men to the Committee, one of whom was Edward Rutter, who recalled in his *Cricket Memories* (1925):

> He had C. E. Green and myself nominated, and we proceeded to sit in conclave with our elderly and reactionary fellow-members. At first we were distinctly ignored and Charlie Green was so utterly disgusted with the supercilious manner in which he was received that he declared he would never serve on the Committee again. Nor did he, but stuck to his resolve. Oddly enough the next official appearance he made in the Club was many years later (1905) when he was elected President.

125

In 1864 FitzGerald increased the entrance fees to Lord's for the Eton v. Harrow match because he had to hire police to prevent the crowd disturbances which had broken out the year before. For the University match too, 'foot passengers paid 1s., persons on horseback 2s. 6d., carriages on two wheels 5s. and on four wheels 10s.'

Only this and the other two glamour games, Oxford v. Cambridge and Gentlemen v. Players were sustaining the club's finances for the membership was only 650 in 1863 and the rest of the fixture list lacked the crack players.

MCC MATCHES IN 1865

AT LORD'S

v. Knickerbockers (*won*)
v. Royal Artillery (*won*)
v. Gents of Yorkshire (*lost*)
v. Surrey Club and Ground (*won*)
v. Civil Service (*lost*)
v. Cambridge University (*won*)
v. Oxford University (*won*)
v. Sussex (*lost*)
1st XI v. Next XXII
v. Harrow and Eton (*drawn*)
v. Gents of Scotland (*won*)
v. Suffolk (*won*)
v. Norfolk (*won*)

OUT MATCHES

v. Bucks (*lost*)
v. Cambridge University (*won*)
v. Surrey Club and Ground (*drawn*)
v. Oxford University (*lost*)
v. Winchester College (*drawn*)
v. Rickling Green (*lost*)
v. Harrow (*lost*)
v. Eton College (*drawn*)
v. Westminster School (*drawn*)
v. Gentlemen of Kent (*lost*)
v. Sussex (*drawn*)
v. Royal Artillery (*lost*)
v. Suffolk (*lost*)
v. Norfolk (*won*)

OTHER IMPORTANT MATCHES AT LORD'S

R.A. and R.E. *v.* Rest of Army
Sandhurst *v.* Woolwich
Household Brigade *v.* Cambridge Quidnuncs
All-England Eleven *v.* United All-England Eleven
Household Brigade *v.* I Zingari
North *v.* South
Oxford *v.* Cambridge
Rugby *v.* Marlborough
Rugby *v.* Charterhouse
I Zingari *v.* Free Foresters
Gentlemen *v.* Players
Eton *v.* Harrow
South Wales *v.* I Zingari

FitzGerald was described by a contemporary as 'sagacious, cheery and amusing', and no doubt he needed all those qualities and more when he urged the Committee, who in 1860 had passed up the chance to purchase Lord's when Dark left, to think again and buy it now, six years later. Thus Mr Moses, who had since changed his name to Marsden, was approached. He had bought Lord's for £7,000; now he wanted £18,313. 6s. 8d. for the freehold.

The MCC members filled Willis's Rooms to vote and responded to the call of the president, Lord Suffield, that the Marylebone Club should hold a position in the cricketing world like that of the Jockey Club in racing, where a 'central authority and a playing headquarters would benefit cricket of all classes throughout the United Kingdom'.

It is hard to see how the members of this most exclusive of clubs could come to be talking about classes other than their own, but the fact is, the money was raised thanks to a loan from Mr William Nicholson, who was to require interest at five per cent. Thus the day came, August 22nd, 1866, when the purchase of the freehold became fact, and the Marylebone Club could call Lord's ground its own. By this time, too, the membership had risen to 980, half as much again as in 1863.

At the anniversary dinner that year, FitzGerald's name was coupled with the chief toast 'Cricket and Success to the MCC'.

Expansion and improvement was FitzGerald's policy. Club practice days were immediately increased from four to six, two-thirds of the ground had been re-levelled. Accommodation was built for the press for the first time and, in 1867, a grandstand was built by a private syndicate of members at a cost of £1,435; but they agreed that the club could purchase it at any time. Two years later the club did so for £1,703. 7s. 8d. On the opposite side of the ground, a new Tavern was erected and the tennis courts restored.

I Zingari team at Althorp, 1868. R. A. FitzGerald is seated in the middle; Hon. S. Ponsonby is on the far right.

Off FitzGerald now went to Paris with an MCC side to play the Paris Cricket Club at the Bois de Boulogne, the MCC winning by an innings and 135 runs. For the Paris Club, a Sergeant McCanlis was top scorer in both innings with 33 and 16. The deciding performances, however, came from Mr Alfred Lubbock, 102, and the bowlers, Russell Walker and A. J. Wilkinson. A mystified Frenchman remarked to FitzGerald after the match: 'It is a truly magnificent game, but I cannot understand why you do not engage a servant to field for you instead of having so much running about to do yourself.'

The secretary's role grew with every project, however; so much so that, in July 1867, FitzGerald indicated that he could no longer continue, and resigned. That most astute planner, the Hon. F. Ponsonby, went into action again, proposing that FitzGerald continue in office, but be paid an annual salary of £400. The annual dinner of 1868 confirmed this appointment of the club's first permanent, paid secretary.

Frederick Ponsonby's name is to be found either proposing or seconding most of the important appointments at Lord's at this time. As a young man he had played cricket for Eton against Harrow, for Cambridge University, and for the Gentlemen. He played in big matches until 1845, at which time he was one of the

I Zingari ('the Gypsies') at Sandringham. An 1866 team which includes HRH the Prince of Wales, later Edward VII.

three founders of I Zingari. He had first established his good sense within the Marylebone Club in the 1830s when the Gentlemen v. Players match was falling into disrepute as a non-contest always won by the professionals. When the MCC Committee refused to sustain the fixture any longer, the Hon. Frederick, supported by Mr Charles Taylor, made strong personal efforts to keep the game going. He was also a long-serving vice-president of Surrey and a trustee at Lord's.

An expanding club needed still more members, and capital schemes needed more membership income. The total by 1868 was over 1,200, but the usual high quota of aristocrats was not maintained. A wider range of men was being put up, with a Committee and its secretary urging priority for good, active cricketers. They were trying to mitigate that other Marylebone Club malaise, the lack of good cricket. It was important to raise amateur standards, and unwise to rely on the popularity of the few great matches.

Inevitably, too, one of FitzGerald's first tasks had been to improve the infamous Lord's pitch. The Lord's surface was still rough and uneven. Of course it suited the faster bowlers like Jackson, Tarrant and Willsher, but no batsman was ever going to get runs unless he could take a lot of bruising and also come down sharply with the bat on the shooter. There were few slow bowlers of the round-arm variety at this stage. All this made W. G. Grace's 134 not out, out of 201 for the Gentlemen against the Players in 1868, an amazing combination of eye, manual dexterity and bravery. W.G. said that it was very much to do with his light bat; he liked a bat of 2lb 5½oz and recommended that weight to everyone.

This particular match provoked the following letter from 'Middle Off' (Mr Gale) to *Bell's Life* on July 4th, 1868, reminiscent of the criticisms of the 1850s:

Had I been wicket-keeper or a batsman at Lord's during the late match, I should have liked (plus my gloves and pads) to have worn a single-stick mask, a Life Guardsman's cuirass, and a tin stomach-warmer ... The wicket reminded me of a middle-aged gentleman's head of hair, when the middle-aged gentleman, to conceal the baldness of his crown, applies a pair of wet brushes to some favourite long locks, and brushes them across the top of his head. So with the wicket. The place where the ball pitched was covered with rough grass, wetted and rolled down. It never had been, and never could be, good turf. I send a speciment or two for your inspection.

I have no hesitation in saying that in nine cricket grounds out of ten within twenty miles of London, whether Village Green or County Club grounds, a local club could find a better wicket in spite of drought, and in spite of their poverty than the Marylebone Club supplied to the Players of England.

In 1869 only one of the major games at Lord's lasted the three allotted days, MCC v. Nottinghamshire, and that was because Richard Daft played 'a marvel' of an innings (103) for Nottinghamshire, slow but sure, and W.G. made 121 for the MCC. Daft began as an amateur, turned professional in 1859, and was a regular in the Nottinghamshire side for twenty years, succeeding George Parr as captain.

Yet not even a mine-field of a pitch stopped the Eton v. Harrow festivities which appeared to be growing in popularity not diminishing. No sooner had that stern Nottinghamshire match ended than Lord's became the scene of social decoration. The grandstand was described by one writer as 'gay as a bank of *Summer Flowers*' and that was because the 'Ladies of England', in costume of brilliant hue, contrasted severely with the 'dark, sombre clad, dense mass' of men who crowded the seats and the pavilion roof. A hundred pounds more was taken at the gate than on any one day's cricket at Lord's before. *Wisden* of that year records:

> As many of the Drags of the 'Four-in-Hand Club' as could gain admission to the ground were grouped together at the NW end of the Pavilion. Around the ground, flanking the ropes, closely clustered (at most parts six deep) were six hundred carriages of the nobility and gentry, each vehicle full, most of them 'fairly' freighted. The tops of the wood-stacks had occupants, so had the window sills of the Racket Court, and the top of Mr Dark's garden wall; and how vast was the number of visitors each day may be estimated from the facts that on the Friday 'about' £770, and on Saturday, 'nearly' £500 was taken at the gates for admission money. In fact the Eton and Harrow match at Lord's has now become one of the prominent events of the London Season; for years and years to come it may so continue to be, and thus materially aid in keeping alive the interest for the fine old game, at present so manifest and general, among its very best supporters, 'The Gentlemen of England'. Eton won by an innings and 19 runs.

FitzGerald continued the levelling of turf, but in 1870 came a tragedy. George Summers, the Nottinghamshire cricketer, was hit on the head by a ball when he was batting. Some thought it pitched on a stone. Platts was the MCC and Ground bowler. Summers scored 41 in the first innings but the second innings card read 'Summers . . . hurt (not out) . . . 0'. Daft, the next man in, walked to the crease with a towel wrapped around his head.

Poor Summers was advised to stay in London for a while, but returned to Nottingham by train where he took herbal treatment and died at his father's house four days after the end of the match. Immediately the MCC bought the gravestone at a cost of £30 with an inscription 'to mark their sense of his qualities as a cricketer and to testify their regret at the untimely accident at Lord's Ground, which cut short a career full of promise, June 19th 1870 in the Twenty-sixth year of his age'. It was an accident that might have happened earlier, and it was particularly sad that it should have occurred when the levelling was already in progress. It was finished by 1875, by which time the groundsman, David Jordan, had been replaced by Peter Pearce.

The club played a strange medley of matches in the early 1870s. In 1871 the MCC and Ground played 'Fifteen Who Have Never Played at Lord's', and at the end of three days in which lightning, thunder and rain howled on a wild north wind, the visitors probably never wanted to play there again. MCC and the Royal Engineers that season conceded the 'frightful' number of 111 extras between them. When Gloucestershire came there was the unusual sight of seeing four brothers in one side, the Graces, E.M., W.G., G.F., and Henry. MCC and Ground played Middlesex and Fitz-Gerald asked if Middlesex would like to play some of their matches at Lord's. They said no because they were well settled at Prince's Ground in what was then 'Hans Place, Kensington', now in Knightsbridge not far from Sloane Square. There was a 'Big Wickets' match in 1872 between the First XI of the MCC and Ground and The Next Twenty – another experiment in which they used wickets an inch taller and an inch wider. Everyone described them as 'ugly' and after Alfred Shaw, the Nottingham slow bowler, had taken 11 of the Twenty's wickets for 25, and because it was thundering and freezing cold, they pulled up the big sticks early and abandoned the trial, unfinished.

Quite easily the most remarkable match of the 1872 season was the one against Surrey. It was postponed by a day because of incessant rain, which led to the covering of the pitch with tarpaulin. Unfortunately the turf turned to mud. The MCC batted first and lost seven wickets before they had scored a single run and *Wisden* called it a 'dead, deceitful pitch' and a 'queer light for batting'. W. G. Grace and Alfred Shaw were among the fallen. The first run was scored by Captain Beecher, coming in at number seven. Beecher got 8, Howitt 2 and Rylott was 6 not out. Total, all out, 16. Surrey responded with 49; MCC staggered to 71 in the second innings and Surrey lost five wickets in getting the 39 required to win.

In 1874 there were Americans at Lord's. Twenty-two baseball players from Boston and Philadelphia came on a mission to spread the knowledge of their own game, but at Lord's they played cricket, Eighteen of America v. Eleven of MCC. The MCC batted first, opening with Mr Lubbock and Mr Courtenay Edmund Boyle against H. Wright (medium, round) and McBride (fast underhand) 'who took three strides and then let fly a tremendously fast grubber that rarely rose from the ground an inch after it pitched'.

Play was suspended at five minutes past two when they retired for lunch. That was the signal for the ground staff to come on to the field to mark out a diamond shape for baseball. So it was baseball in the afternoon, which Boston won. Then the cricket resumed at six o'clock. In the evening there was a dinner with the president of the club, the Marquess of Hamilton, supported by the treasurer, Mr T. Burgoyne, and the secretary, Mr R. A. FitzGerald.

For cricketing skill seen at Lord's, nothing surpassed Alfred Shaw's bowling against the North of England for MCC and Ground that same year. He took all ten wickets in the North's first innings including those of such fine players as Mr A. N. Hornby, Oscroft, Lockwood and Greenwood. Shaw was the finest medium-pace bowler of his day. His action was rhythmical and easy, his arm sweeping round just above shoulder high, and he got enough turn, mainly from the off, but not too much. Many bowlers were swayed to follow an off-theory, but Shaw preferred to keep the ball straight, vary his flight and speed, but above all to maintain the accuracy. W.G. considered that 'the great power of his bowling lay in its good length and its unvaried precision'. He was back at Lord's in 1875 playing for Nottinghamshire, taking 7 wickets for 7 runs against the MCC, his memorable figures being 41 overs, 36 maidens, 7 runs, 7 wickets – 6 were clean bowled.

As secretary, FitzGerald did not escape criticism particularly about the pitch and the match lists, but he always obtained the support of the Committee. Sadly, ill health struck him and he was forced, first of all to spend winters abroad, with the blessing of the club, always hoping to return with fresh vigour, then to retire in 1876. He took refuge at his home in Hertfordshire where he died after years of suffering in 1881 at the early age of 47. The nature of his illness remains obscure.

In his thirteen years as secretary he had seen the membership of the club rise from 650 to 2,080. Apart from securing the future of Lord's by orchestrating the resources of the ground and performing many of the cosmetics on site, he had filled it with cricketers. With the help of his cabal of wise counsellors, a revolution had occurred in the committee-room. His new outlook, linked with the big, bearded doctor performing his miracles under the yellow and orange cap, had led MCC back to an awareness of its public role, and able, if called upon, to perform it.

13 First Century

In spite of the new enthusiasm that built up as FitzGerald brought changes to the club, it would be wrong to see the MCC as a House of Lord's about to assert itself. It was much more the run-down gentlemen's club straining to put its own house in order again – new carpets and curtains and better facilities for the surge of new members which would bring in welcome new subscription money. The Committee still harboured an altruistic care for cricket throughout the country, but it always had to be tugged along by outside invitations to intervene: it was not the initiator and, as in the matter of overarm bowling, sometimes it had to be threatened with revolt before it got a clear view through its own cigar smoke of the cricketing world outside.

Its primary concern was for the club, its members, and the quality of amateur cricket played at Lord's and in MCC and Ground matches elsewhere. Urgently, it needed a prosperous existence outside the glitter of the great social fixtures between the schools and universities. The successor to FitzGerald, as the second paid secretary, therefore, was an important nomination. Once again the Hon. F. Ponsonby got his man, seconded by Lord Verulam.

His choice was Henry Perkins, who took over in 1876 at a salary of £500 a year, a small, slightly built man, usually seen in a grey suit with tail-coat, rubbing his hands together: he could be very friendly, but sometimes fierce. He was no great believer in rule by committee and, even more forcefully than FitzGerald, who had come to rely greatly on committee help and indulgence during his latter years of ill-health, Perkins was inclined to swashbuckle – rather like his batting. He is on record as a 'slashing hitter, making enormous drives on and off, but with not quite a straight bat'. He was born in Sawston, Cambridgeshire; went up to Cambridge University and won a cricket Blue in 1854; and then after graduating he was called to the Bar and became well known on the Norfolk circuit. He also worked for *The Times* and his friends, seeing an excellent career developing, advised him against taking the MCC job. But not only did he respond to that call, he remained the MCC secretary for twenty-one years, all the time continuing

Henry Perkins, Secretary of MCC 1876–97. Amongst his innovations was to install a telegraph to send telegrams on the state of play – to Mincing Lane, Lloyds, Inner Temple, Westminster Hall, the United Universities, Oxford and Cambridge, Army and Navy, and Junior Carlton clubs, and to The Oval.

the policy of growth. In his time the membership rose from 2,000 to 4,000. However, not even 'Perkino', as he came to be called, could have planned or even imagined how much power would fall to the Marylebone Club during his stay.

The MCC was aware that county cricket had a strong following. It had become popular with the watching public, but, also, the professionals could see a good prospect of regular employment on a county staff, employed for a season instead of by the match. There was no formal county set-up, even though Surrey was listed as County Champions for 1864. It was a retrospective title. As Rowland Bowen points out in his *Cricket: A History of its Growth and Development throughout the World*, it was only in 1887 that 'somebody remembered that Surrey were champions for the first time since 1864'. By 1870 the press did publish a county list on the basis of the least number of matches lost. Some counties drew up rules in 1873, but there was no central organisation. In the end a county championship list was brought about only by the invention of newspapers.

Understandably the MCC saw it as nothing to do with them; they were concerned only with their own fixture programme. However, they were not slow to make a plan to cash in on county cricket's popular support: they proposed a knock-out cup competition, all matches to be played at Lord's, for a silver challenge cup – a county championship. The MCC agreed to pay all the expenses.

As Christopher Brookes describes it: 'Six counties were entitled to take part, but only Kent and Sussex accepted.' MCC had even agreed to have the name of the winning team engraved on the cup but, alas, the trophy was never even designed, so Kent and Sussex played in a unique match – part of a cup competition that was never played on a ground which neither of them owned.

Yet because of this lack of central organisation, the counties felt bound to turn to the Marylebone Club, for the immediate need was to obtain an impartial ruling on the qualification of cricketers to play for counties. A conference of county delegates came up with a proposal which the MCC debated at their annual general meeting of 1873. The MCC agreed that:

1. No cricketer, whether amateur or professional, shall play for more than one county during the same season.
2. Every cricketer, whether amateur or professional, born in one county and residing in another, shall be free to choose at the commencement of each season for which of those counties he will play and shall, during the season, play for that county only.

There were suggestions from the MCC and counter-suggestions, about a cricketer's right to play for a county where he owned property, but ultimately, what was carried was –

> 3. Should any question arise on the residential qualification, the same shall be left to the Committee of the Marylebone Club.

The Marylebone men sat back again, another consultancy over. But soon they would have to take notice of the flourishing counties. At the end of his career, W. G. Grace recalled a disorganised 1870 season of twenty-two county matches in all, when the attendances could be counted in hundreds; ten years later, nearly every county game was played home and away with the other seven, thirty-eight inter-county games in all, and the crowds were there in thousands. With Gloucestershire there were Kent, Middlesex, Lancashire, Yorkshire, Nottinghamshire, Surrey, Sussex. To make their own cricket at Lord's continously attractive, the Club needed a county involvement.

Several times in recent seasons the Committee had offered the use of Lord's to the Middlesex club. Every time Middlesex had said no. They were not even tempted in 1869 when they had no ground at all, even though they did, in fact, play Surrey at Lord's that year. When Mr Perkins repeated the offer, Middlesex had been settled at Prince's ground since 1872, and were still reluctant to move. Few people were convinced that there was room for a third first-class cricket club in London along with Surrey and the MCC. The Middlesex captain, I. D. Walker, was opposed to a move, mostly because he was unhappy about the financial arrangements. There was a jibe that he and his brother, R. D. Walker, who scorned pads, would not play at Lord's because it was too dangerous. They would have been safe, however, against the secretary because he still bowled underarm!

Eventually, it was agreed that Middlesex would move, at first only for four matches, with the county taking all gate-money and paying the expenses. Members of Middlesex would have access to the pavilion on county playing days and there would be no charge for the use of the ground. Negotiations went well and Middlesex's presence at Lord's began in the 1877 season. Soon they agreed to make donations to the MCC and later, when firmly established as part of the Lord's scene, the Marylebone–Middlesex liaison was put on a permanent financial basis.

Lillywhite commented: 'There had been for some time to the outside world, an air of monotony and apathy about the cricket at Lord's. The addition of the Middlesex fixtures filled a decided blank in the Marylebone programme, and there was certainly more life in the appearance of matters at headquarters than in the previous years.'

The club pressed on with its development in every possible direction. There were no entrepreneurs like Thomas Lord or William Ward or J. H. Dark to read fashions and risk capital; this was now the MCC, a corporate body, moving daringly forward and acquiring, as it went, a large and complex identity of its own.

A permanent, practical architect and surveyor was appointed at a fixed salary. Adjoining properties were annexed including Guy's Garden at the east end and, later, 45 St John's Wood Road was bought in order to sell luncheons. It was minuted that 'no direct gain could be looked for in the purchase of Guy's Garden, with the exception of £20 which was annually paid to the former proprietor for the exit of carriages through the garden during the Eton versus Harrow match (northern part of the ground). However, it proved of great value as a carriage stand during the inter-school, inter-university contests.'

An inspection of the minutes of the annual general meeting of 1878 reveals who was involved in the growth of the Marylebone Club. The patron was HRH The Prince of Wales; the president, Lord Fitzhardinge; and the treasurer, T. Burgoyne, Esq. There were five trustees, Earl Dudley, Earl Sefton, Hon. F. Ponsonby, R. Broughton, Esq., and W. Nicholson, Esq.

The Committee, which included the trustees, was: Lord Harris, Lord Lyttelton, the Hon. Spencer Ponsonby-Fane (younger brother of the Hon. F. Ponsonby), Viscount Lewisham, MP, the Hon. E. Chandos Leigh, Col. Taswell, Capt. Kenyon-Slaney, R. C. Antrobus, Esq., S. Bircham, Esq., C. E. Boyle, Esq., J. M. Heathcote, Esq., F. Lee, Esq., T. Ratcliff, Esq., A. W. Ridley, Esq., V. E. Walker, Esq., and G. H. Wood, Esq.

The assistant secretary and clerk to the Committee was Mr J. Murdoch.

The professionals engaged at Lord's in 1878 were: Thomas Hearne, senior (captain), Alfred Shaw, F. Farrands, John West, M. Flanagan, Walter Price, R. Clayton, Nixon (of Cambs), A. Rylott, F. Randon, F. Morley, F. Wyld, W. Mycroft, T. Mycroft, G. G. Hearne, junior (son of George), M. Sherwin, John Wheeler, Wilfred Flowers, George McCanlis and William Hearn (of Herts).

Ground superintendent: P. Pearce.

Tennis master: George Lambert (champion).

It was the 91st annual meeting and Mr Perkins, the secretary, was able to report a sum of £4,428 received from matches in 1877 and £2,385 expended. There were 2,304 members and 443 immediately up for election. New buildings included a lodge, a workshop and there was a detail of ground improvement; the report included high praise for Peter Pearce, the groundsman, describing Lord's 'so smooth, so firm, so well covered with herbage'. Unfortunately, it had been a wet summer with heavy rains and the observation added that 'the mucky, messy, muddy wickets played old scratch with true cricket'.

There was one more dimension left. The Marylebone Club, if it was to be the centre of cricket, would have to establish official contact with Australia. The club had always been keen on the fun tours, whether to Canada and America or to Paris, but there had been a build-up of cricket traffic to Australia, even though it took eight weeks to get there by steamer. The tours had been gathered by private individuals or small groups and backed by sponsors. Matches were played against odds. H. H. Stephenson's tour went in 1861–62, George Parr's in 1863–64 and W. G. Grace's in 1873–74. However, in 1876–77, James Lillywhite took a team which played on level terms and, at one o'clock on Thursday March 15th, 1877, Alfred Shaw bowled to Charles Bannerman a ball which was later recognised as the first ball in Test cricket. Perhaps Bannerman sensed the importance because he scored 165, his first Test century, but more likely he was squeezing the most out of a backer who had promised him £1 a run.

Although these teams were not representative, there was an obvious message in Australia's win by 45 runs – their cricket had been underestimated. Lillywhite's men won the other match, also played at Melbourne, but Australia made the oral request that only the best England players should be chosen to tour there in future. The colony and the mother country had begun their healthy but highly combative history.

To be an international cricketer in those days a man needed to be an intrepid seaman. Months at sea was not within everyone's physical capability and no doubt W. G. Grace himself could regale any doubter with grim descriptions of how, as a young man, he virtually hung over the side of the boat all the way to America and back with FitzGerald's team. So the first Australians in England, arriving under the captaincy of D. W. Gregory, needed to be a hardy lot.

No one in England knew much about Australians. H. S. Altham revealed that, before Gregory's men arrived, the president of the Cambridge University Cricket Club was under the impression that they were black (the first tour to England from Australia, in 1868, had in fact been by an Aborigines' team). Australia was still known then as a dumping ground for criminals, and no one has

The Australian touring team of 1878. The reason some people thought they were aborigines was that an aboriginal team had toured ten years earlier in 1868.

put that more vividly than Benny Green in his *Wisden* anthology of the period:

> As late as 1849 the Government of Lord John Russell had most generously sent, absolutely free of charge, a boatload of convicts to Melbourne, whose inhabitants, insisting that a civilised township was no place to dump felons, and thereby implying that civilised townships can usually be relied upon to have plenty of felons of their own, had the whole consignment moved on to Brisbane, an action which most unkindly suggested that Brisbane was not a civilised township.

Most British people imagined Australians to be roughnecked and wild and although Lillywhite would have reported decent cricket out there and James Southerton, the Surrey spinner who had also toured there as umpire with W.G.'s team in 1873, actually wrote praise of several of their players, no one believed that the 1878 visitors were anything but raw beginners. There was little publicity and certainly no praise. They slipped unheralded into Nottingham, and retreated, damp and cold in chilling weather, beaten by an innings and 14 runs. However, a few days later, London crowds flooded to the Tavistock Hotel in Covent Garden to glimpse a new and astonishingly successful breed of cricketers who had just defeated the might of the MCC at Lord's, not only

MCC v. The Australians at Lord's

Played at Lord's, May 27, 1878

Result: The Australians won by nine wickets

MCC

	FIRST INNINGS		SECOND INNINGS	
W. G. Grace	c Midwinter b Allan	4	b Spofforth	0
A. N. Hornby	b Spofforth	19	b Boyle	1
C. Booth	b Boyle	0	b Boyle	0
A. W. Ridley	c A. Bannerman b Boyle	7	b Boyle	0
A. J. Webbe	b Spofforth	1	b Spofforth	0
F. Wyld	b Boyle	0	b Boyle	5
W. Flowers	c and b Spofforth	0	b Boyle	11
G. G. Hearne	b Spofforth	0	b Spofforth	0
A. Shaw	st Murdoch b Spofforth	0	not out	2
G. F. Vernon	st Murdoch b Spofforth	0	b Spofforth	0
F. Morley	not out	1	c Horan b Boyle	0
Extras	Leg bye	1		
Total		**33**		**19**

Bowling

AUSTRALIANS

	FIRST INNINGS				SECOND INNINGS			
Boyle	14	7	14	3	8.1	6	3	6
Spofforth	5.3	3	4	6	9	2	16	4
Allan	9	4	14	1				

THE AUSTRALIANS

	FIRST INNINGS		SECOND INNINGS	
C. Bannerman	c Hearne b Morley	0	b Shaw	1
W. Midwinter	c Wyld b Shaw	10	not out	4
T. Horan	c Grace b Morley	4	not out	7
A. C. Bannerman	c Booth b Morley	0		
T. W. Garrett	c Ridley b Morley	6		
F. R. Spofforth	b Shaw	1		
D. W. Gregory	b Shaw	0		
H. F. Boyle	c Wyld b Morley	2		
W. L. Murdoch	b Shaw	9		
F. E. Allan	c and b Shaw	6		
G. H. Bailey	not out	3		
Total		**41**	Total (1 wkt.)	**19**

Bowling

MCC	FIRST INNINGS				SECOND INNINGS			
Shaw	33.2	25	10	5	8	6	4	1
Morley	33	19	31	5	8	4	8	0

Umpires: A. Rylott and M. Sherwin

by the considerable margin of nine wickets, but also within a single day. In fact, on May 27th, 1878, there is on record only four and a half hours of actual play, beginning at three minutes past twelve and ending at twenty minutes past six. Only 128 4-ball overs and 2 balls were bowled and only 105 runs were scored in the match.

Crowds gathered around the pavilion after the match, shouting out the names of the bowlers who had done the damage, Spofforth and Boyle. *Punch* was not slow with its imagery.

> *The Australians came down like a wolf on the fold:*
> *The Marylebone cracks for a trifle were bowled;*
> *Our Grace before dinner was very soon done,*
> *And Grace after dinner did not get a run.*

The Australians played two more matches at Lord's. They beat Middlesex by 98 runs and, at the close, F. R. Spofforth made an unusual gesture for a hostile fast bowler, by presenting the Hon. E. Lyttelton, who had scored a brilliant 113 for the home side, with a walking-stick. The other match was won by Cambridge University, playing under Lyttelton's captaincy. The game is best remembered for an historic hit by Bannerman off P. H. Morton's bowling. The ball pitched short of the ring but shot up over the low stand on the left of the pavilion, clearing Lord Londes-borough's drag and crashing into the wall behind.

They were outstanding players in the Australian side. Banner-man was a good, natural hitter. W. L. Murdoch and the Irish-born Horan were dependable. However, if they taught lessons it was in the art and inventiveness of their bowling and field-placing. They had a quartet of excellent bowlers, led by Spofforth, fast and hostile, but who also used variations of speed and a break-back off the pitch which gave Boyle many catches at short leg. Boyle, heavily bearded, was right-arm round-arm and fast; Garrett was right-arm and medium-fast concentrating on off-theory, and, lastly, Francis Allan, whose only tour this was, yet who, in Australia, was called the 'bowler of the century' because from a height of 6ft 1in. he whipped the ball down and managed to swing it in the air.

That very next winter the MCC took a look for themselves at cricket in Australia but not in an official way; instead Lord Harris led a team of amateurs out there, assisted by two professionals, Ulyett and Emmett, both of Yorkshire. They played a match as an England team in Melbourne and lost to Australia by ten wickets. Spofforth again was the scourge, taking 13 wickets for 110 in the match, including what has been registered as the first Test hat-trick, removing Royle, Mackinnon and Emmett off successive balls. David Frith's *Pictorial History of England versus Australia* shows

Lord Harris, pictured
in 1872, aged 21.

a photograph of the amateurs on that tour, with neckties and jackets with high revers collars, Lady Harris seated in the centre, Mrs Hornby alongside and a Miss Ingram among those sitting on the floor. Unfortunately, in their match against New South Wales they faced an angry crowd. Murdoch was run out; there was brawling; the crowd invaded the pitch and assaulted Lord Harris himself. Gregory, the home captain, went on to the field to ask that Coulthard, the English umpire, be retired. When it was over Harris said that he would never play against an Australian team again.

Perhaps the boat trip home shook the anger out of him because it was Lord Harris who helped to arrange the big match of Australia's next visit to England in 1880, their first away Test at The Oval.

Somewhere, at this point, the urgent intentions of the MCC to get the best cricket at Lord's, and to be part of the rush of international exchanges with Australia, disappeared because there was no match at Lord's at all on this visit. Perhaps Harris's ire was still rumbling after all, but that seems unlikely. In fact no one had been very keen to give the Australians fixtures after the Sydney riot of 1879. Furthermore, the English professionals were beginning to mutter about the so-called amateur status of the tourists, suspecting that the Australian amateurs were being paid more than the English professionals.

In the end it was only the persistence of the Surrey Club which secured the visit and set up the one Test match. Selection of the England team was always then the responsibility of the home club, and Surrey invited Lord Harris to be the captain.

W. G. Grace scored 152 in England's first innings and Murdoch 153 not out in Australia's second; however the balance was tilted England's way by the support batting of A. P. Lucas, 55, Harris, 52, and A. G. Steel, 42, then by the bowling of Morley, 5–56, and a famous catch by G. F. Grace off a monster hit by Bonnor. E. M. Grace also was in the England side, which is the earliest instance of three brothers playing in the same Test side. England rejoiced in their five-wicket success, but Lord Harris always conceded that the absence of the 'Demon' Spofforth, because of a damaged finger, made a crucial difference.

The next trip to Australia was organised by the business trio of professionals, Alfred Shaw, Shrewsbury and Lillywhite. They lost two Tests and drew two, and if by now there remained any doubts about the quality and competitiveness of Australian cricket they were dissolved next time around in England, at The Oval in 1882. Spofforth was back at his best with 14 wickets for 90 in the match. It was all over in two days. The *Sporting Times* published a mock obituary: 'In Affectionate Remembrance of English cricket which died at The Oval, 29th August 1882, deeply lamented by a large circle of sorrowing friends and acquaints. R.I.P. N.B. The body will be cremated and the ashes taken to Australia.'

Revenge came quickly during the following winter of 1882–83 when the Hon. Ivo Bligh's team won two out of the three Test matches planned. Then a famous story was born that some Melbourne ladies had burned a bail, sealed it in an urn and presented it to the England captain. Ivo Bligh later married one of those ladies; and in 1927 when, as Lord Darnley, he died, he bequeathed the Ashes to the MCC.

The indication that the MCC was much keener to stage a Test match when the Australians returned to England in 1884 was that

The Ashes. They never leave Lord's, whoever has 'won' them.

The England team v. Australia, Lord's, 1884

Mr Perkins acted as the Australians' agent. The Peninsular and Oriental steamer, *Assam*, landed them at Plymouth in March, whereupon Bonnor, as soon as he was on land, proceeded to throw a cricket ball 119 yards and 5 inches having taken a bet on board that he could not reach 115 yards.

Lord's duly staged its first Test match in July, even though just before that, the club's president, the Hon. Robert Grimston, died in office. He had long been associated with the MCC by which, says the annual report, 'he was so justly esteemed as a true friend, a thorough sportsman, and the type of an honourable gentleman.' He was, though, usually reactionary in his advice to the club. He was a devoted Harrovian and a lifelong friend of the Hon. Spencer Ponsonby-Fane. As twelfth man for Harrow, he was recalled as an unusual batsman who took a defensive grip on the bat, the backs of both hands behind the bat handle, and a crouched stance, working on the theory that you had to hold your head down as

Hon. Robert Grimston, a conservative president of MCC, died in office just before the 1884 Test v. Australia began at Lord's. When he was a player he used to employ two bats – one of them was much heavier, for use when facing Alfred Mynn.

Caricature of A. G. Steel.

near as possible to ball level – not all that easy when the bowling is underarm!

England won the Test in which all individual performances were dwarfed by the brilliance of A. G. Steel's 148 in his first innings. In reply to Australia's 229, England had lost five wickets for 135 and Barlow, in his *Forty Seasons of First-Class Cricket*, recalls how Lord Harris, the England captain, said to him as he went out to bat, 'For heaven's sake, Barlow, stop this rot!' He did. His 38 runs helped to make a partnership of 98 with Steel. Two Yorkshiremen played an important part in the victory by an innings and 5 runs, Peate the slow left-arm bowler and Ulyett, the resilient all-rounder, who, among his seven wickets in the second innings, caught a terrific right-handed caught-and-bowled from the mighty Bonnor.

The MCC also beat the tourists by an innings at Lord's. The Lord's pitch had become more generous to batsmen, and three centuries were scored for MCC: W. G. Grace, 101, A. G. Steel, 134, and W. Barnes, 105 not out.

Also in 1884 the Philadelphians made their first visit to England, and there was some serious discussion about playing Test matches against them. Cricket had long been established in the United States, with Philadelphia the major centre. Universal recognition of Philadelphia cricket came in 1878 when they met D. W. Gregory's Australians on even terms and led them by 46 on the first innings. It was a full Australian team which included Spofforth, Blackham, the Bannermans, Murdoch and Boyle. Schools played cricket in Philadelphia and palatial pavilions were built at most of the centres like the Merion Cricket Club; they played a Gentlemen v. Players match which drew crowds of 20,000.

All these stories were told in England by the large number of professionals who went to America to coach. John Barton King, whose career flourished from 1893–1912, was easily their most famous cricketer, a fast bowler who kept up his speed for twenty years and was a master of swing and accuracy.

There was no denying that, however uncomfortable the prospect of travel, the cricketers of the world were on the move. The first English team in New Zealand had been George Parr's in 1863–64, an extension of his Australian tour; the first team of touring Indians were the Parsees who came to England and played at Lord's in 1886. There was an early tour of Englishmen to South Africa in 1888–89, and of South Africans to England in 1894. A year later R. Slade Lucas went on a missionary exercise with his side to the West Indies.

The most ambitious cricket traveller, perhaps, was W. E. Midwinter, who was born in Gloucestershire and played for that county, and yet who settled in Victoria, Australia. He represented both England and Australia in Tests and for a while commuted between the two countries to make a cricket living all the year round.

However, as the nineteenth century began to close, with a universal enthusiasm for the game rivalled only by the Saturday-afternoon soccer crowds which were now piling into the grounds in England – it was clear also that the Marylebone Club had become meticulous about its outward appearance and inward health. It continued the attempts to help the professional player, either by subsidy from the Marylebone Cricketers' Fund – which had been set up by MCC for its own professionals more or less in opposition to the Cricketers' Fund Friendly Society – whose coffers were filled mainly from the Whitsun Monday matches, or by the award of a special benefit match to an outstanding man. Alfred Shaw, for example, received his much-deserved game, North v. South, at Lord's over the Whitsun holiday of 1879. Unfortunately it was washed out by rain for a day and a half, but Shaw made his playing point by routing the South with 6 for 39 and 8 for 21.

Also played for the Cricketers' Fund in mid-September, 1884, was a match between Smokers and Non-Smokers. It was the idea of V. E. Walker, who, apart from wanting to support the Cricketers' Fund, could also see the fun in watching some of the touring Australians play against each other. The Non-Smokers won by 9 wickets, Bonnor got a century for them; W. G. Grace, 5 for 29 in the first innings, Barlow 5 for 24 in the second. The only Smoker to perform with any distinction was Peate who took 6 wickets for 30 in the first innings and the only wicket in the second. Among the other Australians in action were Non-Smokers Bannerman, Murdoch and Scott, and Smokers McDonnell, Giffen, Palmer and Spofforth.

MCC's most serious responsibility was still, of course, the custody of the Laws, and a long time was spent circulating many overseas authorities before presenting a completely new code in 1884. Much of the detail simply brought up to date existing practice – boundaries were formally introduced, five- or six-ball overs were legalised for one-day cricket.

By 1889 the five-ball over was law in all cricket. In England there had been four balls to an over from the 1744 Code of Laws: the move to five was to try to save time, but soon, in 1900, the six-ball over would become law in England. Australia had moved to six in 1887 and, later, in 1922, would adopt the eight-ball over. South Africa waited until 1937–38 for the eight-ball over and

England experimented with eight balls, too, in 1939 but did not continue with it after the Second World War. The object behind the changes was always that of saving time.

The major adjustment for the cricketers themselves was the new law that no bowler could send down two overs in succession, but could otherwise change ends when he pleased. Bowling consecutive overs at each end was not usual practice. In fact the only instance of it to date at Lord's was by Attewell for the Married against the Single, but even then it was accidental, probably after an interval.

There was stern enquiry into the club's domestic organisation, too. A formidable committee under the chairmanship of Lord Wenlock, and including Lord Harris with Messrs Lee, Hemming and Rutter, conducted an enquiry into the 'position of the paid officers and servants of the Club'. They reported in July 1886 that since the business of the club was so extensive, the secretary should be in a position to provide 'active personal supervision' throughout the year. 'We accordingly recommend that he should live in close proximity to the Ground . . . Whilst Mr Perkins remains Secretary the rent and the outgoings should be paid by the Club. We further recommend that all letters addressed to the Secretary should be opened daily.'

They found that the secretary did not exercise sufficient control over the engagement or dismissal of persons in the club's employment. 'We think that a register should be kept showing the dates at which the various servants of the Club are engaged and the terms of such engagement.'

Lord Wenlock's committee also recommended, in order to lighten the work of the clerical staff, that the record of scores of club matches should be printed at the club's printing plant, not kept in manuscript. In addition they suggested: 'an economy of time and labour would be effected by the permanent arrangement of the seats in the Members' Enclosure on block plans.'

There was a strong recommendation that the winter ground staff be reduced, and linked with: 'We think it undesirable that the men should receive the same wages when absent on account of illness as they do when at work.' Instead they thought it possible to establish an insurance scheme or sick fund for the staff's benefit.

On score-card sellers: 'We are of the opinion that the amount (*viz.* ½d. per card) received by the boys for the sale of match cards is excessive.'

Then, apart from small observations about the non-settlement by some members of their tennis-court accounts, and that the billiard room be handed over to the tenant of the Tavern in the winter, the weightier recommendations were for a weekly meeting of the finance committee during the cricket season, and 'looking to the increase of business of the Club since 1880', they thought that the Committee should meet on the second Monday in each month from October to March. Thus the club's rush of activity and responsibility in cricket as well as its increasingly complex domestic arrangements required the sinking of bureaucratic foundations. It was, after all, a hundred years old.

The year 1887 was one of celebration: the centenary of the Marylebone Club as well as Queen Victoria's jubilee. There was a special centenary week of cricket at Lord's in June – MCC and Ground against England, and 18 MCC Veterans (over 40) versus the Gentlemen of MCC.

A dinner was held in the old tennis court, £1 a ticket, when the chair was taken by the president, the Hon. E. Chandos Leigh. Fortunately it is possible to be transported back to 1887 by the nostalgia of Sir Pelham Warner (born 1873) in his history, *Lord's*, published in 1946.

> The first time I saw Lord's was on Friday, May 20, 1887. Only recently arrived in England from the West Indies, I had as a boy devoured the pages of *The Field*, which in those days gave a great deal of space to cricket, *Wisden*, and *The Times*. I had seen in the *Illustrated London News* a group of the Australian team in which G. E. Palmer was wearing a stiff-fronted shirt, and nothing would satisfy me until I was given one exactly like his! The dramatic moments in the famous Test Match at the Oval in 1882, A. G. Steel's 148 at Lord's two years later, Ulyett's wonderful catch-and-bowl of G. J. Bonnor in the same match and Shrewsbury's 164 on a sticky wicket for England against Australia at Lord's in 1886 were vivid in my imagination. I used to dream of cricket! It was, therefore, with a thrill of anticipation and delight that I passed through the main gate and watched the play from a seat in front of the ivy-covered tennis court, with the great clock in the middle, where the Mound now stands. I can recall vividly even now the first wicket I ever saw taken at Lord's – C. Aubrey Smith, from the Nursery end, clean bowling F. E. Lacey with what looked from the ring a very good one.
>
> W. G. Grace was one of the Club side, and during the luncheon interval he passed near by, and I gazed with undisguised admiration, not to say awe, on the greatest personality the cricket world has ever known, or will ever know. With his black beard and giant figure, with an MCC cap crowning his massive head, he bestrode the cricket world like some Colossus, and little did I dream then that one day I should play with and against him.
>
> A month later my preparatory school was taken in a body to see the MCC play England during the Centenary week, in which nearly all the great cricketers of the day were taking part. Of the players in that match none survives today, but I can see Lord Hawke, with his cap worn back to front, and A. J. Webbe catching Louis Hall at short-leg, right under the bat, as if it were but yesterday. I can recall, too, A. E. Stoddart's and Shrewsbury's great first-wicket partnership of 266; Ulyett's powerful hits over deep extra cover's head off Barnes of Nottinghamshire, scattering the spectators in Block A; George Lohmann's artistic and cleverly flighted bowling; and Johnny Briggs at cover. It all comes back 'quick like a shot through the brain'. Here is the score of this great match:

M.C.C. v. England

Played at Lord's, June 13, 14, and 15, 1887

Result: England won by an innings and 117 runs

M.C.C.	FIRST INNINGS		SECOND INNINGS	
Dr W. G. Grace	b Lohmann	5	c and b Briggs	45
A. N. Hornby (Capt.)	c and b Briggs	16	b Bates	6
W. Barnes	b Briggs	8	c and b Bates	53
A. J. Webbe	c Briggs b Lohmann	0	c Pilling b Bates	14
W. Gunn	b Lohmann	61	c Shrewsbury b Briggs	10
G. G. Hearne	b Briggs	8	c Barlow b Lohmann	6
J. G. Walker	c Hall b Lohmann	3	b Briggs	25
Hon. M. B. Hawke	b Lohmann	16	b Briggs	10
W. Flowers	b Lohmann	19	c Lohmann b Bates	43
J. T. Rawlin	not out	18	c W. Read b Bates	4
M. Sherwin	b Bates	17	not out	1
Byes 3, wide 1		4	Byes 4, leg bye 1	5
Total		**175**		**222**

Bowling

ENGLAND	FIRST INNINGS				SECOND INNINGS			
Lohmann	57	29	62	6	32	13	60	1
Briggs	55	22	84	3	39	8	77	4
Bates	5	2	5	1	28.3	15	46	5
Barlow	2	2	0	0				
Ulyett	8	3	20	0	21	8	34	0

ENGLAND

ENGLAND	FIRST INNINGS		SECOND INNINGS
A. Shrewsbury	c Barnes b Rawlin	152	
A. E. Stoddart	c and b Rawlin	151	
R. G. Barlow	lbw Rawlin	0	
M. Read	c Sherwin b Flowers	25	
W. W. Read (Capt.)	c Webbe b Barnes	74	
W. Bates	c Hornby b Barnes	28	
G. Ulyett	c Sherwin b Barnes	46	
L. Hall	c Webbe b Barnes	0	
J. Briggs	b Barnes	9	
G. A. Lohmann	not out	9	
R. Pilling	c Gunn b Barnes	0	
Byes 8, leg byes 12		20	
Total		**514**	

Bowling

M.C.C.	FIRST INNINGS				SECOND INNINGS
Barnes	74.2	30	126	6	
Rawlin	90	39	140	3	
Grace	36	16	65	0	
Flowers	74	29	122	1	
Hearne	9	3	19	0	
Webbe	13	5	22	0	

Umpires: John West and T. Mycroft

G. A. Lohmann of Surrey, a bowler of rare artistry who died in 1901 when only 36.

View of Lord's during play in the Gentlemen v. Players match, July 11th, 1887

It was fitting, later on in the Lord's centenary season, when London was in its pomp for the royal celebrations, bustling with statesmen, soldiers and sailors, that Canada, Britain's oldest dominion, should play against the MCC at Lord's. They drew the match, and it was evident on their tour that they had some talented players. D. W. Saunders, the wicket-keeper, became known as the 'Blackham of Canada'. Dr E. E. Ogden, a clever slow-medium bowler who could spin the ball sharply, took 12 wickets for 163 against the MCC, including I. D. Walker, A. J. Webbe, A. E. Stoddart, C. I. Thornton and T. C. O'Brien. *Wisden* wrote: 'They fairly earned the respect and friendship of their opponents by their modesty in victory, their cheerfulness under defeat and their good-fellowship always.'

In the centenary year, too, after long negotiations, the club acquired Henderson's Nursery, or the Pine Apples as it was often called, adding another 3½ acres to Lord's ground. Apart from

'Lord's in danger.'
The MCC go out to
meet the enemy.' The
enemy was the Great
Central Railway who
wished to build
tunnels under the
eastern fringe of the
practice ground.

William Nicholson, a
member of MCC since
1845 and its president
in 1879. He played an
invaluable role by
lending money to the
club, when it wanted
to buy the freehold
of Lord's, and to
help pay for the new
pavilion in 1890. He
was one of MCC's
few non-aristocratic
presidents, having
made his money from
gin. He had played
for Harrow and
Middlesex, and died
in 1909 after catching
a chill at the Eton v.
Harrow match.

the best pineapples in England, tulips were grown there, too.
Appropriately the Nursery End was born for the practice and
development of cricketers. Up to that time the practice nets had
been on the outfield.

The then Manchester and Sheffield Railway, which later became
the Great Central Railway, promoted a Bill in Parliament in 1890
to acquire Lord's in order to run their line under it. This could
have meant the end of Lord's. The Marylebone men mustered the
members with the most potent political clout, such as Sir Henry
James, a former Attorney-General, and Messrs Bircham, the Par-
liamentary agent for opposing the Bill, and Perkins, and fought
off the threat. A *Punch* cartoon appeared at the time, in which
W.G. on a charger, with pads on and bat in hand, advanced at
the head of a 'battalion' of cricketers to drive off the 'enemy', who
were depicted by a railway engine puffing furiously.

The deal was eventually struck that, for permission to tunnel
under the practice ground, the Great Central gave the club the
site of the Clergy Female Orphanage school which stood on the
corner of St John's Wood Road and Wellington Road.

There remained one further seal to confirm the late-Victorian
self-confidence and conviction that Lord's Cricket Ground would
exist for ever, and that was the building of a new pavilion. The
foundation-stone was laid by the Hon. Spencer Ponsonby-Fane in
September 1889. The mammoth edifice was ready for the club's
annual meeting the following May at a cost of £21,000. Ponsonby-
Fane, brother of the Hon. F. Ponsonby, was popular and respected.
He had been elected a member in 1840 at the age of 16 and because

Effigy of Sir Spencer Ponsonby-Fane, Treasurer from 1879–1915 – one of the terracotta figures on the pavilion balcony.

he was a nephew, by marriage, of Lord Frederick Beauclerk, he was a positive link with MCC's earlier days. For many years (1879–1915) he was Treasurer but, for some unknown reason, strangely declined the presidency, though often asked.

To pay for the pavilion and various purchases at Lord's, the club had to turn once more to Mr William Nicholson for a loan. There was always some reluctance to do this because Nicholson was one of the comparatively new upper class who had made his money from trade, in his case, from gin. Although he had been on the committee in the 1870s, a member since 1845, and also an MP, there was still prejudice in this closed, elite society. He did become a trustee, and was elected club president in 1879, but the list of presidents either side of him emphasised his lack of title. The last untitled president before him was J. H. Scourfield, in 1870, and the one before that, T. Chamberlayne, in 1845. The first after him was V. E. Walker in 1891.

However, as far as membership of the club was concerned, there was a widening cross-section as the membership increased quickly, a new breed of man floating to the top of the pool of social importance, with fortunes made from industry or from urban interests rather than from traditional land-owning. Christopher Brookes in *English Cricket* describes them as 'business aristocrats' and believes they brought fresh vision to an otherwise myopic MCC membership. Certainly since the great educational reforming headmaster of Rugby, Dr Thomas Arnold, had conveyed his

In return for permission to tunnel, the railway company gave MCC the site of the Clergy Female Orphanage School on the corner of St John's Wood Road. A former pupil at the school said: 'How envious we were of those few girls who were allowed to go on the roof of the house with the mistresses to watch a cricket match at Lord's – a privilege granted to rare merit'.

MARYLEBONE CRICKET CLUB – THE NEW PAVILION AT LORDS.
THOMAS VERITY, Architect

message of religion and moral regimen on to which were grafted competitive team games (though not at Arnold's insistence), old schools reformed, new ones competed and a public school education became a real adhesive between old aristocrats and new. It was through the schools that a middle-class father could project his sons into the governing class.

In 1877, out of a total MCC membership of 2,291, the number of titled members of the aristocracy was 337. By 1886 the membership was 5,091 but the titled number had fallen to 327. The MCC was not only growing fast, but it was also changing character.

Perhaps the MCC itself sensed this and wanted in some way to reverse the trend – for when in 1888 it offered one hundred life memberships of the club for £100 apiece to help pay for the new pavilion, it was stipulated that these new members be at least 77 years old. Or maybe the club treasurer was simply making a canny investment? Either way the old titled members from the landed classes were combining with the new urban aristocracy and together were projecting the Marylebone Club into a perilous position of responsibility and power. The pavilion, designed by the architect F. T. Verity, was its symbol, with its two great towers at each end of the huge central structure, both crowned with the monogram, MCC, and adorned with a flagstaff. Members in the Long Room, who perched on high chairs to watch their cricket, took on the appearance of judges. Whispers from the committee room alongside seemed to float secretly into the thick, cushioning walls.

To complete the aura of authority it took only the building of the Mound Stand in 1899 to complete a magnificent backcloth for the game of cricket. Not everyone was pleased, however. Alfred D. Taylor, who wrote an affectionate history, *The Annals of Lord's and History of the MCC* (1903), concluded his romantic tale with a pained observation:

The architect, F. T. Verity's drawing of the new pavilion. From *The Architect*, November 1st, 1889. Also Verity helped to design the Albert Hall (1871).

> The cobbler no longer associates with the Duke, or the farmer with the Squire. The plebs that pays its shillings are marked off with painful distinction from the patricians who are entitled to higher honour. No longer do the 'masses' mingle with society. Picnic days are over; the array of carriages that once lined the southern side of the ground is gone, while the coaches that took up their position at the Nursery end have no inducement. In short, the game is robbed of its old world charm.
>
> The shilling crowd is gradually being ousted by the MCC, and quite three-fourths of the seats are allocated to the club men and the paying public. There are more benches, it is true, but they have not increased in proportion, and the time must come when the admittance to Lord's will be limited. The catering is now done by MCC, and everything considered for comfort and expedience that can be desired: still, for all this, Lord's is Lord's no longer. Are there not 5,000 names enrolled and 9,000 more clamouring for admission? Lord's is transformed out of all recognition. It is an amphitheatre for gladiatorial contests with its massive and mighty circle of seats, stands, boxes and buildings. Old Lord would turn in his grave at the transformation of his favourite spot.

Taylor's conclusion openly declared that 'MCC is a club no longer: it is a national institution.' As, indeed, was the game itself now, and increasingly at the heart of British life and the British Empire.

In Taylor's eyes Lord's had not thrown off the 'anything-for-a-shilling' style of the earlier proprietors, for instance there were still canary shows in the members' dining-room each autumn. On the other hand, the Committee could list their refusals to a Mr Allridge who had wanted to liberate 1,000 pigeons from Lord's, to a Clowns XI who wanted to joke around for charity, or to the Middlesex Volunteers who wished to drill there.

The racquet games were popular with the upper classes. Real tennis had been played at Lord's from 1838, and for many years, 1871–85, the club had been lucky enough to have the champion,

George Lambert, as resident tennis master. When lawn tennis began (1875) the first laws were formed by the MCC tennis committee, Hon. Spencer Ponsonby-Fane, J. M. Heathcote, E. Chandos Leigh, Sir W. Hart-Dyke and the Hon. C. G. Lyttelton. Indeed, the first lawn-tennis singles championship for men was won in 1877 by a MCC member, Spencer William Gore, who beat another MCC member, C. G. Heathcote, in the semi-final.

In the second year Spencer Gore lost to another cricketer, Frank Hadow, but very closely because Hadow, after winning the semi-final, went to watch the Eton v. Harrow game at Lord's and got a touch of the sun. In those days the tennis championships were adjourned over the week-end to allow the great schools' match to take place, otherwise there would have been no crowd at Wimbledon.

Since lacrosse, bowls, baseball and the public schools rackets matches were other games played at Lord's, *Punch*, making a similar case to Alfred Taylor's, suggested, on July 18th, 1900, that the MCC was money-grabbing, not only from those supporters they needed most but from casual passers-by too.

NEW REGULATIONS FOR LORD'S

(Hourly expected)

1. Members of cricketing county elevens will be charged a guinea a head gate money daily.
2. Umpires will pay a fee of five guineas a match of three days.
3. Balloons passing over the grounds will be expected to pay a shilling a second during the passage.
4. Residents of houses surrounding the ground by paying five guineas per annum can avoid the erection of view-impeding hoardings, and thus secure a splendid view of the matches.
5. A small charge (2s. 6d. per person) will be made for the use of the ground during the luncheon interval.
6. Competing county elevens requiring the pitch to be rolled will pay five shillings a time between wickets or three times for twelve and sixpence.
7. After rain sawdust can be secured at four shillings an ounce.
8. Should the crease require re-marking, pipe-clay can be obtained at ten shillings a brush-full.
9. The scoring boards will be erected in a tent, and the public will be permitted to examine them at a shilling a peep.
10. Tickets for gentlemen of the press will be issued at a guinea a day, and accommodation will be found for the ticket-holders behind the chimneys of the grand stand.

If one looks back over the nineteenth century, to both the lowest point of the club's fortunes and to the highest, it can be said that the 1860s – when there was vociferous pressure for the Cricket Parliament, when the pitch was dangerous and the best players had gone – was the trough, but that 1894 was the pinnacle. By then the counties, who had laboured confusedly in their County Cricket Council, stumbled on their own jealousies and dishonesties, tripped on selfishness and a lack of central organisation, and had fallen out with each other. In 1890 the prospects of conciliation had been so utterly exhausted that the chairman dissolved the Council by his own casting vote. Then, in 1894, they turned to the Marylebone Club for sanity and the impartial view; it was their recognition of the MCC as the ultimate arbiter of the game in the country.

Soon the 'Classification of Counties' came from Lord's, as related by the Rev. R. S. Holmes in *The County Cricket Championship* (1894):

> Cricketing counties shall be considered as belonging to first-class or not. There is no need for a further sub-division. First-Class Counties are those whose matches with one another, with the MCC and Ground, with the Universities, with the Australians, and other such elevens as shall be adjudged first-class by the MCC Committee, are used in the compilation of first-class batting and bowling averages. There shall be no limit to the number of first-class Counties. The MCC Committee may bring new Counties into the list, may remove existing ones from it, or may do both.

This arrangement was as easily understood and accepted as was the championship points system – 1 point for a win, 1 point deducted for a loss, nothing for a draw – 'and the county which should have obtained the greatest number of points to the total of finished matches shall be reckoned champion county.'

Plan of Lord's ground, 1891.

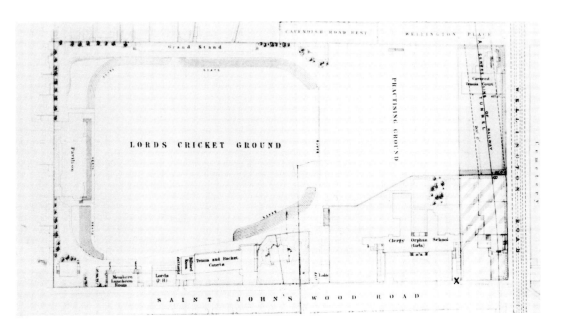

As for Henry Perkins, the secretary, his time in office was almost up, but not before W. G. Grace had played his dazzling Indian summer of 1895, nor before a glorious stream of amateur batsmen began to flow, especially from the universities – K. S. Ranjitsinhji, F. S. Jackson, C. B. Fry, A. C. MacLaren, A. E. Stoddart, R. H. Spooner, R. E. Foster, P. F. Warner, G. O. Smith. He had also seen the MCC refuse to pick Ranji, for reasons of colour, in their Test team against Australia in 1896, even though he was adding a new dimension to the skills of batting. Lord Harris, it was said, did not like choosing 'birds of passage'. Ranji did however score 62 and 154 not out in the following Test at Manchester and, when his cricketing days were over, he did return to his princely commitments by sitting on the Indian Council of Princes and the League of Nations.

The big eight counties were Kent, Lancashire, Middlesex, Gloucestershire, Nottinghamshire, Surrey, Sussex and Yorkshire. They were augmented before Perkins's departure by the admission of Somerset in 1891, then, in 1894, of Derbyshire, Essex, Leicestershire and Warwickshire, and Hampshire in 1895. Only Worcestershire (1899), Northamptonshire (1905) and Glamorgan (1921) were to come.

Henry Perkins resigned in 1897 – he was 65 – but there was an aspect of the pomp and power of this Marylebone Club now which he did not fully realise – his own job, as secretary of the MCC, had moved on a long way from the honorary days when Benjamin Aislabie used to puff and pant his way around Lord's, pen raised to take a subscription in the Red Book or to compose a rhyme for after dinner – to the extent that the club had now to hire the Queen's Hall in Langham Place in order to accommodate 1,500 members to stage the democratic election of his successor.

14 Golden Years

When Henry Perkins, decided to retire in 1897, the Committee was faced with over fifty applications for the secretaryship. It settled on Mr F. E. Lacey, but one of the candidates, Mr J. S. Russel, refused to accept this as a final decision and announced that he was going to seek a majority vote at a special general meeting. Some 1,500 members crowded into the Queen's Hall where Lord Lichfield, the club's president, flanked by a full turn-out of the Committee, prepared to woo support for their nomination.

When Mr Russel withdrew, the stormy debate subsided, and Mr Lacey was voted a salary of £600 a year, and Mr Perkins a pension of £400 as well as election to life membership of the club. There is no doubt that Perkins had been a success, but the role he had played was bravura rather than autocratic, a little eccentric, and his advice to Lacey reflected this: 'Don't take any notice of the damn Committee'. Yet he left the club's business flourishing if not exactly in perfect order.

Lacey, like Perkins, was a barrister, but he possessed a meticulous concern for detail which his flamboyant predecessor had not: he combined patient, hard work with a fine brain. Not that he was at all popular at the start because he introduced pinching economies; a lot of members and staff thought him over-rigid, a cold personality who never dropped his official guard. In truth, Perkins had left the finances dangerously unbalanced. The club had just taken over the catering department which was losing money, and Lacey faced the task of inventing an organisation which could keep a fast spreading business in order. He came up with ideas for splitting the affairs of the club into separate departments run by sub-committees which would report back with recommendations to the main Committee. It was a tighter approach, requiring an absolute observance of the rules and regulations.

Lacey's firmness gave him a comfortable liaison with the dominating presence in committee, that of Lord Harris. The fourth Baron Harris exercised a strong, personal influence over the whole of cricket. Both professional cricketers and amateurs found him dauntingly autocratic, and it was his habit to pass judgment on others, though he was also said to be scrupulously just. Born in 1851, he had learned his cricket in the fashionable way, at Eton, between 1868 and 1870, and at Oxford University. He continued his playing career with Kent, both as captain from 1875–89 and, for a while, as secretary. He was one of the leading batsmen of his day, a forcing player, good against the fast bowlers, a reliable field, and a useful change bowler. Lord Harris led England four times, but quite early he transferred his authority and zeal to the Marylebone Committee rooms.

So, at the time Lacey took office, Harris's best playing days were over. Already, in 1895, he had been president of the club and, importantly, he was at hand as Lacey found himself administering a private club which was being drawn more and more firmly on to the fast-moving roundabout which the cricket world was becoming. Lord Harris was particularly severe on bowlers who did not have legitimate actions. He blasted two Lancashire bowlers, Crossland and Nash, and had Kent refuse to play against them. He wanted all doubtful actions out of the game, and forced two members of his own Kent club side out of first-class cricket. He insisted on the Laws of Cricket, emphasising that they were indeed 'Laws' and not 'rules'. 'Rules,' he said, 'were made to be broken.'

Lacey, too, was not short of cricket intelligence. Born in Wareham, Dorset, in 1859, and educated at Sherborne and Cambridge University, he won a double Blue for soccer and cricket and, later, captained Hampshire between 1888 and 1893. He enjoyed a notable match against Kent at Southampton in 1884, when he scored 211 and 92 not out, and he scored 323 not out v. Norfolk in 1887. So, although now firmly behind a desk, he never lost sight of the game itself or of the playing interests of members. Soon, in fact, he was starting Easter coaching classes for their sons.

The new Mound Stand, replacing the old tennis court, was now ready and, not long after, the tennis courts behind the pavilion. To meet the plea of members who wanted to play squash rackets, a court was added. So it was hardly surprising that, in that year of expansion, 1899, twelve months after Lacey's appointment, the club's liabilities were as high as £26,000, of which £6,000 was owed to Mr Nicholson. By 1904, however, everything had been repaid and the books balanced.

The Marylebone Club was always accused of being slow to change and no one would disagree, but there was plenty of experiment going on too. In 1900 there was an extraordinary plan which would make batsmen run out all of their hits: a net, 3ft high, was put around the ground, except in front of the pavilion and the

Francis Lacey, Secretary of MCC, 1898–1926. In 1902 he started the Easter classes. When he retired, he received the first knighthood in sport.

Mound Stand. A hit over the net was to count three and, should the ball touch the net, two runs extra were to be added to those actually run by the batsmen while the ball was travelling from the bat and in from the fielder. The experiment, which had been devised out of a 'desire to put an end to high-scoring and drawn games', came under immediate criticism. So then it was decided that hits which bounced over the net or went through it, or under it, should count four; hits over, five, and out of the ground, six. Eventually, the whole idea was scrapped, but not before there were many tired batsmen, and entangled retrievers.

At this time, too, when the bat was generally dominant over the ball, the MCC tried out their newly proposed lbw law in seven first-class matches at Lord's and in the second-class championship competition. The proposal was to make Law 24 read – 'If, with any part of his person (except the hand) which is between wicket and wicket he intercept a ball which would hit his wicket, "Leg-before-wicket".' The question was the subject of an historic debate in 1901 when the speakers were the Hon. Alfred Lyttelton, and Messrs John Shuter, W. E. Denison, A. G. Steel, R. A. H. Mitchell and Harvey Fellows. There was a majority for change, 259 against 188, but short of the two-thirds necessary for it to be passed.

There is no doubt what one of the most famous professionals thought of the proposed lbw law, and indeed of the MCC. Arthur Shrewsbury of Nottinghamshire, probably the finest batsman in the country after Grace, thought that batsmen, if their leg had to be between wicket and wicket before they could be out, would simply stay outside leg stump and wait for the ball to break back to them; they would not go to meet it and therefore would not go for the best, most positive and attractive shots. 'It is this kind of blundering leg play which disgusts the spectators,' he said.

But the MCC were nothing if not diligent consulters. Before the great lbw debate at Lord's, they called a meeting of umpires. Shrewsbury wrote a letter to one of those umpires, W. A. J. West:

> Alfred Shaw thought the meeting at Lord's rather a tame affair, inclined to meanness, Mr Lacey's policy is tending rather too much in that direction, except of course the eye looks in the direction of self. My own opinion is that he merely made a make-shift of all of you, he simply had you there so that you could educate him in matters he was ignorant about, so that when he met his committee he could of course speak with some degree of authority. You were giving him a few wrinkles and at the same time paying for the privilege. It don't appear that any of you had sufficient courage to ask for out-of-pocket expenses, and as umpires of today are placed on a high social pedestal – much above the ordinary pro. cricketers – Mr Lacey didn't care to offend their sense of dignity by enquiring into such sordid matters . . .

The opponents of change included A. G. Steel, who thought the proposed law would be difficult for umpires to adjudicate, but even he joined the leading voice for reform, the Hon. R. H. Lyttelton, in condemning pad-play which he described as 'a most deplorable practice'. Meanwhile the proportion of lbw dismissals to wickets taken was rising. In 1870 it was 1 in 40, but by 1890 it was 1 in 17.

The swift escalation of the secretary's role inevitably included a deeper involvement also in international cricket. For the first time the MCC was organising Test matches at home. Test teams had always been chosen by the ground authorities of the Test venue, but their choices could not always be guaranteed to line up the best team in England. For example, A. E. Stoddart had once preferred to play for Middlesex against Kent at Tonbridge instead of for England against Australia at Lord's. Then Yorkshire refused to release Ulyett and Peel for an Oval Test and kept them at home to play for the county against Middlesex. And the MCC itself, of course, had left out Ranji in 1896.

What English Test cricket was now seen to require was a central organiser and a body of national selectors. Only then could there be consistency in policy, and this need became apparent to everybody in 1898 because next year, for the first time, there were to be five Test matches against Australia. Thus the Board of Control came into being, composed of the MCC president, the Hon. A. Lyttelton, MP, and five of the Club committee, who were the Earl of Lichfield, Lord Harris, Mr W. E. Denison, Mr H. D. G. Leveson-Gower and Mr W. H. Patterson.

Added to those was one representative from each of the fourteen first-class counties and one from each county on whose ground a Test was to be played. The Board made rules and regulations for finance, payment, hours of play and appointed a sub-committee of three who would choose a captain and then co-opt him on to the selection committee. The first selectors were Lord Hawke of Yorkshire, H. W. Bainbridge of Warwickshire, and W. G. Grace of Gloucestershire.

They chose W.G. as captain for the first Test, but at 50 he did not hold his place. It was a time when England's batting problems were whom to leave out. The Old Man had played his last Test. A. C. MacLaren took over the captaincy.

The Marylebone Club, now running the national game, was becoming seen as a national institution, for, although communications were slow, it was clear it would soon become the focus of world cricket, too. The colonies looked to the mother country for authority in many matters, why should cricket be any different? It was Lord Hawke, descendant of Admiral Lord Hawke of Quiberon Bay, who announced, 'To no one will I yield my supreme affection for Lord's and MCC. To me, Lord's is the Mecca of cricket, the sanctuary of the greatest game in the world.'

Hawke could claim to know more about overseas attitudes than anyone else. No one had done more to spread the game of cricket and the aura of the Marylebone Club around the world. He was captain of the tenth English team in Australia in 1887–88, and captain in South Africa in 1895–96 and again in 1898–99. He was to help take the game to South America and, domestically, he devoted himself to the Yorkshire club and its players. He devised for the professionals a system of marks for behaviour, discipline and dress; he instituted winter pay. Then, instead of paying over to a player the whole of his benefit money, he insisted that the Committee invest two-thirds of it.

He had considered Perkins, secretary of the MCC, unconventional but clever, though rather carelessly attired. Of Lord Harris he wrote, 'I admire him more than any other in the cricket world.' He saw him as an autocrat but with his heart and soul in the game.

Invitations to join Lord Hawke's touring sides were coveted. He delighted in the spread of cricket and the game was certainly on the move. There was almost a meeting between a West Indian side and South Africans at Lord's in 1900, but the South African war prevented it. The West Indians had come to England under the captaincy of Pelham Warner's brother, Aucher. They did not play any Tests, but the MCC did pay a high compliment to one of their players, George Challenor, by electing him a member of the club, although he had not played the required number of qualifying matches.

England had met the Australians four times within six years and lost every time. It was felt that the honour of English cricket was at stake and the MCC, responding also to a request from Melbourne, undertook to choose the team. Thus it was that, for the 1903–04 tour, MCC took over the running of England's travels abroad. The captain was Pelham Warner and although the team was described as the MCC, in Test matches it played as England. England recovered the Ashes by 3 wins to 2.

At the same time, Mr Lacey was sending out letters to the first-class counties, suggesting that a way should be devised of keeping the MCC in touch with them and vice versa. The collapse of the Cricket Council had left the counties without any representative body. So, in 1904, the Advisory County Cricket Committee was set up, composed of representatives from each first-class county, now fifteen and with Northamptonshire to be elected the following year, three from the Minor Counties who had formed their own association, and with the president of the MCC or one of its Committee as chairman.

Home and away the Marylebone Club stood for organisation and authority, and only by feeding the mass of business into his sub-committees could Francis Lacey take the strain. For example, the claims of South Africa to join the Test fold were becoming obvious. Matches between English sides and South Africa, which started in the 1888–89 season, carried the designation 'Test' match. The inter-provincial Currie Cup began at this time. The English pioneers were led by C. Aubrey Smith of Sussex, and the second visit under W. W. Read went there in 1891–92.

Lord Hawke's first touring team of 1895–96 won three easy victories, but when he returned in 1898–99 South Africa came

Lord Hawke, pictured when Treasurer of MCC, 1932–8. A paternalist captain, much sought after for his tours abroad during the 'Golden Age'.

162

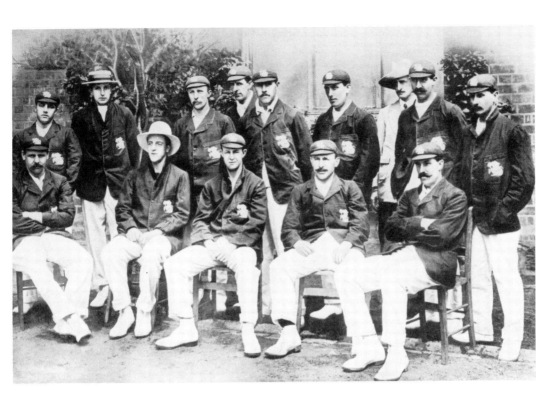

Pelham Warner's MCC team to Australia, 1903–4.

close to beating an England team for the first time when they lost at Johannesburg by only 32 runs.

The first official MCC team to South Africa in 1905–06, led by Pelham Warner, marked the beginning of a period of South African excellence. Much of this was due to their four googly bowlers, R. O. Schwarz, G. A. Faulkner, G. C. White and A. E. E. Vogler. They had learned their skills from the inventor of googly bowling, B. J. T. Bosanquet, but had also improved on his skill. Schwarz, the most successful of them, was unlike the rest in that he bowled only the googly and top-spinners. On the matting wickets he got hefty top spin and therefore high bounce with the sharpest break-back from the off. Aubrey Faulkner, who bowled off- and leg-breaks, was difficult to 'read'. The truth was, the MCC batsmen were bamboozled by them. The South Africans, wild with delight, won their first Test against England at Johannesburg.

After such a win, the MCC could no longer deny South Africa the right to meet England on level terms, so when they came to England in 1907, three Test matches were arranged. England won one, and two were drawn, but more revealing was the tour record of the South Africans. In 31 matches they lost only 4 games and 21 were won outright. The English captain, R. E. Foster, wrote about the 'new bowling' and chose Vogler as the best in the world, but Schwarz was top of the averages, while White and Faulkner spun their usual webs of mystery. It seemed to be one answer at least to the perfect wickets and batting dominance of the 'Golden Age', and after these results it was quite to be expected that the MCC should make plans to include South Africa in the regular programme of Test matches. On July 27th, 1909, the Imperial Cricket Conference was formed, and the following notice appeared in *The Times*:

IMPERIAL CRICKET

Mr F. E. Lacey, the secretary of the MCC, yesterday issued the memoranda of the minutes of the (first) Imperial Cricket Conference, together with the rules for Test Matches and a table showing the practical working of the scheme.

RULES FOR TEST MATCHES

1. Test Matches are those played between representative elevens of England, and of Australia, and of South Africa, also between the elevens of Australia and South Africa.
2. A cricketer who has played in a Test Match for a country cannot play for any other country without the consent of each of the contracting parties.
3. Qualification by Birth – A cricketer, unless debarred by Rule 2, is always eligible to play for the country of his birth.
4. Qualification by Residence – A cricketer, unless debarred by Rule 2, may elect to play for any country in which he is residing and has resided for not less than four years immediately preceding, and thereafter shall always be eligible to play for that country.

SUGGESTED PROGRAMME OF INTERNATIONAL GAMES

Main Principles
1. No team from any country shall pay visits in two successive seasons.
2. Every team shall pay a visit and receive a visit from each other country in every cycle of four years.

TABLE SHOWING PRACTICAL WORKING OF THE SCHEME

Cycle 1909–13			Cycle 1913–17
Year	Months	Countries Meeting	next round
1909	May to August	Australia in England	1913
1909–10	Nov to March	England in South Africa	1913–14
1910	May to August		1914
1910–11	Jan to March	S. Africa in Australia	1914–15
1911	May to August	S. Africa in England	1915
1911–12	Nov to March	England in Australia	1915–16
1912	May to August	Triangular Contest	1916
1912–13	March to April	Australia in South Africa	1916–17

In view of the triangular contest in 1912, South Africa defers its visit in 1911 to 1912, and Australia's visit in 1913 is advanced one year to 1912.

The scheme for the 1912 triangular tournament was that each country would play six Tests each, three against each other. Each country would take half of the gross gate taken at a Test match and the net proceeds of stand money was to go into a pool for the

Key Plate to Messrs. Dickinson & Foster's painting of " Lord's " on a " Gentlemen v. Players " day.

"PLAYERS IN THE FIELD."

1 J. Phillips	5 J. T. Hearne	9 R. Peel	13 J. Maurice Read
2 A. Ward	6 G. A. Lohmann	10 J. Briggs	14 W. H. Lockwood
3 A. E. Stoddart, Esq.	7 W. Gunn	11 John Wheeler	15 W. Attewell
4 Dr. W. G. Grace	8 Arthur Shrewsbury	12 M. Sherwin	

A painting showing
Gentlemen v. Players at
Lord's, 1895, with a
key to those portrayed.

benefit of the ground on which the game was being played and to the counties. This established the principle that Test cricket should not be played in isolation as a major entertainment, but should help to nurture the counties from which it had sprung and, indeed, from which future Test players would have their experience and all players gain their professional aspirations.

The Triangular Tests of 1912 were ruined by wet weather, but otherwise they might have formed a fitting climax to the years between 1894 and 1914 which have been called the Golden Age of cricket. This was not especially a period of England domination on the field, but as far as the Marylebone Club was concerned, it was the time when it stepped up to the pinnacle of power and Lord's provided the finest cricket in the world. For it was undeniably a golden age of batting.

Three old, golden threads still glowed in the new tapestry – Eton v. Harrow, Gentlemen v. Players, and the University match. While Test matches were a tremendous draw, the counties, since their skills were honed on a highly competitive championship, were now much stronger and more attractive to watch.

There were many more heroes than before. W. G. Grace, still playing, must have felt a sea of amateur batting talent swelling around him. Although he enjoyed that prolific 'Indian summer' of 1895, when he was 47 and scored over 1,000 runs in May, his performances were now being overtaken by such players as K. S. Ranjitsinhji, F. S. Jackson, C. B. Fry, A. E. Stoddart, L. C. H. Palairet, A. C. MacLaren, and G. L. Jessop, not forgetting such Australians as Victor Trumper, Clem Hill and Joe Darling. There was a self-confidence about these cricketers which shines out of every old photograph, most of them posing, swarthily handsome behind drooping moustaches, lifting the bat high for the drive for the famous studies of G. W. Beldam (who played for Middlesex) which were used in C. B. Fry's volume *Great Batsmen: Their Methods at a Glance* (1905).

Pitches were improved, Lord's included, by the application of marl or liquid manure, and so helped to enhance these days of the straight bat and high scores. Books and magazines were full of advice on run-getting by such as Ranji or Fry. It was equally an era which produced a lot of tired bowlers. MacLaren used to say that it was the last few hours on a perfect pitch when there was no hope of a result that used to exhaust them. Yet, to get wickets, the best Golden Age bowlers had to be clever and resilient.

H. S. Altham, in his *A History of Cricket*, commends the left-arm spinners, Peel, Peate and Rhodes – all Yorkshiremen, patiently

A. E. Stoddart

working at flight and spin – and Johnny Briggs of Lancashire. There was also, S. F. Barnes (see page 174) who did not play a great deal of first-class cricket, preferring to turn out for his own county, Staffordshire. However Barnes, in 27 Tests between 1901–1914, took an amazing 189 wickets for 3,106 runs, a record unrivalled both for consistency and economy.

B. J. T. Bosanquet was toying effectively with what was called a googly and which in Australia is still called a 'bosie'; while Yorkshire's George Hirst, medium-fast and left-arm (as well as a fine right-handed batsman) virtually discovered how to move a ball in the air. He turned himself from an ordinary fast man into

B. J. T. Bosanquet

a swerve bowler. Of him, one batsman is said to have remarked, 'I don't really see how one can be expected to play a ball which, when it leaves the bowler's arm, appears to be coming straight, but when it reaches the wicket is like a very good throw-in from cover point!'

Many right-arm bowlers were having a tough time, most of them abandoning off-spin altogether, which was not favoured by the lbw law; but the Australian captain and all-rounder, M. A. Noble, did show how experiment brought fresh hope when he found that he could swerve the ball away from the bat even with an old ball.

George Lohmann of Surrey, whose career ended prematurely in 1896 because of ill-health, demonstrated the value of a smooth action because he could slip a fast ball into his medium-pace style without the batsman spotting it. He took 112 Test wickets at a cost of 10.75 runs each. Altogether he took eight wickets or more in an innings twenty-eight times (four times in Tests) and thirteen or more wickets in a match fourteen times. It was, however, of another fine Surrey bowler that one of the great batsmen, Ranji, wrote: 'W. H. Lockwood is the most difficult bowler I ever played against but not because of his speed but because of his slow ball. I do not think it is a slow ball at all when it comes. He does not seem to alter his action in the slightest.'

These fine bowling practitioners tended to be the exception. Generally scores were getting higher and higher and there had been serious complaint about the law of follow-on which made it compulsory for any side 80 runs behind after the first innings. Batting gloves were worn by most, but not all: some wore one only on the lower hand, others wore two, but not necessarily a matching pair. Yet this was not an era when technique leapt forward, more it was one of consolidation for W. G. Grace had explored most of the variations of back and forward play. It was, however, supremely a stylish period.

Many superb batsmen left a rich imprint on cricket at Lord's. K. S. Ranjitsinhji, His Highness the Maharajah Jam Sahib of Nawanagar, had come from Rajkumar College in India to Cambridge University and then joined Sussex. He had little cricket background, nor did he get a Blue until his last year in 1893, but two years later at Lord's for Sussex he made 77 not out and 150. Thereafter he developed the most brilliant batsmanship. Of him, Neville Cardus wrote, 'When he batted a strange light was seen for the first time on English fields'. He was the first batsman to score over 3,000 runs in a season. His performance for Sussex, often with C. B. Fry at the other end, brought him rapturous

K. S. Ranjitsinhji
(*Beldam Collection*)

praise as well as the reputation as the inventor of the leg glide.
Fry always insisted that Ranji was absolutely orthodox, but was
more supple than most in his wrist and body movements, 'as if he
had no bones'.

Wrist-work appeared to be the Indian cricketer's greatest
strength and it usually governed his style. Instead of prescribing
long arcs with the bat, Ranji tended to let the ball come on to his
body and flick it, especially off the back foot, through the leg-side
field. 'He is not a batsman,' said George Giffen, the Australian,
'he is a conjuror!' But however instinctive his game appeared,
Ranji worked hard at it. His career batting realised 24,692 runs
at an average of 56.37 and included 72 centuries. Through the

unlikely medium of cricket, he was the first Indian to make a personal impact on the British public.

Equally distinctive was C. B. Fry's athletic presence and, together with Ranji, he made a breathtaking partnership at Hove. Fry applied a considerable intellect to his games-playing, assiduous in theory and in its application. As Ranji drove, cut and deflected at one end, Charles Fry at the other looked as much concerned with the art of batsmanship as with the runs he had scored. He was a brilliant scholar; for twenty-one years he held the world record for the long jump; he played Association Football for England and at that game won a cup-final medal with Southampton. He edited *Fry's Magazine* and wrote several books of permanent interest, including not only *Great Batsmen* but also *Great Bowlers* with G. W. Beldam. In conjunction with his wife he wrote a novel; he served on the League of Nations, stood as a Liberal candidate for parliament, and trained the young on the *Mercury* on the River Hamble. He was apparently offered the throne of Albania, but declined and King Zog ruled instead. He also wrote an autobiography which expressed his enjoyment of life, *Life Worth Living*. In cricket, Fry's career realised 30,886 runs with an average of 50.

To represent authority at the crease, which was again a hallmark of the age, mention must be made of Lancashire's A. C. MacLaren. 'Magnificence was enthroned at the wicket when MacLaren took his stand there and surveyed the field with comprehensive eye,' wrote Cardus, who as a young man at Old Trafford composed unrivalled word pictures of this man he called 'the noblest Roman of them all'. He saw MacLaren as an England captain by divine right. He was a superb slip fielder, who turned even bending and trouser-hitching into a regal movement. As a batsman MacLaren was erect, bat held high, ready to force the good-length medium-fast ball straight back down the field. He tried to dominate the opposition and matched his firm, sweeping strokes with positive defence. Perhaps he took too many risks to get on top, both as a captain and as a batsman, but then Cardus saw in that the sheer pride in an idea. However, because of the imperious build-up, MacLaren's blunders tended to be big ones. 'He achieved catastrophic miscalculations; he went along the primrose path to the everlasting bonfire.' MacLaren was not, indeed, everyone's favourite: he was haughty, often scornful of other opinions, and certainly no consultant; yet he genuinely reflected this golden age of batting. He played in 35 Tests, and averaged 33.

Leadership was in plentiful supply elsewhere, too, bred in the public schools and refined at Oxford or Cambridge, a process

C. B. Fry (left)
A. C. MacLaren.
(*Beldam Collection*)

personified in the Hon. F. S. Jackson. H. S. Altham writes that he was 'in natural ability, personality and, above all, in his genius for rising to an occasion, a great cricketer'.

Jackson was a strong, well-built man, standing nearly 6ft high, with a full golden-brown moustache. Fry said that 'Jacker' was 'exceptionally good-looking in the Anglo-Saxon, Guards officer way; famous for his impeccable turn-out on the field'. Wilfred Rhodes, who played with him both for Yorkshire and England, said that even after Jackson had scored a hundred he would hardly have a hair out of place. Rhodes also remembers that 'he never appeared without his Cambridge Blue sash neatly folded as a belt round his waist'.

C. B. Fry also records how F. S. Jackson's style helped colour the 'Golden Age'.

> Not only has he an extraordinary number of different strokes of all kinds, but he has a quite notable ability of adapting these strokes without altering them, except in the matter of timing, to all kinds of bowling and to all kinds of wickets . . . Perhaps, among modern batsmen, there is no one who maintains what may be described as perpetual uniformity of style as he does, with the possible exception of Victor Trumper.

F. S. Jackson.
(*Beldam Collection*)

In addition, Jackson was a good change bowler, medium-fast and with the ability to mix in a slower off-break. Like all of these amateurs he was a member of the MCC but, more than they, he was dedicated to the club's affairs. After his playing days were over, he turned his enthusiasm to committee work and became president of MCC in 1921.

Of all the batsmen of the 'Golden Age' it is the Australian Victor Trumper who often seems to be its finest embodiment, living on through the memories, affection and the admiration of his colleagues and contemporaries. Neville Cardus's hero-worship seems almost predictable: he recalls in his *Autobiography* how he used to pray that Trumper would make a century for Australia against England 'out of a total of 137 all out'. But the professional A. E. Knight was, if anything, even more fulsome in his praise of 'this perfect batsman'. In *The Complete Cricketer*, he writes: 'His greatness is of the kind which appeals to the technical no less than to the more human critic. There is no subtlety, no show miracle, but the perfect openness and direct simplicity of a master.' And all this combined with the selflessness and the chivalry which allowed him to make eleven hundreds in the wet summer of 1902, but never to bother to exceed 128.

Lord's and the Marylebone Club were now enhanced not only through the staging of the more important matches, but by this rich seam of batting talent. Nor was there a repetition of the mistakes of the 1880s when the club appeared reluctant to stage matches for the tourists. In 1890, for example, the MCC arranged five matches for the Australians at Lord's: against Middlesex, the Players, England, and two against themselves. In return, Australia and the club gave up part of the gate from the final fixture for the benefit of the Cricketers' Fund. There was no doubt about the crowd getting value for money from two of these matches because they saw the best of the South Australian, J. J. Lyons. He was by no means a leading batsman, but when the pitch was good and

Victor Trumper.
(*Beldam Collection*)

the ball came on to the bat, he could hit as powerfully as any. In the Test he scored 55 in 45 minutes and 33 in 25 minutes as well as taking 5 for 30 in England's first innings. Later, in September, against the MCC, he hit 99 out of 117 in 75 minutes. As though to seal his affection for Lord's, Lyons returned three years later and put up two sensational performances against the club, scoring 149 out of 181 in 90 minutes in the first and in the second, hitting 83 out of 117 in 100 minutes.

The matches between Oxford and Cambridge universities continued to attract the fashionable thousands, the ladies in their

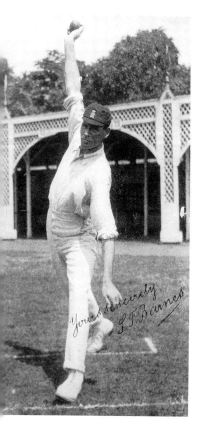

S. F. Barnes. In the background, the arbours, which were hired out for entertaining (see page 237). (*Beldam Collection*)

OPPOSITE
G. L. Jessop, after making 93 for England v. South Africa at Lord's, 1907. One of the first such innings charts. From *The Sketch* July 10th, 1907. (*Illustrated London News*)

finest dresses while no man would think of turning up in anything less formal than a frock coat and top-hat. In 1893, for example, 19,000 people were present on the first day and 20,000 on the second, to watch Cambridge win in two days. On this occasion, though, the spectators left the ground with more than the result to talk about.

Cambridge had batted first, for 182, and Oxford, finding the pitch wearing quickly, faced the possibility of following on with the last two men together, and the 80-run deficit still to clear. But Oxford thought that to follow-on was their best chance of winning because they would be bowling last on a deteriorating pitch. *Wisden* reports:

> Nine wickets were down for 95, and then, on T. S. B. Wilson, the last man, joining W. H. Brain, an incident occurred which is likely to be talked about for a good many years to come. Three runs were added, making the score 98, or 84 short of Cambridge's total, and Oxford thus required only 5 runs to save the follow-on. The two batsmen were then seen to consult each other between the wickets, and it was at once evident to those who grasped the situation that the Dark Blues were going to throw away a wicket in order that their side might go in again.

The Cambridge bowler, C. M. Wells, certainly knew what was happening because he now sent down a couple of round-arm deliveries wide to the boundary. Eight runs! Oxford could not now follow on.

As a result of this, there was a lot of table-banging at the winter meetings of the MCC, but it turned out to be more noise than action. A formal proposal at the annual meeting of 1894, that the side 80 runs behind on first innings 'may be required' but not compelled to follow on, was shelved. By the 1895 season, however, the compulsory first innings deficit before going in to bat again was raised to 100 runs, but even this was not the end of the story.

In the Varsity match of 1896, F. Mitchell, the Cambridge captain, in order to prevent Oxford's following on, instructed E. B. Shine to bowl three balls to the boundary. This time the strategem was unprovoked by any gestures from the batsmen. There were shouts and catcalls all around the ground; members inside the pavilion lost their tempers, many of them booing Cambridge as they came in. *The Times* correspondent did not like the Cambridge tactics, firmly pointing out the difference between Mitchell taking this initiative and F. S. Jackson in the previous match responding to the opposition's gamesmanship. In Jackson's case he saw it as 'diamond cutting diamond'. This new affair, on the other hand, was a disgusting example to the many small clubs who looked to the MCC for their example in conduct and fair play.

THE GIANT OF THE WILLOW: G. L. JESSOP.

Reform of the follow-on law was now demanded. Surely there had to be an option about the follow-on for the side in control at the time? And, because there were good wickets everywhere and much higher scores than earlier, surely change was begging?

MCC acted as it normally did, stolidly against the tide of opinion until the proof for change became overwhelming. By the end of that particular match the members had cooled down because they witnessed one of the great University-match innings by G. O. Smith, who scored a brilliant 132 when Oxford had been set 330 to win. They settled for cheering and for waiting until 1900 for the club to decide that the follow-on figure should be 150 for a three-day match, and also optional.

In 1896 the MCC had played a remarkable game against the Australians, who were astutely led by G. H. S. Trott. The club batted first on a rain-affected wicket and, thanks to some missed catches, reached 219, Stoddart and F. S. Jackson making half-centuries. The club's captain, W. G. Grace, put J. T. Hearne on to bowl at the pavilion end and Attewell at the Nursery end. Hearne quickly took two wickets and, with the score 18 for 3, Grace replaced Attewell with the Leicestershire bowler Pougher. Not another run was made!

There were some famous hits at Lord's notably by A. E. Trott of Middlesex (younger brother of G. H. S.) who landed a ball from his compatriot, M. A. Noble, over the pavilion and into the garden of one of the houses. But the most spectacular hitter was G. L. (Gilbert) Jessop, another amateur, educated at Cheltenham Grammar School and Cambridge University, who had a bent stance which earned him the name of 'The Croucher'. He did not much like that, but it added to the romance and excitement of a batsman who could have people rushing to the Gloucestershire grounds when they knew he was batting. He was also the greatest fielder of his age: no one took a chancy run to him, so easy were his movements and so powerful his throw. As a batsman he was an unusual combination of a hitter to all parts of the ground who possessed a basically straight bat. His contemporaries strongly denied that he was a slogger, as was often claimed. Lord's did see one of his outstanding innings in 1897, for the Gentlemen against the Players. He joined F. G. J. Ford when six wickets were down for 136 in the second innings, then made 39 out of 44 in a quarter of an hour and, altogether, 67 out of 88 in thirty-five minutes, hitting one five and eleven fours.

It was essential to Jessop's punishing style that he could both cut and drive strongly, thereby creating uncertainty in the bowler's mind about length. Jessop looked built for power and was described

MCC v. Australians

Played at Lord's, June 11 and 12, 1896

Result: MCC won by an innings and 18 runs.

MCC

W. G. Grace	b Trumble	15
A. E. Stoddart	st Kelly b Trott	54
K. S. Ranjitsinhji	b Trumble	7
F. S. Jackson	c and b Trumble	51
W. Gunn	b M'Kibbin	39
G. MacGregor	b Trumble	0
G. Davidson	b Trumble	0
F. Marchant	b M'Kibbin	20
A. D. Pougher	not out	9
W. Attewell	b Trumble	7
J. T. Hearne	b M'Kibbin	1
Byes 13, leg byes 2,	no-ball 1	16
Total		**219**

Bowling

AUSTRALIA

Trumble	34	8	84	6
Giffen	9	0	22	0
M'Kibbin	19.2	2	51	3
Trott	13	1	35	1
Eady	8	2	11	0

AUSTRALIANS

	FIRST INNINGS		SECOND INNINGS	
J. J. Kelly	c and b Pougher	8	b Hearne	0
H. Graham	b Hearne	4	b Hearne	5
H. Trott	b Hearne	6	c MacGregor b Hearne	14
S. E. Gregory	b Hearne	0	c MacGregor b Hearne	28
F. A. Iredale	b Hearne	0	b Hearne	0
C. Hill	b Pougher	0	b Hearne	4
H. Trumble	b Pougher	0	b Hearne	0
J. Darling	not out	0	c Stoddart b Hearne	76
C. J. Eady	b Pougher	0	c Grace b Hearne	42
T. R. M'Kibben	c Davidson b Pougher	0	not out	3
G. Giffen	absent ill	0	absent ill	0
			Byes	11
Total		**18**	Total	**183**

Bowling

MCC	FIRST INNINGS				SECOND INNINGS			
Hearne	11	9	4	4	50.3	22	73	9
Attewell	8	5	14	0	10	4	14	0
Pougher	3	3	—	5	28	15	33	0
Jackson					10	3	16	0
Davidson					7	3	15	0
Grace					8	1	21	0

Umpires: W. A. J. West and J. Phillips

F. E. Woolley

J. B. Hobbs. He always said he was twice the batsman *before* the first world war.

by R. A. Paine of Philadelphia as 'the Human Catapult' who wrecks roofs of distant towns when set in assault; but his health was variable. Even so, he lived to be 81.

The Gentlemen v. Players match of 1900 was also an extraordinary game, the Players being set 502 to win and getting them. At half past six, the time for drawing stumps, the scores were tied, but S. M. J. Woods, the Gentlemen's (and Somerset's) captain, decided to have another over. He bowled it himself and Rhodes made the winning hit. The MCC Committee did not approve, because playing conditions had been flouted. As Francis Lacey would insist, rules were rules.

This was a remarkable match for other reasons. It was the first Gentlemen v. Players match for thirty-five years for which W. G. Grace was not chosen. The match was played in tropical heat and R. E. Foster not only scored a century on his first appearance for the Gentlemen (102 not out), but made another hundred, 136, in the second innings. The Players' batting was masterful, however, notably that of their captain, little Bobby Abel of Surrey, who made 30 and 98 accompanied by that precisely technical and most proficient Surrey colleague Tom Hayward, who played a second innings of 111, as well as by J. T. Brown of Yorkshire with 163.

Jessop, in his book, *A Cricketer's Log*, described Foster as the 'English Trumper', quick on his feet with strong wrists. He was a brilliant forward at Association Football and a fine player at rackets and golf. There were many famous cricketing families such as the Walkers, the Lytteltons, the Studds, the Steels, the Fords, the Ashtons and the Gilligans, but none was better, or more numerous, than the Fosters of Worcestershire; so much so that the county was often nicknamed 'Fostershire'.

The Gentlemen v. Players match again offered exceptional amateur batting at Lord's in 1903, although not before the Players had amassed 478 in their first innings, including 139 to A. E. Knight. The Gentlemen were shot out for 185 by Hargreave, Braund and Albert Trott, but, following on 293 behind, they made 500 for 2 declared with some of the greatest batting of the whole era. After Warner had made 27 and Ranji 60, Fry and MacLaren put on 309 in just under three hours, Fry reaching 232 and MacLaren 168, both not out. Cardus had never seen batting of 'such opulence and prerogative'.

By the end of this period, which closed so dramatically with the outbreak of the First World War, the England selectors, usually chaired by Lord Hawke, could call upon Woolley, Hobbs, George Gunn and Joe Hardstaff senior, Philip Mead, Strudwick, as well as Barnes and Rhodes; but it is perhaps an even clearer indication of the style of the 'Golden Age' period that Hobbs was praised by such as Warner because he 'batted like an amateur'. Look at his high back-lift!

It almost goes without saying that the public-school matches continued decorously and profitably at Lord's and there are many pictures which portray the perambulation of the fashionable on the outfield during the intervals of play. Being seen at Lord's, particularly for the two days of the Eton v. Harrow match, was important socially. In 1897, after a third successive match was drawn, a suggestion was raised that a third day be added, but this was vetoed by Dr Warre, the Eton headmaster.

The MCC was always anxious to assist the development of public-school cricket. A notable practical example is given in the annual report of 1913:

> An opportunity occurred of helping Harrow School to purchase land adjoining its cricket ground, and a guarantee not to exceed £1,000 was offered by the MCC to make up the deficit, if any, required to provide £8,500 for this purpose, it being thought that the members of the MCC would welcome an opportunity of assisting a school that plays annually at Lord's to enlarge the area of ground available for playing cricket.

Many fine school games were played at Lord's, but the most famous was the Eton v. Harrow match of 1910, which became known as Fowler's Match.

Eton suffered the indignity of following on. Harrow had scored 232, Eton 67, and then, in their second innings, when the ninth wicket fell Eton were only 4 runs ahead. Manners and Kaye put on 50 for the last wicket, but most people had already left the ground. An unusual and dramatic account of the closing stages of the match was written by Lieutenant-Colonel C. P. Foley, in his book *Autumn Foliage*:

> I was going to spend that Saturday to Monday at Coombe with General Sir Arthur Paget, and not being in the least anxious to see an overwhelming Harrow victory, I left the ground and called in at White's Club to pick up my bag. Providentially, as it turned out, my hair wanted cutting. Half-way through the operation Lord Brackley looked in and said, 'Harrow have lost four wickets for 21 runs' and a few minutes later, 'Harrow have lost 6 for 21'. That was enough. I sprang from the chair with my hair half cut and standing on end, and we rushed together into the street, jumped into a taxi, and said, 'Lord's! Double fare if you do it in fifteen minutes.' We got there in 14 minutes and two-fifths seconds (I carry a stop-watch), paid the man, and advanced on the pavilion at a pace which is called in the French Army *le pas gymnastique*. The shallow steps leading into the pavilion at Lord's form a right-angle. Round this angle I sprang three steps at a time, carrying my umbrella at the trail. A dejected Harrovian, wearing a dark-blue rosette, and evidently unable to bear the agony of the match any longer, was leaving the pavilion with bowed head. I was swinging my umbrella to give me impetus, and its point caught the unfortunate man in the lower part of his waistcoat, and rebounded from one of its buttons out of my hand and over the side rails of the pavilion. The impact

was terrific, and the unlucky individual, doubling up, sank like a wounded buffalo on to his knees, without, as far as I recollect, uttering a sound. I sprang over the body without apology and, shouting instructions to George Bean, the Sussex pro, who was the gate attendant to look after my umbrella, dashed into the Pavilion and up the many steps to its very summit, where I hoped to find a vacant seat.

I arrived at the moment that Jameson was lying on the ground badly cut over, and was told that he had been batting forty minutes for no runs. As he has always been such an exceptionally quick scorer, this is worthy of record. With the total at 29, Fowler yorked Straker for 1 (29–8–1). The excitement reached its climax. I do not think I ever saw or heard anything like it. The roars from the Harrow stand whenever a run was made were heard in the Zoological Gardens. Graham hit a 3 and then Fowler bowled Jameson. He had scored 2 and was ninth man out, and it was a thousand pities that he did not set up a record by carrying his bat through the innings for o! (32–9–2) Alexander* came in, looking horribly confident. The score crept up slowly. By now the cheering had swollen into such a volume of sound that its overtones included Paddington Station as well as the Zoological Gardens in its perimeter. Thirteen priceless runs were sneaked or stolen by the indomitable last pair. How I loathed both of them! And just as things began to look really desperate Alexander edged one to Holland in the slips off Steel, and Eton had won by 9 runs!

Needless to say the scene in front of the pavilion baffles description. I believe, though I do not vouch for it, that Lord Manners, the father of John Manners, who, gallant in his youth as in his manhood, had played such a conspicuous part in the victory, left the ground in despair at lunch-time and retired to his room with strict orders that he was not to be disturbed. It is further said that the butler knocked twice at his door with the object of telling him what his son had done, and so forth, and that he was told to 'Go away' on both occasions. If it is true that the prospect of a Harrow victory was too much for Lord Manners, his regrets that he failed to see the finish must indeed have been poignant. Sir Ian Malcolm, in his recollections of Mr A. J. Balfour, says, 'I can never forget the magnificent finish of the Eton and Harrow match in Fowler's year, when at the close of play, A.J.B., Walter Forbes and Alfred Lyttelton, and two of his brothers, all leapt on to the green bench upon which we had been sitting in the Pavilion and waved their hats and cheered Eton in an abandonment of enthusiasm.' It has always been called 'Fowler's Match'. As he made top score in both innings – namely 21 and 64 – and took twelve wickets, such a designation is entirely justified. His analysis for the last innings was 10 overs, 2 maidens, 23 runs, 8 wickets.

Everyone who plays cricket dreams not only of playing a match like Fowler did for Eton, but also to have Neville Cardus write, 'Their souls entered the Valhalla of cricketers – which is the Lord's Pavilion, noble and murmurous with history.' Nor does it matter whether the aspirations at this time were amateur or professional, for both amateurs and professionals were locked into a deeply set class system. Yet their different routes led on to the same field.

Amateurs, for example, were prepared to consider technique and innovation in cricket. Not only was Fry an irrepressible theorist, but it was out of Eton that the young Bernard Bosanquet came.

* Later Field Marshal Earl Alexander of Tunis.

Lord's Ground.

ETON v. HARROW.

FRIDAY & SATURDAY, JULY 8, 9, 1910. (Two-Day Match.)

HARROW.

	First Innings.		Second Innings.	
1 T. O. Jameson	c Lubbock, b Fowler	5	b Fowler	2
2 T. B. Wilson	b Kaye	53	b Fowler	0
3 G. W. V. Hopley	b Fowler	35	b Fowler	8
4 T. L. G. Turnbull	l b w, b Fowler	2	c Boswell, b Fowler	0
5 G. F. Earle (Capt.)	c Wigan, b Steel	20	c Wigan, b Fowler	13
6 W. T. Monckton	c Lubbock, b Stock	20	b Fowler	0
7 J. M. Hillyard	st Lubbock, b Fowler	62	c Kaye, b Fowler	0
8 C. H. B. Blount	c Holland, b Steel	4	c and b Steel	5
9 A. C. Straker	c Holland, b Steel	2	b Fowler	1
10 O. B. Graham	c and b Steel	6	not out	7
11 Hon. R. H. L. G. Alexander	not out	2	c Holland, b Steel	8
	B 18, l-b 2, w , n-b 1,	21	B 1, l-b , w , n-b ,	1
	Total	232	Total	45

FALL OF THE WICKETS.

1-15	2-84	3-88	4-121	5-133	6-166	7-191	8-201	9-215	10-232
1-0	2-8	3-8	4-21	5-21	6-21	7-26	8-29	9-32	10-45

ANALYSIS OF BOWLING.

Name.	1st Innings.						2nd Innings.					
	O.	M.	R.	W.	Wd.	N-b.	O.	M.	R.	W.	Wd.	N-b.
Fowler	37.3	9	90	4	...	...	10	2	23	8	...	...
Steel	31	11	69	4	...	...	6.4	1	12	2	...	...
Kaye	12	5	23	1	...	...	3	0	9	0	...	...
Stock	7	2	12	1	...	1	...	...	...	...	...	...
Boswell	8	4	17	0	...	...	...	...	...	...	...	...
	...	...	...	...	...	...	...	...	...	...	...	...

ETON.

	First Innings.		Second Innings.	
1 R. H. Lubbock	l b w, b Earle	9	c Straker, b Hillyard	9
2 C. W. Tufnell	b Hillyard	5	l b w, b Alexander	7
3 W. T. Birchenough	c Hopley, b Graham	5	c Turnbull, b Jameson	22
4 W. T. Holland	c Hopley, b Hillyard	2	st Monckton, b Alexander	5
5 R. St. L. Fowler (Capt.)	c Graham, b Jameson	21	c Earle, b Hillyard	64
6 A. I. Steel	b Graham	0	c Hopley, b Hillyard	6
7 D. G. Wigan	c Turnbull, b Jameson	8	b Graham	16
8 A. B. Stock	l b w, b Alexander	2	l b w, b Earle	0
9 Hon. J. N. Manners	c Graham, b Alexander	4	not out	40
10 K. Lister Kaye	c Straker, b Alexander	0	c Jameson, b Earle	13
11 W. G. K. Boswell	not out	0	b Earle	32
	B 10, l-b , w 1, n-b ,	11	B 2, l-b , w 3, n-b ,	5
	Total	67	Total	219

FALL OF THE WICKETS.

1-16	2-16	3-26	4-34	5-36	6-57	7-62	8-64	9-66	10-67
1-12	2-19	3-41	4-47	5-65	6-107	7-164	8-166	9-169	10-219

ANALYSIS OF BOWLING.

Name.	1st Innings.						2nd Innings.					
	O.	M.	R.	W.	Wd.	N-b.	O.	M.	R.	W.	Wd.	N-b.
Earle	12	9	4	1	...	...	17.3	3	57	3	1	...
Hillyard	19	9	38	2	1	...	23	7	65	3	1	...
Graham	9	7	3	2	...	...	18	12	33	1	...	...
Jameson	4	1	4	2	...	...	9	1	26	1	...	...
Alexander	4.1	1	7	3	...	...	14	4	33	2	1	...
Wilson	...	...	...	...	...	...	2	2	0	0	...	...
	...	...	...	...	...	...	...	...	...	...	...	...

Umpires—Moss and Whiteside.   Scorers—G. G. Hearne and Newman.

ETON WON BY 9 RUNS.

Scorecard of Eton
v. Harrow, 1910,
'Fowler's match'.

In the 1890's, the Eton v. Harrow match was one of the social occasions of the year. (*The Golden Age of Cricket by David Frith*)

At first he was a medium-pace bowler and strong batsman, good enough to win an Oxford Blue. It is said that he discovered the possibilities of a googly when playing 'twisty-grab' on the billiard table. He first tried it out for Middlesex at Lord's in 1900, his first victim being Sammy Coe of Leicestershire who was stumped off a four-bouncer!

Professional cricket, on the other hand, had a proletarian image rather like professional football, but cricket could never quite go all along the road to the cloth cap precisely because the amateurs were an integral part of the game.

Jack Hobbs, whose career for Surrey began in 1905, said that he was attracted to professional cricket because £5 a match appeared to be handsome payment and also he thought it would be a dream fulfilled to bat with Tom Hayward. Newspapers and magazines and the new idea of cigarette cards spread the fame of the best players which helped in turn to attract large crowds. The population of the country had quadrupled during the nineteenth century, the census of 1911 revealing a total population in the United Kingdom of 45 million. There was more leisure time now for watching the game because working hours had shortened, paid holidays were beginning to come in, people were generally living longer, and also there was unemployment.

Because of his independence of the county club, the amateur was thought to be the better man to captain a side. Yet there was serious respect for the professional, constantly declared by none less than Lord Harris:

> A more discerning body of men it would be difficult to find. Their work, especially among those who do not rise to the top of the ladder, is very hard; they are always expected to be keen ... It would be a distinct loss if such a body of men were to be withdrawn from our cricket fields. Therefore let us by all means encourage them to persevere in their professions so they may do their part towards the welfare of the community.

K. S. Ranjitsinhji also wrote about the social position of the professional in the early years of the twentieth century.

> Now, I should be the last to say that a man of ability should give all his time to cricket. That would be quite absurd. But I do not think that the life of one who devotes himself to cricket is neither altogether wasted nor quite useless to his fellow men, for the simple reason that cricket provides a very large number of people with cheap, wholesome and desirable entertainment.

The majority of professional cricketers came from working-class backgrounds. Cricket was not a high-flying career, but it could be a steady job for a while. And, gradually, its status improved. Cricket became a sort of craft, and professionals fell into the artisan class of modest wages for a hard day's work.

Amateurs, of course, were not paid to play, but some found it necessary to accept expenses. Hotel and travel were paid, and perhaps some form of compensation for loss of business, but otherwise the public-school ethic dominated, that of competitive games, heroic service in some far-off outpost of the Empire, or of school-mastering itself, all requiring self-discipline and obedience, but above all nobility of purpose.

Surprisingly, perhaps, the public schools had a subtle influence on secondary state education, too. For example, public-school stories had a vogue in the years before the First World War, written by such authors as Talbot Baines Reed, Frank Richards, even P. G. Wodehouse with *Mike* (1910). Richards's stories in the *Magnet* and the *Gem* emphasised the glamour and the snobbery of public-school life, and much of it was read by working-class children. Thus the public schools began to shape character in the state and secondary schools to the extent that grammar schools had houses, prefects and colours for rugger and cricket. This was the concept also of C. B. Fry's training ship *Mercury* for poor

1914 – the first centenary of Lord's. Lord Hawke is speaking with King George V. Also in the picture, the Prince of Wales, later King Edward VIII, and the Duke of York, later King George VI. (*The Golden Age of Cricket by David Frith*)

children – that they should be taught by the method of the public schools to be, one day, commissioned as officers in the Royal Navy.

The MCC sent the public-school ethos speeding through the game of cricket wherever in the world it took root. Cricket consumed it and offered back its own imagery for the teachings of life, 'playing a straight bat', or 'that's not cricket', for example. Sometimes this became somewhat exaggerated, as when it was proclaimed from the pulpit:

> Aye, and when on the resurrection morning you come out of the pavilion, leaving your playing clothes behind you, and robed like your glorious Captain-King, you and all the hosts of God will see and understand your score as you cannot now, and your joy will be full as you hear the Captain, 'the unnumberable company of angels' and the whole redeemed Church of God greet you with the words, 'WELL PLAYED, SIR!'

More famously, under the influence and euphoria of war it was proclaimed patriotically by Henry Newbolt in *Vitaï Lampada*:

> *There's a breathless hush in the Close tonight –*
> *Ten to make and the match to win –*
> *A bumping pitch and a blinding light,*
> *An hour to play and the last man in.*
> *And it's not for the sake of a ribboned coat,*
> *Or the selfish hope of a season's fame,*
> *But the Captain's hand on his shoulder smote –*
> *'Play up! Play up! and play the game!'*

After the First World War, in 1923, only 6 per cent of the country's children were at public schools, but a large cross-section of the nation, while resolutely keeping to its social place, was touched by the ripples of these schools' teaching. Thus cricket, and the Marylebone Club which governed it, became a sort of precious flagship of the wealthy minority as it spread its influence and its ethos to county cricket ground, village green, park, school yard and back lane.

15 War and After

It was the autumn of 1915. A large man with a big grey beard was fondly doing the seasonal work in the large garden of his home called Fairmount in Mottingham in Kent. He was 67 years old, but his movements were brisk and boyish, and the splendid garden was evidence of diligence and green fingers. Yet he had not been well for many months and surprisingly, for a man so determined and fearless in all he had done in public, the noise of Zeppelin raids worried him. Suddenly he had a stroke. Dr W. G. Grace was dead.

The German press claimed him as an air-raid victim; it made excellent propaganda, and indeed, at home, the death of The Champion removed the war news temporarily from the newspaper headlines.

Immediately the obituary writers began to log his last appearances in public on the club cricket field for Eltham; at a Lord's match for the benefit of Jack Hobbs, switched from The Oval which had been put to military use. The previous year, 1914, he had attended the Lord's ground centenary dinner where Lord Hawke was in the chair and C. E. Green spoke affectionately of him and where he was given a spontaneous standing ovation.

W. G. Grace had been wholly loyal to the Marylebone Club, always ready to explain to doubters that only by its slowly moving legislation could the club avoid the greatest danger for cricket – impulsive legislation that could carry the game in the wrong direction.

The last sighting of W.G. in public, and what he saw to be his final duty, were poignant. It was at a cricket match played at Catford Bridge on Whit Monday 1915 in aid of war charities. W.G. was not well enough to play, but he did go around the ground collecting contributions. But nearly a year earlier, a few weeks after the war had broken out, old W.G. had felt dismayed that cricket was still being played while men were losing their lives in France and Belgium. Accordingly he wrote to *The Sportsman*, a letter dated August 27th, 1914:

> There are many cricketers who are already doing their duty but there are
> many more who do not seem to realise that in all probability they will have

186

to serve either at home or abroad before the war is brought to a conclusion. The fighting on the Continent is very severe and is likely to be prolonged. I think the time has arrived when the county cricket season should be closed, for it is not fitting at a time like this that able-bodied men should be playing day by day, and pleasure-seekers look on. There are so many who are young and able, and are still hanging back. I should like to see all first-class cricketers of suitable age set a good example, and come to the help of their country without delay in its hour of need.

This call to duty was promptly heeded but, as Eric Midwinter comments in his biography of Grace, W.G. himself, who was simultaneously the virtual creator of modern cricket and the least political of men,

must have been forcibly shaken by the immediacy of the Great War. The alarums of war had, throughout Grace's life, been indistinct and distant, faintly sounding from South Africa or Sudan. Now it involved reported atrocities just across the Channel, and the need to succour victimised Belgians through charity cricket matches. So W.G.'s last duty on cricket's behalf was to bring it to a halt.

He saw war in simplistic terms. The endeavour directed towards cricket now had to be redirected towards the war-effort. Just as the early eighteenth-century aristocracy might have seen cricket as a substitute for battle, so the morality and courage of the cricketer, with Victorian heroism grafted on, could not think of playing a match while men were dying.

Grace was buried at Elmers End cemetery; he left behind him £10,000, a sizeable fortune, and a game which he had transformed by personal example, by deep thought and commitment, and with a fistful of natural talent.

When the fighting began, Lord's, like The Oval, was used for military purposes. Accommodation was found there for units of the Territorial Artillery, the Army Service Corps (Transport), the Royal Army Medical Corps, as well as classes in wireless instruction and military cooking. No. 2 Grove End Road was let as headquarters to the Royal Volunteer Battalion (London Regiment).

When the RAMC left, the War Office used the buildings and practice ground as a training centre for Royal Artillery cadets. In the pavilion, the staff and some members occupied their spare time making hay nets for horses, and more than 30,000 were sent to Woolwich.

It has often been written that the mood of the British people during the First World War was retrospective, harking back to the good times; but although the war was uniquely close to home for the first time in living experience, it was still seen to be at the

THE NEW TEAM AT LORD'S! GOING TO THE NETS.

THE CLOSE OF THE INNINGS: "FIELDERS" RETURNING TO THE PAVILION.

bottom of the garden more than on the doorstep: a sanguinary break, so to speak, before the restoration of Pax Britannica. As far as cricket was concerned, however, there was nothing to do but look backwards and remember the golden runs and wonder whether favourite players, called to arms, would stay alive.

Before the start of hostilities, Mr Alfred Lyttelton, MCC President of 1898, died, and so did A. G. Steel, the recorder for Oldham, who had been one of the small band of all-round cricketers, with W. G. Grace the greatest, who had sent English cricket soaring in the 1880s. For the remembrance of Alfred Lyttelton, the University match of 1913 was stopped, precisely at midday, the hour of his memorial service at Westminster. *The Times* reported, 'The umpires took off their hats. The 13 cricketers in the field did the same and stood reverently to attention. Then everyone in the pavilion, which was filled in all three tiers, rose, as did the spectators in all parts of the ground, and all remained standing for some minutes in unbroken silence.'

Of course, the list of cricketers killed in action is the most poignant, although there were only three Test players among them: Sergeant Colin Blythe (Kent Fortress Engineers, attached King's Own Yorkshire Light Infantry) was killed in France in 1917 and Lieutenant Kenneth L. Hutchings (King's Liverpool Regiment, attached to the Welsh Regiment) was killed in action, an instantaneous death when he was struck by a shell. Both of these Kent players had finished with Test cricket, but Second-Lieutenant M. W. Booth of Yorkshire (West Yorkshire Regiment) who fell on the Somme in July 1916, was only 30 years old and had played just two Tests. His England debut in South Africa in 1913 was thought to presage an outstanding career as an all-rounder.

The deepest loss was of the younger generation of bright talents whose future Test selection had been strongly tipped, such as A. Jaques (Hampshire), Percy Jeeves (Warwickshire) and D. W. Jennings (Kent). A. E. J. Collins, the Clifton boy whose 628 not out is still the highest individual score ever made, was a war casualty. John Howell, the outstanding Repton schoolboy cricketer, was killed in Flanders. Australia lost their famous fast bowler Albert Cotter, and South Africa two of the googly quartet, R. O. Schwarz and G. C. White.

By the time hostilities had ended, other cricketers had died. A. E. Stoddart, the outstanding double international, alas shot himself at the age of 52. Albert Edwin Trott also ended his life with a bullet, in his lodgings in Denbigh Road, Willesden Green, in London. His elder brother, G. H. S. Trott, died in their native Melbourne,

Lord's in the first world war. No cricket. 'Geese not ducks'. (*Illustrated London News, September 8th 1915.*)

Victoria, and was remembered as a most sporting Australian Test captain. In fact Ranji thought 'Henry' Trott a better captain than Joe Darling, which was praise indeed. Trott's finest innings was made at Lord's in 1896. The pitch was poor and the bowling of Tom Richardson fast and dangerous, but, with Gregory, he put on 221 for the fourth Australian wicket, his share being 143. But, now, Tom Richardson was gone too; not by a suicide as was for a long time imagined, but of a heart attack while walking on holiday in St Jean d'Arvey in France when only 41.

Sadly for Australia, their most brilliant batsman and that most modest, popular man, Victor Trumper, died in his thirty-eighth year. It had been at Lord's, in 1899, his first visit there, that he first announced his high class by scoring 135 not out for Australia against England, and still fresh in people's minds was his amazing season in 1902 and his chivalrous style and nature. In 1913, Australian cricket had done him proud with a benefit of £3,000, but soon after he fell victim to Bright's disease.

While the war was still going on, the club continued to send out sides to the public schools, but there was no thought of using Lord's for games until later on, and then only to raise money for the war's casualties. In 1916, at the request of the Canadian contingent, a baseball match was played at Lord's in September between the Canadians and London Americans, for the benefit of a fund which helped the widows and orphans of Canadians who fell in battle. But there was an impatience to play cricket again, which revealed that the public conscience had moved away from the anti-sport mood of 1914 when W. G. Grace's call had struck such a public response. The editor of *Wisden*, in 1917, recalled a conversation he had with the Surrey secretary, Mr W. Findlay, two years earlier about whether the nets would be put up for practice that season. The reply was, 'The nets will be put up, but don't expect our fellows will use them much. They will be afraid of being jeered at by the men on the tram cars.' Such fears passed away, prompted to some extent by the support of football, for public boxing which hit a boom, and professional billiards matches which were played in the hottest weather.

There was another motivation which led to cricket's resumption – the need for some distraction from war. It was thought an excellent idea, therefore, when Captain P. F. Warner, supported by the MCC, arranged Services matches for charity as a way to play cricket without wrestling with the national conscience.

In 1917 two matches were played at Lord's, the one an English Army XI v. an Australian Army XI; the other, a Combined Army and Navy XI v. Combined Australian and South African Forces team. Some £1,320 went to two funds, the St Dunstan's Hostel for blinded soldiers and sailors, and Lady Lansdowne's Officers' Family Fund.

In 1918 two more charity games took place at Lord's. An England XI played a Dominion XI on both occasions. King George V attended the second and saw a large crowd, coloured by the khaki uniforms of home and overseas servicemen, with a sprinkling of the blue uniforms worn by the wounded and hospitalised. A report of this second match appeared in *The Spectator*:

> A band played, thus accentuating the fact that the match was for charity – for whoever heard of a Test Match at Lord's being accompanied by a band! It was provided no doubt, with the best of intentions, but in truth we somewhat resented it. When 'Plum' was facing Docker it seemed sacrilege to hear 'The Merry Widow' waltz on a band.

But, of course, there was no escaping the atmosphere of war. A glance down the score-card revealed only one name which was not prefixed with a military rank. Was it make-believe or perhaps a firm statement that the ritual of cricket was imperishable? Whatever it was, these Lord's matches of 1917 and 1918 were enthusiastically played out by good players such as Australian Lieutenants Kelleway and C. T. Docker and Warrant Officer Macartney, and for England by Corporals Makepeace and J. T. Tyldesley, Private Hendren, Lieutenant Fender, Captain Warner and Lieutenant-Colonel J. W. H. T. Douglas. The writer's (E.B.) conclusion was:

> We seem to see beyond the smooth turf and the group of white figures, and the still crowds where the 'great game' is being played, to those fields in France and Flanders, in Italy and in Mesopotamia, and the spaces of the seas where the greatest and ghastly game is being played in which many also who wielded bat or ball at Lord's have played their last ball and closed a noble innings.

As far as cricket itself was concerned the death of W.G. emotionally sealed the war period, and this was evidenced later, in July 1923, in the form of handsome new gates, erected at the members' entrance at Lord's and bearing the inscription:

TO THE

MEMORY OF

WILLIAM GILBERT GRACE

THE GREAT CRICKETER

1848–1915

THESE GATES WERE

ERECTED BY THE MCC

AND OTHER FRIENDS

AND ADMIRERS

The Grace Gates

Not surprisingly, perhaps, following the end of the war, the MCC found it difficult to trace all of its members. Eventually, in 1922, Francis Lacey, still the secretary, sent out a mass of letters and made a public announcement about the findings.

The club had written to 5,014 candidates entered in the books between 1889 and 1896 in order to find out if they still wanted to be elected. Of these, 1,300 said yes; 268 wished to have their election postponed; and 158 said yes, but did not afterwards apply; 1,650 did not reply at all; 760 letters were returned by the Post Office; 294 said no to election; and the committee were informed that 614 were either killed in action or otherwise deceased.

When cricket resumed in 1919 there were gloomy prophecies that the game could never be the same again, and these were reflected in the adoption of a suggestion by Mr Ludford Docker, president of Warwickshire, that county matches should be limited to two days, but with longer hours being played each day. This idea was made plausible by the new 'daylight saving'. In 1916, Germany had started a daylight saving scheme for light and fuel economy, and this influenced Britain's Summertime Act, passed on May 17th, 1916. On Sunday May 21st the clocks throughout

W. G. Grace in his MCC cap;
a portrait in oils by Archibald Stuart Wortley, 1890.

Francis Lacey became Secretary of MCC in 1898. When he retired in 1926, he was knighted, the first knighthood in sport. In 1902 he started the Easter coaching classes.

Sir Pelham Warner; a portrait made in 1949, presenting him as he was when still playing. He retired from the captaincy of Middlesex in 1920 and began publishing *The Cricketer* the following year.

LORD'S GROUND.

M.C.C. v. HERTFORDSHIRE,
JUNE 22nd, 1814.

1st Innings.	HERTFORDSHIRE.		2nd Innings.	
Mowbray, c Ward	4	b Beauclerk	1
H. Bentley, not out	33	run out	0
Bruton, b Budd	7	b Osbaldeston	17
S. Carter, b Budd	0	st Vigne	0
Sibley, b Beauclerk	6	c Budd	1
Taylor, c Beauclerk	6	run out	2
Denham, b Budd	10	st Vigne	21
T. Carter, b Budd	1	b Osbaldeston	0
J. Sibley, c Beauclerk	6	not out	3
Freeman, c Beauclerk	2	run out	5
Crew, b Beauclerk	0	st Vigne	0
Byes	4	Byes	5
Total	79	Total	55

M.C.C.

Mr. A. Schabner, c J. Sibley	55
Hon. D. Kinnaird, b S. Carter	1
Mr. C. Warren, b Taylor	25
Mr. E. H. Budd, c T. Carter	36
Hon. E. Bligh, b Bentley	6
Mr. T. Burgoyne, run out	0
Lord F. Beauclerk, b Taylor	3
Mr. G. Osbaldeston, b Mowbray	18
Mr. W. Ward, run out	10
Mr. T. Vigne, b Bentley	2
Mr. J. Poulet, not out	1
Byes	4
Total	161

TOM BROWNE & Co (NOTTᵍ) LIMITED.

The Centenary of Lord's, 1814–1914.
The match, MCC v. Hertfordshire, the first played at the new ground,
was repeated and this illuminated scorecard for the
1814 fixture was printed as a souvenir.

A composite painting, by H. Barrable and R. Ponsonby Staples, which imagines a match in the MCC's centenary year, 1887. In 'A' Stand (replaced in 1958 by the Warner Stand) the Prince and Princess of Wales (later King Edward VII and Queen Alexandra) are approaching the seats while the actress Lillie Langtry is sitting just to the right of the pillar. On the field W. G. Grace is batting, F. R. Spofforth bowling, and T. W. Garrett is bending to field the ball.

Fifty-one years later than the previous subject, Charles Cundall painted the scene of Lord's during the England v. Australia Test match of 1938. This detail shows the pavilion completed in 1890, and the Grandstand, with 'Father Time' aloft, completed in 1926.

Dennis Flanders' watercolour drawing of the Long Room, 1953.

A selection of cigarette cards from different companies and in varying styles, which cover the years 1900–39.

the country were put on one hour in advance of Greenwich time, extending the hours of daylight for the whole of the summer months. Although originally a wartime measure, it was found to have so many advantages it was continued and made permanent in 1925. (Interestingly the experiment was echoed in the Second World War with 'double British summer time' during and after the war, but no one was suggesting two-day matches then.)

The scheme had its opponents and that might well have included the cricketers because, as *Wisden* of 1919 states, 'The advocates of the two-day match overlooked the needs of the human stomach . . . the craving for food had as a rule become stronger than the passion for cricket.' Play used to end at 7.30 p.m.

The two-day system failed also because wickets were good and games therefore were uncompleted. At Trent Bridge only one match was finished that summer. By the end of the season there were as many people against the scheme as there had been for it, so it was stopped, and the three-day first-class game returned in 1920. The MCC had no part in the two-day scheme: the Gentlemen v. Players match and Oxford v. Cambridge were still of three days' duration, and if anyone had kept optimism for cricket afloat right through the war it was Lord Harris. He steadfastly maintained that the old charm would still exist for an enthusiastic public after the war, and he can seldom have been more correct. In the 1920 season, the interest in cricket appeared greater than ever before; large crowds attended county games. Where there used to be 7,000 or 8,000, now there were 20,000 and sometimes, at Lord's, even 30,000. It was much the same at The Oval and at Old Trafford where, in the Lancashire v. Yorkshire 'Roses' match, all records were broken.

Fast-moving social changes were being reflected in cricket. The high proportion of unemployed people boosted crowds. After 1925, at Lord's, they could find free, covered seats; only the ground admission of 3 shillings had to be paid or half-price after tea. County revenues were comfortably bolstered by these fast accumulating shillings. From post-war days too dates, for many and complex reasons, a decline in the number of Gentlemen cricketers, and there was a withdrawal of patronage because the taxation laws against the wealthy were becoming severe. For the amateur there was no more drifting from one country-house cricket match to another.

However, cricket was being played ever more widely at the universities, the public schools, in most parts of England, the more anglicised parts of Wales such as Glamorgan, and the eastern areas of Scotland. As popular interest boomed, a star system

V. T. Trumper and W. W. Armstrong, from contemporary cigarette cards.

developed: cricket personalities and Test matches were national news. It was back to the 'national game' again: even soccer was eclipsed. Cigarette cards had been popular before the war – the clear eyes of the heroes stared out with scarcely a trace of a smile beneath their tight-fitting county caps or under ribboned boaters. The cards were passionately collected by schoolboys, although the obvious intention of Wills and Capstan or John Player was to induce adults to purchase their cigarettes. These cricket cards began with the head and shoulder portrait: neat and tidy J. T. Hearne of Middlesex, or flamboyantly amateur, Mr R. E. Foster of Worcestershire. The Australians, erect and formidable, all in green blazers with yellow trim and Test caps – V. Trumper, NSW, wearing a white polo-necked sweater, looking not unlike the boyish W. W. Armstrong, Vic. The firm of Godfrey Phillips Ltd. went for straight photography with attention to the county players, including R. C. Robertson-Glasgow of Somerset, later such an attractive writer on the game whose autobiography was entitled *46 not out*; Alec Skelding of Leicestershire; and C. W. L. Parker of Gloucestershire who posed with cap and ball at stumps without bails.

Wills included H. Larwood, in a straight portrait; the late R. Kilner, solid and cheerful, left-arm over the wicket; and Mr K. S. Duleepsinhji in Cambridge-blue blazer. Players offered cartoon action sketches of the lively bowling activities of Mr J. M. Gregory, NSW, Mr P. G. H. Fender of Surrey, and Mr G. O. Allen, a youth with hair roughly parted in the centre, called on the reverse of the card, 'Young Allen', and rated 'a tearaway bowler with possibilities, and a free bat with a good variety of strokes'.

There was an increasing press coverage of Test matches through the 1920s and, by 1930 Test matches were being broadcast on radio, the first commentary having been given in 1924–5 in Australia. Quickly names like Hobbs, Sutcliffe, Hammond, Woolley, Chapman and the Australian Don Bradman became far more widely known than all other contemporary sportsmen. Cricket attracted writers, journalists, even poets, which would never have happened with a more proletarian game – not that good writing had only to do with snobbery. Much more, it was because cricket was a longer game, a point which Bernard Hollowood makes persuasively in his *Cricket on the Brain*:

> I am devoted to open rugger, modern soccer (a brand of animated chess), tennis, golf, squash, baseball, billiards, ping pong and almost every other ball game. But cricket seems to me to be richer in potential ... The game lasts long enough to be affected by changes in cloud cover, light, humidity, temperature, the consistency of the pitch and the 'speed' of the outfield; long enough for ritual and pageantry to be welcomed; long enough for individual

character to unfold, for boys to become men, for reporters to write worthy prose, for casual meetings to ripen into lasting friendships, for luck to dart in and out of the proceedings and raise hopes that seemed shattered – and shatter hopes on the wing. A cricket match is a campaign rather than an encounter.

In the middle 1920s the name of a sports journalist came to notice in the north of England, and later to the world. He wrote under the name 'Cricketer' in the *Manchester Guardian* and when his first collection of essays was published he revealed his name as Neville Cardus. He wrote stylish prose and elevated cricket to the level of artistic ritual. He inspired an affection for cricketers, and those who were happy victims in his golden words did not object if he left the play without every detail of the score-card at his command.

As for cricket periodicals, the Americans, who had paved the way with *The American Cricketer* from 1877, were just about to drop out of circulation both as cricketers and cricket-readers. Philadelphia cricket was dying and the magazine ended in 1929.

Cricket, later called *The World of Cricket*, began in 1882, but was a casualty of the First World War, so the way was open for a new regular publication on the game. It was P. F. Warner, on his retirement as a player, who brought out the first edition of *The Cricketer* on April 30th, 1921.

In his third issue, however, he carried words of complaint against Lord's and the Marylebone Club for failing to cope with the increase in the number of matches played and the enthusiasm of the game's post-war following.

The arrangements made at Lord's for coping with the great crowd, which everybody who has followed cricket at all closely during the last few years knew would assemble for the Test match, were very bad indeed. There was a most frightful crush outside the ground on the first day, ticket-holders and those who had no tickets being inextricably mixed up. It is not pleasant to see women fainting in a crowd, and the authorities at Lord's cannot escape criticism for not making better arrangements . . .

The number of turnstiles has been increased since last year, but there are even now, only six or seven at most, and in order to ensure a large crowd getting into the ground, twice that number of turnstiles is necessary. It is also most unfortunate that all the turnstiles are in St John's Wood Road. MCC own nearly all the property around Lord's, and one would have imagined that on this occasion entrance for ticket-holders might have been made through the gardens of some of the houses at the back of the pavilion and on the north and north-east side of the ground. There were certainly not enough police to control the crowd on Saturday, and altogether the confusion was appalling, many people who were ticket-holders waiting literally hours in the queue before they could obtain admission to the ground.

On the first two days the gates had to be closed, and we venture to suggest that for future Test matches, the MCC must keep in view a crowd of at least 40,000. The present stands at Lord's are far too low, and hopelessly out of date.

The interest in cricket today is greater than it has ever been, and the MCC must, in their own interests, move with the times . . . Lord's is the Mecca of cricket, and MCC should do everything in their power for the comfort of the crowd, who, after all, supply the sinews of war. The cricketing world will look with confidence to Col. the Hon. F. S. Jackson, MP, the President, to put matters right in future.

Although the tone of these comments was more of sorrow than anger, they led to *The Cricketer* being withdrawn from sale at Lord's for three days while tempers cooled.

England's Test performance after the war was dismal. Three series were lost on the trot to Australia and the Ashes were only regained in 1926, but there cropped up meanwhile names in school and university despatches which were to have impact on the MCC's affairs in the years ahead. An outstanding cricketer was noted at Oxford, called D. R. Jardine, and the exceptional bowling strength at Cambridge had much to do with G. O. Allen. Pelham Warner vividly recalled Allen's bowling against the Australians in 1926: 'He obtained the last four wickets for 11 runs (his full analysis was 5 for 63) in each case sending a stump somersaulting, and in Australia's second innings he again ripped a stump out of the ground.'

More important for England, Jack Hobbs was in full swing again – eight centuries in 1919, eleven in 1920, four for MCC and England in Australia, in 1920–21. However, it was Hobbs's habit to say, 'I was never half the player after the First War than I was before'; but those who watched him in 1919 and 1920 saw him still truly great. Although he was now in his late thirties he continued to score prolifically, completing 197 first-class centuries by his retirement in 1934 in his fifty-second year. As late as 1932, despite a torn leg muscle, he scored 1,764 runs at an average of 66 per innings. Douglas Jardine described his 161 not out at Lord's in his last Gentlemen v. Players match as 'a great personal triumph'.

Many records stand to Hobbs's name: his aggregate of 61,237 runs; his total of 197 centuries, 98 scored after the age of 40; the highest score in a first-class match at Lord's (316 not out); the highest score (266 not out) in the Gentlemen v. Players matches, at Scarborough, his 16 hundreds in those matches (beating Grace's 15), and his 12 against Australia. Just as W.G. was called The Champion, J. B. Hobbs was revered by his generation as The Master.

There was genius too in the tall, stylish left-handed batsman of Kent, F. E. Woolley. He played for England from 1909–34. In all first-class cricket he scored 58,969 runs, an aggregate second only to Hobbs, and also took 2,068 wickets. He scored 145 hundreds.

George Challenor, the finest of the early West Indian batsmen, pictured in 1923. On the previous tour in 1906, he was elected a member of MCC, even though he had not played the requisite number of qualifying matches.

Even though his record in Tests is described by H. S. Altham as 'uneven', the Lord's crowds always made a vivid tale of his 95 and 93 scored against Australia there in 1921 with 'almost negligent majesty'.

Woolley said his farewells in 1938 at the age of 51 with a revealing observation:

> I doubt whether English cricket has really recovered from the effects of the war. You see, we missed half a generation, and since then young men have found many other ways of occupying their leisure hours. Those were the days when plenty of amateurs could spare time for cricket. I do not think there are so many good players in the game now as before the war. In the old days we were probably educated in cricket in a far more serious way than now. For the purpose of giving younger people my idea of the difference I will put up Walter Hammond, England's captain, as an example. Before 1914 there were something like thirty players up to his standard and he would have been in the England team only if at the top of his form. I make these remarks without casting the slightest reflection on Hammond. He is a grand player and one of the greatest all-round cricketers since the war – in fact, the greatest.

W. R. Hammond, as it happened, had a certain difficulty in getting started at all. He had been born in Kent, a technicality which Lord Harris seized upon to keep him out of county cricket for the whole of the 1922 season in order to fulfil MCC's registration laws. Not that Harris always got his own way with the counties in their Advisory Committee. His long objection to Glamorgan being given first-class status was ignored, and in 1921 the seventeenth and youngest county to date was admitted.

In the mid-1920s a new and permanent problem arose for the MCC, the expansion of cricket throughout the Empire. More and more tours were called for and other countries wanted to join England, Australia and South Africa at official Test level. The West Indies, who had toured England before the war and in 1923 without playing Tests, arrived first, in 1928. They came under the captaincy of R. K. Nunes and lost all three Tests by an innings. George Challenor was now 40 and past his best, and weak slip fielding let down the promising fast attack of Constantine, Griffith and Francis. Constantine did not bat well in the Tests, but his fielding made a sensation; and against Middlesex at Lord's he scored 86 and 103 and, in the second innings, took 7 wickets for 11 runs in 14 overs.

At this time the England team was strong, chosen perhaps from Hobbs, Sutcliffe, E. Tyldesley, Hammond, Woolley, Jardine, Leyland, Hendren, Chapman, Tate, Larwood, Geary, White, Duckworth, Freeman; but in 1929–30, when the MCC sent teams concurrently to the West Indies and New Zealand, the former under the Hon. F. S. G. Calthorpe, they could only draw a series of four matches. Five years later the West Indies beat R. E. S. Wyatt's MCC side 2–1.

New Zealand were the next to be admitted to Tests. They had done well on an earlier tour in 1927. Then in their inaugural series against A. H. H. Gilligan's team in 1929–30 they drew three matches and lost only one. They impressed with cricketers like T. C. Lowry, C. S. Dempster, M. L. Page, R. C. Blunt and W. E. Merritt.

India played their first Test match at Lord's in 1932, the only Test of the tour. Their tour captain was the Maharajah of Porbandar although, on the field, the leadership was eventually entrusted to C. K. Nayudu. England won by 158 runs, but not without a hiccup or two. Jardine's resolute batting, 79 and 85 not out, eased a tricky situation as Mohammad Nissar, Amar Singh and Jahangir Khan took reasonably priced wickets.

The picture of Test cricket between the wars can most easily be seen from this list:

DATE	SERIES	TESTS
1920–21	Australia v. England	5
1921	England v. Australia	5
1921–22	South Africa v. Australia	3
1922–23	South Africa v. England	5
1924	England v. South Africa	5
1924–25	Australia v. England	5
1926	England v. Australia	5
1927–28	South Africa v. England	5
1928	England v. West Indies	3
1928–29	Australia v. England	5
1929	England v. South Africa	5
1929–30	New Zealand v. England	4
1929–30	West Indies v. England	4
1930	England v. Australia	5
1930–31	Australia v. West Indies	5
1930–31	South Africa v. England	5
1931	England v. New Zealand	3
1931–32	Australia v. South Africa	5
1931–32	New Zealand v. South Africa	2
1932	England v. India	1
1932–33	Australia v. England	5
1932–33	New Zealand v. England	2
1933	England v. West Indies	3
1933–34	India v. England	3
1934	England v. Australia	5
1934–35	West Indies v. England	4
1935	England v. South Africa	5
1935–36	South Africa v. Australia	5
1936	England v. India	3
1936–37	Australia v. England	5
1937	England v. New Zealand	3
1938	England v. Australia	5
1938–39	South Africa v. England	5
1939	England v. West Indies	3

Very much concerned with their international role, the MCC also
sent tours during this time to the weaker cricketing countries:

1922	Denmark
1922–23	New Zealand (pre-Test status)
1925	Denmark
1925–26	West Indies (pre-Test status)
1926–27	India (pre-Test status), Burma and Ceylon
1926–27	South America
1928	Holland
1933	Holland
1937	Canada
1939	Denmark

When Pelham Warner captained the MCC side to Australia in
October 1911 he was concerned lest his men would get stiff on the
voyage; so he sent a wireless message to the Colombo Cricket Club
asking that a match be arranged between MCC and Ceylon when
the SS *Orvieto* dropped anchor in Colombo. No English side had
played in Ceylon for seventeen years, and the local club was
delighted. Warner commented on the excellent grass wickets, the
capacity crowd and on the hospitality and enthusiasm.

> Cricket has become more than a game. It is an institution, a passion, one
> might almost say a religion. It has got into the blood of the nation, and
> wherever British men and women are gathered together there will the stumps
> be pitched. North, South, East and West throughout the British Empire, from
> Lord's to Sydney, from Hong Kong to the Spanish Main, cricket flourishes.
> It is the policy of the MCC to encourage the love of cricket in every possible
> way, and in playing at Colombo we were but carrying out that policy.

Warner's delight in Ceylon cricket led to Colombo becoming a
regular stopping-place for MCC sides on their way to Australia in
the years between the wars.

Where Warner's paean errs is that it implied that the MCC
fostered cricket only within the British Empire. In fact, as the tour
list between the wars reveal, its influence went far beyond. Two
years before Warner's side played in Colombo, Viscount Brackley
took the MCC on a tour of Egypt with G. H. Simpson-Hayward,
one of the last great underarm or 'lob' bowlers, captaining it on
the field and with another Test player, Captain E. G. Wynyard,
in the party. Then, while Warner was preparing to return from
that tour of Australia, Lord Hawke was making his way to Argentina with a strong MCC side which included A. C. MacLaren,
E. R. Wilson, C. E. de Trafford and W. Findlay. Of the three
international matches played, Argentina won the first and the
MCC won the other two.

Cricket was not new in Argentina. The first evidence of its being
played there dates back to 1806. By 1823, 3,000 Britons lived in

Buenos Aires, so there was no shortage of players. In 1864 the Buenos Aires Cricket Club opened its new ground at Palermo Park and celebrated with a match between the home club and HMS *Bombay*. Six days later, unfortunately, the *Bombay* caught fire and sank.

The MCC were back in South America in 1926–27, this time taking in matches in Chile as well as Argentina. It was a strong side, too, with G. O. Allen, J. C. White and Lord Dunglass (later Sir Alec Douglas-Home, Prime Minister). More importantly for the prestige of Argentina, the country was invited to play the MCC at Lord's in 1926 and 1928. There is little evidence, however, that the game was spreading beyond the English expatriate communities.

In the Netherlands, cricket was being played in the middle of the nineteenth century and in 1883, eighteen clubs formed the Nederlandsche Cricket Bond. In 1921 the famous De Flamingo's Club was formed.

Cricket was first played in Denmark also in the nineteenth century and the first international match of any kind took place in 1887 when K.B. Club, Copenhagen, beat a side drawn from the crew of the Prince of Wales's yacht, *The Osborne*. In spite of this unexpected success, cricket in Denmark lived in the shadow of soccer and other games. The stimulus it needed was provided by the MCC, and by one of the club's noted members, Richard Prescott Keigwin. Keigwin was a magnificent all-round sportsman, who represented Cambridge at cricket, soccer, hockey and rackets. He played county cricket for Essex and Gloucestershire, as well as international hockey and county tennis. When in France for a time he became an expert at pelota. He was a master at Clifton, his old school, for sixteen years and, later, was warden of Wills Hall at Bristol University.

Most significantly, perhaps, he was the foremost translator of Danish literature into English and an authority on the works of Hans Christian Andersen. He was made a knight of the Order of the Dannebrog for his services to Danish literature, but he served Danish cricket just as well. It was at his instigation that the MCC sent a side to Denmark in April 1922. Keigwin himself led the party which included two Hills – Vernon Tickell, the father, and Mervyn Llewellyn, the son. Hill junior won admiration for his splendid wicket-keeping for Somerset and Glamorgan and was to tour India, Burma and Ceylon with the MCC side of 1926–27. Also in Keigwin's side was J. C. Clay, then a fast bowler with only one first-class season behind him, but with a long career of off-spin ahead.

In 1925 Keigwin led a second MCC side to Denmark where all six matches were won. The club maintained regular contact with the game in Denmark between the wars right up to 1939 when the MCC team under G. C. Newman and accompanied by Pelham Warner 'celebrated fifty years of cricket in Denmark'.

There had long been cricket contact with Canada dating back to 1785, and to W. G. Grace's trip there with R. A. FitzGerald in 1872; but the first official MCC side went there in 1937. G. C. Newman's side played nineteen matches and were beaten once.

Rhodesia always received a visit when MCC teams toured South Africa, but if there is to be a serious criticism of the MCC's propagandising, it was its failure to take official teams across to America where the game had once been strong and yet was now reduced almost to extinction, due principally, in Philadelphia at least, to the growing popularity of lawn tennis.

In domestic cricket in Britain between the wars the story is essentially about the shift of success in the county championship from south to north. There was a run of success for Yorkshire who were champions four times in a row. In 1925 they won eleven of their 21 victories by an innings and were unbeaten. Then came Lancashire, who in five years were beaten only five times while they were collecting 64 wins. Between 1926 and 1930 they were champions four times. After that, apart from two seasons, Yorkshire were to take the title right up to the Second World War.

Eton v. Harrow still attracted large crowds, but the indications were that they were becoming essentially social occasions; and as such attracted the attention of writers and cartoonists. For example, A. P. Herbert in *Punch* in 1923:

> I love Lord's. I love Eton and Harrow. I love the sunny green, the happy crowds, the coaches, the frocks, the pretty ladies, the grey top-hats, the cultured talk, the little walking-sticks of the boys, the ribbons on the walking-sticks, the flowers in their coats; I love to feel that this is England, this is the national game, a manly dangerous game; and I think with pity of the effeminate dagos who can only play pelota, basket-ball and lawn-tennis. Fops!
>
> Joan is as keen on cricket as I am, and she was the best-dressed woman there. We sat on a very hard seat for the greater part of a hot day and saw hundreds of frocks. The wicket was 'plumb', the batting orthodox, and if there is anything more boring than orthodox batting on a plumb wicket I suppose it is professional billiards . . .
>
> But personally I go to Lord's for the conversation; and as soon as I pointed out some of the badder balls to Joan I settled down to enjoy some of that charming idiocy which only flourishes at Lord's. This year there was prevalent a sort of pose of being interested in the cricket; and everybody I sat in front of was commenting bitterly on the conversation of the people behind them. And the sum total of these comments was like the sound of a Cairo bazaar in the American season.

The dialogue would not go well on stage, I dare say; but that is because it's true.

'How that fellow jaws!' said a male voice bitterly. 'My hat, that's a bad ball!'

'Tommy said they were bowling rather well.'

'They're bowling muck. Muck. I never saw such muck. Look at that!'

'Oh, I missed it,' said the lady, waking from a stupor. 'What is it?'

'A long-hop. Ought to have gone for four . . . Did you hear that?'

'Hear what?'

'This fellow behind me –'

'The one with the moustache?'

'No, the one with the nose –'

'Yes?'

'Well, he's been telling a story about some girl or other. It was after a dance and – damn it, how was he out?'

'Afraid I didn't see. Bowled, somebody said.'

'Always the way. As soon as you say a word, a wicket falls. Well, this girl's terribly proper, it seems – been kept very close by her mother and all that. That lad wasn't bowled, he was caught – caught Number 4. Who's that?'

'Crossman.'

'No, Crossman's Eton. It's Stewart-Brown. And one night, in the country, or somewhere after a dance or something, they play hide-and-seek. Only this girl was supposed to be in bed. And she was found in a cupboard with Major Somebody or other. Rather funny?'

'Do you mean she was found by her mother?'

'I don't know. I didn't catch that. This fellow's been telling the story for the last quarter of an hour. That's all they come here for, most of these people.'

'I know. I like that black frock in front.'

'Jolly. I never saw such bowling. It's about time they had another lemonade.'

Not that the matches between Eton and Harrow were idly fought. They engendered an extreme partisan following from everyone who understood the game. *The Times* leading article on July 8th, 1927, was entitled 'On Being a Good Hater', referring to the 'annual orgy' of the Eton v. Harrow match and concluding that it is 'a satisfactory spiritual outlet to indulge once a year in a good, clean, thorough-going hate'. Like the Oxford v. Cambridge matches they were cockpits of partisan rivalry and full of good cricket. It was definitely the shouting that made the match different from others, like a prolonged uproar which crescendoed now and again. Fridays, they report, were tolerably controlled, but Saturdays were a heady mix of hope for a win and the terror of losing.

Such a competitive atmosphere bred fine players, and the schools gave Lord's many of its greatest days. However, Lord's and the Marylebone Club had to change quickly to keep pace with the demands of domestic and international cricket. In the first thirty years of the twentieth century few institutions could have made more changes; it had to, in order that the tornado spread of cricket could blow through the committee room without tearing the

An unusual view of
Lord's on June 27th,
1930, with the flags out
for the England v.
Australia Test match
(and perhaps to stop
other agencies taking
pictures!). Overhead,
the airship R101.
(*BBC Hulton Library.*)

pictures off the walls and bringing this particular 'establishment'
down.

The only part remaining of Thomas Lord's third ground was
the turf itself. There was drainage under it, but otherwise it was
the same as had been brought from Dorset Square and North
Bank a century before. Otherwise the ground had been developed
into a spacious venue for big matches; the finances were in order;
MCC had a playing ground staff of its own; the club had 6,000
members. The Marylebone Club acted as a court of appeal to the
whole cricket world, and as such was flooded with correspondence.
It ran the County Championship, selected Test teams and organised the England tours abroad. It had formed governing bodies
at home and an imperial conference to keep close connections
throughout the Empire. Lord's was now an administrative club,
with business spinning off into many sub-committees.

The man whose job it had been to implement business on all
sides was the secretary, F. E. Lacey. After his retirement in 1926,
having given twenty-eight years of service, he was knighted: the
first knighthood in sport. This underlined how everything seemed
grand and powerful in the MCC world; but now Australia was
producing a batting genius, who was beginning a career as astonishing as those of Grace or Hobbs and, indirectly because of him
and his commanding skill as a player, the club would be drawn
into a storm of accusation and slur.

16 Bodyline and the LBW Law

Donald Bradman was born on August 27th, 1908, at 89 Adam Street, Cootamundra, in New South Wales, Australia. It was at the house of the local midwife, Ellen Scholoty, but neither he nor his parents actually lived in Cootamundra: the family cottage was at Yeo Yeo, between Wallendbean and Stockinbingal. Don's brother, Victor, was just over 6ft tall, like their father, and his three sisters, Islet, Lillian and May, were all above average height; but Don himself was just 5ft 6¾in, the same height as his mother. When Don was two, the family moved to Bowral, in the hope that the climate of the southern highlands would help his mother's variable health. So his father gave up wheat and sheep farming and became a carpenter. Don Bradman was a country lad of sturdy stock.

He was raised in a close family life; his sister taught him the piano, his mother bowled left-armers at him in the backyard and when bowlers were not available, he took a small stump and hit a golf ball as it rebounded from the brick base of a water tank. He was a choirboy at St Jude's Church, Bowral. When he left school he played tennis for a couple of years and then thought he might become a house decorator.

Eight years earlier than Bradman, in 1900, Douglas Jardine was born in Bombay. His father, M. R. Jardine, who had scored a century for Oxford in the University match of 1892, was a barrister at the Bombay Bar. Douglas himself was tall and upright. His early life was so rooted in law and Empire that he was left in no doubt about the relationship of Britain to its colonies: this left him with a hint of patronage, even contempt, when it came to relationships with other people. Outwardly he was cold. He was sent home to be educated, at Horris Hill School, then at Winchester, and quickly embarked on the amateur cricket trail. At Oxford he won his Blue as a freshman but was never captain. Afterwards his Oxford Harlequin cap became a badge of identity.

Don Bradman used to keep the score for Bowral, then, at the age of 17 he got a game for them against Wingello. It was the close of the 1925–26 summer and W. J. 'Bill' O'Reilly was on the other side. Bradman scored an amazing 234 not out on the first Saturday on the Bowral ground. The following Saturday when the match continued at Wingello, he was soon out to O'Reilly, but the news had already spread. He followed it with an innings of 300 against Moss Vale. Very quickly his prolific scoring in the bush brought him trial nets at the Sydney cricket ground and he was soon in the New South Wales side for the 1927–28 season. At Adelaide against Victoria he went in at number seven and scored 118.

D. G. Bradman

It was just after his twentieth birthday that Don Bradman made his first contact with the MCC. He had only once seen a Test match and as far as he was concerned the MCC was England. Now in 1928 he was in the New South Wales side against A. P. F. Chapman's side and Walter Hammond was in regal flow, scoring a glorious 225 in the MCC score of 734 for 7. Young Bradman made 87 in the first innings and then, when New South Wales followed on, saved the match with an unbroken stand of 249 for the fourth wicket with A. F. Kippax: Bradman, 132 not out.

At Oxford, Jardine played six innings without success in three Varsity matches, missing out 1922, his third year, because of injury. However, he did score excellent centuries against the counties. He played his first game against an Australian side in 1921. Armstrong, the tour captain, had insisted on a two-day game only against Oxford, so that his team would have plenty of time for travel and rest before the Test match. Jardine was 96 not out when the match ended. Many writers have suggested that Armstrong upset Jardine by refusing to bowl an extra over for the undergraduate to get his century, but it is hard to see the truth in that – in the first place the MCC, with Lords Harris and Hawke keeping the conscience of cricket's laws and regulations, was unlikely to sanction false time-keeping; second, even if a nod from the umpires would have fixed it, Jardine was not the kind of man to take such presents. Nor, for that matter, was Armstrong the sort of captain to give them.

Nonetheless it was early proof that Jardine was a fine batsman. When he went down from Oxford he set out to be a lawyer like his father and, hampered by limited financial means, made only irregular appearances for Surrey. By now true amateurism was becoming a less convincing posture than before the First World War. Even so, in 1927 and 1928 Douglas Jardine headed the English averages with 91.09 and 87.15, respectively. His first Tests were under A. P. F. Chapman against the novice West Indians in 1928. He was considered a superb player of fast bowling.

So these two cricketers, Bradman and Jardine, from opposite ends of the earth in many senses, took the same field to represent their countries at Brisbane in the first Test of the 1928–29 series. Jardine saw the young Bradman on his debut come in late, score 18 and 1 and get left out of the second Test; but he also saw him return for the last three to score 79, 112, 40, 58, 123 and 37 not out. Jardine held his own place, in a very strong side, with innings of 35, 65, 28, 62, 33, 1 and 98, 19 and 0. England won the Ashes convincingly 4–1.

D. R. Jardine

Nothing had happened so far to suggest that Bradman and Jardine would have anything in common other than cricket: it was a little too early for anyone to match their sanguine natures – Bradman the merciless and remorseless destroyer of bowlers; Jardine, the cold commander who would stop at nothing within the law. The story developed with Bradman's exceptional talent. After the 1928–29 tour, Jack Hobbs and Percy Chapman, the England captain, had both identified Bradman's danger to England, and when the Australians toured in 1930, spectators in England saw it for themselves.

At that time the fastest bowler in the world was England's Harold Larwood. He was the third important element in a gather-

H. Larwood

ing storm. His was a humble background – the son of a Nottinghamshire coal-miner, who learned his game on the coal-tips and in the back streets before joining the Nottinghamshire staff, beginning his first-class career in 1924. He was not tall, about average height, but his run-up over eighteen yards was a crescendo which never lost its smooth rhythm and ended in whirling arms. He was very successful until his path crossed Don Bradman's in England in 1930. Bradman in those Tests scored 68 not out and 131 at Trent Bridge, 254 at Lord's, 334 at Headingley and 232 at The Oval. During the whole tour the young Australian prodigy scored 2,960 runs at an average of 98.66. Harold Larwood withdrew painfully with four wickets only, costing 73 runs each, to ruminate over the feather-bed pitches they had played on. Australia won the Ashes.

Bradman had immense natural skill as well as huge concentration of mind. He had physical strength, extreme fitness and a cool temperament. Pelham Warner thought he detected too 'an idealism which urged him to learn everything he possibly could, and to profit by the lessons learnt'.

As a teenager, Don Bradman had been a sprinter, a champion runner, never beaten. His footwork at the crease matched the speed of his eye; he could move quickly to off stump and hit the ball to leg; he could be orthodox; his defence was rocklike. And then there was that almost brutal avarice for runs – bowlers were clinically demolished.

When the England selectors prepared their teams for the 1932–33 tour to Australia, the key question was, what to do about Bradman? At Lord's, the Board of Control announced that the England selectors would be Pelham Warner, chairman, who had led two MCC sides to Australia, P. A. Perrin, and T. A. Higson. The firm advice which usually came from Lord Harris was missing this time, because the fourth Lord Harris of Seringapatam and Mysore and of Belmont had died on March 24th, 1932. However, Harris had favoured the elevation of Jardine, who had done well enough with Chapman's side in Australia and who was thought at Lord's to be a diligent student of the game, a sharp observer, and not afraid to make positive contributions to MCC committees.

Furthermore, Jardine had already confirmed the hopes of his supporters by leading England to victory over New Zealand in 1931 and India in 1932, although the opposition was admittedly well below the standard expected to win back the Ashes. Jardine was chosen. Bradman, the selectors considered, had looked vulnerable against leg-spin, but R. W. V. Robins of Middlesex, whom everyone wanted to go, regretted that he could not leave his business; Ian Peebles, also of Middlesex, had lost his form; and so Tom Mitchell of Derbyshire was chosen as well as the young amateur F. R. Brown of Surrey. Jardine also had Verity to bowl left-arm spin, but more importantly there were four fast bowlers: Larwood, who had a distinguished wicket-taking record in county matches and earlier Tests; Voce, his Nottinghamshire partner, burly and left-handed; the tall Yorkshireman who wore glasses, Bowes; and G. O. Allen, the amateur who played for Middlesex. It was quite a battery, with Tate joining later.

Everyone knew that real speed could win matches. There were still vivid memories of Australia's fast bowlers of the early 1920s, Gregory and McDonald, the finest pair to date. The editor of *Wisden* in 1922 records, 'some of our batsmen, knowing that they would have to face Gregory, were out before they went in. Since Knox bowled his fastest in 1906 I have never seen batsmen so obviously intimidated. McDonald struck one as being really the finer of the two, but Gregory was by far the more alarming.'

Once the 1932–33 tour had started, Larwood, Voce and Bowes were soon in demolishing form in a match against 'An Australian XI'. It was ferocious bowling which included a number of short-pitched balls directed much more to leg stump than to off as was the custom. To accommodate this, there was a steady reinforcement of the leg-side field. R. E. S. Wyatt was captain in Jardine's absence. Woodfull suffered a painful blow over the heart; Bradman was out cheaply. Bradman failed again for New South Wales in an equally intimidating match. Bouncers were usually called 'headers' then, but the Australian press invented the emotive word 'bodyline'.

FIRST TEST, SYDNEY.
Bradman was ill and did not play. England won by ten wickets and by relatively plain tactics. Sutcliffe, Hammond and Pataudi scored centuries, but the fabled innings was the 187 scored by Stan McCabe. He attacked the fast short-pitched bowling even when Larwood bowled to six fielders on the leg side. Voce bowled short and on leg stump, and he opened the bowling in the second innings with five short-legs, but both bowlers fell prey to McCabe's inspired hooking. However, the Australian crowds let it be known that they did not like the element of physical intimidation contained in the 'leg-theory' bowling. In the first innings Larwood took five wickets, Voce four and Hammond one; in the second Larwood again got five, Voce and Hammond two, and Allen one. The match was played to the accompaniment of almost non-stop, raucous barracking.

SECOND TEST, MELBOURNE.

This took place over New Year, and Bradman was fit. England dropped Verity, the only spinner in their first Test side, substituting Bowes. There had been a protracted argument in selection. Neither the vice-captain, Wyatt, nor Allen, both amateurs, could see the sense in taking the field without spinners. In the dressing-room before the game, Jardine came and sat by Allen. He wanted him, he said, to bowl more bouncers and have a stronger leg-side field. Allen says he refused: Jardine persisted. Allen replied, 'Well, I'm not going to, and if you don't like the way I bowl, you'd better leave me out – but I would add that if you do, every word you've said here today will be made public when I get home.' Jardine accepted the situation. It was an oddly aggressive statement by Allen, amateur to amateur, even though he suspected that Jardine planned to use his new brand of leg theory in the middle.

The Melbourne pitch was slow. Larwood had exasperating trouble with his boots and actually had to go off twice. Bradman played on to Bowes for 0 in the first innings, but scored a rehabilitating century, 103 not out, in the second. Voce and Bowes had bowled fast and short to a leg-side field, and Larwood increasingly followed. Australia won by 111 runs, thanks mainly to their spinners.

THIRD TEST, ADELAIDE.

Peaceful Adelaide, a city of half a million inhabitants. Some 39,000 paid to watch the first day's play, barracked the English without mercy, and saw England totter to the brink of collapse before Leyland, Wyatt, and Paynter grafted to a respectable 341. Around 50,000 watched the second day, Saturday, the biggest crowd to date at the Adelaide Oval. Fingleton went quickly, caught by Ames off Allen. Enter Bradman. Larwood was at his fastest and none of his contemporaries ever thought they saw a faster bowler.

Larwood had raised complaints on the previous tour, 1928–29, for his leg-stump bowling in a match at Sydney. In the biography, *Sir Donald Bradman*, by Irving Rosenwater, is reproduced part of a letter written by Warwick Armstrong to the MCC at that time – 'Yesterday and today he appeared to be bowling deliberately at the batsman. He has great pace, and could afford not to bowl at the man . . . If he continues these tactics the spectators here might think there were more sporting ways of getting results.' Now in 1932, after the first Test, Pelham Warner, chairman of selectors and tour manager, already had confided in a letter home, 'personally I am terrified of some horrible incident.'

At Adelaide, the last ball of Larwood's second over pitched on

W. M. Woodfull
(*Central Press*)

the wicket, not a lot short of a length; it got up fiercely and hit Woodfull over the heart, just as had happened in the game against 'An Australian XI'. Woodfull followed the Australian habit of moving a long way across the stumps as the bowler let the ball go. He was hurt, dropped his bat and staggered away from the wicket. The crowd howled.

It was unusual for a Test batsman to be hit. Jardine is said to have proclaimed, 'Well bowled, Harold.'

At the start of his third over, right in the middle of his run-up, Larwood was stopped by Jardine who conspicuously moved the slips to the leg side to make a circle of five short-legs. The crowd was almost out of control and Jardine, erect, with his silk neckerchief intact, wearing as usual his Harlequin cap, was the perfect English target for the barrackers.

In *The Bodyline Controversy* by Laurence Le Quesne, every detail of the play has been skilfully explored and exposed. The author considers this incident to be the 'moral turning-point' of the series, 'the point at which Australian opinion swung finally and overwhelmingly to condemnation of the English bowling tactics'. For now, in the fifth over of Australia's first innings at Adelaide, Jardine stopped Larwood in his run-up and called in his leg-trap.

Australia were 222 all out, but the wound against Woodfull was a wound against the whole nation. For Warner it was particularly desperate. His visit to Australia could have been a gentle lap of honour, full of pleasant reunions with old friends, with a few despatches sent back for publication in London. As it was, with all Australia shouting 'bodyline' he could please no one, and this would have hurt him more than the events themselves. He was called the manager, but there was no precedent for a tour manager's superseding the captain in any matter. On the day that Woodfull was hit Warner went to the Australian dressing-room to commiserate with the captain and to apologise for England's tactics. He was spurned by Woodfull. 'I don't want to speak to you, Mr Warner. Of the two teams out there, one is playing the game, the other is making no effort to play the game of cricket.' Many versions of this remark were reported. Whatever the exact wording, this was a shattering rejection for Warner. Bowes was later to recall Warner's returning to England's dressing-room like a broken man, repeating incredulously, 'They turned their backs on me – they wouldn't speak to me.'

Yet the peace mission also lost him the loyalty of many of his own side. Certainly his deteriorating relationship with Jardine hardened still further and temperamentally, the strong, terse captain, of Scottish descent, involved in the battle on field, was unlikely to find common ground with such a gentle, courteous, paternal diplomat. Warner's position of weakness was emphasised all the more when the England team got together and signed a statement of support for Jardine.

When Jardine made that switch to 'bodyline', bringing in the short-legs, pandemonium had broken out in the crowd. Wyatt, who was fielding close to the bat, heard the news from an England boundary fielder that 200 armed police had moved in. From this point on, it was the opinion of both Wyatt and Allen that the escalation of a tactical cricket war was elevated into a slanging match between the two countries by the press.

On Monday, Ponsford batted, bulging with padding, and Oldfield supported him. Voce had an injured ankle: the pitch was easy. At 194 Ponsford was out. There had only been minor blows to the body. At 200 the new ball was available and soon taken by Larwood and Allen. Grimmett was out to Allen at 212 and then Oldfield, at 218, trying to hook Larwood, was hit on the head so badly he had to retire. He took no further part in the match. Larwood had been bowling a lot of leg theory during the innings, but in fact was not bowling it when either Woodfull or Oldfield received their injuries. Observers said that they were both hit by balls aimed at the wicket, though obviously short of a length. Oldfield himself said afterwards that it was his own fault that he was hit. Indeed he was no easy victim with the bat; and he had made 41 when he was hurt.

After Oldfield had been helped off, the next man, O'Reilly, had trouble in getting through the crowds to the middle. He recalls,

> The crowd were yelling mad, standing on seats, rushing around the outfield. It took me ten minutes to fight my way out of that tiny passage to get as far as the grass and when I saw daylight across the other side of the ground, I was amazed – mounted police had drawn up in a line as if to battle-charge over at the far gate. When I got to the middle Larwood was a mile away back at the start of his run, sitting on the floor, bouncing the ball on the ground, waiting for the crowd noise to go down. When he ran in – it must have been now fifteen minutes from the moment I had stood up to leave the dressing room – I can tell you, I gave him a good sight of my stumps. Always did. It only took five balls.

O'Reilly, no great respecter of rank or position, used to call Jardine 'Hiawatha', because of the totem-pole line of Jardine's forehead and nose.

> I got to like him. It was only on the next tour of England that I discovered how shy he was. Sutcliffe, the senior pro., was the unpopular one with the Australians. He would call for a leg-theory field before Jardine. On the Saturday evening of the Adelaide Test I went to the England team hotel to meet someone. Jardine saw me in the foyer and asked me to go for a drink in the England team room. I did not particularly want to but I felt I ought to

go. They gave me a fine time. I stayed most of the evening. I really enjoyed myself.

The crowd bayed right through the match, Jardine increasingly their target. In their view, Larwood was only the captain's missile. Whereas Allen, an amateur, could refuse to bowl to order, Larwood, the professional, could not. Amateurs belonged to cricket's governing class, travelling first-class while the professionals went second or third, lunching at separate tables. Joe Darling, the former Australian captain, said he had heard amateurs address professionals like dogs.

The events at Adelaide closed with an England win by 338 runs. Larwood and Allen had taken 15 wickets: England were 2–1 up in the series. The match ended in a mood of conciliation as far as the teams were concerned; but by then the fascination and the fury had already shifted from the field of play into the orbit of the MCC Committee.

Australia's first move was simply for their Board members at the ground in Adelaide to convince Warner, and the assistant manager, R. C. N. Palairet, that bodyline tactics should be discontinued. The manager replied that they were not responsible for playing policy. The Australian Board of Control despatched a cable, therefore, to the MCC. It was drafted with the approval of the chairman, Dr Allen Robertson, in Melbourne and was sent on January 18th, 1933, the fifth day of the match:

> Bodyline bowling has assumed such proportions as to menace the best interests of the game, making protection of the body by the batsmen the main consideration. This is causing intensely bitter feeling between the players as well as injury. In our opinion it is unsportsmanlike. Unless stopped at once it is likely to upset the friendly relations existing between Australia and England.

The cable was received with shock and disbelief by the MCC. Australia questioning England's sportsmanship – that for an MCC committee was a heinous affront and, as for the breakdown of relations between Australia and England, surely they meant cricket relationships.

The cable was unbelievable in England because no one there had a realistic picture of the cricket that was being played. Communications between the two countries took a long time. A letter in those days, just before the introduction of a full air-mail service, took 27–29 days by sea, there was no air service and the telephone system was scant and rudimentary. But there were cables, not an easy form of communication.

The principal interpreters of the cricket for the English public were three correspondents of the London evening papers: Bruce

Harris of the *Evening Standard*; Warwick Armstrong, the former Australian captain, for the *Evening News*; and Jack Hobbs for the *Star*. Jack Hobbs's was the voice everyone wanted to hear. No cricketer commanded wider respect and everyone recalled how he had protested against excessive bouncers during a Surrey–Yorkshire match the previous August at The Oval. Hobbs was not a fluent writer: his reports passed through the hands of a ghostwriter, Jack Ingham. Yet Hobbs above all others offered some perspective – 'There is enough to put up with playing in Australia without a feeling that your own people at home are against you.' Hobbs knew: he had toured Australia four times. He was convinced too that only leg theory could stop Bradman. What he saw and recognised was Test cricket being played hard, to a design which, not for the first time, included intimidation. Australian crowds were bound to barrack louder than ever, so it was essential that the England party stick tightly together.

Armstrong was unusually placed as an Australian reporting for an English paper, and he managed to extract from his comments many strong, subjective old rivalries, arguing instead the impoverishment of cricket when the game is reduced to a tedious spectacle of batsmen ducking and weaving, unable to play strokes.

The debate was joined at both ends of the world. In England most thought that it was chauvinism, Australian crowds viciously partisan and full of bad grace. F. R. Foster, one of the finest of left-arm fast bowlers, was indignant, however. Although he had been consulted by Jardine about field placings for leg theory which Foster had often bowled, he judged that the performance in Australia had developed contrary to the spirit of the game.

In Australia, one of the home opening batsmen, Jack Fingleton, was later able to explain the difference between leg theory and the new bodyline. 'A leg-theory field had its men distributed evenly on the leg side. A bodyline field had a cordon of short-legs and fine-legs with an outer cordon to cover them.' The object was to give batsmen three choices – to prod protectively, to hook, or to be hit.

Both Wyatt and Fingleton had one instinct in common – they thought that the seed of bodyline bowling had been sown at The Oval in the final Test in 1930. It rained, but not before Bradman and Archie Jackson were in complete control with the bat. When the rain stopped the umpires took the teams back on the field at 6.25 p.m. with time for just one Larwood over. Bradman and Jackson dawdled to the wicket and were booed for their reluctance to play. Larwood dug the ball in short, revealing a Bradman no one had seen before. He backed away.

Cartoon by Low, from *Evening Standard* feature, January 21st 1933, which shows the temperature of the Bodyline controversy. (*Express Newspapers*)

The feller's a cad, sir! Tisn't Cricket, sir! Play the game, sir!

LOW'S PATENT CRICKET SUIT, suitable for coping with the new game as played in the match GENTLEMEN v. SLAYERS, Australia, 1933.

Five days after the Australian Board's cable arrived at Lord's the Marylebone Committee assembled – half a dozen members of the peerage, four knights, the Speaker of the House of Commons, a chairman of the Unionist party and an ex-governor of Bengal, a cabinet minister, a lord mayor of London, a former England captain, Sir Stanley Jackson, and half a dozen who had played cricket at first-class level. Pelham Warner was their representative on the tour.

There is no way in which they could have had a realistic idea of what had happened in Adelaide and their reply to the Australian Board, based on a draft by Lord Lewisham, the president, and Sir Kynaston Studd, was unyielding:

January 23rd, 1933. We, Marylebone Cricket Club, deplore your cable. We deprecate your opinion that there has been unsportsmanlike play. We have the fullest confidence in captain, team and managers and are convinced that they would do nothing to infringe either the Laws of Cricket or the spirit of the game. We have no evidence that our confidence has been misplaced. Much as we regret accidents to Woodfull and Oldfield, we understand that in neither case was the bowler to blame. If the Australian Board of Cricket wish to propose a new Law or Rule, it shall receive our careful consideration in due course.

We hope the situation is now not as serious as your cable would seem to

223

indicate, but if it is such as to jeopardize the good relations between English and Australian cricketers and you consider it desirable to cancel the remainder of the programme we would consent, but with great reluctance.

MCC immediately released the contents of the cable to the public.

There were rumours of a split in the England touring party, but Herbert Sutcliffe, the senior professional, compiled a statement to the press:

Members of the England team do not desire to enter into public controversy, for they deplore the introduction of any personal feeling into the records of a great game.

In view, however, of statements which have been given space in some sections of the press to the effect that there has been dissension and disloyalty in their team, they desire to deny this definitely and absolutely.

They are, and always have been, utterly loyal to their captain, under whose leadership they hope to achieve an honourable victory.

On January 30th, 1933, the Australian Board of Control came up with a reply better designed to be understood 8,000 miles away.

We, the ABC, appreciate your difficulty in dealing with the matter raised in our cable without having seen the actual play. We unanimously regard bodyline bowling, as adopted in some of the games in the present tour, as being opposed to the spirit of cricket, and unnecessarily dangerous to the players.

We are deeply concerned that the ideals of the game shall be protected and have, therefore, appointed a committee to report on the action necessary to eliminate such bowling from Australian cricket as from beginning of the 1933–34 season.

We will forward a copy of the Committee's recommendations for your consideration, and it is hoped co-operation as to its application to all cricket. We do not consider it necessary to cancel the remainder of the programme.

At the time of the Adelaide Test, a new governor of South Australia was appointed, Sir Alexander Hore-Ruthven, scion of an ancient Scottish family and a soldier with a distinguished military record. He was a MCC member.

Hore-Ruthven went to the Dominions Office and suggested to his chief, J. H. Thomas, that he should get in touch with the MCC and try to take some heat out of the situation. As a result, a MCC deputation of four called at the Dominions Office on February 1st, 1933, Lord Lewisham, the president, Jackson, Studd and Lord Bridgeman. Also present were Hore-Ruthven and Sir Thomas Inskip, the Attorney-General, who was a keen cricketer.

There was no report of the meeting but, as Le Quesne points out, this meeting probably created the rumour that bodyline was being discussed in the British Cabinet. On the following day the MCC Committee sent their second cable.

We, the Committee of the Marylebone Cricket Club, note with pleasure that you do not consider it necessary to cancel the remainder of the programme, and that you are postponing the whole issue involved until after the present tour is completed. May we accept this as a clear indication that the good sportsmanship of our team is not in question?

We are sure you appreciate how impossible it would be to play any Test Match in the spirit we all desire unless both sides were satisfied there was no reflection on their sportsmanship.

When your recommendation reaches us it shall receive our most careful consideration and will be submitted to the Imperial Cricket Conference.

There was never any danger of a cancellation. Brisbane would not have wanted to lose its Test whatever happened in Adelaide. Queensland had been admitted to full membership of the Sheffield Shield only as recently as 1926–27 and only one MCC touring party, that of 1928–29, had so far played a Test there.

Six days afterwards back came the Australian Board's third cable, dated February 8th, 1933. It was conciliatory: gone was the accusation of England being unsportsmanlike. The Board sensibly joined Warwick Armstrong's lead and put concern for cricket above their anger.

We do not regard the sportsmanship of your team as being in question.

Our position was fully considered at the recent meeting in Sydney and is as indicated in our cable of 30 January.

It is the particular class of bowling referred to therein which we consider is not in the best interests of cricket, and in this view we understand we are supported by many eminent English cricketers.

We join heartily with you in hoping that the remaining Tests will be played with the traditional good feeling.

For Jardine and his men, it was off to Brisbane to try to win the Ashes in the fourth Test; there could be no draw because all Tests in Australia were then played to a finish. Here the Australian team went to the crease wearing cork heart-protectors and with three conspicuous methods of playing Larwood – Woodfull ducking and moving quickly to the off; Victor Richardson hooking; and Bradman stepping back outside leg stump and square-cutting. Australia, batting first, were 340 all out: England replied with 356, a lead of 16. Larwood had taken four wickets, three of which were top batsmen and included Bradman. His fiery performance also helped Allen, Hammond and the two spinners in the side, Verity and Mitchell. Voce, injured, was not playing.

In the second innings, Larwood again got Bradman's wicket as well as the wickets of two bowlers in his three. Australia scored 175, England knocked off the runs for the loss of four wickets, the Ashes were won, and appropriate speeches made by Woodfull and Jardine.

In the fifth and final Test, Jardine refused to drop bodyline, for in doing so, he would have gone some way towards conceding that it was outside the law. McCabe was hit, so was Bradman for the only time in the series – a painful crack on the upper arm. In fact

Larwood bowls to Woodfull, who takes evasive action, in the fourth Test at Brisbane, with a battery of short legs.

Larwood broke down because of his foot becoming injured on the hard Australian grounds, but Jardine kept him in the field until Bradman was out. Bradman was by no means a failure, but with a series average of 56.57 his run-getting had at least been reduced to manageable proportions.

One red-hot issue of bodyline bowling was daily ignited by the cricket crowds who were used to yelling banter or abuse at matches and by an Australian press which delighted in putting the colonial boot into the austere snobbery of Jardine. They had mocked his stiff-upper-lip appearance and Harlequin cap on Chapman's tour and continued to do so. But if bodyline was brutal and unacceptable, what was the cricket intelligence behind it?

The run-getting of Bradman had created the bowlers' frustration and so it needed to be checked if possible; but the root cause of batting domination lay elsewhere, in the lbw law. A bowler could only be awarded an lbw decision if the ball pitched within the imaginary parallel lines, wicket to wicket. This meant that, when the ball pitched outside off stump, the batsman could safely step across to cover his stumps with his pads knowing that, if he missed it, he could not be given out lbw. However, the accepted way then to take wickets was still to attack the off stump and wait for the snick or miss. To play the ball deliberately with the pads was considered extremely unsporting, but there had been an increase of pad-play, even since it had been condemned by such players as Arthur Shrewsbury, and the Australians appeared to move much farther across in front of their wickets than did the English batsmen. The obvious tactic to stop them was to keep them on leg stump, make sure that their stumps were at least visible and force them to play in a tucked-up style, close to the body. Jardine's analysis was completely correct.

But it was not original. There had already been a history of leg-theory. F. R. Foster of Warwickshire, like Voce, bowled fast left-arm from around the wicket when he was with Warner's team in Australia in 1911–12. In fact he used a leg-trap which ranged from silly mid-on to leg slip, just like Larwood; it was almost identical. Fred Root, of Worcestershire, was also well known as a leg-theory bowler.

Larwood and Voce had certainly bowled bodyline for their county, Nottinghamshire, and their captain, A. W. Carr. Most accounts give credence to a famous dinner at the Piccadilly Hotel grill-room in early August 1932 at the end of the traditional Surrey v. Nottinghamshire Bank Holiday fixture at The Oval, where Jardine discussed short-pitched fast bowling with Carr, Larwood and Voce. This may not have been such a clandestine plot against Australia: any intelligent captain, about to take the MCC on tour, would have been seriously lacking if he had not taken the Nottingham fast men and their skipper out for a working dinner. And it would have needed only a very short speech by Larwood on the combination of perfect batting wickets and the increasingly defensive styles of batting, involving the use of pads as a second line of defence, to persuade Jardine that the most profitable line for his men to bowl in Australia was at leg stump.

In fact, during the August of the previous season, it was recalled that Larwood and Voce bowled short, fast and on leg stump to a ring of close fielders in county matches against Essex and Glamorgan; but this did not produce any proof of future devastation because, for Glamorgan, Maurice Turnbull scored a brilliant 205 against them at Cardiff, very much in the attacking style of McCabe at Sydney.

Jardine's planning no doubt came back to Bradman, and it seems probable that bodyline bowling, as it was only later called, started as a defensive strategy. Jardine was a detailed thinker and a fine captain; it was obvious that the leg stump had to be the target if initial breaks failed – or, better still, to have Larwood and Voce, and perhaps Bowes too, aiming there, but with Allen placing it outside the off stump where tucked-up or intimidated batsmen, over-eager, might go for their shots. Bodyline may have evolved, but Jardine had it in his mind all the time.

He had other factors to consider. His concept of keeping Bradman quiet according to diagrams drawn on a napkin at the Piccadilly Hotel grill might appear workable, but it depended entirely on the quota of skill his fast bowlers could muster. Larwood's superb achievement was that he sustained not only speed but an accuracy which made anybody standing in front of leg stump a target. From the batsman's end he was fearsome. He was not very tall and so the short-pitched balls skidded into a flat trajectory up off the pitch towards the batsman's chin. He could bowl a yorker when he wanted; he was impassive, loyal to his captain and, quite simply, the fastest bowler in the world. Pitches in Australia may have been hard and fast, but they were not generally as sound as in England. There was a lot of uneven bounce.

Jardine's battle plan was finely thought out and absolutely within the laws of the game. It was new only in that there was a full semicircle of short-legs and another covering ring behind them. However he took the game to the very brink of gamesmanship and, for the home crowds, the mere sight of an Australian green cap battling painfully in a ring of England fielders proved intolerable.

On April 28th, 1933, a new cable arrived at Lord's from the ABC. It was a flagrant challenge to the Marylebone Club as the law-maker of the game. It suggested that:

> Any ball delivered which, in the opinion of the umpire at the bowler's end, is bowled at the batsman with the intent to intimidate or injure him shall be considered unfair and 'no ball' shall be called. The bowler shall be notified of the reason. If the offence is repeated by the same bowler in the same innings he shall be immediately instructed to cease bowling and the over shall be regarded as completed. Such bowler shall not again be permitted to bowl during the course of the innings then in progress.

The Australians had adopted this new law in their cricket straightaway without waiting for the MCC even to discuss it.

It was mid-May 1933 before the MCC Committee met to consider this proposal and hear also the tour reports of Jardine, Warner and R. C. N. Palairet, joint manager with Warner. They also interviewed Larwood, Voce and Ames.

Incredibly they still did not seem to grasp the mental picture of bodyline, or perhaps they high-handedly refused to move from their preconception that it was no more than leg theory with some unusual patterns of field-placing. William Findlay, the secretary, was as unmoved as any. When Allen turned up at Lord's after holidaying in Vancouver, Findlay uttered some criticisms of Australia and made the comment, 'I refuse to believe that any Englishman ever bowled at a batsman.'

'If that's what you think,' replied Allen, 'the sooner you find out what really happened the better.' Neither Allen, nor Wyatt who shared his views, was summoned to the Committee.

The MCC Committee eventually made their reply in a haughty headmaster manner. They said they considered the word 'bodyline' to be 'misleading and improper', a confusion between the short, bouncing ball and leg theory. Surely bodyline means an attack on the body? They replied 'that such an implication to any English bowling in Australia is improper and incorrect'. They even had the impertinence to explain that 'the present habit of batsmen who move in front of their wicket with the object of gliding straight balls to leg, tends to give the impression that the bowler is bowling at the batsman, especially in the case of a fast bowler when the batsman mistimes the ball and is hit.' All that without having seen a ball bowled, yet in possession of Warner's criticisms – which were severe.

The MCC did not consider the proposed new law 'practical'. It would give an umpire far too much power over the game. So, promising merely to keep an eye open for unwelcome trends, the Committee then gave the Australians a reprimand.

> Barracking has, unfortunately, always been indulged in by spectators in Australia to a degree quite unknown in this country. During the late tour, however, it would appear to have exceeded all previous experience, and on occasions to have been thoroughly objectionable. There appears to have been little or no effort on the part of those responsible for the administration of the game in Australia, to interfere, or to control this exhibition.

And then the reclaiming of the initiative – 'unless barracking is stopped, or is greatly moderated in Australia, it is difficult to see how the continuance of representative matches can serve the best interests of the game.'

The Marylebone men were unbending because they completely failed to understand the exact nature of Larwood's attack, never once referring to the length of the fast bowling or how it followed the batsmen outside leg stump. The Australian Board was treated like an impudent upstart child.

The aftermath of the bodyline tour was full of intrigue.

First, on the field. The West Indies came to England in the summer of 1933 and in the second Test at Manchester Constantine and Martindale, their very fast bowlers, were accused of bowling bodyline. Constantine was later to say in 'Cricket in the Sun', his section of *The Changing Face of Cricket (1966)*: 'We were playing the bodyline match, as MCC wanted to see what it was like after the 1932 rumpus in Australia.'

So, was the Test match apparently turned into an experiment, presumably because the club had a conscience about Australia's complaints, and felt it safe to do so because the West Indies were far short of England's standards?

Indeed Constantine and Martindale ruffled a number of batsmen; but the ultimate irony was that one England player stood firm, bravely behind the rising balls, dropping them lifeless to the ground and punishing the wayward ones, for neither Martindale nor Constantine was as accurate as Larwood had been. He scored 127, and he was the captain, Douglas Jardine, reappointed for the 1933 series.

Then at Lord's in July, in the Varsity match, Kenneth Farnes bowled something akin to bodyline for Cambridge, fast, often short, with four fielders up near the batsman on the leg side. It became a battlefield as Tindall was hit on the body, Oldfield bowled off his neck and Townsend was hit on the neck before falling on his wicket.

Between Australia and the MCC, there now followed conciliatory cables which cleared the way for Australia's visit to England in 1934. After long discussions, Jardine was made MCC captain for the tour of India, 1933–34. Larwood was unfit and Voce rested. Even so, the serious problems of selection lay ahead. Should Jardine and Larwood be chosen against Australia again?

In January, Pelham Warner was writing letters to Hore-Ruthven in Adelaide with whom he had kept in touch:

> The real trouble is *Jardine*. Is he to be captain? At present I say 'No' unless he makes a most generous public gesture of friendliness and then I am not sure I would trust him. He is a queer fellow. When he sees a cricket ground with an Australian on it he goes mad! He rose to his present position on my shoulders, and of his attitude to me I do not care to speak. It is hoped he may retire at the end of the Indian tour but in many quarters here – where they do not know the truth – he is a bit of a hero. If he is captain in the first Test and is not friendly, he will not captain in the second, but I would not have him at all . . .

Hore-Ruthven, soon to be promoted to the peerage as Lord Gowrie, replied: 'If you want the game to be played in the proper spirit and the whole controversy buried once and for all, keep Jardine out of the picture on any plea you can find.'

In the end, Warner resigned from the Selection Committee, Jardine stayed on in India after the tour, and at the end of March 1934 he announced to everyone's shock: 'I have neither the intention nor the desire to play cricket against Australia this summer.'

Jardine returned home, became engaged to be married and played no more first-class cricket. The Marylebone Club, for all their support of him, sighed with relief.

As for Harold Larwood, his injury was repaired, but he never again bowled as fast. First, he said he would bowl leg theory again and that he did not think the MCC would stop him. Then he published opinions in the *Sunday Despatch* to say that he was convinced that he could not be allowed to bowl leg theory for England, that an official conspiracy had been orchestrated by the MCC. He went on to challenge the club, saying that they had never admitted he bowled at the batsman and not at the stumps, that they had found nothing in the Laws to prevent his bowling and could not, unless they had the courage to change the Laws.

The Marylebone Club decided to play without Larwood. There was a swell of support for both him and Jardine. Were they the price MCC was prepared to pay for the easy resumption of good relations with Australia?

So, first, the MCC had put up a stonewall defence against Australian complaint and argument, and against their proposed law change; but now there were indications that the dimensions of the bodyline controversy were slowly sinking in. Mostly the club, in its usual style, had made slow-footed reactions to events, but at last had come an initiative, in the forming of a sub-committee on October 8th, 1934, to discuss direct attack by bowlers and how to eliminate it and also to consider the lbw law. 'Thus,' as Le Quesne observes, 'did the two streams which had flowed parallel courses for many years at last come together.'

When, in the spring of 1935, the MCC issued its 'Instructions to Umpires' the point had been reached when bodyline was officially outlawed in cricket. The Committee defined 'direct attack' as 'persistent and systematic bowling of fast, short-pitched balls at the batsman standing clear of his wicket'. A guilty bowler would get two cautions, and then, if he infringed again, he would be taken off and not allowed to bowl again in that innings.

As for the lbw law, there was a change made to include a ball pitching outside off stump which would have hit the wicket, but is intercepted by part of the striker's person which was between wicket and wicket at the moment of impact. It was an experimental law, recorded in score-books as 'lbw (n)' until 1937, when it was permanently adopted.

In 1935 South Africa won their first Test in England at Lord's. Bruce Mitchell's 164 for the visitors was by a long way the most heroic performance of the match, in which Herbert Sutcliffe played the last of his fifty-four Tests. All seven of the lbw decisions in the Test were given out under the new experimental law, lbw (n).

G. O. Allen took MCC's next side to Australia in 1936–37. He was Australian born himself and it was the spirit engendered by him and the home captain, Bradman, which eventually healed most of the bodyline scars. The chief topic of conversation once again was cricket.

17 Club, and Ground

To celebrate the 150th anniversay of the MCC in 1937 two special matches were arranged: first, North v. South (see over); second, the MCC Australian Eleven beat the Rest of England by 69 runs. On May 25th *The Times* published a special number of twenty-four pages, profusely illustrated, in fine binding and containing a message from the president of the club, Colonel the Hon. J. J. Astor.

In the same year, Pelham Warner was knighted. Since he retired from playing, no one had seen his journalistic career, as cricket correspondent to the *Morning Post* or with his own *The Cricketer* magazine, as in any way contradictory to the interests of the MCC, for whom he had been a committee man and often a selector of the Test team. To most people he was 'dear old Plum', championing cricket which had been so good to him, and recommending the code which the MCC propagated – hierarchy, fairness, tolerance. He was at the centre of cricket and loved the aura of Lord's above all things. Yet Sir Pelham had his critics. Some saw him as over-concerned with how others saw him, others believed his behaviour as manager of Jardine's tour was deft, if not actually devious. Yet, without question, he was devoted to the game as painted on the largest international canvas and through every class of society. He could see no order to English county cricket without the amateur and yet no one was more fulsome in his appreciation of the professional player. He once wrote, 'Few, if any, men owe more to the professional cricketer than I do. I have travelled with him the world over and played with and against him in this country. I have always found him loyal to a degree and a splendid, happy companion both on and off the field.'

Walter Hammond, also believing that the amateur should be in charge – and perhaps with a nod and a wink of official encouragement – declared his intention of transferring from the professional ranks. Once he had done this, he was appointed captain of England in 1938.

As the elevations of Warner and of Hammond were being warmly greeted, the death of Martin Bladen, seventh Baron Hawke, saddened the corridors of the Marylebone Club. He was

North v. South

Played at Lord's, May 22, 24, and 25, 1937

Result: The South won by six wickets

NORTH	FIRST INNINGS		SECOND INNINGS	
E. Paynter	b Gover	3	b Robins	51
L. Hutton	c Robins b Langridge	102	b Farnes	15
J. Hardstaff	c Ames b Robins	71	c Robins b Farnes	4
M. Leyland	c Barnett b Todd	31	c Ames b Farnes	5
R. E. S. Wyatt (Capt.)	c Ames b Gover	23	lbw b Farnes	49
H. E. Dollery	b Farnes	11	b Farnes	4
C. R. Maxwell	b Farnes	5	b Gover	30
A. V. Pope	c Compton b Robins	15	b Robins	10
H. Verity	st Ames b Robins	2	not out	4
W. Voce	not out	0	c Ames b Gover	1
E. Hollies	lbw b Robins	0	b Gover	0
Byes 5, leg bye 1, no-balls 2		8	Byes 6, leg byes 2, no-balls 3	11
Total		**271**	Total	**184**

Bowling

SOUTH	FIRST INNINGS				SECOND INNINGS			
Gover	20	6	49	2	15	5	40	3
Farnes	21	6	35	2	17	8	43	5
Todd	15	4	48	1	5	0	28	0
Hammond	10	4	17	0				
Langridge	15	4	37	1	5	1	7	0
Robins	16	2	54	4	13	4	47	2
Compton	5	0	23	0				
Barnett					3	1	8	0

SOUTH	FIRST INNINGS		SECOND INNINGS	
C. J. Barnett	c Hollies b Verity	22	c Maxwell b Hollies	22
H. Gimblett	b Hollies	20	c Maxwell b Voce	10
W. R. Hammond	c Voce b Pope	86	not out	100
L. Ames	st Maxwell b Hollies	24	b Verity	2
L. J. Todd	c Maxwell b Verity	3	b Verity	5
D. Compton	b Verity	70	not out	14
W. J. Edrich	c Dollery b Voce	19		
J. Langridge	lbw b Pope	0		
R. W. V. Robins (Capt.)	lbw b Verity	38		
A. Gover	not out	1		
K. Farnes	c Verity b Hollies	0		
Byes 9, leg byes 7, no-ball 1		17	Leg byes	5
Total		**300**	Total (4 wkts.)	**158**

Bowling

NORTH	FIRST INNINGS				SECOND INNINGS			
Voce	19	3	43	1	10	1	43	1
Pope	22	4	59	2	11	2	24	0
Hollies	23.2	3	73	3	10	0	47	1
Wyatt	2	1	5	0				
Verity	24	5	66	4	14	4	23	2
Hutton	6	0	37	0	2.2	0	16	0

Umpires: F. Chester and F. Walden

another who had made his presence felt for the good of cricket world-wide. His own colours, light blue, dark blue and yellow, a combination of Eton and the Cambridge University Quidnuncs, were known through most of the cricket world; his tours were legendary, his dinner parties the envy of those never invited to his London home. Yet much nearer the nerve of the game, Hawke had taken Yorkshire's professionals in hand, tidied their dress and their drinking habits, and helped to create a promising and prosperous future for the county. For MCC he admitted emotional attachment; from 1914 and throughout the First World War he was its president.

As old stars faded, younger ones glittered, but now there was the impending background of another war. However in 1938 W. R. Hammond set the highest score against Australia at Lord's, 240, assisted by Paynter with 99. Although the attack looked weak, the new ball being bowled by McCormick and McCabe, and the old one spun from the overworked fingers of O'Reilly and Fleetwood-Smith, it still represented a magnificent recovery from the dismissal of Barnett, Hutton and Edrich for 31.

The innings provided a fond recollection for Ronald Mason, in his biography of Walter Hammond.

> The Lord's Test of 1938 attracted a vast and absorbed crowd as it always does when Australia are there: the sun shone gloriously upon the opening overs, the excitement was tensed beyond any that had been felt in that place for four years or more. Perhaps it was screwed a point higher by the obscurely sensed international unrest; Austria had gone down before Hitler in the early spring and in the background of many minds must have lurked the doubt, even as the immemorial plane-trees rustled in the June heat and the great ground lay open to the sunshine, packed as it had hardly ever been before, whether this might be the last time for years or for ever that the English would be permitted the deep pleasure of this classic rivalry and content.

Hammond played all his majestic strokes with unemotional impudence, flowing style, breathless power. But then, two matches later, the young Leonard Hutton of Yorkshire, in only his sixth Test, shattered all records. In an innings of 13 hours and 17 minutes he amassed 364 runs, the highest individual Test innings; his partnership of 382 with Leyland (run out for 187) was a record for any England wicket against Australia, and the England win was by a record margin for all Test cricket – an innings and 579 runs. But neither Bradman nor Fingleton could bat in Australia's two innings.

There were two other youngsters in the 1938 sides, W. J. Edrich from Norfolk, and D. C. S. Compton, a London lad, both of whom had found their way into the Middlesex side through the Marylebone Cricket Club ground staff.

THE ENGLISH AND AUSTRALIAN TEAMS IN THE SECOND TEST AT LORD'S IN 1938

Back row, left to right : D. Compton, M. G. Waite, W. J. Edrich, A. G. Chipperfield, D. V. P. Wright, F. Ward, E. Paynter, S. Barnes, W. Ferguson
2nd row, left to right : J. H. Fingleton, L. Hutton, W. A. Brown, C. J. Barnett (Eng.), E. White, A. W. Wellard, W. J. O'Reilly, L. O. B. Fleetwood-Smith, J. Hardstaff, E. McCormick
3rd row, left to right : L. Ames, B. A. Barnett (Aus.), K. Farnes, W. H. Jeanes, W. R. Hammond, D. Bradman, Col. R. S. Rait Kerr, S. J. McCabe, H. Verity, C. L. Badcock
On the ground, left to right : A. L. Hassett, C. W. Walker

The England and Australia teams at Lord's for the second Test match, 1938. (*Sport & General*)

The arrival of these two teenagers in Test cricket just before the Second World War gave prominence to the 'school' which had trained them. The Marylebone Club was by now maintaining a pool of young cricketers who continued the traditional role handed down of bowling to members, keeping the ground in good repair and joining in MCC and Ground matches whenever wanted. However, because the MCC ground staff and the Middlesex professional staff were interchangeable, these boys harboured aspirations of their own in the professional game. They were the true heirs of Thomas Lord, whose adventure in cricket began as a practice bowler to the Marylebone Gentlemen when they were at the White Conduit Fields. Also, J. H. Dark's association began as a practice fielder. As soon as the MCC began to exist so did its ground staff, however small.

The MCC attracted extraordinary loyalty from many families whose sons followed fathers into the service of the club and the stories handed down from generation to generation offer pictures of the life on the Lord's ground staff over a long period of time.

In 1914, William Slatter, the Clerk of Works, was asked to pen his reminiscences:

> I know that our family's service extended over a period of 200 years – father, Stevey, 40 years, myself (to 1914) 51 years, brother Steve about 40 years, son Stephen 18 years (this was written before poor Steve died in 1913); my maternal grandmother died at the age of 89 a pensioner of the MCC, having been employed as a charwoman for a great number of years. My paternal aunt also died a pensioner at the age of 92, also having been employed in the cleaning department at the same time as my grandmother and after her death, my mother did the laundry work for upwards of twenty years, and my eldest sister who was born in the rooms at the rear of the old Pavilion (1847) is still in charge of the Mound Stand Ladies Room.

William Slatter was first taken on as an attendant in the pavilion dressing-rooms, but he had already, as a schoolboy, sold score-cards around the ground. Playing cricket was not his great strength, although he was an excellent fielder, and whenever the 'real tennis' master, George Lambert, 'dobbed' up his tantalising slows, he always wanted young Slatter out in the deep field for the catch. His best performance for MCC and Ground, he thought, was against Essex in 1878 on a new ground at Herongate: on a poor pitch, all four innings were over in a day, but after a top score of 27 by Nixon of Nottinghamshire, Slatter's 19 came next.

Perhaps it was not surprising, therefore, that the strength of his service to the club was on the ground – first in charge of the painting and decorative department before being promoted in 1900 to general foreman, and then, with wider responsibility again, to Clerk of Works with full charge of all building and repairs: 'In the winter of 1902–03 I designed and built the luncheon arbours surrounding the practice ground, to accommodate 120 luncheon tables, each one supplied with water, waste and a wash-up sink, cutting board and lock-up cupboard. (In 1912 each arbour was supplied with gas and ring for heating water.)' Slatter's father, Stevey, had emerged from the odd-jobbers to be groundsman, and in summer he was helped by four boys who would 'clean the ground every morning where the sheep had been; roll the wickets; long-stop while practice was on and hold horses.'

Horses, Slatter recalled, were an essential source of a ground-boy's income. On match days, the boys would tie ropes between the trees at the back of 'A' enclosure for tethering horses while the owners were watching cricket, the idea being to squeeze as many reins as possible on to your rope because it was worth one shilling a horse. Workers at Lord's depended almost entirely on tips. Slatter senior, groundsman-in-chief, received 21s. a week, of which 7s. was repaid to Mr Dark as rent.

There were older members of the ground staff, specialist bowlers, who were permitted by Lord's to earn their whole living off the ground, but because they were rarely engaged for a member's practice before midday, earlier they had to give their services for odd jobs free of charge to the club. Sometimes bowlers were retained at Lord's during the winter, but for very little pay; for a long time, the rate of pay was fixed – bowlers, 2s.; long-stop 1s.; fielder 6d. 'I myself long-stopped for six or seven hours after doing a morning's work.'

In the second half of the nineteenth century the number on the ground staff had built up to sixty. The illustrious Alfred Shaw was among them with a strong contingent from Nottinghamshire, until the Nottinghamshire Club formed its own ground staff in 1897.

By now there was a community feeling about the resident workers at Lord's, and they had cricket activities of their own. Round about 1868, they made up what they called ground boys' matches, home and away. The major encounter was against The Oval, although the Surrey staff was smaller and they had to import some bowlers. The expenses for the matches were met by posting members' subscription lists at Lord's and The Oval. Slatter re- membered, 'We always had a dinner after the match on both grounds, with music and songs afterwards. As a rule we made the journey to Kennington in a van lent by our corn chandler. The van was drawn by our roller horse and driven by Johnson (Yorky).'

Later it was replaced by a team they called the St John's Wood Ramblers, the inspiration for this being George Lambert, the tennis professional, who had developed into one of the hardest hitters of the ball on the leg side anyone had seen.

Then in 1880 a club was formed by the juniors at Lord's called, at the suggestion of Jimmy Fennell, the new tennis master, the Cross Arrows. It was so successful that they decided to open the club to all employees and friends and, by 1907, the Cross Arrows had over a hundred members and twenty matches a season.

At the end of William Slatter's published recollections there is a note which provides the link between his day and that of Compton and Edrich: 'Prior to 1896 lawn tennis was played for many years on the match ground when there was not an MCC match being played. Often five or six courts were in use on Saturday afternoons. Dick Gaby who has charge of the south score-board was lawn tennis marker.'

This Dick Gaby joined Lord's at the age of 15 in 1875 as a ground boy, and he did every menial job until he became a lawn-tennis professional and was put in charge of the Mound score-board. He was with the MCC for sixty-three years, retiring at the age of 78. It was his son, Dick junior, who stood young

Compton and Edrich to attention when they joined the Lord's ground staff in the early 1930s and handed them, not a cricket bat, but a broom, and delivered a swift, brief lecture: 'If you learn to use a broom properly then you'll learn to use a bat properly.' No young cricket enthusiast could see the point, but the apprenticeship was hard, the traditions long.

Dick Gaby has his own memories of the great social matches between the wars, Oxford v. Cambridge, Eton v. Harrow. 'The large West End clubs, the Carlton for example or the Navy and Military, would have large marquees on the Nursery ground; members wore top hats and frock coats, even hostlers and servants wore black jackets and bowler hats. The club's employees wore best suits.'

He recalls crowds of 12,000 or so promenading around the ground. It got so congested under the grandstand that rails had to be installed to streamline the traffic. Often it was difficult to get the crowd back off the pitch for play to restart, so they tried herding them off with big ropes:

> After these matches there were always fights, fathers and sons involved, though it always seemed to be good-humoured stuff. A lot would try to invade the pavilion. We did have some policemen, not many, at the most a sergeant and six constables. Next day the lost property office would be full of toppers: it was a fine sight to see the staff trying them on.

Dick Gaby junior's first job at Lord's, at the age of 21, was as a telegraph boy, and he started work at the beginning of the week of the Eton v. Harrow and Universities' games. It was chaos. His job was to take and send the members' telegrams, most of which concerned racing. At the back door of the pavilion was an Extel machine. The tape would come up with the runners, the members made their selections and Gaby's job was to ring through to their bookmaker. It cost them twopence for the call and although he did not get a commission, he found that as most calls would be directed at the same bookmaker, he could reel off ten or twelve bets for a single twopence, and make a fine profit. 'Most bets I handled in a day was 175, all the business done half an hour before each race and then join in a tremendous scrum to find the results.'

One of the unforgettable characters at Lord's was the manager of the refreshment department, George Portman, remembered by Dick Gaby as 'the whistling chocolate maker'. He used to make boxes of handmade chocolates sold in silver foil with the MCC monogram.

He was an ice-cream maker par excellence, a superb cook, and a baker of Bath buns. Long queues used to form outside his Lord's shop along St John's Wood Road to buy 'Bradman's' cake. He would provide anything to order for the arbours during big matches, salmon and lobster being his lunch-time specialities.

The attitude between the members and the professionals, Dick Gaby remembers as being very good. 'The boys sometimes had some fun choosing a "difficult members XI" and they would never rush to the nets to bowl at the poor tippers: they called those "stumers".' In winter some boys went coaching to South Africa, a few got a job with the Lord's works department. As for Denis Compton?

> I remember Compo well, a most forgetful lad. On one occasion he forgot to pick up his wages for four days and so Jimmy Cannon, who looked after Middlesex affairs, told him to tie a piece of black string around his finger to remember next time, but when he looked, he found there was already some string around it to remind him to take home his dirty laundry. Good lad though. Very unassuming, Compo; obviously a brilliant cricketer but always did everything the other lads did.

Denis Compton was born in Hendon on May 23rd, 1918, went to the local Bell Lane school and played all his cricket on the road outside his house in Alexandra Road. He was offered a professional chance by Pelham Warner who had seen the promise in the dashing lad when he scored 112 for the London Elementary Schools against C. F. Tufnell's XI at Lord's. He turned up at the start of the 1932 season and was registered as a 'fourth-class boy' at a wage of 30s. a week for sixteen weeks.

Manual work always took precedence over cricket. From 8 a.m. there was a session of pulling Lord's giant roller with eleven other lads, then some sweeping, cleaning, odd jobs and errands. It was around this time that the ground staff was mobilised to defend Lord's from an unexpected and subversive attack. In February 1935 the Committee had even to resort to buying an 'exterminator' to deal with the invader.

Two hot summers and a mild winter had turned Lord's into an ideal breeding ground for the leather-jacket, the larva of the crane-fly, or daddy-long-legs, and this had reached plague proportions with the larvae gradually munching their way through the grass roots of the hallowed turf.

Various remedies were tried but none proved completely effective and most resulted in the staff having to sweep the dead grubs off the grass every morning. Inevitably the leather-jackets left their mark, large bare patches appeared and undoubtedly played their part in the outcome of several matches. By July *The Times* was prompted to offer its solution in a fourth leader; it was quite simple, had it not been proved that the leather-jacket was the favourite food of the starling, so why not import some from

Lord's ground staff on the giant roller, including Laurie Gray (in front), the Middlesex bowler, later an umpire, Sid Brown (second from right) and Alex Thompson (fourth from left). Groundsman Harry White in charge. A photograph from *The Cricketer*, June 29th, 1935.

Trafalgar Square? 'Small boys might be forbidden to ask for autographs until they could prove that they had brought one or more starlings to Lord's. Some grandiose political scheme might include the organisation of the unemployed into corps of beaters to drive the starlings up Regent Street and Portland Place into the Regent's Park, and so to Lord's; and flocks of starlings, collected overnight in cages, might be released each morning at the beginning of play . . . the starling might be to Lord's what the goose was to the Capitol'.

For Compton, a more pleasant chore was to assist inside the grandstand score-board, because the hopping up and down to change the details of the wickets and bowlers kept him active and also because he could see some cricket.

He was not the most diligent score-card seller, although some of the other boys saw it as the way to earn extra cash. Queues sometimes formed outside Lord's at 5 p.m. on the evening before a big match. So by 6 a.m. crowds were all around the ground, five deep – a score-card seller's bonanza. The MCC tried to persuade captains to announce their team selections on the day before a match to facilitate the printing of the cards, but the boys preferred a delay until the morning. Then the members would be in such a hurry to get to their seats they would not wait for their change. Compton recalls, 'We earned ½d. commission on a score-card sale. We'd pool the money and take home about £5 a head. There was one exception in 1934, England against Australia, when every boy went home with the giant sum of £14 for the day's work, nearly ten times his weekly wage.'

As for cricket, Compton, the fourth-class boy, was tutored twice a week in the nets by the Lord's coaches George Fenner and, subsequently, Archie Fowler. In three years, he had lightning promotion to first-class-boy status, which meant more cricket and fewer ground labours.

Percy Fender used to want Compton to bowl to him in the nets. Fender was popular, not only because of his own prominence as a cricketer but because he often gave Lord's boys a winter job corking bottles in his wine business. Meanwhile, a couple of nets away, a newer ground-staff lad was flinging wild bouncers through the whiskers of a less popular member, Lieutenant-Colonel Ethelred Dimwitty-Smythe. The bowler's name was William Edrich.

Compton was given his first major MCC match in 1935 against Essex at Felixstowe. He remembered to turn up, but forgot his kit. He was out first ball in the first innings, batting in size 11½ boots, two sizes too big, and trousers 7in too long, but belonging to George Brown, the old Hampshire all-rounder. His kit arrived overnight and he scored 110 in the second innings.

Bill Edrich, born on March 26th, 1916, recalled being in his parents' house in Lingwood, Norfolk, when a friend of the family, Michael Falcon, the Norfolk captain, gave him the straightforward advice, 'Go to Lord's. That's the place to be. The eyes of those who matter will be upon you, and you'll enjoy it immensely.'

Young Edrich had a trial in 1934. The day before, he split his right hand unyoking a horse on the family farm, but he turned up. By the time he came out of the net, blood had seeped into his batting glove. George Fenner saw this and recognised an extraordinary competitor.

Compton and Edrich batted together for the first time for the MCC at Beaumont College. 'What do you do?' enquired Alec Waugh, the captain and well-known author. 'We're bowlers,' Edrich replied. Compton was put to bat at number ten, Edrich at number eleven. The side was saved, after a collapse, by a formidable last-wicket stand.

Three years later, in 1937, in the third Test against New Zealand, at The Oval, Denis Compton was one of three debutants along with A. D. G. Matthews of Glamorgan and C. Washbrook of Lancashire. For the first Test at Trent Bridge in 1938, there were also three newcomers, R. A. Sinfield of Gloucestershire (his only Test), D. V. P. Wright of Kent, and W. J. Edrich. Two of the most famous ground-staff boys were on their way. Both went to South Africa the following winter, but their careers were to be interrupted and, in Edrich's case markedly, by war.

18 Wartime Democracy

William Findlay,
Secretary of MCC from
1926–36, who came
out of retirement to
help Sir Pelham
Warner, Acting
Secretary, during the
second world war.

Britain declared war on Germany on September 3rd, 1939. Immediately Lord's cricket ground, usually stately and ordered, became the scene of hurried departures and arrivals. The secretary and assistant secretary, Colonel R. S. Rait Kerr and Mr R. Aird, cleared their desks and headed for military service, so did members of the administrative and playing staff. The practice ground was requisitioned and the Royal Air Force was preparing to move into the buildings; pictures were taken down in the pavilion to be secreted in a country rectory and the Ashes urn was removed from its glass case, the ultimate retreat. Lord's became a thoroughfare for military personnel but this only mirrored what was happening outside the walls where London was filling up with troops on the move, and evacuating the young to different parts of the country to be safe from air attack.

Lord's cricket lovers, like others, accepted the inevitable decision to abandon both Tests and county cricket and settled behind blacked-out windows 'for the duration', left only with memories of talented cricketers, now absent in uniform, such as Denis Compton and his brother Leslie, Bill Edrich, Jack Robertson, not to mention Yorkshire's Len Hutton, Doug Wright of Kent, Joe Hardstaff of Nottingham, the amateurs G. O. Allen and R. W. V. Robins; and what of the great Walter Hammond? Hopes for the future were mixed with fears that some might never play cricket again.

Lord's ground was like a great and distinguished ocean liner being rapidly refitted for active service. All that remained now was for the clarion call to be sounded – *dulce et decorum est pro patria mori* – just as W. G. Grace had delivered it to cricketers before the First World War.

Yet, this time, it was different: the call was to keep playing; and into the Lord's bustle walked a lean man, 66 years old, with firm tread and a familiarity with the surroundings which suggested he was quite looking forward to playing the role of temporary secretary to the MCC, Sir Pelham Warner. Running Lord's meant more than keeping the minutes of a cricket club; it was the management of an estate.

Barrage balloon at Lord's. The RAF took over in 1939. Little damage was done by enemy action. An incendiary bomb fell on the pavilion roof in 1940, and Father Time was toppled by a balloon cable.

Sir Pelham had no particular experience in that direction. Since his cricket-playing ended, he had busied himself with publishing *The Cricketer* magazine and with other cricket writing, books and journalism. So to help him the former secretary, W. Findlay, came out of retirement on a one-day-a-week basis. Both of these gentlemen had a clear recollection of how the British had abandoned their cricket to concentrate on war in 1914 and how, month by month, year by year, to 1918, the need grew stronger to fetch the bats out from the boxrooms. The public, after concentrating grimly on war, had found the need for distraction, however artificial or momentary. There had been a touch of defiance about it, too – as if the sound of a bowler pounding in at Lord's was the heart-beat of the nation itself. So Lord's, come the 1940 season, stayed open for cricket; and even more surprising perhaps than the decision to play, was the high quality of cricket produced.

Two teams, the London Counties XI and the British Empire XI, were formed in 1940 by independent organisers, one of whom was Desmond Donnelly, later MP for Pembroke. They toured to keep cricket going where possible, and on certain special occasions played against each other, all the time raising money for the Red Cross and other charities. Because the most populated nest of migrant servicemen was in London, Lord's became a natural venue. They were one-day matches, large crowds watched. Even Frank Woolley was talked out of retirement on August 10th to play in front of 13,000 spectators who saw familiar faces reporting for cricket duty and under new caps, including Private J. G. W. Davies, Aircraftsman P. F. Judge, and Dr C. B. Clarke who had been in the West Indies team in 1939. In particular they saw Sergeant D. Compton, c. Eastman, b. Woolley, 60; and Woolley c. and b. Compton, 38. Compton took 6 for 81, rather expensively in 10 overs.

MCC matches against the schools were kept going by a brave band of members, mostly too old for call-up, and it was a familiar sight to see them arriving back in London late at night after a tough day in the field, cursing the lack of taxis and trudging miles through darkened streets, cricket bags on their shoulders.

The Universities still played, except in 1940. Eton v. Harrow did not play, but the public-schools matches otherwise continued as usual in August except in 1944 when the risk of flying bombs was thought by headmasters to be too great a danger. There were new matches at Lord's invented to match the buoyant mood, such as the Cadets of Dartmouth against the Cadets of the Royal Air Force. Alas, there was a sad irony in the match between the Surrey

The Long Room during the war. A repository, but the pictures were removed to a country vicarage.

Home Guard and the Sussex Home Guard: Andrew Ducat, a former Surrey player, collapsed and died.

As for county cricket, the club secretaries did attempt to keep a fabric of local matches going, but it was almost impossible. To give an example, *Wisden* included a short account of Nottinghamshire affairs in 1940:

> In an effort to provide as much cricket as possible Nottinghamshire played six matches, three with Royal Air Force teams and one each with Derbyshire, Leicestershire and the Notts and Derby Border League. Not only did these games show that leading county players now in the Services retained their skill, but they brought to light some promising talent. Particularly noteworthy was the work as opening batsman of R. T. Simpson, a young policeman, of whom competent judges formed a high opinion. Among members of the county side who joined the forces were: J. Hardstaff, C. B. Harris, H. Butler, all sergeants, and J. Knowles (Army), and F. G. Woodhead and E. A. Meads (Royal Air Force). W. Voce undertook munition work. The 1940 accounts showed a surplus of £43, but repairs and painting have not been done at Trent Bridge since the war began, and there is a bank overdraft of £525.

The Royal Australian Air Force, operational in Britain, formed its own cricket team and played many times at Lord's from 1943. They included a dynamic batsman who, also, was just beginning to bowl very fast, Sergeant (later Flying Officer) K. R. Miller, a handsome six-footer, with film-star looks and an unruly mane of black hair. Miller had not only established himself as a powerful batsman with the Victorian team in the late 1930s, but he carried the diverse reputation of being a lover of horses, handsome women and classical music, and a hater of formality, pretentiousness, rules and regulations. He rarely brought all of his kit to a match, preferring to borrow bats, odd socks and did not worry if he had only one batting glove. So having Miller play at Lord's was rather like taking Tarzan to church. As he came in through the Grace Gates with a few Australian team-mates Sergeant Miller took a first look at Lord's which he has always been able to recall very sharply:

> 'So this is the great Lord's,' I thought. 'What a crummy little ground.' That was my first thought. It was the summer of 1943. I had been summoned from RAF South Cerney in Gloucestershire to play for the RAAF in a one-dayer. Having come from Melbourne, Victoria, with the huge stands and crowds of 87,000 at the MCG, this was a big let-down. But more than that, what seemed ridiculous; what made my Aussie mates look on Lord's as a bit of a joke – the pitch and the whole field was on a decent-sized slope.
>
> In wartime matches, both teams used the same dressing-room. It was crowded. I pushed someone out of the way, quite firmly, to get to my gear. 'Excuse me, sport, can you hop out of the way?' I was taken aside and told sternly that I had shoved the celebrated 'Plum' Warner!
>
> Australians always prefer having a shower to a bath. In those days Lord's had only huge-sized baths. I once asked the room attendant, Jack O'Shea, if Lord's did have a shower. 'Follow me,' said Jack. He led me upstairs, along

Cecil Pepper and Keith Miller going out to bat for Australia in the fourth 'Victory' Test of 1945. Miller's 185 for the Dominions against England this same year was his most memorable innings. Twenty years later, Pepper played an interesting role as an umpire in the 'throwing' controversy. Miller, who became both 'darling and demon' of Lord's reappeared there in 1948, 1953 and 1956.

corridors, somewhere towards the middle of the Members' Stand and there was a single shower which looked as if it had been installed when the pavilion went up in the last century. I laughed. O'Shea was serious. He warned me not to tell others about it. I didn't, but I often wondered why.

This broadening of the base of the cricket teams available led naturally, by May 1945, when victory in Europe was achieved, to Sir Pelham Warner's setting up some truly international cricket – five three-day 'Victory' Tests, England v. Australia, three of which were to be played at Lord's and the others at Sheffield and Manchester.

A superb series ended up level, with two wins each, and the cricket played was a delight. Huge crowds, starved of cricket, feasted on centuries by Hammond, Hutton, Washbrook and by the Australians, Miller (2) and Cristofani. Five bowlers took five wickets in an innings – Colonel J. W. A. Stephenson (Essex)

247

playing his first game since 1941, George Pope (Derbyshire), Dick Pollard (Lancashire), W. E. Phillipson (Lancashire) and, for Australia, D. R. Cristofani again.

There was one other international match at Lord's in 1945 and those who saw it forever after regaled those who missed it with tales of wonderful cricket. England played against the Dominions and were beaten by 45 runs with only eight minutes to spare. Walter Hammond, with so little emotion on show, at first went through an exercise of hitting the ball very hard to fielders, then, without noticeable adjustment to stroke or mood, began hitting it very hard into spaces. He scored a magisterial century in the first innings. As if that was not enough to send boys home in a dream, a young New Zealander called Martin Donnelly, left-handed, scored 133 in a most confident and cultured way: obviously a class player likely to project his country towards a more substantial international reputation.

Doug Wright, the Kent leg-spinner, who had made his Test début in 1938, took five Dominions wickets in both innings. His was an unusual action for a spin bowler. Bounding and bouncing off a lengthy run of about a dozen paces, he twirled the arm over quickly and obtained the most tantalising fast loop in the flight. Then, wonder of wonders, Hammond got another superb century in the second innings, this time adding a brutal nudge to his drives, sending the ball crashing into seats and even through the pavilion door to scatter the Long Room.

Only shattering brilliance could have won this match for the Dominions – who, by the way, were led by Learie Constantine in place of Lindsay Hassett (who had been captaining the Australian teams) who cried off with an injury – and this came from Keith Miller. His innings of 185 had an orthodox base, good straight driving, pick-ups to leg, strong, chopping cuts off the back foot, yet there was a ferocity about it all which turned the ball into a missile clattering into the furniture of Lord's and even threatening to knock a stone or two out of the eternal structure of the pavilion. One six off Eric Hollies had the radio commentator, Rex Alston, choking on his words and ducking in the commentary box high up on the roof-top. The ball stuck in the guttering. A higher hit than Trott's, they said.

England v. Dominions attracted a record crowd for a three-day game at Lord's of 90,000 and with it first-class Test cricket seemed to have come home again.

Of course the occasional pleasures of wartime cricket had been under the threat of enemy bombers, the raucous soaring air-raid sirens and life lived both precariously and on a ration book.

England v. The Dominions

Played at Lord's, August 25, 27, and 28, 1945

Result: The Dominions won by 45 runs

THE DOMINIONS

	FIRST INNINGS		SECOND INNINGS	
D. R. Fell	c Griffith b Wright	12	b Davies	28
H. S. Craig	c Davies b Phillipson	56	c Hammond b Davies	32
J. Pettiford	b Davies	1	b Wright	6
K. R. Miller	lbw b Hollies	26	c Langridge b Wright	185
M. P. Donnelly	c and b Hollies	133	b Wright	29
L. N. Constantine (Capt.)	c Hollies b Wright	5	c Fishlock b Hollies	40
C. G. Pepper	c Hammond b Wright	51	c Robertson b Hollies	1
D. R. Cristofani	lbw b Edrich	6	b Wright	5
R. G. Williams	lbw b Wright	11	c Hammond b Wright	0
R. S. Ellis	b Wright	0	st Griffith b Wright	0
C. D. Bremner	not out	1	not out	0
	Leg byes 3, wides 3	5	Bye 1, leg byes 8, no-ball 1	10
	Total	**307**	Total	**336**

Bowling

ENGLAND	FIRST INNINGS				SECOND INNINGS			
Phillipson	16	2	40	1	2	1	1	0
Edrich	9	1	19	1	3	0	13	0
Wright	30	2	90	5	30.1	6	105	5
Davies	22	9	43	1	13	3	35	2
Hollies	20.2	3	86	2	29	8	115	3
Langridge	6	1	24	0	8	0	57	0

ENGLAND

	FIRST INNINGS		SECOND INNINGS	
L. B. Fishlock	c Pettiford b Ellis	12	run out	7
J. D. Robertson	lbw b Constantine	4	c Fell b Pettiford	5
James Langridge	lbw b Cristofani	28	b Pepper	15
W. E. Phillipson	b Pepper	0	run out	14
S. C. Griffith	b Williams	15	c Pepper b Pettiford	36
W. R. Hammond (Capt.)	st Bremner b Pepper	121	st Bremner b Cristofani	102
H. Gimblett	c Pettiford b Cristofani	11	b Pepper	30
W. J. Edrich	c Pepper b Cristofani	78	c Pepper b Ellis	31
J. G. W. Davies	b Pepper	1	b Pepper	56
D. V. P. Wright	lbw b Pepper	0	b Cristofani	0
E. Hollies	not out	0	not out	0
	Byes 7, leg byes 6, wides 2, no-balls 2	17	Byes 6, leg byes 5, no-balls 4	15
	Total	**287**	Total	**311**

Bowling

THE DOMINIONS	FIRST INNINGS				SECOND INNINGS			
Miller	1	0	2	0	5	—	28	0
Ellis	4	3	4	1	20	4	54	1
Williams	22	4	49	1	2	4	54	1
Cristofani	23.3	4	82	3	21.3	1	64	2
Constantine	15	2	53	1	6	0	27	0
Pettiford	5	0	23	0	14	3	45	2
Pepper	18	3	57	4	33	13	67	3

Umpires: A. Fowler and G. Beet

The players lying flat as a V1 flying bomb cuts out close to Lord's, 1944.

Happily, Lord's itself escaped disaster though it was scarred. The first bombs in the area fell in the Wellington Road, in September 1940; then on October 16th, an astonishing incident – an oil bomb fell on the outfield at Lord's, not far from the Nursery End sight-screen. It burst open on landing revealing a photograph of a young German officer, written across which was 'With Compliments'. There were other near misses, but the only direct hit was on one of the club's houses, 6 Elm Tree Road, which was destroyed. On July 29th, 1944, the Army played the RAF at Lord's. This was the match during which a flying bomb looked like landing at the Nursery End and all the players lay flat on the ground. The 'doodlebug' eventually came down near the Zoo, and when play resumed, Jack Robertson hit R. E. S. Wyatt's second ball, a long-hop, for six. 'Rousing cheers,' as Derek Lodge, a boy at the time, recalls.

There was a bizarre sight on top of the grandstand when dear old Father Time got caught up in a barrage balloon cable and was tugged from his lofty perch down on to the seats; also the Home Guard was reported to the Committee for using the garden at No. 2 Grove End Road for 'bomb-throwing' practice. One freakish incident on the field of play was when Gubby Allen was given out, 'handled the ball', the first batsman given out that way at Lord's since J. Grundy in 1857. Major Allen picked up a ball which had spun off his bat and lay still at the base of his stumps; in gentlemanly fashion, he tossed it back to Roper, the RAAF bowler, whose shout of 'owzat', because he thought the ball had hit the stumps, was enough to do the job.

As the seasons of war passed, the old favourites, one by one, returned to the cricket field: Sergeant Hutton after a successful operation which slightly shortened his left forearm; Flying Officer

K. FARNES

H. VERITY

Kenneth Farnes, Hedley Verity and overleaf Maurice Turnbull, all casualties of the war.

Wyatt, Flying Officer T. W. Goddard of Gloucestershire, Squadron Leader Edrich, Squadron Leader R. W. V. Robins, Sergeant D. Brookes (Northamptonshire) and Lieutenant-Colonel S. C. Griffith; while some new faces appeared, including Lieutenant T. E. Bailey, RN, Flight-Lieutenant R. T. Simpson, Sergeant T. G. Evans and Flight Sergeants E. A. and A. V. Bedser. Even Sergeant Instructor D. C. S. Compton would soon be back from India, where he had made a double century for the Holkar State side. Yes, and Squadron Leader Walter Hammond at last got home from Egypt. Alas, though, not everyone did come back, among them, three Test cricketers.

Kenneth Farnes was lost first, in 1941 – the tall fast bowler of Cambridge University and Essex, a schoolmaster. He had played for England as early as 1934, but was still only 30 when, after a month of night-flying, his plane went down on a training flight. He was modest and popular, recognised as a bowler of surprising ferocity off a reasonably short run. His height, 6ft 5in, gave him sharp lift: an awkward bowler to play and a very good close field. His 720 first-class wickets had cost him only 20 runs apiece.

Then two years later Hedley Verity died of wounds. A captain in the Green Howards, he was shot while leading his men in a cornfield at Catania in Sicily. His men last saw him on the ground, hit in the chest, his head cradled by his batman, Private Thomas Reynoldson of Bridlington. He died in a prisoner-of-war camp.

As the war began, almost at the end of the 1939 season, Hedley Verity was spinning out Sussex at Hove with figures of 7 for 9. He was from Headingley and a true inheritor of the rare Yorkshire skills of slow left-arm spin as handed down by Peate, Peel and Rhodes. He was 38 when he died: there may have been no more Test cricket to add to his forty appearances, but how he had adorned England cricket with his high, easy action, the whip through of the arm, and marvellous control. R. C. Robertson-Glasgow described his bowling as 'a pensive variety', going on to say that, 'he combined nature with art to a degree not equalled by any other bowler of our time'. He took 1,956 wickets at an average of just under 15. Famously, he had taken 14 wickets in a day against the 1934 Australians at Lord's, ending with a match analysis of 15 for 104 and, by doing that, joined Wilfred Rhodes as the bowler taking most wickets against Australia in a Test match. In addition Hedley Verity could bat well enough to open the innings for England in the Adelaide Test of 1936–37. He had been, they said, a man of quiet dignity.

Then in August 1944 at Montchamp in Normandy, a Welshman was hit through the head by a sniper's bullet and died instantly.

251

M. J. TURNBULL

Maurice Turnbull, Glamorgan's captain, from his schooldays at Downside, was an outstanding gamesplayer – cricket for England, rugby football for Wales and hockey, too; a holder of the Welsh squash rackets championship. He had captained Cambridge at cricket, was a member of the Test Match Selection Committee and had been captain and secretary of Glamorgan since 1930. He was 33 when war broke out and might have added to his nine Test caps. He was a fine batsman and an outstanding captain, but more than his performances on the field, it was as secretary of Glamorgan that, as J. C. Clay recorded, 'he turned a shambling, shamefaced, bankrupt into a worthy and respected member of society with a bank balance of £1,000'.

The war over, where would cricket go now? After the First World War, the MCC's Committee running the domestic game, the Advisory County Cricket Committee, had hurriedly organised a county championship of two-day matches. This time the MCC were able to plan well ahead, more confident than usual in the role of initiator. First, the senior members, including Sir Pelham Warner as acting secretary, could recall the pessimism of the first post-war years and shun any idea that things were not going to be what they used to be. The popular appeal of wartime cricket had dispelled any such fears, and the counties were hungry for a sight of the best players in the championship. As early as 1943 a select committee, chaired by Sir Stanley Jackson, was appointed to advise how the game could be restarted. Sir Stanley's committee was representative of all parts of the game, including county representatives, cricketers and umpires.

Their scheme was for a championship reduced to twenty-six matches per county instead of a variable number of matches and scoring by percentages. This was intended to make room for touring teams and Test trial games and also to allow for a knock-out competition. It was this idea of a cup which attracted most of the press, but, because the government at that time was considering a ban on mid-week sport to encourage more production, the idea was dropped.

That was a pity, as far as some counties were concerned, because a cup could have opened the way for commercial sponsors. The MCC realised that individual patronage was gone, that counties would have to live by the profit at the turnstiles, all reflecting the social disturbances of the age. Post-war administrators, raising their antennae, were feeling the instinct to grab the commercial nettle.

Democracy had clearly been at work in different ways in the

Lord's Committee Room even before the election of the Labour Government of 1945. There was talk about democratisation, collectivism, egalitarianism and the greater involvement of the state in everyone's life, but it was too early to affect the MCC even if the swell of such a movement could be enticed through the Grace gates. The MCC was still an elite club, with 7,000 members elected almost entirely from public school or aristocratic background. Britain was still the greatest imperial power in the world. Figures from *Britain since 1945* reveal that, for all the governmental talk, by 1950, 54 per cent of the capital wealth of the country was owned by a mere 1.5 per cent of the population, and 62 per cent of the population were property-less. Most people in 1945 remained and were to remain in the class into which they were born.

For the majority of MCC members, talk of inviting outside commercial interests into first-class cricket must still have been heresy. George Orwell, a socialist old Etonian, described what he thought to be the essential quality of British society when he wrote in December 1940:

> England . . . is a family in which the young are generally thwarted and most of the power is in the hands of irresponsible uncles and bedridden aunts. Still, it is a family. It has a private language and common memories, and at the approach of an enemy it closes its ranks. A family with the wrong members in control – that, perhaps, is as near as one can come to describing England in a phrase.

The MCC stood for upper-class control of cricket – a game administered by amateurs and led on the field by amateurs. Yet the country did feel a surge with the change of government, at least towards a lessening of class difference. Above all, there was peace.

A subtle social shift affected cricketers. The allocation of service commissions in the war had separated them. For example, CSMI Denis Compton would have saluted Squadron Leader Bill Edrich. When they returned to county cricket they would both be in the professionals' room again, along with many other professionals who had received commissions. There were two principal effects. First, some of the commissioned may have wanted to become amateur cricketers following the pre-war example of Walter Hammond, partly for the social status but more because they wanted to be leaders in civilian life, too, and they knew that only amateurs had become county captains. Second, the return of cricketers from the Services to the pavilions after the war made a nonsense of social separation by rank. It would be a sensible time to remove the social divide. Quite contrary to its reputation, Lord's agreed with this and led the way. The MCC decided to discontinue the separate dressing-rooms for amateur and professional and in Middlesex's first game after the war, the openers Robertson and Brown not only walked out to bat from the communal room within the pavilion but also got to the field by the amateur route, down through the Long Room and out by the centre pavilion gate. The old professional gate to the north side of the pavilion was abandoned and the accommodation there was given over to the junior playing staff.

Amateurs were no longer referred to as 'Mr' on the score-card but differentiation was still kept in that amateurs had their initials before their names, the professionals after – a response to the public's desire to know who was who, rather than snobbery, is the point made in *Lord's 1946–70* by Diana Rait Kerr and Ian Peebles, a 'sequel' to Sir Pelham Warner's history.

Sir Stanley Jackson's committee condemned any proposals to tamper with the basics of the game. They were wholly in favour of three-day county cricket as opposed to the two-day experiment of 1919. Sunday play was unanimously turned down.

The changes were the return to the six-ball over, for a new ball to be available after 55 overs instead of after 200 runs, and for the right to declare to be at any time on the first day of a three-day match after a side had scored 300 runs. Above all, the committee emphasised the need for enterprise from captains to counter the signs that were appearing just before the war, of dull, defensive play. Many attributed the decline in entertainment to the lbw (n) law, giving the batsman out to balls pitching outside off stump as long as he was standing 'between wicket and wicket' when the ball hit him; it was leading to too much in-slant bowling and defensive pad play, the front foot stretched safely outside the off stump with no stroke attempted.

Alec Bedser, undoubtedly a great bowler.

The particular error of the Jackson committee was to think that a new ball after 55 overs would help this situation. Of course it made it worse: there was always plenty of shine on the ball for the inswinger, and there were in-slant bowlers of ordinary talent who were flattered by these conditions. There was one, however, whose manipulation of swing and seam put him above them, and would have done so whatever the lbw law, A. V. Bedser of Surrey. He was tall, over 6ft and burly: his action was a model of absolute bodily commitment into the delivery stride, the front foot thumping down on a straight, firm left leg. His outstanding skills were developed in the wrist. Whereas most bowlers signalled which way they were trying to swing the ball by an obvious plane of arm action, Bedser, soon known affectionately as 'the Big Fella', brought his arm over lower than the vertical prescribed by coaches, but altered the angle of the wrist to control the direction of swing.

Inswing was his stock ball, but he could send a ball down well outside the off stump which would swing in so sharply over the last few yards that few batsmen had time to work out the fine geometry of the lbw law. With a similar arm action, but with fingers gripping across the seam, he could revolve the ball in flight to make it cut away from the batsman from leg to off. For a batsman expecting the late inswinger, it was an uncomfortable feeling.

The cricket ball itself changed during the 1950s and as it did Bedser's skills became even more potent. The stitching, or seams, which held together the outside leather case became more raised, easier for fingers to grip and also giving the growing army of medium-fast bowlers, who were profiting from the lbw law, the extra advantage of movement off the seam: a ball landing on the seam often moved laterally, one way or other, when pitching.

A cricket ball had always been made of a cork centre, wrapped in twine and encased in leather which was stitched tightly around to form the sphere. It had therefore changed little in appearance since the Code of Laws of 1744 which specified that it must be between 5 and 6 ounces. Later in 1774, the weight was reduced to between $5\frac{1}{2}$ and $5\frac{3}{4}$ ounces and that is how it is to this day.

As far as the ball's circumference was concerned, the first specification came in 1838, between 9 and $9\frac{1}{4}$in, and that remained until 1927 when the measurements were reduced to 'between $8^{13}/_{16}$ and 9 inches'. The smaller ball was supposed to help the bowler and so was the last enlarging of the stumps, in 1931, to 28 by 9in. Indeed, in 1947, Douglas Jardine wrote a letter to *The Times* advocating the introduction of a smaller ball still – the sort used by junior schoolboys; but the idea was never taken up.

In 1946, when first-class cricket restarted, the MCC had to interest themselves in much more mundane matters than the composition of the ball. The problem was how to buy a ball at all. These were the post-war days of shortages, rationing and clothing coupons. A major point on the Committee's agenda was how to obtain towels for the pavilion. They considered asking members for clothing coupons because they had heard of such schemes working with the counties – county secretaries were accepting coupons to buy boots and flannels for the players. The Indians were touring in 1946 and, because they always relied on English-manufactured kit, nearly started off their matches wearing grey flannels. To buy a ball you needed a certificate, and there was a waiting-list for the reblade of a bat. Emergency controls affected the development and repair of buildings and a crisis loomed at Lord's when it was thought that the Mound Stand would not be ready for the Australians in 1948.

Portrait of Diana
Rait Kerr, the first
Curator of Lord's,
appointed in 1945. She
was the daughter of
the Secretary, R. S.
Rait Kerr, and with
Ian Peebles wrote the
sequel to Pelham
Warner's *Lord's,
1787–1945* which
carried the story
up to 1970.

In 1947, the MCC Committee approved the final draft of the new Code of Laws which had been the result of three years' careful preparation by Colonel Rait Kerr, happily back in the secretary's office along with his assistant Ronald Aird. Graceful exits had been made by Sir Pelham Warner and his latest helper, Lieutenant-Colonel Hugh Henson, later secretary of Gloucestershire, as well as by the wartime president, Stanley Christopherson, who had been so enthusiastically involved in all of the cricket. His nominated successor was General Sir Ronald Adam. For the first time the MCC had appointed a curator, Diana Rait Kerr, the secretary's daughter.

Thus, through such planning ahead, domestic first-class cricket started up in 1946 without any problems, save appalling weather. In 1947, however, which was a golden year of lovely weather and brilliant batting, Lord's was at the centre of it. The names Robertson, Brown, Edrich and Compton became as famous as any top four names in any batting order. Runs flowed, crowds bustled to Lord's. On Saturdays and Bank Holidays signboards would go up in the Underground saying 'Lord's ground full'. Middlesex won the championship not only by weight of runs but by the patient slow left-arm bowling of Jack Young, attacking batting by George Mann and especially by the sure, often inventive, tactical touch of the captain, R. W. V. Robins; but above all, there was Compton and Edrich, the 'Terrible Twins'.

These two appeared to spend the whole season batting together and they excited the whole country. Compton scored 3,816 runs and Edrich 3,539. Compton was extravagant and lavish in his stroke-play, the darling of the nation, handsome as he smiled from posters advertising Brylcreem: Edrich looked pugnacious and was short, with a small man's aggression, never to be terrorised by bouncers, only inspired by them into a more resolute stance. Not since Bradman in the 1930s had anyone come up with such an array of strokes as Compton. Ian Peebles, the former Middlesex and England leg-spinner who had played against Bradman and also with Compton, was able to compare them.

Although very different in temperament and approach, they shared an extraordinary stamina in unrelenting pursuit. The chief difference lay in the fact that Bradman always applied himself with a cool, unwavering concentration, while Compton seemed to be borne along by a carefree joy. This difference was best illustrated in the running between the wickets. Bradman was fast, decisive and an unfailing judge of speed and distance. Compton was so joyously haphazard that J. J. Warr (later to play with Compton for Middlesex) remarked that 'his call was merely an opening bid'.

As for Compton and Edrich, they had only a sound orthodox defence in common. Edrich was firmly right-handed, strong on the pull, the cut and the hook: Compton would often dance down the pitch and invent. If he had a hallmark, it was the sweep, which he played brazenly fine.

An extra, royal adornment was given to Lord's in this glorious summer by the attendance of King George VI and Queen Elizabeth at the Test match against South Africa. The two princesses were there with them and that set the crowd speculating about a likely engagement between Princess Elizabeth and the tall, handsome lieutenant at her side, Philip Mountbatten. Later in the season, the Eton v. Harrow match, still a great draw, was made even more glamorous by the presence of the newly engaged couple alongside the King and Queen and Princess Margaret up in one of the Clock Tower boxes above the swirl of elegant debutantes and top-hatted escorts.

The Varsity match this year was well attended, but there was a dressing-down for the Cambridge team for not dressing properly. The Cambridge opening batsmen did not wear light-blue caps. Instead, one wore the Crusader and the other a Quidnunc cap, both university caps but not good enough for E. Rockley Wilson, the former Cambridge University and Yorkshire amateur, now a schoolmaster at Winchester. The students offered the excuse of clothes rationing which Mr Wilson thought feeble. Why had they not borrowed from Old Blues, he wanted to know. Whereupon the Cambridge pair fell silent.

The Marylebone Club, by leading the country back to first-class cricket so thoughtfully, had immediately confirmed its role of service to the game. Membership of the club had always been associated with privilege for the few, a self-perpetuating playground for the landed classes and the public schools: the yellow and orange striped tie was seen as a badge of exclusiveness, even snobbery. In its dealings with Australia after the bodyline tour, the club had lived up to its high-hat image and only repaired the affront, which Australians obviously felt, retrospectively and taking care not to lose face by public concession. Now, through the Second World War and straight after, there was evidence that the club was taking on a new persona. Indisputedly it had emerged as the game of cricket's patron and servant, concentrating on building a framework in which cricketers at home and abroad could enjoy themselves. However, the arrangements at home, in spite of war, turned out to be much easier to get right than those for the resumption of international play.

To begin with, the MCC believed that a reduction in the number

257

'Quite simply the best English batsman most people had seen'. Walter Hammond's majestic cover drive, photographed in Sydney by Herbert Fishwick in 1928. (*Sydney Morning Herald*)

of tours and Test matches was essential: players were being asked to commit themselves to far too much cricket – professionals would become stale, amateurs would be unable to get away from their occupations. Also the increase in the number of Tests would debase their value.

Yet the MCC found itself swimming against an international tide. In their work for the Imperial Cricket Conference, they found a queue forming of countries who wanted to join the Test match rota. Even Australia appeared to be over-keen to get Tests going again. It took a lot of pleading by Dr Evatt, Australia's Minister for External Affairs, in 1945, to persuade the MCC to send an England side out there in 1946–47, rather before England felt ready.

W. R. Hammond was the captain but England, with a somewhat elderly side, were outplayed and saved from a five-match defeat only by the new regulation, agreed between the countries, that Tests in Australia should no longer be played to a finish, but limited to thirty hours' play, which meant six days in Australia and five in England. The final Test could, however, be played to a finish if the margin of advantage either way was only one win. England lost three Tests with two somewhat fortunately drawn. The closing hours of all those Tests were broadcast live back to England on radio.

Hammond himself suffered ill-health, though his 50,000th first-class run came up with an innings of 188 against South Australia. He could not play in the fifth Test, Norman Yardley took over and Hammond retired at the end of the tour in New Zealand.

Walter Hammond had been quite simply the best English batsman most people had seen. Although born in Kent he had been to school at Cirencester Grammar. His play was often daring and extravagant, his bowling most effective as a 'wobbler' of the new ball, and he was an outstanding slip fielder. His first international recognition was as a member of the MCC team which toured the West Indies in 1925–26 where he scored 733 runs at an average of 45.81. He was ill and unable to play at all in 1926, but in the following summer he scored 1,000 runs in May and, in the season, 2,969 runs, averaging 69.05. The slightly impulsive Hammond fined down his art and his temperament to become a golden example of authority and magnificent control at the crease. Neville Cardus wrote about a 'style ripened to an almost statuesque nobility, easy and powerful of stroke-play but absolutely correct in its observance of first principles'. Of his 167 first-class centuries, 9 were against Australia, 6 against South Africa, 4 against New Zealand. He skippered England against

Australia and the West Indies in England in 1938 and 1939, against South Africa in 1938–39, against India in 1946 and in Australia in 1946–47. In all, he played 85 Tests.

The Imperial Conference first met after the war on January 15th, 1946, at Lord's, a lapse of seven years. The representatives of England, Australia, South Africa, New Zealand, West Indies and India agreed a seven-year programme of international tours which included, for the first time, matches between the West Indies and India and India and Australia. Yet the MCC stood firm in its conviction that there was too much cricket: only in exceptional circumstances would two overseas tours take place in successive winters by England and that priority would go to the co-founders of the Imperial Conference, Australia and South Africa. The only suggestion of compromise with New Zealand, India and West Indies was an agreement to keep sides going to those countries to ensure the development of the game there, but not an England first team. They would offer an 'A' team which the receiving country could accept or reject once the team was chosen. The club soon had to appreciate, however, that it was playing a King Canute role. The programme of tours increased rapidly and the evidence rushed in of the high quality of cricket being played by more countries.

In 1947–48 the MCC sent a makeshift party to the West Indies, hoping to camouflage the rawness of promising young players and the absence of seasoned players unwilling to make another tour so soon after the war, with the experienced leadership of G. O. Allen. Allen's men ran into a virtual blitzkrieg by young West Indian talent – Worrell, Weekes, Walcott, later known as the 'Three Ws', Gomez, Stollmeyer and Goddard. The West Indies won the four-match series 2–0, despite Hutton being sent out to reinforce the team at mid-stage.

New Zealand, two years later in the English summer of 1949, were invited to play four three-day Tests and proved they deserved longer matches by drawing them all comfortably. They revealed as they went around the country, under the shrewd leadership of Walter Hadlee, the outstanding batting talents of Bert Sutcliffe, Martin Donnelly and of the young, belligerent John Reid as well as new-ball bowling from the 37-year-old Jack Cowie, which could still trouble England. On the whole tour, eight New Zealand batsmen made over 1,000 runs and Tom Burtt, the left-arm spinner, collected 128 wickets. So both the West Indies and New Zealand had made their point; who was going to deny them regular Test matches now?

India too had signalled their claim for recognition. Their first tour to England after the war was in 1946, led by the Nawab of Pataudi (senior), once an England player. His side won eleven and lost only four matches including one of the three Tests which, as it happened, lost them the rubber; but the vice-captain, V. M. Merchant, in a very wet summer, made 2,385 runs at an average of 74.

The partition of India and the creation of Pakistan in 1947 presented the ICC with a major issue. Pakistan set up its own board of control. At first it was hoped that India and Pakistan would still combine to form one Test team, a wildly unreasonable concept; and in 1952 the inevitable took place, Pakistan received her full membership of the ICC, proposed by India and seconded by the MCC.

Yet in spite of this flurry of international machinations which was leading as sanely as possible to a filigree pattern of multi-international engagements, it was the appearance at last of the Australians in England in 1948, after an absence of ten years, which persuaded cricket-lovers at home that cricket was again as they remembered it before war intervened. To begin with 'the Don' himself was back, as captain, also the man who had so impudently brightened up Lord's during the war and the 'Victory' Tests, Keith Miller. Lindwall and Miller were established as the two fastest bowlers in the world, and they were supported by the fast, versatile left-armer Bill Johnston. This trio was backed by three kinds of spin and, on top of that, was especially helped by the change in regulations which had so much amused Bradman by allowing him to take a new ball every 55 overs. Bradman would unleash Lindwall, Miller and Johnston, then the accurate Toshack would keep the game tight before Bradman fired in the new ball again. England could only make slow progress. On average Australia called for a new ball before 130 runs were on the board: twice it was taken before 90 runs.

The Australian batting order was a line-up of breathtaking ability. Indeed W. A. Brown, acknowledged as a specialist in English conditions, was squeezed out for three of the Tests. The top of the batting order was one which can still be reeled off by those who saw them play, Barnes, Morris, Bradman, Hassett, Miller, Harvey. These were the first five-day Tests played by an Australian side in England. Australia won four and one was drawn.

Miller, who had only turned to bowling during the war, had developed into a roaring, spontaneous performer with the new ball, strong and powerful. Sometimes he would turn to begin his run-up after only a few paces back and still be able to bowl as fast as off his long run. He might throw in a spinner, a bouncer or any

The undefeated
Australian team in
England, 1948. (*Sport
& General*)

shock ball. In the first Test at Trent Bridge he ran up and bowled a perfect length googly. His 'bumper' was not all that short and he had many batsmen ducking unwisely. Of course Miller was also a magnificent attacking batsman and an extraordinary character, as John Arlott explained in one of his written sketches:

> Keith Miller, he is the direct opposite of Don Bradman in one important respect – a respect which indicates a fundamental contrast between the two. Don Bradman, as a public figure, has taken seriously his duty to the public. Keith Miller, finding himself a public figure, shrugs his shoulders and continues to be Keith Miller. The Keith Miller he continues to be is happy, comradely and often humorous. He has discovered that the world is his oyster and he proposed to swallow it without caring a damn what anyone thinks. Before the oyster can be swallowed, however, it has to be opened – Keith Miller likes to open oysters for himself – and, if he has to do so with his bare hands, then that is exactly the sort of challenge he relishes.

Ray Lindwall, too, was a rare cricketer. In 1948 he was 26, an intelligent fast bowler of remarkable control. He kept the ball well up to the bat, a sensible adjustment to his practice on harder Australian wickets where there was more bounce. He was admired for his smooth crescendo of a run-up, rhythmical and gathering momentum, and the slinging action which looked as impromptu as a boy hurling a ball down the street, but was refined to the fingertips to produce and control swing. There was a similarity with Larwood in the streamline approach, although Lindwall's bowling arm went through a flatter trajectory. His wrist stayed behind the ball and, like Bedser and other masters of swing, it was the wrist angle at delivery which determined the swing and made it difficult to anticipate. Len Hutton, England's best opening batsman of the era, said that Lindwall was the finest bowler he ever faced.

These Australians came to Lord's four times. They crushed a respectable MCC side by an innings and won the June Test by 409 runs. Then in July they beat Middlesex by ten wickets and finally, at the end of August, they saw off the Gentlemen of England in a day and a half. Don Bradman's last performance in Tests is fabled. He went to the crease at The Oval requiring just four runs to take his Test career aggregate of runs to 7,000 and his average to 100. He was given a standing ovation to the crease; then Norman Yardley, the England captain, raised his cap and called for three cheers, a spontaneous appreciation of a great adversary whom

Lindwall's beautiful bowling action, photographed at Oxford in 1948. (*BBC Hulton Library.*)

they had briefly caged in the 'bodyline' series but had never tamed. However, cricket, the coy mistress of all aspiration, gave Don Bradman a final reminder that, although he had dominated the game of cricket, he did not rule it. Eric Hollies' second ball to him was a googly; the ball turned between bat and pad, Bradman was bowled for nought, and a career of staggering achievement was over.

His farewell to Lord's came in the match against the Gentlemen of England. This time, appropriately, he got 150. He gave his wicket away and so delivered the final coup to English bowling – a demonstration of mercy.

Bradman's century coincided with his fortieth birthday. To celebrate it, the Lord's caterer, George Portman, created one of his tremendous birthday cakes. Thus the 1948 Australians departed unbeaten and, in the next New Year's honours list, Don Bradman was knighted. At that time he wrote to the secretary of the MCC:

> I felt that our last tour was a great success from your point of view as well as ours. We may eliminate playing results because I am convinced we had a particularly strong side, but there is no doubt a splendid feeling existed, and I shall certainly continue to work for this spirit of goodwill between our countries.

The postscripts were these – the BBC broadcast all the Tests for a fee of 250 guineas a match and the radio broadcasts went around the world, causing such a heavy rise in electricity consumption there was a power failure in New Zealand. There was a record crowd for the Lord's Test: 132,000 and the highest-ever receipts of £43,000.

Also, the celebration of Australian greatness inevitably left the question about the quality of England's cricket. Where were the young boys coming along and especially, where was the help for Alec Bedser with the new ball? Was there young talent locked at the bottom unable to come through? Everyone knew how excellent the playing conditions were in the public schools and in most of the grammar schools, but there were two million elementary and secondary schoolboys who had little or no opportunity to play cricket properly. For the boys who failed the Scholarship examination at the age of eleven, the only pitch was the road or the yard or a pitch which was poorly attended by local councils' mowers. The treasurer of the MCC, Lord Cobham, announced an MCC enquiry into youth cricket.

This enquiry was very much the concept of G. O. Allen, who had been on the MCC Committee since 1935, but who was only just fighting his way through its reactionary attitudes. Fortunately, the chairman of the enquiry was H. S. Altham who, as a master at Winchester, had been devoted to youth cricket. Allen and Altham were helped by livelier and progressive committee men such as Twining, Stanyforth and Newman and, as the result of their work, the MCC Youth Cricket Association was formed in 1951. Immediately it began to recommend organised practice schemes, instruction for coaches, instructional films and ideas for the organisation of cricket for boys between school-leaving age and National Service. Altham became chairman of the Youth Cricket Association and also, in 1950, became the treasurer of the MCC. This was the most important role at Lord's because the treasurer was the one permanent committee member with a right to sit on every committee and to work with the secretary on every aspect of the club's business.

Sorting out the finances was not so simple, and Altham came to office facing a deficit for the first time since the war. Capital expenditure had to be kept to a minimum. It was worrying to think that there was no money for a youth scheme. Eventually, members came up with a once-for-all capital grant of £15,000 to launch a central youth organisation and the counties were asked to contribute to regional projects. It was also agreed to publish a book to support these objectives, called the *MCC Book for Young Cricketers* and, in 1952, the first edition of the standard manual of tuition came out after very careful preparation, *The MCC Cricket Coaching Book*. Altham and Allen were very much the collaborators in the writing of this book, Allen predominating on the technical aspects of play and Altham in the writing. Allen had a remarkable eye for technical soundness in players and it so happened that he did not like one of the illustrations for the first coaching book, the forward defensive stroke, drawn by the artist J. A. Broad. He wanted to change it even though Altham said it was due at the printer's the next morning and he would not co-operate with any late change. Late in the evening, Allen was in his car, out into a night of thick snow and off to the artist's house in Kingston in order to pose for the 'correct' forward defensive. It was duly redrawn, Allen was home by 2 a.m., and the substitute illustration was included with the remainder of the text in the morning.

Other financial problems were solved by an increase in membership. The MCC expanded to 8,000 by 1950, and Middlesex extended their numbers too, from 1,500 to 2,000.

Three more actions remained, which were to seal off the past and prepare for the future. First, the MCC gave honorary membership of the club to famous retired cricketers. The idea was new and had arisen in conversation between G. O. Allen and Len Hutton in the West Indies. It was not passed without opposition, but in July 1949 the president of MCC, Prince Philip, Duke of Edinburgh, announced the following honorary elections: S. F. Barnes, C. J. Barnett, W. E. Bowes, L. C. Braund, G. Duckworth, A. P. Freeman, G. Geary, G. Gunn snr, J. W. Hearne, E. Hendren, G. H. Hirst, J. B. Hobbs, H. Larwood, M. Leyland, C. P. Mead, E. Paynter, W. Rhodes, A. C. Russell, A. Sandham, E. J. Smith, H. Strudwick, H. Sutcliffe, M. W. Tate, E. Tyldesley, W. Voce, F. E. Woolley. Truly the professional was now arriving in the same field as the amateur.

Next, Gubby Allen was also behind the selection of Harry Altham as treasurer. Sir Pelham Warner had wanted a banker of no cricket experience, Sir Eric Gore Browne, to take on the job. In the event, Altham stepped perfectly into the shoes of Ponsonby-Fane, Harris, Hawke, and Cobham who had made the office one of such importance within the web of committee structure.

Lastly, Colonel Rait Kerr, now past his sixtieth year, retired as secretary at the end of 1952. The increasing load of administration had put a strain on his health. During his term of office he had set high standards of behaviour and left behind a new code of laws as a testimony of his diligence. Ronald Aird, who had been at Lord's as an assistant since 1926, was the automatic choice to succeed. Under him was appointed S. C. Griffith who previously had been both captain and secretary, as well as wicket-keeper, of Sussex.

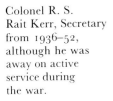

Colonel R. S. Rait Kerr, Secretary from 1936–52, although he was away on active service during the war.

19 Different Approaches

In the early 1950s the MCC found itself caught up in an extraordinary cricket contradiction. It concerned methods of teaching the game to the young, especially batting and the indoctrination of future players with an English approach.

From 1948 the MCC had been resolving their plan of action – to train schoolmasters and youth leaders to give basic cricket instruction in schools and clubs where facilities for coaching were non-existent; to appoint a director of coaching, H. P. Crabtree who had played for London Counties during the war and since then for Essex as an amateur; and to standardise techniques and the basic skills. Locating the boys would not be difficult because the sort of boys they were talking about were in all the lower-middle and lower classes of Britain – society was still severely structured even if there were more layers in this post-war period than before. They would be from secondary schools and youth clubs. Cricket lessons began with group coaching, boys set out in rows and rows, in school yard or gymnasium, all going through the motions of the forward defensive stroke or back as preached by the particular Crabtree evangelist; some lads had real bats, probably reblades, some just stumps to use as bats, but all leaned earnestly into the forward defensive stroke.

Group coaching – a useful but arguably too formal an answer to a real problem. (*Sport & General*)

The contradiction was this: a team of West Indians came to Britain in 1950 and as the British coaches in their gyms were persuading the lads' bats closer to their pads, and sloping backwards so as not to give catches at slip, Caribbean cricketers such as Frank Worrell, Everton Weekes and Clyde Walcott were demonstrating, in Test Matches, a completely opposite approach to batting. It was a more mental opposite than a technical one.

The West Indian schoolboy was learning his cricket in the backyard or on the beach, or on any piece of flat ground among the palm trees; and he wanted to hit the ball farther and bowl the ball faster than ever Learie Constantine had done. The West Indians relied on exuberance and natural gifts; there was no gradual grinding down of the opposition: total annihilation at every moment was the hot pulse of all island players.

The West Indian batsman, as the bowler's arm went over, was ready to hit the ball hard for runs. If he recognised it halfway down the pitch, as of good length, not right for hitting, he stopped it. That rejection was not so much a studied defence as outright rejection of the ball.

In the British youth club hall the British boy would be listening to the coach saying: 'If you get to the perfect forward defensive position and then you feel it is a half-volley, all you do is follow through.' Defence first: attack second. The West Indian boy was putting one foot down the pitch, looking to play brutal drives even if the bat ended up a long way from the pad. Attack first: defence second.

This is an oversimplification because there were *studied* players in the West Indies side. Not only had the great George Headley only just retired; but there were openers like Allan Rae and Jeffrey Stollmeyer, as well as Goddard, Gomez and Christiani. Even so, the dramatic players were Worrell, Weekes and Walcott. They added a bravura dimension to batting which not even Bradman possessed. Bradman thought about batting and was able to put his theories into voracious practice: the three 'Ws' did little theorising: batting itself was their language.

Thus the West Indies touring team brought to England in 1950 more of a cultural explosion than a cricket event; their whole style and approach posed a giant question about the English defensive game and this right in front of the compilers of the *MCC Cricket Coaching Book*, at Lord's.

The West Indian batsmen had enjoyed prolific run-getting on their tour of India in 1948–49, and by the time they were in England in 1950 they had grafted on a couple of young players, unknown even to their own side. The spinners Ramadhin and

The three Ws – Frank Worrell, Everton Weekes, and (behind) Clyde Walcott. 'A bravura dimension to batting.' (*Roger Wood*)

Valentine had played only two first-class games in their lives. They made their Test debuts at Manchester when England won, without any surprise, by the margin of 202 runs.

The success of the West Indies over G. O. Allen's MCC side in the Caribbean back in 1947–48 was generally thought to have been because of the second-eleven side which England had taken out there. This first Test at Old Trafford now appeared simply to be confirmation of the ancient balance of power between the countries. However, there was one warning note – Alf Valentine, with orthodox left-arm spin, took 8 wickets for 104 in England's first innings, in fact, the first eight to fall: Hutton, Simpson, Edrich, Doggart, Dollery, Yardley, Evans and Laker. The game was decided, however, on a crumbling pitch by England's spinners, Berry with nine wickets in the match and Hollies with eight.

The scene of the second Test, at Lord's, was astonishing. West Indian cricket-lovers living in London had never before turned out in such numbers. They saw Rae and Stollmeyer begin the first innings. Rae possessed the more solid attributes and Stollmeyer the elegance: they combined to provide excellent ballast for the prodigious attacking styles to follow. In fact, for England, Yardley's strategy was strongly based on keeping the tourists in check at one end by bowling Bedser for 40 overs, and alternating many spinners at the other: John Wardle of Yorkshire, who could bowl either orthodox left-arm slow spin, or wrist-spin; Roly Jenkins of Worcestershire, right-arm leg breaks and googlies; Bob Berry of Lancashire, slow left-arm; or Yardley himself, medium-pace swing. Edrich was the only seam bowler to assist Bedser. In these post-war years he performed most effectively as a fast bowler, particularly in 1947, but his jerky, slinging, almost tearaway action soon caused him severe enough back trouble to prevent him bowling.

Rae scored a superb century in the first innings and Walcott a mammoth 168 not out in the second, but the shock performances came from the youngsters, Alf Valentine, 4 for 48 and 3 for 79 and Sonny Ramadhin 5 for 66 and 6 for 86.

England were bowled out for 151 and 274; the West Indies won by 326 runs and, in fact, lost only 6 wickets in their second innings. It was their first Test win in England.

As the climax approached, the West Indian supporters brought to Lord's what commentators referred to afterwards as crowd participation. They beat out cricket's rhythms on makeshift drums, pointed up the tempo by clapping. Guitars gave intonation to what was otherwise a magical cacophony of jubilation. Nor was the human voice ignored. While the MCC member was precisely unwrapping his cucumber sandwiches from a hamper napkin, groups of West Indians were loudly inventing calypsos as England wickets fell. The triumph of the occasion was that everyone enjoyed it. It was joyous, not offensive: a cordon of policemen arrived solemnly and left full of smiles. A great sporting event had occurred. It gave the Caribbean Islands huge delight to beat the mother country at her own headquarters.

The calypso of the day, later formalised by Egbert Moore, Lord Beginner, with the Calypso Rhythm Kings, was on the lips of West Indians and British alike:

> *Cricket, lovely cricket,*
> *At Lord's where I saw it;*
> *Cricket, lovely cricket,*
> *At Lord's where I saw it;*
> *Yardley tried his best*
> *But Goddard won the Test,*
> *They gave the crowd plenty fun;*
> *Second Test and West Indies won.*
>
> CHORUS
> *With those little pals of mine*
> *Ramadhin and Valentine.*

There were two more Tests to play. The West Indies won by the vast margins of ten wickets, and an innings and 56 runs. A new major force had emerged in world cricket.

This 1950 series was brilliant, full of strokes of quite new shapes. So often the batsmen would move as if to hit an off-drive, but then allow the ball to come alongside them and hit it with a wristy flourish past point. Weekes was the poker-faced genius who could be patient as well as demolishing; he could stare defensively down the pitch with the blackest look and then unleash a trail of starlight across the turf – because Weekes did not hit the ball in the air. As for Frank Worrell, he possessed a silken touch with the bat and, with his left-arm seamers over the wicket, sent down lissom overs with the new ball. Walcott was an astounding asset as a number five batsman and wicket-keeper as well. All this the West Indies had, as well as the outstanding leadership of John Goddard and the flint-hard all-round qualities of Gerry Gomez.

England could not truly complain that they were suffering the losses of war, although only experienced players got centuries, Washbrook (two), Hutton and Evans. The truth was, the West Indians presented a superior concept of the game.

Australia 1950–51. 'Hearts as big as Freddie Brown's.' (*Sport & General*)

How the 19-year olds, Ramadhin and Valentine, enjoyed themselves! Valentine was coached in Jamaica by one of the finest former English county bowlers, Jack Mercer of Sussex and Glamorgan. Valentine took 33 wickets in the series including Hutton's three times. Yet it would be right to say that, as the batsmen were fully stretched to gauge his flight at one end, they found themselves trying to solve a conjuring trick at the other. Not since South Africa had brought their four wrist-spinners to England in 1907 had there been so much theory about spinning.

Sonny Ramadhin was an orphan and was helped in his early cricket by a Barbadian inter-colonial cricketer in Trinidad. His selection was a gamble because his deception was based on a finger-trick, not on a tutored method. He bowled with an upright wrist, palm facing the batsman. His middle finger was bent as if he had the ball clamped in on top of it by the other fingers: he looked like a small boy about to flick a pellet across the classroom. When his arm came over, the sweep of it across his body suggested leg spin: very occasionally it was, but often it was as sharp an off break as anyone could bowl. Few could 'read' Ramadhin, but add to his finger deception a surprising maturity of flight and length and you had an innovator as worthy of a place in the record books as Bosanquet. He always bowled in a cap and with his sleeves buttoned down.

After losing to the West Indies, England went on to lose the Ashes in Australia, 4–1, in 1950–51, despite the bold and popular leadership of F. R. Brown. Lindsay Hassett was by now leading Australia, who had Miller and Lindwall still, the class of Morris and Harvey and the superb wicket-keeping of Don Tallon. Freddie Brown was recognised in Australia as the most inspiring England skipper they had seen. His side suffered considerable bad luck with the weather and with injury – and both Washbrook and Compton, with his knee trouble, were out of form – but no circumstances were substantial enough to mask the Australians' huge superiority even over an eleven which England could scarcely better – Hutton, Washbrook, Simpson, Compton, Sheppard, Bailey, Brown, Evans, Bedser, Wright and Tattersall – the side for the fifth and final Test, which at last England won.

Yet somehow, despite this unpromising launch into the 1950s, the world of the Marylebone Club looked bright by 1953; eight years had passed since the war, a new generation of players was coming along, including two first-rate fast bowlers: Freddie Trueman, from Stainton in Yorkshire, who had routed the Indians by taking 29 wickets in the four-match series at home in 1952; and Brian Statham, from Lancashire, a Manchester Central Grammar schoolboy who had made his Test debut on Brown's tour when it moved on to New Zealand. A couple of spinners, Tony Lock, orthodox left-arm, and Jim Laker, a tall off-spinner, complemented each other profitably for Surrey at The Oval and were soon together in the England side. The most promising young batsmen were Tom Graveney of Gloucestershire, upright and elegant, and Peter May, a high-scoring schoolboy batsman at Charterhouse and at Cambridge University who made his Test debut against South Africa in 1951 at the age of 21.

The relief of the MCC Committee Room now came on August 19th of this particular year, 1953, when the news was borne across from The Oval that England, under the captaincy of Len Hutton, had wrested the Ashes from Australia after they had been held for a record period, counting the war, of 18 years and 362 days. There were many fine performances in this series. Alec Bedser, for example, who under Brown in Australia had become the first England bowler since Larwood to take 30 wickets in a series, began the campaign with 7 for 55 and 7 for 44 at Trent Bridge, normally enough to win a match, but Australia were saved both by their captain, Hassett's long first innings, 115 in 394 minutes, and by rain. The next three matches were also drawn and it was left to the fifth at The Oval to decide the outcome. At last there was help for Bedser. On a humid first morning, Bedser 3 for 88, and Trueman 4 for 86, did the damage. Then in the second innings, it was spin, Lock taking 5 for 45 and Laker 4 for 75. England's batting, led by Hutton's 82 was solid enough and it was Compton who hit the winning run to set 15,000 spectators delirious. The Ashes were back again. Yet there was one day's cricket earlier in this series when the advantages looked to have gone to Australia, during the second Test at Lord's in June.

Australia, batting first, made 346; Hassett, although troubled by cramp, still made a century. Then Hutton and Graveney in a demonstration of the most elegant batting put on 168 together for the second wicket. They helped England to lead, 372 to 346. After Miller's highly responsible 109, and 89 by Morris, plus Lindwall's fastest 50, England needed 343 to win, 80 more than their highest-ever winning fourth innings at home. On the final day Hassett's bowlers, Lindwall, Miller, Johnston, Ring, Benaud, Davidson and Hole, had six hours to clean up the last seven wickets for under 322 because the English score-card already read

Hutton, c. Hole b. Lindwall 5;
Kenyon, c. Hassett b. Lindwall 2;
Graveney c. Langley b. Johnston 2.

Three wickets had fallen for 12.

The famous rearguard action began between Willie Watson, a calm Yorkshire left-hander playing his seventh Test, and the more experienced Trevor Bailey. The situation suited Bailey whose eyes always twinkled in a tight corner when defensive batting was the order of the day. He scored 71 runs in 257 minutes. The exercise was perhaps more challenging for Watson, a most elegant touch-player. Yet he quietly whistled his way through 346 minutes' batting for his 109 and their fifth wicket partnership realised 163 runs. They joined each other at 12.42 and parted at 5.50, just forty minutes from the close. The game was safe, give or take some lusty hits by Brown. And it enabled the Ashes to be won.

Yes, 1953 was full of good omens. It was Coronation year. Queen Elizabeth acceded to the throne on the same day that Hillary and Sherpa Tensing scaled Everest. There was an unprecedented knighthood for a professional cricketer in the Coronation honours – Sir Jack Hobbs. Lord's itself at this time was undergoing radical 'surgery'. During the winter the new Coronation garden had been laid out behind 'A' Stand (where the Warner Stand now is) and a weeping willow tree was planted with a circular seat around it in memory of the retired club secretary, William Findlay.

The Imperial Cricket Memorial Gallery was opened by HRH the Duke of Edinburgh, in the presence of the High Commissioners of those countries represented at the ICC, along with a gathering of distinguished cricketers. The Memorial Gallery was dedicated by the Bishop of London, Dr Wand, and Prince Philip in his speech emphasised the unchanging and unifying qualities of cricket throughout the Commonwealth. The tablet laid reads: 'To the memory of Cricketers of all Lands who gave their lives in the Cause of Freedom. 1914–1918; 1939–1945, secure from change in their high-hearted ways'. This last line, by James Russell Lowell, was chosen by the Hon. George Lyttelton.

In the same year, 1953, the ICC welcomed for the first time a representative of Pakistan, Mr S. Nazir Ali. It was twenty-seven years since the founder members – England, Australia and South Africa – had welcomed India, New Zealand and the West Indies to the fold. The following year Pakistan made its first tour to the U.K.

Again in 1953, the new inn sign outside the ground was restored; the MCC president, the Duke of Beaufort, unveiled the Tavern, a handsome board created by Cosmo Clark, R.A., who painted Thomas Lord on one side and Alfred Mynn on the other. In this year London Transport named an electric locomotive Thomas Lord; two famous cricketers had 80th birthdays – Sydney Barnes and Sir Pelham Warner. Up in Staffordshire where Barnes worked even at that advanced age as an engrosser of legal documents with his beautiful script, his county club commissioned a portrait by Harry Rutherford, which was later presented to the MCC.

A new stand, to be called the Warner Stand, was designed by Sir Kenneth Peacock. It was urgently needed by an expanding membership. The Warner Stand – when it was finally built and opened in 1958 – impressed some but not all. It was a two-tiered stand with cafeteria-style facilities on the first floor. The large window gave good viewing for those with a pie and a pint or a cup of tea. But the press and the television commentators were upset because their angle of view on the game now shifted to extra cover and long leg.

The only noticeable change around the ground at this time was the sight-screen at the Nursery End which was painted duck-egg blue, instead of white, to reduce the glare.

In 1955 the bicentenary of the birth of Thomas Lord was duly celebrated. To the cricketers of Thirsk, in Yorkshire, Lord's birthplace, the MCC presented an oak plaque, handed over by the president, Lord Cobham, at the Thirsk cricket pavilion. Also, at West Meon, on a beautiful August day, a MCC team walked in procession with the cricketers of West Meon and Warnford from the cricket pavilion to the churchyard to pay respects to Thomas Lord at his grave, to drink a pint of beer in the renamed Thomas Lord Inn, and to visit the house where he spent his last years. In a commemorative match MCC beat the local players by 142 runs.

In 1955 too E. C. 'Ted' Swannell, who had joined the staff in 1923, succeeded Austin Martin as head groundsman. Real tennis was still a feature and in 1955 Jack Groom, the reigning professional, was presented with a medallion to recognise his thirty years at Lord's.

Membership was a continuing problem. It was possible for a candidate to be put up and to wait thirty years for election: it meant that some people would be lucky to be elected during their lifetime. There was a tightening-up of this through a resolution that a member could propose and second only one candidate a year. The minimum age too for a candidate went up from 14 to 17. Then, in 1958, came an idea to raise money by admitting 2,000 to associate membership – a new category. There were certain restrictions on these members, for example they could not use the pavilion during Test matches, but their annual subscription was £4 as opposed to the £6 of full membership. Next came the insistence that all members should become associate members first, but playing members were the exception; these had to undertake to play ten days' cricket for the club over two years.

Candidates were very much on trial both as cricketers and as personalities. They could apply to match managers and ask to be considered for games, but it was not always easy to break in. The match manager would then report to the club on the candidate's behaviour off the field and form on it. All members were allowed to wear the club tie, however. In the late 1950s a new 'City' tie was introduced for the first time because the club tie proper was considered too gaudy by many and unsuitable for formal wear. The 'City' tie had a repeated motif of a red and gold MCC monogram on a navy blue background, or as the manufacturers described it, a monogram in marigold and buttercup.

Honorary membership, too, was widened, so that in exceptional circumstances a professional cricketer still playing could be awarded honorary membership. Indeed, after his victories in Australia in 1955, Len Hutton was met off the liner *Oronsay* at Tilbury Docks by Ronnie Aird, the secretary, who handed him his MCC member's pass and tie.

At this time, and over the next twenty-five years, the MCC was fortunate in its chairmen of the Test Selection Committees. From 1955 until 1981 there were just four, G. O. Allen (1955–61), R. W. V. Robins (1962–64), D. J. Insole (1965–68) and A. V. Bedser, who began in 1969, the year that the Test and County Cricket Board took over the control of professional cricket from the Marylebone Club. His tremendous stint took in the last overseas tour to travel under the MCC name in 1977.

The history of Test selection had begun in 1899 with Lord Hawke, Dr W. G. Grace and H. W. Bainbridge. At the turn of the century and until 1928, Test series in England were played at two- and three-year intervals. The appointment of a selection committee was therefore not an annual procedure.

In 1938 it was decided to increase the number of selectors to four, including two captains of county teams, so that for the Australian series that year A. B. Sellers of Yorkshire and M. J. Turnbull of Glamorgan joined their illustrious seniors, Sir Pelham Warner and P. A. Perrin.

In 1950 Leslie Ames of Kent became the first professional cricketer to be appointed. An ideal committee was one whose members covered a large geographical spread, but whoever they have been they have always been criticised by players because they cannot possibly see enough cricket, committed as they inevitably are to their working lives outside the game. It was Doug Insole's opinion that a selection committee is as good as its chairman: he is the man who pulls together the ideas, who is, or should be, in contact with county coaches and captains and with any cricket judgment he thinks worth taking on board.

G. O. Allen first became a selector at the end of the 1954 season in time to have a say in the choice of the MCC side to tour Australia under Len Hutton. There were two inspired selections made, Colin Cowdrey and Frank Tyson, both young talents untried. Gubby Allen always held the conviction that class counted most when players of even performance vied for places and in Cowdrey, the Oxford undergraduate, he saw an easy style and exceptional timing. He preferred Tyson to Freddie Trueman because Trueman had not performed abroad as well as he had at home: on the previous tour in the West Indies, Trueman's 9 wickets had cost him 46 runs each.

However, it was as chairman of the selectors the next year that Gubby Allen applied himself with the utmost dedication to shaping England's Test cricket. To begin with, he had been in correspondence with Sir Donald Bradman about the respective over-rates during the 1954–55 tour of Australia which Hutton's side had won, but not without criticism. This was the evidence – Australia's over-rate, translated in six-ball overs, was 19.6 an hour and England's was only 14.74. A comparison of the bowlers of each side gave England no excuse for any time-wasting: Australia had Lindwall, Miller, Davidson, Benaud and Johnson; and England fielded Tyson, Statham, Bailey, Appleyard and Wardle.

Allen's co-selectors were Leslie Ames, Brian Sellers and Wilfred Wooller. They appointed Hutton captain for the home series against South Africa, but minuted their concern about his approach at a meeting on May 21st, 1955.

> It was decided to appoint Len Hutton captain for the series against South Africa but before doing so obtain from him a definite undertaking to speed up the team in the field in accordance with the wishes of the Board of Control expressed at the meeting in March of this year. [Hutton was told that this would be enforced] even to the extent, in any extreme case, of omitting a player who, after being warned, had not given his full co-operation: furthermore the reason for the omission would probably be given to the press.

As it happened, Len Hutton retired because he had back trouble and Peter May began a run of thirty-five consecutive Tests as England captain. He was the outstanding batsman of his generation and, though still only 25, the outstanding candidate for the leadership. Happily he and the chairman of selectors were temperamentally suited, too, and they had a successful run on the field, apart from the surprise failure in Australia in 1958–59. On Gubby Allen's committee over these years was one common factor, the Glamorgan captain, Wilfred Wooller. Wooller had long been

Len Hutton. England's first professional captain won back the Ashes in 1953 and kept them in 1954–5. (*Central Press*)

known as a brilliant sportsman. An outstanding schoolboy rugby player at Rydal School, he was a Welsh international three-quarter even before he went up to Cambridge. There he won a double Blue. He was a big man, competitive to his toe-nails and captain of Glamorgan from 1947–60. His understanding of the game was as complete as could be; he was a match for Gubby Allen in debate and also his chairman's supporter.

The Essex captain, Doug Insole, served for three years, Tom Dollery and Cyril Washbrook for two years each. Leslie Ames, by now retired, was a close friend and playing colleague of the chairman and he gave three years of the most valuable advice.

As far as the players were concerned it was imperative that the selectors were seen to be in touch with county cricket and the practice of having senior current players involved in selection was greatly approved. Yet there was a conviction that Gubby Allen personally ran England cricket. All cricketers who played at Lord's wanted to do well, not just because they were on an historic ground, but because they felt they were laying out their talents for inspection. Up in the press box were cricket writers who reported the game for national newspapers, several of them old first-class cricketers and most of whom would very rarely in their working season get to see a match on the county fringes or in the unfashionable corners. Finally there was also Gubby Allen.

The player out on the pitch might well glance towards the window of the Committee Room at the left end of the pavilion to see if the chairman of selectors was there. Allen's favourite seat was to the extreme left as the cricketer looked from the pitch. On fine days the window could be up and the fielder on the pavilion boundary could see members of the MCC Committee, some sitting in high chairs, a lectern alongside on which was placed the latest score-card and, behind them, the stern visages of old oil-painted presidents and secretaries, deities in the holy of holies.

There is a television set in the Committee Room which is often switched on during Test matches, but otherwise is reserved for occasional horse races. It was a waste of a brilliant stroke if played in the middle of a Derby or one of the great races: Mr Allen would be looking the other way.

In 1956 Gubby Allen and his selectors, Ames, Washbrook and Wooller, faced with a strong but ultimately flawed Australian side touring England under Ian Johnson, applied some brave and successful thinking. In the first Test at Nottingham, they put together two new openers, Peter Richardson, the young amateur from Worcestershire, and Colin Cowdrey, who had never opened in his brief career of eight Tests or for Kent. They put on 53 in the first innings and 151 in the second. Richardson particularly had a superb debut with scores of 81 and 73 against an attack which included Lindwall, Miller, Davidson, Archer, Benaud and Johnson. The match was drawn.

The second Test, at Lord's, was decisively won by Australia. The pitch was lively, especially when Australia batted first, but a tenacious opening partnership of 137 by McDonald and Burke helped the tourists to 285. England, with the exception of Peter May, who got 63, failed and were out for 171. Apart from their obvious skills, Australia produced two performances of brilliance: Richie Benaud, when fielding in the gully, held a catch of astounding instinct, a slashing shot by Cowdrey off Mackay which was flying above Benaud's head. Then, in Australia's second innings, while Mackay defended endlessly, Benaud attacked in a most belligerent way. He was caught off a skier for 97. Trueman had bowled superbly and ended with 5 for 90, Bailey 4 for 64, but the England batting failed again. Gil Langley, the wicket-keeper, established a world Test record at the time when he made his ninth dismissal of the match.

Yet there was even more genius. The 36-year-old Keith Miller, for so long both the darling and the demon of Lord's, apart from his contribution of 58 runs in the game took ten wickets, five in each innings. He got more life from the pitch than anyone else. It was typical of him that he should nip off a bail as a souvenir at the end, but even more in character that he tossed it to the crowd as he left the field.

Australia had won by 185 runs and the Selection Committee had problems. They were positive about their changes. Out went Graveney, Watson, Wardle and Statham; in came Oakman of Sussex, Insole of Essex, Lock of Surrey and, to everyone's astonishment, the 41-year-old Washbrook of Lancashire. Washbrook, of course, was one of the selectors, but more to the point, he had not played in Tests since 1950–51 in Australia.

England batted first at Leeds. Washbrook came in with the score at 17 for 3, survived a massive appeal for lbw, and then he and Peter May put on 187 for the fourth wicket, May 101, Washbrook 98, and Lock with seven wickets did most to bowl out Australia twice to win the Test by an innings and 42 runs.

Washbrook naturally retained his place, but for the next Test, played at Old Trafford, the selectors were still not satisfied with the form of everyone in the side. Out went Insole and Trueman, in came Statham, on his home ground and, another shock, the Rev. David Sheppard, who had not played for England since 1954, nor had he been able to free himself from church duties to play

Laker bowling
against India at
Lord's in 1952.
(*Sport & General*)

much for Sussex. In fact Allen had met him before the 1956 season
when Sheppard said he was going to take a holiday playing cricket
at the end of the summer. The chairman persuaded him to take
his vacation earlier than later in case England should need him.

David Sheppard scored 113, coming in first wicket down, following an opening partnership of 174 between Richardson and
Cowdrey. All the inspirations were paying off. What happened
after England had scored 459 is now cricket history. Jim Laker,
on a dusty turning wicket, took 19 Australian wickets for 90, all
from the Stretford end, while Tony Lock took only one at the
other. No one had ever taken more wickets in any first-class match
in cricket's history and this was also the only instance of all ten
wickets falling to one bowler in a Test innings. Laker was a tall
man, broad-shouldered, with a model action, high and sideways
at the moment before delivery. He had superb patience when he
was bowling, without histrionics or hurry. He was Yorkshire born,
educated at Salt's High School, Saltaire. He had come to the
forefront with Surrey, whom he joined after the war in 1947.
Although in the England side for three Tests against the 1948

Australians he was not a permanent choice for England in spite of his regular success at The Oval. In fact this 1956 series and the 1956–57 series in South Africa were the only ones in his career in which he would play every game.

So now 2–1 up, surely the selectors would choose the same side for the final Test at The Oval. Not at all. The omissions this time were Bailey and Oakman and the inclusions were Tyson and, lo and behold, minus a knee-cap after his latest operation, the 38-year-old Denis Compton. Like Tyson, he had not played a Test that summer but, relishing the renewal of combat with his old adversaries, he completed the selectors' success story by getting the top score of 94 in England's first innings and 35 not out in the second. The match was drawn and the series won.

Just to emphasise, too, that they had chosen the right captain, despite his inexperience – he was not yet captain of Surrey – May gave a remarkable lead with the bat, with scores in the series of 73, 63, 53, 101, 43, 83 not out and 37 not out. May's batting style was classically straight and a delight to watch. It was complemented by an inflexible temperament which always ensured his progress to a big score if he had managed to get in. He was not a man to throw his wicket cheaply. His leg-side strokes were a model for all young cricketers, and photographs of the famous May on-drive have been used many times in the MCC and other coaching manuals.

There was a break in May's career when he was ill on the tour of the West Indies in 1959–60. He reappeared in the 1961 home series against the Australians, played one Test under Colin Cowdrey and then took over again but retired at the end of the season.

Although a selection committee might choose their team, the full MCC Committee could veto any selection. It was a rare occurrence, but, as the selectors were preparing to form their side to tour Australia in 1958–59, J. H. Wardle of Yorkshire informed them that he would not be available, for family and business reasons.

Wardle then changed his mind, and his name was included in the fourteen selected, yet within three days, the startling news came from Headingley that the Yorkshire committee had decided to terminate Wardle's engagement at the end of the season – obviously not for any decline in his talent. Unhappily his dismissal was followed by a series of newspaper articles appearing under his name in the *Daily Mail*, highly critical of the Yorkshire committee and his captain J. R. Burnet. In the face of this criticism Yorkshire sacked him immediately.

Before making any decision the MCC Committee invited War-dle to Lord's to state his case. Next day, they announced that his invitation to tour had been withdrawn, the Committee explaining that they felt they had a duty to support the welfare of cricket as a whole in terms of loyalty and behaviour.

In so many instances involving the discipline of players who, for example, could be fined for any breach of good behaviour on tour, the MCC is portrayed as high-handed. Yet MCC could argue that it had the drawing-power to attract the very best men for its cricket sub-committee – which in the mid-1950s was made up of eight England captains, five active county captains, as well as Trevor Bailey, the Rev. David Sheppard, Peter May and Colin

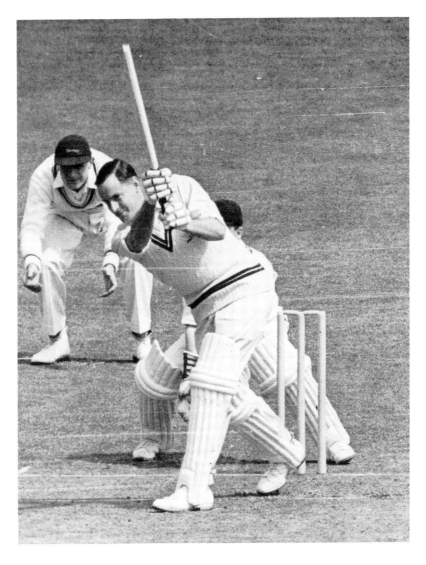

Peter May, a classical
stylist (1957).
(*Sport & General*)

Cowdrey. The club was certainly not out of touch in cricket matters. Similarly, a more personal accusation was made against Gubby Allen that he was a dictator, but when every sub-committee was subordinate to the Advisory County Cricket Committee, which ran domestic cricket, and to the Board of Control, which ran Tests at home, how could that be?

In 1960 additions were made to the list of honorary life members of MCC: Godfrey Evans, Jim Laker and Cyril Washbrook, and in 1961 Alec Bedser. Unhappily, within a couple of months of his election, Jim Laker had a book of memoirs published in which his Surrey Club believed he had misrepresented their staff and officials. Surrey withdrew his pass from The Oval and it was with regret, after he had been given the chance to state his case, that MCC felt bound to support the principle of a player's loyalty to his county and suspended his membership. When, later, Laker made his peace with Surrey, his membership of MCC was restored.

At this time county cricket in England seemed to have lost the enthusiasm and *brio* which had rekindled it after the war. It seemed to be settling into a defensive torpor which gave rise to constant reports of slow play and dogged professionalism. The MCC's view was that an independent body such as they were was the best to shake cricket from its sloth. At the start of the 1960s they were hopeful that the examples of Richie Benaud and Frank Worrell, two superbly imaginative captains of Australia and West Indies, would act as a catalyst throughout the game. Benaud and Worrell were in opposition in Australia in 1960–61 and the cricket their teams played fitted the old descriptions of manly, heroic and sporting, especially in the first-ever tied Test, played at Brisbane, in which Australia required 233 to win in 310 minutes, and lost their last wicket to a run-out off the seventh ball of the last over, the scores level. Indeed, of the last four wickets to fall, three were by run-outs in a brilliant demonstration of West Indian determination and skills in the field.

Yet, nothing of this spirit was seen to rub off on England. Indeed, by 1965–66 when M. J. K. Smith of Warwickshire led the MCC to Australia, his manager, S. C. Griffith, the MCC secretary, was given authority to dictate affairs on the field. This was a wholly unrealistic move which, even before the tour began, undermined the authority of the captain in public. Nor was Mike Smith a captain short of enterprise. He had been an outstanding schoolboy cricketer at Stamford School, who played for Leicestershire in the school holidays, and his three years at Oxford were memorable. He was also an England international rugby player,

The two captains of the tied Test in 1960–61 between Australia and the West Indies – Frank Worrell and Richie Benaud. Why did their example not seem to rub off on English cricket?
(*Sport & General*)

an outside half, tall and willowy, with a long, flowing stride. In 1956 he joined Warwickshire whom he captained from 1957–67 and where he was a prolific scorer. He was such a skilful hitter to leg, he appeared almost to choose his spot on the boundary and hit the ball there wherever it pitched. 'Good player,' he was apt to say, wrinkling his nose under his spectacles, 'plays on the man's side of the wicket,' expressing his approval that someone else shared his predilection for on-side play.

His fifty Tests did not find him in such dominating form,

however, but his captaincy was intelligent and unobtrusive, respected by his players and his fielding close to the wicket on the leg side was brave and athletic for such a tall man.

Had it not been for the understanding natures of both Mike Smith and Billy Griffith, the MCC's dictate could have been a disaster. It was much more important to match temperamentally a manager with a captain than to have an off-field leader. However, *Wisden* of the following year was to record:

> Australia achieved their objective. They retained the Ashes which they have held since 1959, but, really, who took the honours? Surely MCC. In planning the tour, the Committee concerned themselves in matters of broad principle with the image of Test Matches on tour. MCC were anxious that each game be approached in a positive way: that a challenge be accepted if a faintest chance of winning existed: that the team would never contemplate tactical time-wasting. To make sure their wishes be carried out, MCC appointed their secretary Mr S. C. Griffith, manager, and granted him authority to override the captain in matters of tactics but it seems only rarely did Mr Griffith find it necessary to criticise adversely.

In desperation MCC set up a major enquiry in 1966 into pitches, players' conduct and approach, playing conditions and future structure of the game. It became known as the Clark Report after the committee chairman David Clark, the former captain of Kent. It came out with a long list of recommendations. In the county cricket programme, a reduction of three-day matches to allow for more one-day cricket competition in addition to the Gillette Cup, begun in 1963: also two separate championships organised, one of 16 three-day and another of 16 one-day games. Even more controversially, the Clark Report suggested a revision of points to include an added incentive on first innings.

As for overseas players in county cricket, it recommended that the registration rules be amended to allow one of the two overseas players who could be registered for each county to play after twelve months and not wait the usual twenty-four.

Acknowledging modern methods for raising money for cricket and accepting wholly that sufficient cash was never likely to flow, it recommended that sponsors be found for every competition.

The Clark Report also developed the theme that each county should be responsible for the condition of every one of its pitches. The adjudication of pitches would be made by both umpires and captains and if they were adverse would require the home club to appear before a pitches sub-committee at Lord's to make an explanation of why it was bad and what they intended to do about it. Pitches ought to be hard and fast.

Much time and energy was expended on this Clark Report, but the counties moved slowly on it. They were suspicious of one-day cricket even though *Wisden* of 1967 confirmed that support for the County Championship had dwindled to next to nothing.

There was a confused public too: there had been too many changes in the regulations governing play. For example, during the twenty years from 1946 to 1966 a new ball could be taken after 55 overs (1946), 65 overs (1949), 75 overs (1956), and 85 overs (1961), and/or after 200 runs. Also limits had been set to the numbers of fielders on the leg side, and no two years seemed to pass without the follow-on rule being altered.

The Clark committee did not get its revolution, but its work did lead to the extension of one-day cricket when the Sunday League, a 40-over-a-side competition, sponsored by John Player, started in 1968.

The increase in one-day cricket meant that cricketers were for ever on the road. Luckily for them Britain was developing its motorway system which speeded up the travel, but club committees were afraid that their players, driving when tired, were in danger of accidents on the road. Modern cricketers, like those of William Clarke's All-England circus a century or more before, were becoming a caravan of entertainers always on the road to the next show.

It was inevitable that some of the game's arts should be eroded by the negative bowling skills and defensive field settings required to win one-day, limited-over matches. Instead of swing and seam, flight and spin, bowlers were now applauded simply for stopping the batsman from scoring; a maiden over was a precious commodity. Batsmen were always facing diminishing possibilities of shaping a long innings as the overs expired. Games were won more by big hitters than by stroke-makers. This worked well in that batsmen had to be aggressive, but limited-over cricket, especially the short 40-over Sunday game, became a poor breeding nursery for youngsters who had yet to learn a sound technical game. Many critics believed that the proliferation of one-day cricket, especially after the initiation of the Benson and Hedges competition in 1973, was responsible for a later decline in Test-match standards.

The playing adjustment of real impact and value, however, came in 1968 – an addition to the lbw law designed to stop batsmen from padding the ball away outside the off stump without offering a stroke. That law, which stands today, now reads:

> The Striker shall be out lbw even if the ball is intercepted outside the line of the off stump, if, in the opinion of the Umpire, he has made no genuine attempt to play the ball with his bat, but has intercepted the ball with some part of his person and, of course, if the ball would have hit the wicket.

Gary Sobers (above and right) a great all-rounder. (*Sport & General*)

Without doubt the English game received a rush of outstanding talent when two overseas players qualified for each county. The great Barbadian, Gary Sobers, went to Nottinghamshire, the most brilliant, natural all-round cricketer of his day. His batting, left-handed, was technically sound but also breathed originality and was coloured by a breathtaking range of attacking strokes. He took over a hundred catches, mostly at short leg, in Tests and he could bowl in three ways: fast left-arm over the wicket with venomous swing and movement off the seam; left-arm orthodox spin; and a Chinaman-googly variety. Sobers was a most popular cricketer, modest and generous, and the cricket world was delighted to see two of the most inspiring West Indian cricketers later knighted – Sir Frank Worrell and Sir Garfield Sobers.

Among the fine overseas players on show in daily county cricket were the South Africans Barry Richards and Mike Procter, West Indians Rohan Kanhai and Lance Gibbs, Australians Graham McKenzie and Greg Chappell, and the Pakistanis Majid Khan, Asif Iqbal, Mushtaq Mohammad and Zaheer Abbas.

It took many seasons for the Board of Control for Cricket to appreciate, however, that the influx of foreign talent would impede the development of home talent. In the early 1980s a move was made to phase out overseas cricketers from county cricket, by reducing the number to one per county.

The MCC did not neglect its contact with cricket countries abroad. Unfortunately the centenary match between Holland and the MCC, as part of the Royal Dutch Cricket Association's centenary in 1983, was ruined by rain. Not that rain dampened the celebrations, because it had never been forgotten how the MCC helped the revival of the game after the war in the form of fund-raising efforts and by the gift of much-needed equipment.

Danish cricket was also flourishing with a regular link between the MCC and the Danish Association. In 1961, MCC beat Denmark at Lord's in August by 115, but a young man called Henrik Mortensen, with 4 for 57, won favourable comment. He was later to captain Denmark and to manage the side in the ICC Trophy in 1968.

In 1963 at Hjorring, MCC made 201 for six declared and 148 for three declared and Denmark were bowled out for 127 and 129. In the first Danish innings, John ('Pom-Pom') Fellows-Smith, the South African Test cricketer, took all ten wickets for 41. In 1971, the MCC side included Bob Gale of Middlesex, Jack Bailey, the club's secretary, and Alan Moss also of Middlesex, but Tom Provis, a leading sports journalist, wrote in *Aktwelt*, 'This is a team

we must beat to ensure they send a stronger one next time.' The 'Test' match was drawn.

The East and Central African Conference is younger than the Danish Cricket Association by three years. Initially, it was based in Nairobi and drew its players from Malawi, Tanzania, Uganda, Zambia and Kenya, but in 1980 Kenya withdrew to form its own association which became an associate member of the ICC the following year. The pattern was being repeated that local enthusiasm, which is always based on individual enthusiasm, is to be nurtured by the MCC. It was Mr A. Davies of Kenya Kongonis who persuaded the MCC to send a team to East Africa for the first time at Christmas 1957. It was a formidable side led by Freddie Brown, with Billy Griffith as manager. In the side were Jack Bailey, Hubert Doggart, Colin Ingleby-MacKenzie, Peter Richardson, Dennis Silk and John Warr. The MCC followed this tour with others as the game developed there.

Thus, all over the world, the MCC presence has been felt and the people who sustain the game know that they have the encouragement and backing of those at Lord's

Ronald Aird, Secretary of MCC 1952–62. In the background, Dick Gaby (left) and C. H. Wray. Aird was always worried by dull play, especially on television.

288

20 The Health of the Game

In spite of a thriving club, an improving ground and a most desirable membership card, the MCC was so deeply involved now in the running of cricket world-wide and at all levels that it could never relax and pull the blinds down in the Committee Room, let alone take a snooze. Even when England under the leadership of Len Hutton had been winning the Ashes in 1953, and defending them successfully in Australia in 1954–55, the basic English county game was in decline. There was an urgent need to discuss the health of domestic county cricket and within it, certain technical flaws in the game which were arousing more and more wrath among the players.

The general health of the game was always a concern, and rightly so. In 1953, when Ronald Aird had taken over as secretary of the MCC from Colonel Rait-Kerr, he issued a warning in his maiden speech to the counties against complacency. He thought television coverage of cricket had its dangers. If what was shown on television was dull and defensive the viewers would never dream of turning up at the grounds or becoming county members. Television might even turn people away. So the MCC tried to limit television coverage because they detected, or thought they had, a vicious circle. Players, like actors, need audiences to bring out the best of their talents. Without spectators, would they ever play exciting cricket?

Many saw the answer to dull cricket in the encouragement of more amateurs to play. Sir Walter Monckton, later Viscount Monckton of Brenchley, when he was the club's president in 1956, thought the objective should be to enable amateurs to play more cricket, then they would have the spirit of adventure ensured. At the end of that same year the Altham Committee was set up with the wider brief of looking at the whole game.*

By that year, admittedly a wet summer, attendances had dropped by half a million to a figure which was half of the

---

* The members of the Altham Committee, in addition to H. S. Altham, were G. O. Allen; M. J. C. Allom; B. K. Castor; E. D. R. Eagar; C. A. F. Hastilow; Lt.-Col. H. A. Henson; J. H. Nash; C. H. Palmer; Col. R. S. Rait-Kerr; R. W. V. Robins; G. O. Shelmerdene; and Wilfred Wooller.

attendance of 1947. Altham's committee was seriously perturbed by the tempo of first-class cricket which, they saw, was frequently being played without any zest for victory. With over-rates dropping, and crowds disappearing, they were considering a proposal that county cricket should be played at weekends only.

The lbw law was also high on their agenda. But no one thought a reversion to the old pre-1935 law would get the strength of the game back to the off side, so the committee explored such possibilities as limiting the number of fielders allowed on the leg side, recommending that only two be allowed *behind* square on the leg, because this would help to make leg-side attack less profitable. Next, they suggested an experiment, for one season at least, of limiting the number of overs in the first innings to 85. They thought this would inject the urgency into the batsmen and, also, the spectator would see both sides bat in a day; but it was turned down by the counties who, instead, went for the Middlesex proposal that first innings points be reduced from four to two, but then upped again by two bonus points if they had scored their runs faster on a runs-per-over basis. This was brought into practice in 1957, and Surrey showed just how much they enjoyed it by hurtling to their sixth successive championship win, 94 points ahead of the second side, having collected 48 bonus points.

Time-wasting was another malpractice, which the Altham Committee dealt with by allowing umpires to censure any sluggish over-rate or careless time-wasting under Law 16, as unfair play. The 75-yard boundaries were introduced, in the hope that more batsmen would try to hit sixes. Slow pitches were condemned. The concept of a knock-out cup was again advanced, only to be turned down because no one could see an answer to the problem of unfinished matches.

Underlying all these problems, the professional player of the 1950s was a cautious animal. His income depended on form and on performance. On top of a basic salary there was appearance money for first-team matches and a win bonus. Then at the end of the season most county clubs handed out extra cash rewards according to each individual's success. To stay in the side, the professional of average ability tended to seek safe, percentage performances. Of course captains could insist on a more adventurous approach, but that particular command was more likely to come from an amateur than from a professional, because the amateur was not on the pay-roll.

The one recommendation to receive public acclaim was the idea for a knock-out cup. But how often before had the MCC heard the cheers and the objections? Although the idea was again shelved, the clock would not stay still and later, in 1961, the counties voted for a cup competition to be dovetailed into a reduced first-class programme in 1963. Gillette were the sponsors and, to solve the problem of unfinished matches, the number of overs per side was limited – in this competition to 60 overs.

The problems faced by the various MCC committees in the 1950s are fascinating because they belie the club's reputation for being retrospective. There was an alertness and a realism about their discussions at this time which served cricket well: they might so easily have coasted serenely onwards in the wake of England's success at international level rather than taking note of the financial discomfort of certain counties and the falling attendances at county matches. There were counties who covered their losses at the turnstiles by the creation of county supporters' clubs which ran football pools and other fund-raising competitions under the Lotteries Act; for example, Warwickshire not only built up considerable reserves of wealth in this way, but generously helped out counties less fortunate. However, if the financial troubles were the still, muddy waters of the game, there were the three streams of argument on its playing surface – 'dragging', throwing, and amateur status.

Bowlers who 'dragged', landed their back foot legitimately behind the bowling and inside the return crease, but then, before releasing the ball, slid over that crease balanced by momentum on their back toe. In that way they stole a lot of ground and in effect shortened the 22-yard pitch. In Australia, in the first Test series after the Second World War, Ray Lindwall was found to drag. His action was filmed; he sat down and watched the evidence; and by the time he came to England in 1948, had added a pace to his run-up. He was no-balled for overstepping by umpire Paddy Corrall, the former Leicestershire wicket-keeper, in 1953, but his problem was under control.

The bowlers who suffered most were the fast ones. Those who arrived at the crease with a jump and coil of the back had no troubles. The drag was only possible with bowlers who had a 'run-through' delivery. Freddie Trueman of Yorkshire blasted his way on to the international scene and was spotted as a dragger. In Australia Pat Crawford was an offender and after England's tour of 1954–55, it was not long before other Australians were pointed out; and Frank Tyson, too.

At Lord's in 1955 the MCC began two experiments – the first to adjudicate a no-ball on the front, or popping, crease, the second allowing the bowler to ground his foot by the extent of the estimated drag behind a mark placed 18in to 2ft behind the bowling crease.

A panel of observers evaluated the experiment including members of the MCC Committee, the South African Test cricketer K. G. Viljoen, who was the South African tour manager that summer, and two umpires, Laurie Gray, the former Middlesex quick bowler, and Frank Lee, ex-opening batsman of Somerset. The umpires decided that it was easier to give a decision on the front foot.

England and Australia agreed to differ. England chose the front-foot adjudication, Australia the back. More meetings took place, including a conference at which the Australians – Sir Donald Bradman, Jack Leeward, secretary of the Australian Board, and Mr W. J. Dowling – insisted that, although they wanted a back-foot ruling, they were against the arbitrary drawing of lines behind the bowling-crease – although, later, it was they who introduced the white disc to fulfil that purpose. They may well by then have been prompted by English criticism of one fast bowler, Gordon Rorke, who played in the last two Tests against the MCC in 1958–59.

By placing a white disc down behind the bowling crease the Australians reckoned to allow a measure of legalised drag because they thought that the front-foot rule was not only too difficult for the umpires to judge, but also that it made no sense to have a bowler charging in and then being no-balled for overstepping the tiniest fraction over the front line. Sir Donald conceded that Australian opinion might well change with proof of the experiments to be carried out in England where there were more umpires of first-class experience than in Australia.

Eventually, in 1962, at the Imperial Cricket Conference, there was agreement subject to the confirmation of the various boards of control, that the front-foot rule controlling drag should be an experiment in all first-class matches, including Test matches, not later than 1963–64. Although the West Indies would not agree to this experimental rule during their 1963 tour of Britain, all cricket in 1963 in the home county championship followed the front-foot rule, i.e. the front foot had to land behind the popping crease and the back foot inside the return crease.

There were many complaints from fast bowlers, all of whom had to retreat to the practice nets to remeasure their run-ups. Nor has it ever been a wholly satisfactory law. It only requires a little straining for extra effort, or a loss of rhythm, to upset a bowler's calculations. However, the front-foot rule effectively killed off dragging; and it was an important piece of legislation too because dragging had spread downwards to county and league cricket. Emulating Lindwall, Trueman and Tyson was the instinct of every young fast-bowling aspirant in the country.

Whereas dragging had been an annoyance, an illegality to be

eradicated, throwing was looked upon as a positive evil. So much so that a stigma attached to all of the bowlers under suspicion. They were viewed not just as fraudulent but as criminal. This was both unfortunate and unfair. In every country in the world there were young boys hurling balls down in back streets, without benefit of early tuition, who incorporated a throwing kink into their actions without knowing it, and so honestly never knew whether they were throwing or not. The names of the famous throwers have been posted by history as if in a chamber of horrors. No voices were stronger than those of G. O. Allen and Sir Don Bradman, who both urged umpires to stick to Law 26 more firmly, yet they both showed compassion rather than scorn for the offenders.

Tony Lock of Surrey had been no-balled for throwing in England and in 1954, in both a Test and a colony match in the West Indies. However, encouraged by the rough pitches at The Oval in the 1950s, Lock began bowling his left-arm round-the-wicket spin faster and faster. His bent arm was seen to be the signal of the permanent thrower. He bowled in much the same style until the

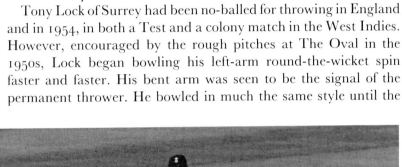

Tony Lock bowling, 1961. He had completely revised his action after seeing it on film. (*Sport & General*)

end of the 1958–59 series in Australia. Then, it is said, the evidence of a film of his bowling taken in New Zealand changed him. Having watched it he decided, of his own volition, to end the controversy by taking action.

Australia paid attention to their own suspect players, especially after complaints from Peter May's touring party of 1958–59. During that tour, all sorts of throwers appeared, the names including Slater, Burke, Rorke and, above all, Meckiff.

Ian Meckiff's was the most notorious and the saddest story. He was a left-arm fast bowler who played his way from South Melbourne first grade into State and Australian cricket, who toured South Africa, India and Pakistan, but who then was branded and dismissed from the game in extraordinary and cruel circumstances. In retrospect, many aspects of his treatment by the administrators of cricket, players, press and public seem alarmingly insensitive and his family endured a nightmare.

Throwing the ball instead of bowling it with a straight arm is an extremely difficult exercise at speed. When the controversy raged at its hottest around 1960, professionals used to experiment in the nets by trying to 'throw' or 'chuck'. Most found it impossible. Unless a kink in the arm had implanted itself at an early stage it was unlikely that anyone could learn to throw well enough to win a place in a Test team. Sir Donald Bradman saw 'chuckers' as to victims of a most complex problem.

Ian Meckiff was first no-balled in 1959, for certain odd deliveries at Adelaide and Brisbane. No great seriousness was attached to it. Those with longer memories could recall the tall, blond South African fast bowler, Cuan McCarthy, being no-balled, when he was an undergraduate at Cambridge University, by umpire Paddy Corrall.

It was during the 1958–59 MCC tour of Australia, led by Peter May, that inflammatory criticisms arose of Meckiff. Australians have since described Meckiff as having anatomical irregularities. Jack Pollard in *Australian Cricket* writes:

> Meckiff bowled with a left arm that has a permanent bend in it and could not be fully straightened, letting the ball go from a bent elbow wind-up. He achieved his pace from double-jointed shoulders and from extremely thin wrists. Originally he made very little use of his front arm but when the chucking controversy raged he started to use the front arm more, throwing it up higher. The action of his bowling arm remained the same but the change in the use of his front arm made some critics believe he had altered his bowling action. Ironically, Meckiff had a poor throwing arm when fielding.

Peter May, in his reminiscences *A Game Remembered*, recalls his first sight of Meckiff. MCC were about to begin a match against

Ian Meckiff. His action was always doubtful, but he was badly treated. (*The Photo Source*)

Victoria at Melbourne and May was looking out of the dressing-room window at the opposing side practising.

> One of them, a left-hander, whom we knew to be Ian Meckiff, was throwing the ball at the batsman. This seemed an odd way for a bowler to limber up. A few minutes later he was out in the middle bowling to Peter Richardson with exactly the same action. I was fascinated.
>
> He soon removed Richardson but he was so inaccurate that he caused little concern. Arthur Milton and Raman Subba Row made what were to be their highest scores of the tour, and although Meckiff had played in the previous winter's series in South Africa, we could not believe that a bowler as wild as he would be picked again.
>
> I soon realised that one of the characteristics of the thrower is his wildness. But in this lies some of his effectiveness, for the batsman has few hits at the ball, even in an eight-ball over. There is no rhythm about the action, the line and pace are unpredictable – just a sudden jerk and the ball arrives.

In the Test at Melbourne, England were bowled out for 87 in their second innings, Meckiff 6 for 38 in 15.2 overs. Yet it is the first innings that May remembers most vividly. 'Next day I reached 113 and was thinking that there were plenty more to come when Meckiff, with the new ball, produced an absolute thunderbolt from somewhere. My bat was still in the air when it shattered the wicket.' Meckiff was cheered from the ground after that Melbourne Test but soon the question of throwing was on the agenda all over the world. G. O. Allen was in a position of considerable power at Lord's as chairman of the cricket sub-committee, chairman of the Test selectors, and chairman of the umpires' committee. In spite of his urgings in 1957 about the need for Law 26 to be stringently enforced, no one was called for throwing in 1958, but, at international level, with the furore about Meckiff particularly and the no-balling of Tony Lock in 1959, the Imperial Conference of 1960 made throwing a subject of prime importance. There could not have been more dramatic evidence of a flawed bowling action than that of the young South African fast bowler touring England that summer, Geoff Griffin.

Geoff Griffin was just 21 years old. He was blond and athletic, but an accident at school left him with a crook in his right elbow and unable at any time to straighten his arm. There had been rumbling complaints about his action. He had been no-balled for throwing twice before in provincial matches at home, in February and March 1959 while playing for Natal against Transvaal and also against a Combined Border and Eastern Province XI. Then in 1960, in the South African match against the MCC at Lord's, he was called for throwing once by umpire Frank Lee and twice by John Langridge, although both umpires said that they thought his basic action fair.

Strangely enough, four games earlier, in the tourists' match against Derbyshire, Paul Gibb the old Yorkshire, England and Essex wicket-keeper-batsman, now an umpire, no-balled the Derbyshire fast bowler Harold Rhodes six times for throwing, but Griffin's action was considered satisfactory.

Griffin's nightmare continued in his next match after the Lord's game. At Trent Bridge he was no-balled in the match against Nottinghamshire eight times, and no-balled for dragging seven times. Griffin took advice. He went to Alf Gover, and the former England fast bowler, well known now for his indoor cricket school in Wandsworth, coached a modified action into young Griffin. Griffin played in the first Test at Edgbaston, which England won by 100 runs, and took the wicket of Subba Row in the first innings and those of Parks, Walker and Statham in the second.

Alas, the Gover treatment which held up then, collapsed in a match against Hampshire at Southampton. Griffin was called for

Geoff Griffin, in action in 1960. Cricketers generally felt sympathy for him. (*The Photo Source*)

throwing six times. Undeterred, the South Africans played him in the second Test at Lord's. This became a fiasco. England won by an innings and 73 runs with over a day to spare, but the game was made memorable because Geoff Griffin became both the first South African to achieve a hat-trick in a Test match and the first player to be no-balled for throwing in a Test match in England.

Griffin was called eleven times during the England innings, all by Frank Lee, the umpire standing at square-leg. Then when the match ended at 2.25 p.m. on the fourth day, an exhibition match was played and Griffin's only over consisted of eleven balls. Umpire Syd Buller no-balled him for throwing four times out of five. On the advice of his captain, McGlew, who had spoken to Buller, Griffin changed to underarm, but was promptly no-balled again by Lee for forgetting to notify the batsman of his change of action. Griffin's last three balls were all underarm. It was his last bowl in Test cricket.

Cricketers everywhere felt sympathy for Griffin. The opinion throughout the game was that he threw almost every ball, but it was sad that his disgrace was so public. He completed the tour as a batsman and fielder only.

The Imperial Cricket Conference was a solemn affair. Throwing had not been underestimated by anyone. For the first time Australia actually sent delegates over: normally they had their English-based representatives. Sir Donald Bradman came with W. J. Dowling and they heard the president of MCC, Harry Altham, promise that MCC would exclude from international cricket all bowlers whose actions they considered suspect.

First, the delegates agreed to recommend a definition of the throw to their countries:

> A ball shall be deemed to have been thrown if, in the opinion of either umpire, the bowling arm, having been bent at the elbow, whether the wrist is backward of the elbow or not, is suddenly straightened immediately prior to the instant of delivery. The bowler shall nevertheless be at liberty to use the wrist freely in the delivery action.

The next move, in November 1960, was the announcement of a moratorium between England and Australia before Australia's tour to England of 1961. On that tour, they agreed, no one would be called for throwing in a match involving the Australians until June 7th, 1961, and if an umpire thought any touring bowler threw he would simply report that judgment to Lord's. The report would be sent to the president of MCC and a copy, through MCC, to the management of Australia.

The umpire's report was set out as follows:

UMPIRE'S REPORT

To the President,
MCC

I beg to report that I officiated at the match Australia .... played on
.... (date) at ....

    In my opinion the Australian bowler .... (name) infringed Law 26
(Throwing) in this match to the following degree:
    Basically – that is every ball
    Frequently
    Occasionally
    Very rarely
(Please mark category thus 'X' and make any comments you may wish and
especially any which may help the bowler concerned.)
    Yours faithfully,

The truce was not popular with everyone. For example the umpires were unhappy and Leslie Smith, linked with the Association of Cricket Umpires, saw the moratorium as a move which made the umpires 'hold in abeyance their interpretation of what constituted fair and unfair bowling . . . which to my mind reflected no credit on the authorities of the two senior cricketing countries'.

There were Australians like H. L. Hendry who urged the Australian selectors to admit that there were 'chuckers' in their camp and not to pick them for the 1961 tour of England. The selectors did not pick them, and this put the onus emphatically on England to put her own house in order and to consider what action to take against professional bowlers who had recently been called for throwing: Rhodes of Derbyshire, White of Hampshire, and Bryant of Somerset. Lock, by now, had changed his action and was selected for three of the five Tests, but he was only included with a stricture from the chairman of selectors, G. O. Allen. The Selection Committee minute was revealed for the first time in *Gubby Allen, Man of Cricket*, by E. W. Swanton: 'It was agreed that the Chairman should speak to Lock on the eve of the match and obtain from him an assurance that he would not bowl his "away-swinger" or his "chinaman" as both were regarded as "suspect" and, in the circumstances, no possible causes for concern can be given.'

Lock took 3 wickets for 250 in three Tests. It must have been like going into battle and finding that you have left half of your ammunition behind.

The saga of throwing now shifted back to Australia: the season was 1963–64; the South Africans were due to tour and Richie Benaud was the captain of Australia.

In the Australian twelve for the first Test was Ian Meckiff. The Australian selectors were Sir Donald Bradman, Jack Ryder and

Meckiff follows throught, right arm high. He is bowling to Milton in the third Test at Sydney, 1958–59. Bailey is the non-striker. (*The Photo Source*)

Dudley Seddon. Bradman at least knew exactly how Benaud felt about throwers. It was during England's visit in 1962–63 that Sir Don had taken the opportunity, when he found all of the Sheffield Shield captains in Adelaide before a Test, to invite them to his home to watch some cricket movies. He had strung together a film of suspect or unusual actions. Present were Bill Lawry of Victoria, Barrie Shepherd of Western Australia, Ken Mackay of Queensland, Benaud of New South Wales and, because it happened to be in Adelaide, Les Favell, although not in the Test team, was also at hand.

Film had become accepted evidence, indeed the prime evidence, in throwing adjudications. At the end of the evening Benaud made the dramatic announcement that he would not continue to bowl anyone in a match who had been called for throwing by an umpire, and, as he wrote in his memoirs, *Benaud on Reflection*, 'I intend to go a step further and not continue to bowl anyone I considered to have a suspect action.'

A few days before the meeting Benaud had worried about Gordon Rorke's action in a match against South Australia. He asked Neil Harvey to take a look from square-leg. Harvey agreed with Benaud's doubts that, every so often, when Rorke bent his back, he let the ball go with a bent arm.

A dressing-room discussion with Dudley Seddon, the chairman of the New South Wales selectors, ended in confrontation. The selectors insisted they would pick the team and Benaud's job was just to lead it; Benaud's reply was that if in future he found in the New South Wales side anyone with a suspect action he would not bowl him but open the batting with him.

So now, some eleven months after the main squabbles and discussions, and in the new season, on December 6th, 1963, at Brisbane, Richie Benaud was leading Australia, winning the toss and batting first. Brian Booth made 169, and South Africa had a hard time of it in the field as the Australians scored 435.

Trevor Goddard and Eddie Barlow opened for South Africa. Graham McKenzie and Meckiff took the new ball for Australia. When Meckiff bowled, the umpire at square-leg, Colin Egar, called him for throwing on the second, third, fifth and ninth deliveries. Benaud took Meckiff off and, sticking to his threat, never bowled him again in the match.

Why did Benaud not bowl Meckiff at the other end? Would the other umpire, Lou Rowan, have adjudicated differently? Benaud sat out the fourth rain-soaked day, coping with the press and a multitude of questioners in the pavilion rooms. He described what then happened:

I was sitting in the luncheon room next to the dressing-room, musing on life in general and wondering if it were all worth it, when suddenly a strangely garbed figure appeared in front of me. It was Jock, the team masseur. He had on his masseur's clothes but over the top he had a plastic raincoat and he was wearing a hat, something I had never seen him sport previously. He was also carrying a copy of a pink newspaper, the *Melbourne Sporting Globe* which, in banner headlines, asked why I hadn't bowled Meckiff from the other end, with a secondary story of police protection being provided for the captain.

Jock looked a bit strange. The whites of his eyes were showing and he said, 'Why didn't you bowl him from the other end?' 'Jock,' I said. 'Please go away, I've got enough problems at the moment.'

All of a sudden he whipped away the pink *Sporting Globe*, cocked the gun he had in his right hand and said, 'You should have bowled him from the other end.' The story of my life went before me as he pulled the trigger of the gun producing a bright flash from the barrel.

It took me a couple of seconds to realise nothing had penetrated the area adjacent to my heart and as I slumped in a wave of relief, I caught sight of the figure rolling around on the floor outside the luncheon room. It was Bill Lawry. He had pulled off one of the greatest practical jokes of a cricket lifetime.

With hindsight Benaud wrote:

It is very sad because it had a most detrimental effect on one of the nicest men ever to step on to a cricket field. Ian never played first-class cricket again. It had an effect on his family because it put enormous pressure not only on him but also on his wife and his children and it left a hollow feeling with everyone who had taken part in that game – it was an awful day and it seemed slightly unreal.

It was the end of Ian Meckiff's career. His children were subjected to taunts of 'chucker' at school, the family became sad and unhappy, and all over a game of cricket. It is hard to understand how the Australian Board came to persevere with Meckiff after 1958–59 when they knew his action was suspect. How much public humiliation they could have spared him. Peter May, again in his reminiscences, agreed with Benaud and Harvey about both Rorke and Meckiff:

> He [Rorke] was erratic but he was the fastest we met and made the ball bounce a lot. His action, although not the purest, was not as open to criticism as Meckiff's, but in combination with the amount he was allowed to drag down the pitch he was the most difficult of all to play. I never batted in a cap except under a hot sun and I cannot believe that I would have taken readily to a helmet if helmets had then been in vogue. But if I had ever worn one, it would have been to Rorke.

The throwing controversy was not over yet, however; there was more agonising to come, involving a running doubt and ultimate condemnation of the bowling action of the West Indian Test cricketer, Charlie Griffith.

Charlie Griffith, a big burly West Indian, played his first Test, at home, against the England touring side of 1959–60 in the fifth Test at Port-of-Spain. He took one wicket in a drawn match and gave no indication of the problems he was going to cause batsmen in the future. In fact, the West Indies selectors were not aware of it either, because he did not get a game when he went to Australia in 1960–61 nor even in their next series, at home against India. In fact he had to wait for Frank Worrell's team to visit England in 1963. Then, in harness with Wesley Hall, he began to get batsmen hopping uncomfortably around the crease, and not only with the new ball. He took 32 wickets in the five Tests, the West Indies winning the series 3–1 with one match drawn. The captain of England was Ted Dexter.

As a rather nervous joke, batsmen used to say that Griffith bowled only yorkers or 'throat' balls, the latter being a ball hurled in short of a length which then rises sharply towards the face: more seriously, many professionals believed that Griffith sometimes threw. They took as proof the position of his body before delivery; he was like a javelin thrower at the point of release. Griffith opened up his action, landing in the delivery stride with left leg splayed out, foot pointing towards cover, the leading knee bent, left shoulder dropped, chest facing squarely down the pitch

Charlie Griffith, West Indies fast bowler, 1963. He was said to bowl only yorkers and 'throat' balls!
(*Sport & General*)

and the arm bent, poised to release the ball. This was when he put in an extra effort to send down a really fast ball. At other times the Griffith arm made a gentle, orthodox revolution and then he was usually not quite quick enough to cause trouble.

It was when Australia went to the West Indies in 1964–65 that suspicions came out into the open. Ted Dexter wrote a newspaper column which stated that, if Griffith bowled at the Australians with the same action he had used in England in 1963, the results would be as meaningless there as they had been in England. Richie Benaud was by now a travelling cricket correspondent and he castigated Griffith too, backed by three of the leading players on that tour, Simpson, the captain, Lawry and O'Neill. They considered Griffith's action so dangerous that they said openly they would never play against him again or against any team in which he was included.

Nothing was done about Charlie Griffith's action, however; indeed, the West Indies could fairly argue that no umpire had acted against it in England, and that only players had grumbled.

Yet that was not the case. In 1965 there was a revelation in the *Daily Mail* in London which reopened the dispute and rocked confidence in the MCC. The club, which had led the march against throwing, was said to have been involved in a plot to give Griffith a peaceful passage through England in 1963.

It transpired that Charlie Griffith had been named as a thrower by Cecil Pepper, the jovial leg-spinner and big-hitting Australian Services cricketer, who, by now, was a first-class umpire in England. Three exhibition matches had been played between England XIs and the West Indians ('Sir Frank Worrell's XI'), at Scarborough, Edgbaston and Lord's in 1964. Pepper wrote to the MCC to say that he had been asked by Trevor Bailey, who had captained in two of these matches, to go easy on the front-foot rule, which was still foreign to West Indies bowlers, but he added that he would have had no hesitation in no-balling Griffith for throwing, had these not been exhibition matches.

The MCC wrote back to Pepper:

> Thank you for your letter of September 8th giving us your confidential comments on the action of Charles Griffith. I entirely approve of the steps you have taken in this matter since undoubtedly it would have caused unnecessary unpleasantness if you had called him in an exhibition match of this sort. The matter will be considered by the MCC committee in due course.

The composer of the letter was Donald Carr, replying in the absence of the secretary of the MCC. How the letters arrived on the editor's desk at the *Daily Mail* has never been fully explained: allegedly they were in a brief-case which was stolen from Pepper at Taunton eight months after the event. What were the MCC up to? If Pepper or any other umpire had called Griffith in England, the furious controversy which hit the Australian tour of the West Indies in 1965–66 would never have occurred. It also follows that, if Dexter and Benaud had not come out with their condemnations, then it also would not have emerged at all.

Surely, what the MCC should have done was to pass Pepper's report on to the West Indies and Australian cricket boards of control so that the series in which they were about to take part would be played in the full knowledge that Griffith's action had been queried, not only by the umpire who had once called him for throwing in Barbados, Cortez Jordan, but by an umpire in England as well.

In the autumn of 1965 MCC's cricket sub-committee spent a lot of time on the throwing subject. F. G. Mann was the chairman of a group which included G. O. Allen, Doug Insole, Raman Subba Row, Trevor Bailey, Ted Dexter, and the umpires Charlie Elliott and Fred Price.

They set up an adjudication committee, which was to watch and judge each reported bowler. Harold Rhodes of Derbyshire, who had been no-balled by umpires Buller and Elliott, was thought to be the main offender. He was filmed, photographed and at one time even painted – the black and white arm showed up much more clearly on film. Medical evidence was gathered of how his elbow was double-jointed and could bend back below the horizontal, so that when it was brought over quickly the lower arm could act as a whip. Rhodes had first been called in 1960, and it took a shameful nine years to clear his name and to declare that his basic action was fair.

In May 1966, when Charlie Griffith was back in England with the West Indies, he was called for throwing at Old Trafford – only the second tourist to be called in England. Eventually the Mann Committee rewrote the definition of throwing and with a later preamble from Australia it read as follows:

> Umpires must be satisfied beyond all doubt that the ball is bowled. If they are so satisfied no other question arises. The ball shall be deemed to be thrown, if in the opinion of the umpire, the process of straightening the bowling arm, whether it be partial or complete, takes place during that part of the delivery swing which directly precedes the ball leaving the hand. This definition shall not debar the bowler from the use of the wrist in delivering the ball.

Throwing had been a crime from the start, ever since Tom Walker was criticised at Hambledon, and later, at Lord's, when John Willes left the field in a huff, to leap on his horse and ride out of the game for ever. The harshness of the system now set up by the MCC was that it hounded men out of the game when they were adult and found it almost impossible to change their actions; whereas the emphasis needed to be on catching offenders when young, which required much greater alertness in the regions where the Youth Cricket Association schemes were being run. Similarly, in other countries, it had to be accepted as a responsibility of organising international cricket that attention be paid to the childhood game where bad habits could take root.

Yet there was encouragement, too. Harold Rhodes, painfully wounded by his long trial after playing two promising Tests for England in 1959, eventually got his clearance and Tony Lock, who completely reshaped his action, became a bowler of slower flight, higher trajectory and was able to add another dimension to his Surrey and England career. He emigrated to Perth, Western Australia, and was hugely successful both as a captain and a bowler. Then, between 1965 and 1967, he found time to play in English county cricket again, this time for Leicestershire whom he also skippered with success. Even then his career had not run its course. In 1967–68 Fred Titmus, the England off-spinner, was seriously hurt in a boating accident on the MCC tour of the West Indies. Tony Lock was called to replace him. So now, loudly appealing in an Australian accent, he began wheeling away again with flight and spin for England in two more Test matches.

Charlie Griffith played the last of his twenty-eight Tests for the West Indies at Lancaster Park, Christchurch, New Zealand in 1969 at the age of 30. He had been able to prolong his career because he had never been a thrower of every ball.

The other running debate of the 1950s was about the amateur in first-class cricket: his breed was thinning out, not quite to the point of rarity, but there were obvious signs that he was under threat of extinction. This was happening at the very moment when six-day-a-week county cricket was grinding along in front of decreasing crowds, with bowlers emphasising the containment of batsmen – and with batsmen replying through the chanceless accumulation of runs.

Amateurs had always been seen as standing for adventure and purpose, even when they defended with the tenacity of Bob Wyatt. Such attitudes were easier to adopt because they were not tied to their counties by cash rewards. Thus, much of the argument at Lord's was emotive like Walter Monckton's earlier aim to foster the amateur. The images of Lords Harris and Hawke, 'Jacker' Jackson and Archie MacLaren were called up; and through the 1930s, of course, the counties had been led by amateurs – A. B. Sellers, the benevolent dictator of Yorkshire, R. E. S. Wyatt in Warwickshire, A. W. Carr at Nottinghamshire, the Hon. L. H. Tennyson with Hampshire, T. N. Pearce and D. R. Wilcox in Essex, M. J. Turnbull with Glamorgan, F. T. Mann and R. W. V. Robins at Middlesex, A. W. Richardson in Derbyshire – these were long-standing captains.

Just before the war, when Walter Hammond turned from pro-fessional to amateur, this paved the way for his captaincy of Gloucestershire and England. Bill Edrich, after the war, did the same and became joint-captain of Middlesex in 1951. No one quite managed the amazing duality of Dr W. G. Grace, who had played out his career enjoying the social position of the amateur yet, at the same time, treating cricket and his fame as a cash business.

The amateurs had always been an elite brigade whose background of public school and/or university gave them little in common with the professional player other than the game itself. Consequently, amateurs usually kept their own company often in different hotels, travelling first-class on the railways, while the professionals went third-class, and at most county grounds had a separate dressing-room. Everything was done within the game to provide the amateurs with the privileged touches they normally received outside it, and no one complained, certainly not the professionals who relished the presence of amateurs so long as they were leaders worth following. The professional player was happy not to carry the responsibilities of running his county's cricket.

The amateur-professional relationship was akin to that of unpaid executives and paid servants of the same organisation and, since the glorious 1890s, the amateur role had been a heroic one. So it was a shock to find that the Welfare State, Britain's taxation system, and the post-war mixture of social adjustments now offered little scope for a young cricketer to concentrate on sport for five months a year, without monthly recompense, and often at considerable cost. Some accepted jobs with time off from firms who accepted that the cricketer's name was of business value; others took administrative employment within the game, which gave them the freedom to play regularly.

In 1956, when the MCC set up the committee under Sir Walter Monckton's chairmanship, it had advised against change in amateur status. Diana Rait Kerr, joint author with Ian Peebles of *Lord's 1946–1970*, explains how, by the mid-1950s, the 'popular' newspapers were leading the call for the abolition of the amateur, while the 'heavies' argued the retention. She herself in that book expressed the view as it was felt within the MCC membership and its Committee.

> If MCC, as the Governing Body of cricket, strove to keep the true amateur in first-class cricket it was not, as was popularly stated, for the sake of the 'old school tie', but with a sincere desire to regain and preserve the unfettered spirit of high adventure, which, since the Golden Age, had been the amateur's priceless contribution to cricket. The modern game was gripped to a point of suffocation in an iron band imposed by the gospel of containment, shackling the players so that they could not break out of their prison even if they would. Never had a leaven of lightness and joy been more sorely needed, for while there had been times in the past when cricket had been in the doldrums and survived, dullness had never been allied in quite the same way with social and economic pressures. Enterprise was not a sine qua non for survival.

In the meantime, two professional players demonstrated that amateur captains were not absolutely necessary. In 1949 H. E. Dollery of Warwickshire became the first professional county captain and not only did he lead his team to the county championship in 1951, but they were considered a popular, well-managed side. Then, in 1952, the Test selectors chose the first professional captain of England, Len Hutton. He led the side at home, in Australia, New Zealand and the West Indies, with success. He knew how to win matches and pursued his end with firm and often private determination. This he did on top of his career burden of carrying England's batting as an opener. He scored over 40,000 runs in a career extending altogether from 1934 to 1960, nearly 7,000 runs in Test cricket, and 129 centuries in all. In his batting technique was the most captivating marriage of method and touch, technique and artistry. For his international achievements he received a knighthood in 1956.

Although neither he, nor any other professional, was yet to captain Yorkshire, his, and Dollery's, elevation reflected the changing times. It was all very well for the MCC to encourage amateurs such as Peter May, Colin Cowdrey, Hubert Doggart, Trevor Bailey, the Rev. D. S. Sheppard and the other talented cricketers, but the retention of amateurism for its own sake attracted some whose talent did not gain the respect of the professionals. Some amateurs who were schoolmasters, for example, would join their county sides during the summer holidays. If they were unpractised and failed to succeed, they became ripe targets for the darts of the professionals who had been left out of the side to accommodate them. Above all, the professional body of cricketers could not abide 'shamateurism', which included a cricketer's employment by those firms which never expected to see him, and turned out to be no more than commercial sponsorship.

After the Monckton Committee, there followed one in 1957 chaired by the Duke of Norfolk, the reigning president. It investigated the mood of the professionals. They wanted the retention of the amateur. So the Norfolk Committee recommended that, at home, an amateur was entitled to repayment of genuine out-of-pocket expenses and, abroad, allowed broken-time payment. They decided that an amateur could be paid by a county club for an administrative role, but any payment, direct or indirect, for playing cricket, was improper and not permissible. A standing committee was formed to examine individual cases as they arose. Among amateur cricketers there was a number of county club secretaries and assistant secretaries, among them Trevor Bailey of Essex, Desmond Eagar of Hampshire, and Wilfred Wooller of Glamorgan; while Donald Carr was with Derbyshire before he joined the MCC administration.

Then, a year after his committee had tried to ensure the workability of amateur status, the end came very suddenly. The Duke of Norfolk announced: 'Try as we may to retain it, amateur status as we have understood it, is at an end . . . the Special Committee had hoped the recommendations in their report would work, but, sadly enough, they have not . . . Now is the time for reconsideration.'

The final decision to abolish the amateur was made by the counties on November 26th, 1962. The actual proposition came from Glamorgan to the Advisory County Cricket Committee, that all players in first-class cricket should in future be called cricketers, and that any financial arrangements with them would be the sole concern of their respective counties.

This was a commitment by a society which, since the war, had widened the channels of advancement, mainly by educational opportunity and, conspicuously, the system of state scholarships which took many more grammar-school boys into Oxford and Cambridge. Yet still, within Lord's, lurked fear of the changing order, suspicion of professionalism in cricket, immutable allegiance to the amateur and the old hierarchy. Lord Frederick Beauclerk still ruled! The last roll on this battle-drum was sounded by Diana Rait Kerr:

> At the gateway to a new decade the first-class game in England has become wholly 'professional', and the vitality which it so sorely needs is sought by the recruitment of stars from overseas, to the ultimate discouragement, one would think, of cricketers born and bred in Britain. Cricketers all, they arrive at Lord's like City commuters (only they don't have a five-day week). For what? So often it is just another day's cricket; another day at the office. And who can blame them if, as they take the field in front of a handful of spectators, the edge of their enthusiasm is blunted, and they play as soberly as City accountants balancing a ledger?

The MCC Committee had strongly urged, and tried to arrange for, the retention of the amateur. Not for the first time in its history, the club had been dragged along by social change into a new life and style.

21 A New Role for MCC ?

S. C. Griffith succeeded Ronald Aird as Secretary in 1962. In the same year Sir Pelham Warner, in declining health in his eighty-ninth year, retired as a Trustee of MCC. In fact there was a change in the term served by a Trustee: it used to be for life, now it was for a term of five years. So Sir Pelham became the first life Vice-President of the Marylebone Cricket Club.

Billy Griffith proved a most caring Secretary, particularly concerned with brighter cricket: to replace the amateur he was always looking to encourage the man of independent spirit. He constantly questioned boring play, politely and with complete understanding of the cricketer's problems as might be expected from someone who had played for Cambridge University, Sussex and England. Yet although he could not have known in at the time, Billy Griffith had started out into an administrative minefield.

At first, however, he enjoyed pleasant days of progress. In 1964 there were the celebrations for 150 years of the present Lord's. MCC sent a full tour, if not a first-choice team, to India under Ted Dexter, and the queue of countries wanting to tour England was eased by the acceptance of the principle of 'twin tours' during an English summer in which each visiting country would play three Test matches.

As it happened, Billy Griffith was away in Australia as manager of the MCC tour of 1965–66 when, for the first time in the club's history, the members threw serious doubt on the wisdom and judgment of their elected committee. It was over the redevelopment of the south-west corner of the Lord's ground.

A redevelopment sub-committee had long been shaping plans for a new stand on the site of the Tavern. The more they talked with the club's architects, the wider the possibilities appeared, and the plan grew to include, as well as a new stand, a new Tavern, a 300-seat restaurant, and a tower block of flats at the corner of Grove End Road and St John's Wood Road. The financial objection was straightforward: the club's reserves were £300,000 and the projected scheme would cost as much. The members' fury, immediately fanned by the press, was that the Tavern and its clock-tower, one of the most famous landmarks in cricket, would be demolished. Gone, too, would be the members' dining-room and the changing-boxes behind their wrought-iron balustrades.

It was important to get started on the block of flats in case the local authority issued a compulsory purchase order, because the site had been derelict for some time. In 1965, the Committee had accepted an offer of £150,000 from Messrs W. T. Chown for a 99-year lease with permission to build a twelve-storey block of flats and a penthouse, now called Century Court. Other urgent problems were the Tavern catering, which was losing money, and also the heavy outlay required to repair the crumbling Tavern buildings. The Committee therefore moved on to the next stage, a four-deck stand, designed by the MCC architect, Kenneth Peacock, which would stretch from the Tavern site to engulf a large section of the 'Q' enclosure. In the plan, the ground-level concourse and the top tier would be for members and friends, and the two middle tiers for hospitality boxes. For this stand, £305,000 was needed.

A meeting of members was called but *The Times* and the *Daily Telegraph* were full of letters from members demanding that others refuse to approve such a grandiose scheme, and that they should not even turn up to listen because the Committee had given them insufficient notice. The meeting did go on, in which the President, Lieutenant-General Sir Oliver Leese, was supported by the treasurer and Messrs G. C. Newman and M. J. C. Allom, chairmen respectively of the sub-committees responsible for development and catering. They offered a lucid explanation of all the stages of redevelopment, but only one stage was approved, the sale of the corner site for flats.

The MCC, rocked by the strength of the opposition, produced a booklet explaining their scheme, stage by stage, and for the second meeting in January 1966, the Seymour Hall had to be hired to cope with the large number of members attending.

In the end the Committee had its way, the day being won by Sir Bernard Waley-Cohen whose amendment asked for a modified new stand, costing less than the money envisaged. The Committee had to decide whether to omit the top terrace at a saving of £20,000 at the expense of 1,500 seats, or whether to limit the boxes to one tier, saving £33,600 and losing twenty-one boxes and their revenue. They chose the latter. Aesthetically they might well have stumbled on an acceptable solution – otherwise the stand would have dwarfed every other building on the ground. On financial grounds, however, it was probably an error. Yet again the MCC's antennae were not properly tuned to the shifts and drifts of the future. Cricket was entering a commercial age in which the letting of

Sir Pelham Warner, in his 85th year, speaking at the opening ceremony for the Warner Stand, May 7th, 1958. With him is the Duke of Norfolk, President, who performed the ceremony.

boxes at major matches would become a handsome source of income.

It was scarcely noticed, as Lord's was virtually turned into a building site in 1966, that the Grace Gates had to be resited. However, on June 13th, 1967, a week before the Test against India, Mr Billy Griffith drew the first pint at the new Tavern as he had drawn the last at the old. Unfortunately he was going to need more than a couple of pints of beer to refresh him through the radical debates that were to follow – involving, first, South Africa, and, then, the withdrawal of the MCC from the control of British cricket. The South African issue, although spread over many years, came to a head in the D'Oliveira affair.

Basil Lewis D'Oliveira was brought up playing non-white cricket in the Signal Hill area of Cape Town. He was Cape Coloured, one of South Africa's four groups, alongside African, Indian and White. He played for his father's cricket club, St Augustine's. It was poor cricket played in deprived circumstances. On the morning of a match he would walk ten miles or so to roll the wicket hard and flat for the mat to go on top. Twenty-five teams shared the same open space and players were always in danger of getting a bump from a nearby contest.

As a Cape Coloured he had little to do with white people, but whenever he could, he would go to Newlands to watch the white players in Test matches. D'Oliveira was an outstanding player, and he had dreams. One day he sat down and wrote a letter to the only cricket man he knew in England, John Arlott, whose radio voice and loving word-pictures of professionals in action had made him the voice of English cricket all over the world. Arlott responded generously with letters of encouragement, but it was impossible for clubs to evaluate D'Oliveira's eighty centuries in Cape cricket. So it was two years later before there came the offer of a contract with the Central Lancashire League Club, Middleton, one season only for £450. Since part of his fee would have to pay for his air fare, he was on the verge of turning it down but various collections helped to raise another £450.

Basil D'Oliveira arrived in England on April 1st, 1960. Five years later he joined Worcestershire and in his first season made six centuries and a 99. Worcestershire retained the county championship. A year later D'Oliveira was playing for England.

Basil D'Oliveira was popular and talented. There were plenty of jokes about his date of birth which he purposely kept obscure, but eventually he agreed to being 35 years old when he first played for England in 1966. He batted in the middle of the order where he could show a determined defence if required, but was happier playing pugnacious strokes. He was at his most dangerous fighting his way out of a collapse. His swing and seam bowling of gentle medium pace was subtle and a useful change for his county and often at Test level too. He went on to play 44 Tests, scoring 2,484 runs at an average of 40.06, including five centuries, and taking 47 wickets. It is a sadness that D'Oliveira is not remembered solely for what he himself made of cricket; his name is indelibly marked in MCC history, however, for what others made of him.

As far back as 1961 South Africa had decided to leave the Commonwealth and, by definition, ceased to be a member of the Imperial Cricket Conference. However, Pakistan, the newest ICC member, was the first to say that South Africa's future association with ICC teams should depend on a change in its domestic policy of separate racial development: apartheid.

Obviously, the departure of South Africa was mourned by England and Australia because these three countries had first formed the ICC in 1909 to promote their own international programme. But from 1960 there had been a swell of opposition in England to South Africa's racial and racist government. The Rev. David Sheppard refused to play against the touring South Africans in 1960 and in 1965, and John Arlott refused to broadcast their matches.

There had been public demonstrations during both those tours. D'Oliveira, understandably, became the champion of all nonwhites in South Africa, but also unwittingly for all those outside trying to change the South African government's policy by sporting propaganda. The sequence of events leading to crisis has been frequently described. D'Oliveira performed modestly for England in the West Indies in 1967–68, held his place for the first Test against Australia in the home summer of 1968, but was dropped after England's heavy loss. Many claimed that he had been left out for political reasons and certainly the events of the eighteen months before, as recounted in D'Oliveira's autobiography *Time to Declare*, make dramatic reading.

January 1967 – Britain's Sports Minister, Denis Howell, told a cheering House of Commons that the 1968–69 tour to South Africa would be cancelled if there were any moves to ban me.

In the same month South Africa's Minister of the Interior, Mr Piet le Roux, said, 'We will not allow mixed teams to play against our white teams over here. If this player is chosen, he would not be allowed to come here. Our policy is well known here and overseas.'

April 1967 – South Africa's Prime Minister, Mr John Vorster, said that apartheid principles would be relaxed in so far as they affected teams from overseas countries 'with whom we have traditional sporting ties'.

September 1967 – Derek Dowling, a South African Test selector, told me he was sure I'd be allowed to go on tour, if selected.

Basil d'Oliveira.
(*Sport & General*)

March 1968 – Sir Alec Douglas-Home met Mr Vorster in South Africa and came to the conclusion that my chances of being allowed to tour South Africa were favourable.

A few weeks later Lord Cobham, a former President of the MCC, was asked to visit Mr Vorster while in South Africa. He later said, 'Mr Vorster gave me to suppose that if D'Oliveira were selected, the tour would probably have to be cancelled.' Lord Cobham passed his opinion on to the appropriate MCC officials.

June 1968 – Wilfred Isaacs, a prominent man in South African cricket, came to see me at Lord's and talked warmly about the forthcoming tour. He offered me his flat and hospitality whenever I wanted it on the trip. Yet when he returned to South Africa a few weeks later, he forecast to the Press that I would not be selected. He also later denied he'd spoken about the tour to any MCC officials.

A high ranking official told me on the eve of the Lord's Test that I could get everyone out of trouble by making myself available for South Africa *not* England. I angrily refused.

D'Oliveira was left out at Lord's in favour of Barry Knight, of Essex. This made definite cricket sense to D'Oliveira: 'At Manchester I was the third seamer which was surely wrong; I should always be a batsman who could be the sixth bowler as a bonus.' He had batted at number seven. At Lord's the England line-up was Edrich, Boycott, Milburn, Cowdrey, Barrington, Graveney and Knight; very powerful, but there was no room for D'Oliveira to force himself in as a specialist batsman at this stage.

In August 1968, before the fifth Test, there was a meeting between D'Oliveira and a Mr Tiene Oosthuizen, an official working with a tobacco company. Oosthuizen offered D'Oliveira £40,000 in a ten-year contract, as well as a car and house, to coach in South Africa, provided he was unavailable for the South African tour.

Along came the final Test against Australia when R. M. Prideaux, of Northamptonshire, withdrew because of illness. D'Oliveira replaced him, made 158 in the first innings, though not without giving chances, and was asked by Doug Insole, chairman of the selectors, whether he was available for the tour. Colin Cowdrey told him that in his opinion he should be chosen.

He was not chosen; instead T. W. Cartwright of Warwickshire was selected. Immediately D'Oliveira accepted a commission from the *News of the World* to cover the Tests in South Africa. Mr Vorster came back with 'Guests who have ulterior motives or who are sponsored by people with ulterior motives usually find that they are not invited.' He accused the *News of the World* of making D'Oliveira a political football.

The fates were not finished yet. Cartwright withdrew from the tour because of a recurring injury to his shoulder. D'Oliveira was chosen. But why was he now replacing a bowler when he was originally rated a batsman? And where was Barry Knight, who was a lively seam bowler, first, and a batsman, second? Just before the fourth Test a lurid article appeared in a Sunday newspaper in which Knight said his marriage was broken, his business bankrupt, and he had contemplated suicide. In short, he was not in the best frame of mind for the tour.

So the processes in which D'Oliveira was chosen were extraordinary. John Arlott wrote: 'It is difficult to think of any step taken by the cricket establishment more calculated to mar the image of the game.' No one doubted the integrity of the selectors, Insole, May, Bedser, Kenyon, Cowdrey, the tour captain, and Ames, the manager, or those sitting with them, A. E. R. Gilligan, the MCC President and G. O. Allen, the treasurer. However, when D'Oliveira was first omitted, some MCC members resigned, and a group led by the Rev. David Sheppard demanded a special general meeting.

The MCC had let loose forces they did not truly understand. Their every decision reeked of political expediency because the cricket argument for excluding D'Oliveira and then including him was tenuous. Like wildfire, apartheid spread well beyond the cricket world as the MCC declared its naïvety in political matters, an attitude which shocked everyone. Here was the great club – which had spent over a century and a half proclaiming that cricket was more than a game, a way of life, even a code of honour – shrinking away from the role of national institution back into that of a private club.

Quickly, the South African representatives, Arthur Coy and Jack Cheetham, flew to London, but they could not save the tour. The South African government refused to accept D'Oliveira, and the MCC could not accept dictation of their selection. The tour was off.

Then MCC's agonies began. They were obliged to hold a special general meeting at Church House, Westminster, and the Committee faced three votes of censure. There, the president, Ronnie Aird, the former secretary, paid tribute to the 'great dignity which Basil D'Oliveira had maintained throughout the whole business' before he and his Committee faced their accusers among the gathering of over 1,000 members.

The Rev. David Sheppard led the accusers. He argued the MCC's mishandling of affairs with cool reason. His seconder was J. M. Brearley, the Middlesex and England batsman, later to be an outstanding captain. Brearley had toured South Africa with the MCC in 1964–65 and believed the Committee to be guilty of mistaken priorities. Both thought that MCC's wish to retain links with South Africa was outweighed by the club's wider responsibilities to non-white cricketers throughout the world. They also emphasised the image of the MCC which was now one of political cunning and conniving: not at all the image which the Committee believed they were projecting.

The defenders of the MCC debated as emotionally as the Sheppard group had been clinical, stumbling into personal attacks against Sheppard and losing the day in all but the final vote. The Committee survived the vote of no confidence.

What had happened to Lord Cobham's earlier information that D'Oliveira could not be allowed with an MCC team in South Africa? It transpired that the Committee had withheld this information from the selectors in order not to prejudice them. This revelation came at the very moment that the information of D'Oliveira's coaching offer was eventually let out. Had the MCC hoped he would go away quietly? Again the club incited mistrust, and the president, treasurer and secretary were targets of heavy criticism. Billy Griffith felt the pressure too great and offered to resign but, accepting the Committee's warm vote of confidence, he stayed on.

In fact his South African nightmare had only just begun, even though the other major event of these years, the shifting of responsibility for British cricket from the MCC, had taken place by 1969. In that year, the club's direct control of first-class professional cricket in the UK had been transferred to a 'Test and County

S. C. Griffith, Secretary 1962–74. Very sensible of the problems of cricketers.

Cricket Board'. Indeed all of the MCC's public role, save the custody of the Laws, was removed and split three ways.

First, amateur cricket, that is all non-first-class cricket, was taken over by the National Cricket Association (NCA) in 1965. It was an autonomous body but still run by the MCC secretariat. Then in 1968, professional cricket became the responsibility of the Test and County Cricket Board (TCCB) which would be the ultimate authority, but again, the paperwork was done by the MCC staff. This Board was very much the new 'Parliament' of the professional game, but initially, and at the time of the impending South African tour of 1970, the chairman and vice-chairman of the TCCB were the president and treasurer of MCC. The third element in cricket was MCC itself.

These three elements now operated under an umbrella organisation called the Cricket Council. The Cricket Council had its roots in the Wolfenden Report of 1963, *Sport and the Community*, which confirmed that cricket was in need of a national body 'to canalize views and promote the interest of all cricketers and above all to negotiate with government in such fields as taxation, grant assistance, rating and the extension of facilities for play'. To fulfil this role, the MCC themselves felt they were not suitable.

So when the South Africans were due to make a full tour of England in 1970, it was the Cricket Council and the TCCB who had to meet the considerable opposition, most prominently a group of protesters and disrupters called the 'Stop the Seventy Tour' which was orchestrated principally by a South African-born student Peter Hain. That winter, 1969–70, a South African rugby tour of Britain had been considerably disrupted by demonstrations; some games had to be stopped because demonstrators put tin-tacks on pitches or dug trenches. The Springbok rugby players had no fun. They moved secretly from town to town, trying not to reveal the whereabouts of their hotels, rarely stepping off their team bus. There was a constant and huge police presence. It soon became obvious that to defend English cricket grounds would be even more difficult, and probably impossible. The Rev. David Sheppard formed a Fair Cricket Campaign dedicated to non-violent protest against a Springbok cricket tour. In response Lieutenant-Colonel Charles Newman led an appeal to raise £200,000 in a cricket fund, approved by the Cricket Council, to finance the protection of the South Africans and the cricket grounds. It never came to that, however. In response to a request from the Home Secretary, Mr James Callaghan, the tour was called off on May 22nd. The cancellation was received with anger by the many who saw it as their democratic right to play cricket

Before the South African tour of 1970 was cancelled, MCC had to be prepared to defend Lord's, and the wicket in particular, against sabotage. (*Topix*)

with old friends, and yet with relief too, as the MCC ground staff put away their 300 reels of barbed wire. The cost of defending a three-day match with a large police force and other protections had been estimated at anything up to £18,000.

Cricket contact with South Africa had been severed.

As the government's National Sports Council began to dispense financial grants for leisure activities in the mid-1960s, so the MCC saw it right that cricket should be among the beneficiaries. However, the sports councils throughout the United Kingdom did not recognise private or professional clubs for grant aiding. They saw that cricket deserved some money, but the ramshackle arrangement of cricket clubs, associations and organisations owing vague allegiance to a private club, did not suit their strait-jacketed criteria.

The MCC, however, was forced along the path because it could not play the role of financial benefactor any longer. Thus they evolved a new structure for cricket. The first move had been the creation of the National Cricket Association (NCA) with its responsibility to look after the interests and aspirations of all cricket which was not first-class. Its headquarters was Lord's and the MCC secretariat did the administration: one of the assistant secretaries, J. G. Dunbar, handled their affairs.

Two years later the MCC could still not report a healthier balance-sheet, indeed the biggest annual deficit in the history of the club was recorded, £14,204 in 1968. This must have fanned the urgency for the second, but much more revolutionary, move, the formation of a body to run all first-class cricket and MCC tours abroad, the Test and County Cricket Board administered by another assistant secretary, Donald Carr. This rearrangement left the MCC, in effect, with only the custody of the Laws of Cricket.

Thus the administration of cricket was divided three ways and, to complete the requirements of the government and the recommendations of the Wolfenden Report, the ultimate authority of British cricket, the Cricket Council, was formed as a sort of umbrella over the top. Its component parts were five representatives from each of the MCC, TCCB and NCA. This particular split was the idea of MCC so as to prevent any one group's interests dominating the others'.

By 1974 J. G. Dunbar and Donald Carr had left all MCC responsibility to set up individual staffs for the NCA and the TCCB respectively. Also, at the same time, the mightily overworked secretary, Billy Griffith, retired and was succeeded by J. A. Bailey who had been the assistant secretary at Lord's responsible for public relations and promotion.

Yet this was not quite the disentanglement from the MCC which it appeared to be on paper. All of the new bodies were housed at Lord's free of charge, the Cricket Council met at Lord's, and Lord's itself, although not responsible for the major funding of the Council, paid its part. Lord's suddenly began to resemble one of the modern-day, converted cinemas. Instead of one show there were three, all on the same premises but in different theatres. Where Lord's differed, however, was that, instead of its three shows having different actors, it had three shows featuring similar casts! Some members of the TCCB were the members of MCC committees. There appeared to be a few men trying to wear a number of hats at the same time. These were the circumstances which led not to a peaceful shift of power but to difficulty and deadlock in the 1980s; it became more a jockeying for position and a fight for control.

It is fair to remove the NCA from the political squabbles which followed. There was smooth progress to report under the secretary,

Brian Aspital. Its national coaching scheme is run with tender, loving care by Keith Andrew, the former Northamptonshire and England wicket-keeper. He is an example of the perfect man for the job, absolutely enveloped in the quality of cricket taught to youngsters, sympathetic to the needs of amateur players and quite content not to be jostling along the corridors of power. He organises six full-time regional coaches and the NCA, by close links with sponsors – who really are more like good, old-fashioned patrons because they expect little in return, such as the McAlpine Trust, Wrigleys, and Agatha Christie Ltd – sets up competitive cricket, both domestic and international.

The problems have been between the TCCB and the MCC. More and more the conversation has been about the role of the MCC in cricket and initially about the desirability of the secretary of the MCC being the chief executive of the Cricket Council.

One group wanted management consultants to review the whole new structure because it looked cumbersome and incestuous in a cricket world that was fast-moving commercially and required a sharp business sense as well as affection for cricket's old standards.

Then, in 1977, there was a forced union between the TCCB, the MCC and the International Cricket Conference, once the Imperial Cricket Conference, but still known as the ICC. There was a revolution among the top cricketers of the world, who joined a professional circus based in Australia called World Series Cricket. Behind the breakaway was Mr Kerry Packer and also, as cricket adviser, Richie Benaud, the former Australian Test captain.

It is a matter of opinion as to who wanted the breakaway more, the players or Kerry Packer. As far as the cricketers were concerned, they had been for several years unhappy both with the status of their profession and with the actual remuneration. They looked sideways at the best golfers, tennis players and footballers, and saw more profitable, respected lives. What they needed was a billionaire to finance the breakaway from the established game.

Kerry Packer, on the other hand, was living with his own frustrations in Australia. He owned a go-ahead television company called Channel 9, but he had found it impossible to invade the cosy relationship which the Australian Board of Control for Cricket had with the Australian Broadcasting Corporation and could not get his hands on the television rights of Test matches.

In May 1977, thirty-five international players announced that they had signed for World Series Cricket and would only be available for traditional Test matches in the months when his contract did not bind them. More followed to form three international sides, Australia, West Indies and the World XI.

The involvement of MCC was as the secretariat of the ICC. When the annual meeting of the ICC took place in the summer of 1977 the mood of the member countries was belligerent. The rival Packer series was viewed with contempt, not as competition, and this intransigence led to protracted dispute in the High Court between cricket's authorities and Packer's players.

The ICC passed unanimously a change in their rules to excommunicate players from the authorised version of cricket: 'No player who after 1 October 1977 has played or has made himself available to play in a match previously disapproved by the Conference shall thereafter be eligible to play in any Test match (without the express consent of the Conference).'

In effect, players who had signed for Packer were given until October 1st to withdraw from those contracts or face a ban from Test and county cricket. It meant a ban at Test and first-class levels. This ICC resolution was a grave mistake.

The West Indians, Jeffrey Stollmeyer and Allan Rae, had strong reservations which turned out to be well founded. The ban was judged by Mr Justice Slade as illegal restraint of trade and indeed there was also the strongest suggestion that players were being induced to break their contracts, also illegal.

The judge's ruling on all points in favour of the Packer players and against the cricket authorities meant that the latter had to find a quarter of a million pounds to pay the costs of the action.

The World Series experiment in cricket will always remain fascinating for those who saw it. Because the established grounds of Australian cricket, under the control of the Board, were barred to Packer, artificial pitches were manufactured in hot-houses in concrete troughs and lifted by crane into holes dug in the centre of showgrounds and football stadia. Floodlit cricket, with a white ball, black sight-screen and players in coloured clothing became the Wednesday night television rage.

Families had barbecue nights at home just to watch the World Series matches. The games were poorly attended at the start, but eventually built up a following as the West Indies in maroon stripes, met the World in light blue and Australia in green and yellow; 50,000 people watched a match at the Sydney cricket ground. The Australian Board of Control was under pressure and, after a year, had to reach an agreement with Packer.

For its part, the ICC was led skilfully in debate by the MCC secretary, Jack Bailey, and helped towards a sane conciliation by the different presidents in this period – W. H. Webster, David Clark and C. H. Palmer – and the treasurer, J. G. W. Davies, and,

The Indoor Cricket School, opened in 1977. (*Patrick Eagar*)

again, David Clark who took over in 1980. The ICC had always committed itself to seeking a broad agreement with World Series Cricket which could be assured of the full support of all the Test-playing countries. By sticking to that commitment the settlement took a long time to come and involved Jack Bailey in a great deal of travel around the world. In the end there was criticism of Australia's speedy settlement, but Bailey admitted that unresolved issues had to be left to the good sense of the Australians who were much more under fire than any other country.

There is no doubt that the TCCB received a shock and one of its immediate reactions was to form a working party to examine the long-term administrative structure of cricket in Britain. The official comment was: 'The recent High Court action would seem to have lent weight to the view that responsibilities are not very well defined and that the process of decision-making is too often protracted.' This was an attack on the age-old committee process which, some believed, clogged the Committee Room of Lord's like a fungus. Three men were chosen to produce a report, which they did in July 1978, Cedric Rhoades, Ossie Wheatley and Raman Subba Row, who was chairman.

Cedric Rhoades was the chairman of Lancashire, a forthright man, who had been determined in his efforts to overturn the Lancashire committee which he and the huge majority of members saw to be out of date. He was not one to pay lip-service to MCC's history, in fact, in his view, there was no reason why the Board should not operate from Nottingham or Birmingham which at least would be central.

Ossie Wheatley, chairman of Glamorgan, had been a fine bowler with Cambridge University, Warwickshire and later as captain of Glamorgan. The third, Raman Subba Row, was a former Surrey and England batsman now in the business of managerial public relations. All three men were keen to streamline cricket and none was prepared to consider as more than a great red herring the future role in cricket of MCC.

Indeed, their report recommended the virtual demise of the MCC. They envisaged a United Kingdom Board of Cricket Control, consisting of seventeen first-class counties, eight representatives from the NCA, one for all the universities, Scotland and Ireland. The last three would not have voting powers. MCC's position as custodian of the Laws was recognised only by the concession of one representative.

The scheme was turned down by the counties, but it did lead the way to another reorganisation which was announced in 1982. The supreme authority in cricket would still be in the Cricket

Council, but the TCCB would have the weight of authority with eight members, the NCA five, and the MCC now reduced to three. The TCCB was invested with total authority to run all aspects of the professional game affecting English cricketers, and the NCA confirmed to be in charge of amateurs. The MCC's copyright of the Laws was acknowledged and it was also charged with organising cricket tours to minor member countries of the ICC which, of course, it always had done.

The mathematics of representation on the Cricket Council was now important. If the MCC and the NCA voted together they could still be outvoted by the TCCB with the casting vote of the chairman who, again, might be their choice. It was a move which was brought to the attention of the whole cricket world because it persuaded G. O. Allen to resign from the Cricket Council, although he had been one of the two men who had set it up. He sent a letter of explanation to the Council's chairman, C. H. Palmer:

> Billy Griffith and I were responsible for the foundation of the Cricket Council because we felt there should be a governing body for cricket, representative of all levels of the game. At its inception we were in favour of MCC having the largest representation, as both the TCCB and NCA were in their infancy and we thought they might need guidance. Later, when both those bodies had found their feet, we suggested the 5–5–5 representation.
>
> In the discussion on the current reorganisation, I made it absolutely clear that I was not opposed to a reduction in MCC's representation if that was the consensus of opinion. But it is my firm conviction that a national body cannot be controlled by one faction, in this case the professional side of the game, regardless of how much money it may in its generosity provide for the recreational side of it.
>
> Further, at no time has anyone explained to my satisfaction either the reasons for or the advantages of TCCB having control of the council, bearing in mind that under the new constitution both it and the NCA have been delegated absolutely the control of their respective activities. It certainly cannot become a more effective body . . .

The MCC, which once ruled the whole world of cricket, the private club with the public role, now ruled little and had little public role. The shift put a strain on the relationships of the secretaries, Jack Bailey and Donald Carr, who, for a long time, worked at opposite ends of the Lord's pavilion. Jack Bailey, as a fast bowler, had captained Oxford, played for Essex and then went into industry before arriving at the MCC in days when the club bore the whole burden of cricket administration. By the time he took over from Billy Griffith, the job had changed. Certainly he had become the manager of a large estate in north-west London, but he had little authority in cricket matters.

Donald Carr was from Derbyshire. Primarily a batsman, although it was more as a left-arm bowler that he had been chosen as a schoolboy for one of the 1945 'Victory' Tests, he had been both a county captain and secretary. He had also been an Oxford captain and led England in one Test in Madras in 1952 when the tour captain, Nigel Howard, was ill. After moving to Lord's in 1962 he managed three overseas tours. By nature he was always cheerful, but sometimes agonisingly diplomatic, although this perhaps helped him to get through a testing run of legal and racial wrangles over South Africa in an atmosphere of reasonable calm.

The approach of Jack Bailey to his job was as a zealous defender of MCC's historical sway and actual rights. Rather than supervise the eclipse of the club which many saw to be the inevitable course of events, the secretary began to hammer home the club's serious contributions to cricket.

In the first place, Lord's was a Test-match ground which contributed as much as 40 per cent to the TCCB Test income; second, MCC provided the chairman and secretary of the International Cricket Conference; third, the MCC was responsible for the framing and updating of the Laws of Cricket. Also the club could offer high-calibre people to contribute to committee discussion and a skilled administrative corps; it was giving both the TCCB and the NCA considerable focus by allowing them to stay at Lord's and, perhaps more important still, it could continue to offer what it had done traditionally, an independent mind. The fear was that the 1982 reorganisation would lay cricket open to the petty jealousies and often selfish views of the counties. This had happened before, in the 1890s, when the counties self-destructed their own County Cricket Council and handed the first-class game back again to MCC. Might it not happen again? In the context of a 200-year history of the MCC, the Board was a mere infant, and who was to guarantee its continuity?

The inherent danger of the Board's business concept of cricket administration was that all its initiatives would simply be responses to market values. Australian cricket, which, after Packer, has been promoted by the PBL Marketing Agency, went headlong for night cricket in coloured clothes and a hard-sell in the market-place. Should cricket legislation necessarily follow market forces, which might anyway be temporary enthusiasms?

What control is there over the quality of representatives sent from the counties to the TCCB? What calibre of person will control the Cricket Council? At present, the cross-fertilisation of well-known and respected men, nearly all MCC members, works well but what if others replace them who do not have the feel for cricket and its place in British life? Does MCC not have responsibility at this to express its fears?

The Library

Although Lord's and the MCC is a private club, the TCCB feels it should have much more control over who runs Tests at Lord's, who allocates the hospitality boxes, issues invitations, and governs the media. MCC, while recognising TCCB's overall responsibilities, has maintained that there is an absolute practical need for MCC to be in charge at Lord's. Thus MCC is accused of fortress politics and the secretariat seen as jealous of the low ground of power. That this squabbling has taken so long to settle is because, as Geoffrey Moorhouse points out in his *Lord's* (1983), the TCCB is the cuckoo in the nest. It resides at Lord's, puts on its best shows there, but has no sway there.

There are similar situations around the world. In India the Cricket Club of India staged Tests at the fine old Brabourne stadium in Bombay. However, the Indian Board of Control could not get the control over Tests they wanted on the ground, nor the percentage of income they believed they deserved, so they removed the Bombay Test matches to the Wankhede stadium not a mile away. The Brabourne stadium is now a sad, grand relic.

In Australia the Sydney Trust runs the Sydney cricket ground for the New South Wales government. There is currently no cricket representative on the Sydney Trust, and the NSW Cricket Association, unhappy about its treatment in many aspects, has also aired the idea of playing some of its games on a different ground.

Could it happen that the TCCB takes Tests and one-day finals away from Lord's? It has the power to do just that, although it would be the first to admit that the Natwest final at Edgbaston, for example, would not feel the same great event.

Is it possible that Lord's will be humbled in this way?

In the meantime, as these crucial matters are fought over, it is business as usual. Improvements are being made all the time. In 1977 the Lord's indoor cricket school was opened by G. O. Allen. It had been carefully planned by a steering committee under the chairmanship of E. W. Swanton, whose enthusiasm for the project was matched by his thoroughness.

The internal playing area of the school measures 120ft by 88ft. Not only are there nets in rows, but also, when they are drawn back, there is enough space for six-a-side cricket with its own clever rules. At the social end of the school there is a raised balcony above the dressing-rooms and a lounge and bar where, in the winter, the club holds discussion evenings. The school was raised at a cost of £200,000 but, to the relief of the club, £75,000 of that was donated by Sir Jack Hayward, the British businessman resident in the Bahamas. The school's interior is known therefore as Hayward Hall.

The chief coach Don Wilson, formerly of Yorkshire, recruits other current or former professionals to help him with the supervision. Thousands of schoolchildren pass through there every year. The school is used for hospitality during Test matches, and the occasional knowing member takes a good breakfast upstairs before the start of Test-match play.

In 1980 a new Code of Laws was introduced by the MCC. It was the conscientious work of the former secretary, Billy Griffith, who acknowledged the help of T. E. Smith, a previous general secretary of the Association of Umpires. With repeated consultation with every international member of the ICC they, with many re-draftings, managed to reduce the Code of Laws of 1947, from 47 to 42. There was one new Law headed 'Timed Out. Law 31'. This Law made it possible for a batsman to be given out on appeal if he wilfully takes more than two minutes to reach the wicket. S. C. Griffith ended his introduction as follows:

> Cricket, like every other art form, is constantly evolving, and in due course, this code, like its predecessors, will stand in need of modification. Yet it is only the fourth full revision to be undertaken of the original Laws of 1744. It is my earnest hope that the code of 1980 will stand the test of time as well as those that have gone before.

The MCC Committee in session (1978).
(*Patrick Eagar*)

More recently, on the field of play itself, Sri Lanka played their first Test match in England, at Lord's in 1984. It was their twelfth in a short history. In it Sidath Wettimuny matched himself with many of the great players who have excelled against England there. He scored 190, Sri Lanka's highest-ever individual score, and the seventh-highest score against England at Lord's. It was a match of varied achievement – Ian Botham equalled S. F. Barnes's world record by taking five wickets or more in an innings for the twenty-fourth time and Allan Lamb's fourth Test hundred of the season equalled the record shared by H. Sutcliffe (1929), D. G. Bradman (1930), and D. C. S. Compton (1947). The match was drawn.

Ground development has seen an extension and fresh building behind the pavilion to house the TCCB and the NCA in separate quarters and also to create space for a new library. This was built with sympathetic financial assistance again from Agatha Christie Ltd, through Dame Agatha's grandson, Mathew Prichard, who had

Crowds attending the one-day cricket cup finals invariably have plenty of action to shout and enthuse about. This occasion is the Benson & Hedges Final at Lord's in 1982. (*Patrick Eagar*)

a sweet-sour taste of Lord's himself when, as a schoolboy in 1962, he was run out for 95 for Eton v. Harrow.

The official crowd capacity at Lord's has been 27,000 but that is increased now that the new Mound Stand has been erected. Included in the building are twenty-seven boxes of which thirteen will be leased either on an annual basis with a minimum fee of £20,000 or for a period of five years in return for an interest free loan to the club in excess of £150,000. In addition there are 520 seats on the third level of the stand with associated bars and dining facilities available to members on debenture basis. In return for an interest-free loan to the club of £1,000 for a period of three years, the debenture holder may purchase a ticket enabling him to occupy a seat in this area for all major matches at Lord's. The debentures are being offered in pairs and members may purchase only one pair.

This is but one example, of which there are so many in the history of the MCC, of how the club, by nature suspicious of change, has been prepared to embrace change once it is shown to be necessary, and to meet commercial sponsorship more than half-way.

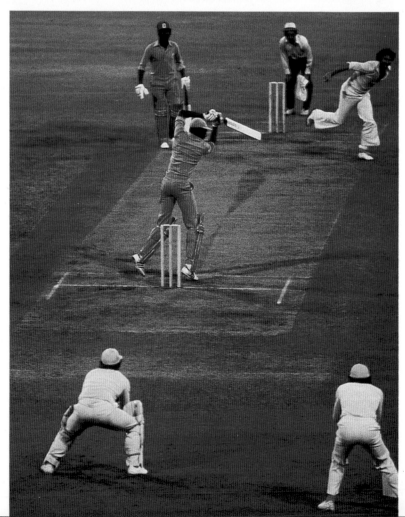

World Series cricket
in Australia:
above – a night match
at Victoria Park,
Melbourne;
below – Australia v.
West Indies,
Sydney 1979.
(*Patrick Eagar*)

Centenary Test at Lord's, 1980, v. Australia:
Wood, st Bairstow b Emburey 112.
(*Patrick Eagar*)

OVERLEAF A memorable gathering at Lord's of former Test
cricketers and current players from England and Australia
at the Centenary Test, 1980.
(*Patrick Eagar*)

22 Club and Country; a personal view

The MCC began its life with some gentlemen employing workaday professional cricketers. But as this gentleman's club flourished and took charge of the Laws and conditions of the game, there still remained the two necessary elements in the game's membership – the gentlemen who lived for sport and the players who 'sported' for a living. This was symbolised in 'Gentlemen v. Players' being one of the 'great' games of early organised cricket.

The first such fixture was in 1806, and although the match was often a non-contest in purely cricket terms, the fixture survived and kept a validity for some 150 years. Interestingly, however, the contest was at its best during W. G. Grace's time when that colossus swung the results back in the favour of the Gentlemen. In his own day he managed to bestride the great gulf between the amateur and the paid player: he was a Gentleman who made money from the game. Yet when the Gentlemen v. Players match was in decline in the 1950s and ended in 1962, it was the false status of many of the country's amateurs which lost the fixture its validity and once the public, sensing that artificiality, ceased to regard the match as 'great', the fixture died. Professional captains had proved they were effective leaders; and all of us 'cricketers', as we were now called with the abolition of amateur status, needed to earn our livings.

As it happened I was involved in the last Gentlemen v. Players match, at Lord's in 1962. I knew it was a famous old fixture but was unaware then of its historical significance. To us in the game it looked more like another Test trial match. But I had noticed too how the University match, another very old fixture in which I played from 1960–62, was also dying from lack of spectators.

I had grown up in Neath in South Wales, a long way both from Lord's and the MCC. Just like Don Bradman at the age of twenty, I had no idea what the MCC was even when I saw the red and yellow stripes on a sweater. Most cricket clubs in my area represented towns or villages, welfare associations or works, and usually they shunned club colours, preferring badges and shields on blazers or sweaters. Consequently when, in my middle teenage, I saw two red and yellow banded sweaters adrift in this sea of

The MCC monogram and the cricket balls which for a heraldic crest at the top of the Lord's pavilion towers are not easily descried by the naked eye. (*Patrick Eagar*)

337

club heraldry, I wondered what sort of men could be wearing the colours. They turned out to be Captain W. M. S. Trick of Neath, a superb left-arm spinner, one of the Glamorgan county's amateurs, and J. D. H. Riches of Cardiff, son of the county captain in the 1920s, N.V.H., and himself the skipper of the Glamorgan seconds. The MCC was then explained to me by someone only slightly less ignorant than myself, as a big club in London which ran everything.

Even when I had my first sight of England playing in 1950, I still had no idea that the MCC was anything to do with Test cricket. We were at The Oval. My father had squeezed me down on to the grass, mid-wickets on the gasometer side, to watch the fourth and final Test against the sensational West Indies side. I can remember having to leave by tea-time to get back to my aunt's house in Eaton Socon in Huntingdonshire and I saw only one wicket fall, that of J. B. Stollmeyer when the score was 72. After that I was treated to endless, easy batting by Allan Rae and Frank Worrell who were about to compose a partnership of 172. I read the next day that both had scored centuries.

Thirty-four years later, in 1984, I was chatting in the concourse just inside the Grace Gates at Lord's with the same Jeffrey Stollmeyer and the man who had dismissed him all that time ago, Trevor Bailey. I claimed total recall of that lbw dismissal and felt I had to tell them that, although only twelve at the time, I felt sure that the ball would have gone over the top of the stumps. Jeffrey beamed. 'Absolutely right. I have never reconciled myself with that decision,' he said. We looked at Trevor, who already appeared to be deep in thought, his nose wrinkled up, eyes totally closed. Eventually he announced, 'Plumb'. Then he smiled puckishly and added, 'Well, near enough anyway.'

The details of the MCC's contribution to Test cricket were never explained to me as a boy, or later – how they chose selectors, planned the programme of tours, handled the revenue, organised the England tours abroad and considered every possible problem which arose. It was much easier simply to accept the blanket description that the whole of cricket was run by Lord's.

Yet if Lord's was remote to me in South Wales, so was it to millions of others living away from London and the Home Counties, let alone overseas. It is easy to imagine the importance of Lord's in the school lives of those trying to make the First Eleven of Eton or Harrow, or Cheltenham or Haileybury, Clifton or Tonbridge, Beaumont or Oratory, Rugby or Marlborough; but outside the privileged circle of those schools who played annually there, Lord's ground was another planet. Indeed it has now become so for those schools too: only Eton and Harrow play at Lord's in the 1980s and that is a one-day match.

Lord's, the cricket ground, grows on you, I found, as the treasure-chest of cricket you see and play there becomes more precious. At first sight, and empty, it can seem unimpressive, as Keith Miller had found. I was lucky enough to appear there in three University matches, in that last Gentlemen v. Players, for the MCC in various games, and in contests for Glamorgan against Middlesex. Yet, like many young men in the 1950s, my first opportunity to play at Lord's came during National Service. Some, but not all, of the inter-service games were at Lord's and they continued to be so until 1972. The Combined Services match against the Public Schools indeed still is there. At one time the Army and Navy sides were so strong that, in 1914, in the centenary week celebrations of the Lord's ground, the match between them was selected as the second match. When compulsory call-up ended in 1962 the services underwent a reduction in numbers and the cricket standards fell. Now the inter-services matches take the form of a three-day festival at a service station; but when I was representing the Royal Air Force and Combined Services, from 1957–59, there were many fine players among the regulars, including A. C. Shirreff, M. L. Y. Ainsworth, J. H. G. Deighton, G. G. Tordoff, and M. D. Fenner, while few can say that they were not once bowled out by one of Commander Martin's big in-swingers in a match against the Royal Navy.

In my first Lord's match I felt no hair bristling on the back of my neck. I recall the big ground being empty and the crack of bat on ball echoing around the stands. The dressing-room seemed incredibly spacious with tables and sofas and a row of wash-basins; the players' nervous walk out to bat, down the stairs and through the Long Room made me feel like an errand boy who had wandered by mistake into a club reading room and could not wait to get out the other end. The floor had a rubberised smell. At the crease however, I enjoyed being able to see my score go up on the large boards, on both sides of the ground; it was reassuring, somehow.

One of the Combined Services captains, J. H. G. Deighton, knew his way around the Lord's pitch better than most. In 1947 he took a hat-trick there for the Army against the Navy, and the next season performed a second hat-trick on the ground but this time for the MCC against Cambridge University. This was an exceptional performance because Lord's was a reliable batting pitch, that is until 1958, when a ridge was first reported. County batsmen complained that it was dangerous batting at the Nursery End, especially as Middlesex had a tall, fast bowler who could exploit it, Alan Moss. J. J. Warr, the Middlesex captain and also a quick bowler, thought that the frequent incidence of shooters as well as of balls which lifted might be caused by subsidence rather than a ridge. By 1961, however, batsmen wanted some action by the MCC. In the Lord's Test that summer, Australia beat England by five wickets and after the match, the club called in consultant surveyors who eventually proved the existence of a ridge at the Nursery End, but a slight one too at the pavilion end. Their findings emphasised the great merit of the 130 scored in that match by the Australian opener, W. M. Lawry. The next highest score on either side was 66: most batsmen had been intimidated by Trueman and Statham, or by Davidson, McKenzie and Misson. The solution to the ridge was thought to be annual levelling with top-dressing, but the MCC heeded the players' cry, removed the turf, and relevelled and relaid the offending area.

In 1962 came the ultimate demise of the amateur in first-class cricket and therefore the conclusion of the Gentlemen v. Players series of matches. In the years immediately after the Second World War there was no decline in the attraction of the fixture. 28,000 watched the 1948 match, when Len Hutton's century led to a win for the Players. The reduction in the number of outstanding amateur cricketers able to take time away from their occupations meant, however, a growing ascendancy in match results for the Players, almost as in the early days, in fact. The Gentlemen only recorded three wins in all the matches played at Lord's after the First World War.

In 1950, C. J. Knott of Hampshire did the hat-trick for the Gentlemen, but the last two batting for the Players, Hollies and Wright, held out for a draw. It was Hollies again in 1957 who held out with the bat, this time with Trueman, to save the professionals. So there were hard-fought matches, yet they ended up less as great occasions, more as convenient Test trials.

The last Gentlemen v. Players match in 1962 was an example of this. It was fanfared in the press as a showdown between Colin Cowdrey, captain of the Gentlemen, and the Rev. David Sheppard playing under him, for the leadership of the forthcoming MCC tour of Australia. Cowdrey withdrew from the side and, unexpectedly, the captaincy of the Gentlemen was given to E. R. Dexter, an outstanding Cambridge University batsman who had taken up the captaincy of Sussex two years earlier.

The game was attended by three or four thousand people who saw Freddie Trueman lead his players to within sight of an exciting victory after declarations, when the rain came down. H. S. Altham recorded: 'Enterprising and attractive play by J. H. Edrich, Parfitt,

GENTLEMEN

	FIRST INNINGS		SECOND INNINGS	
Rev. D. S. Sheppard	c & b Titmus	112	b Titmus	34
E. J. Craig	b Trueman	4	c Titmus b Trueman	0
E. R. Dexter	c Trueman b Shackleton	55	run out	1
M. J. K. Smith	run out	44	not out	15
R. M. Prideaux	b Trueman	14	b Shackleton	109
A. R. Lewis	lbw b Shackleton	2	c Andrew b Titmus	10
R. W. Barber	run out	0	not out	3
D. B. Pithey	run out	30		
T. E. Bailey	c Walker b Shackleton	5		
A. C. Smith	c Sharpe b Shackleton	33		
O. S. Wheatley	not out	10		
Byes 4, leg-byes 6		10		
Total		**323**	Total (5 wkts., dec.)	**172**

Bowling

PLAYERS	FIRST INNINGS				SECOND INNINGS			
Trueman	13	6	59	2	10	6	8	1
Shackleton	38	9	101	4	19	8	38	1
Walker	28	4	64	0	9	2	21	0
Titmus	20	6	46	1	24	5	69	2
Gifford	14	4	43	0	7	0	36	0

PLAYERS

	FIRST INNINGS		SECOND INNINGS	
M. J. Stewart	c A. Smith b Bailey	0	c A. Smith b Wheatley	3
J. H. Edrich	b Bailey	19	not out	77
P. H. Parfitt	c Sheppard b Dexter	9	c Dexter b Barber	63
T. W. Graveney	b Craig b Wheatley	21	c A. Smith b Bailey	41
P. J. Sharpe	c & b Barber	39	not out	12
P. M. Walker	b Bailey	15		
F. J. Titmus	c Dexter b Bailey	70		
F. S. Trueman	b Wheatley b Barber	63		
K. V. Andrew	c A. Smith b Bailey	17		
N. Gifford	c A. Smith b Bailey	2		
D. Shackleton	not out	1		
Byes 4		4	Byes 1, leg-byes 10	11
Total		**260**	Total (3 wkts.)	**207**

Bowling

GENTLEMEN	FIRST INNINGS				SECOND INNINGS			
Bailey	30.3	10	58	6	13	1	45	4
Wheatley	19	6	37	1	12	1	46	1
Dexter	18	2	49	1	7	0	43	0
Barber	21	7	90	2	7	0	43	1
Pithey	8	2	22	0	4	0	27	0

Umpires: H. Yarnold and A. E. Rhodes

Freddie Trueman – a great fast bowler with a flowing action.

and Graveney carried them well ahead of the clock, but then the clouds opened, and the Gentlemen and Players left the field at Lord's together for the last time'.

I was among them on that occasion as some good form in the Cambridge University side had gained me selection. I recall David Sheppard's solid century and Ted Dexter's approach to batting. In the dressing-room while waiting to go out to bat Dexter took up an imperious stance in front of the mirror, went through the motions of imaginary drives, all the time repeating loudly, 'These cocks can't bowl'. I was padded up, kneeling nervously on the sofa-end, taking an occasional peep at the progress of our men against Trueman and Shackleton whom I knew most definitely could bowl. It was a mighty surprise to Sheppard, to Cowdrey and, I believe, to Dexter too, when, during the match, Dexter was summoned to the Committee Room to be informed that he was the captain-elect for Australia. In the second innings, he was applauded to the crease by the Players. Dexter's public image as Lord Edward, who loved horse racing and practised golf swings at cover-point, covered a most thoughtful nature and a cricket mind enraptured by theories of many sorts, but sharp enough to get to the truth of the matter. He was a magnificent athlete, a scratch golfer, good at rugby football; and he excelled because he matched talent with an independent spirit, the sort of spirit Billy Griffith was always looking for. Among slight eccentricities, Dexter once stood in Cardiff as a Conservative candidate for Parliament, he flies his own aircraft, zooms to Lord's on a motorbike, and races greyhounds. By nature he was an attacker of bowlers and the one innings that always goes with his name, though there were many others, was the 70 he scored at Lord's against the West Indies in 1963, when he blasted the fast attack of Hall and Griffith. Dexter was also a lively medium-fast bowler, who caught the eye with a remarkable performance – 5 for 8 and 3 for 47 – for the Gentlemen against the Players in 1957.

In many ways we, the young cricketers of the second half of the 1950s, were the cheated generation: we had been weaned on the sight of full county grounds and an established order at Lord's, but throughout the decade the old order was changing fast – the great matches were in decline and amateurism was constantly under threat. Yet the plan for young amateurs was still that they should pass through Oxford or Cambridge and go on to captain their counties. Although Sir Len Hutton had been the first professional captain of England, and H. E. Dollery had risen through the ranks to lead Warwickshire, the ideal still seemed to be the amateur in charge of the professionals. Consequently some amateurs were recruited from outside the first-class game who otherwise would not have made a regular career of county cricket.

There still persisted the artificial separation of amateurs and professionals. Major grounds, like The Oval and Old Trafford, had amateurs' changing rooms; R. W. Barber, briefly captain of Lancashire, often had to follow the club tradition of staying at different hotels from the rest of his side; amateurs lunched in committee rooms or at least on separate tables. However, the differences had become misty and confused when, for example, some amateurs remained so only because they were being sponsored indirectly by business firms, or were on the county club payroll as secretaries. Equally a professional who had been commissioned during wartime service was unlikely to leave the officers' mess and turn round and whiten the amateur's boots. In fact, the senior professional players came into their own in this year, 1962, willingly taking responsibility for discipline within the team, controlling the junior staff, and being outspoken about the team's tactics whenever they thought the skipper was getting them wrong.

Not surprisingly, as social fashion changed so radically, the University match, that third original 'great' match, was also in decline, no longer part of the social season, although there were still good sides. For example, as a freshman, I played in C. B. Howland's Cambridge side of 1960. We beat three counties in the build-up to the Varsity match but found ourselves opposed to one of the strongest possible Oxford teams. Their line-up of future county and Test players was intimidating: A. C. Smith; D. M. Green; A. A. Baig, a young Indian who had scored a century against England on his debut at Old Trafford in 1959; Javed Burki, soon to lead Pakistan; the Nawab of Pataudi, junior, talented and well schooled at Winchester, about to begin a Test career of 46 tests for India; C. A. Fry, grandson of C.B.; C. D. Drybrough, who would be Middlesex's captain, joining a trio of spinners with Piachaud and Duff; Sayer and Corran, as fast as any undergraduates could be. Cambridge were saved by rain and a rearguard action.

Generally, however, the Universities lacked bowlers, although O. S. Wheatley, later to captain Glamorgan, took a record 80 wickets with his away-swing during a Cambridge term. M. J. K. Smith of Oxford scored a century at Lord's in every one of his three years. Three centuries in two years were later scored by R. J. Boyd-Moss for Cambridge in 1982–83. The highest Cambridge innings in the history of the game was by Gamini Goonesena, 211 in 1957, and, for Oxford, 238 not out by the Nawab of Pataudi, senior, in 1931.

Pataudi junior scored a superb 131 as a Freshman in 1960 in his first University match. The next summer, tragically, he was involved in a motor accident in Hove and damaged an eye which left his sight impaired for the rest of his life. His recovery revealed a most competitive character, a man of dignity and humour who never believed that cricket was all of life. His personality came through to those who knew him well. In one Test match in Madras in 1973, when he had been called back into the Indian side to the delirious approval of the Indian public, he began to bat nervously but survived furious shouts for lbw and catches off bat and pad. He looked in trouble but then, quite regally, he stroked away his first single. As he trotted up to the non-striker's end he veered out to me at mid-on and gave me a poker-faced look as if to complain about the actions and reactions of the close fieldsmen in my side. He said, 'Hey chief! I am not getting a nought today.' He laughed and the nerves eased. Pataudi too, like Dexter, was to his fingertips an independent spirit.

Exactly the same could be written of the Khan family: of Majid Khan, who led Cambridge with such authority and batting genius and of his father, Jahangir Khan, a fast bowler, who played for Cambridge and who in 1936 against MCC bowled a ball which killed a sparrow in flight. (The ball, ceremoniously if rather ghoulishly mounted complete with the poor bird on top, is on view in the MCC museum.) Majid averaged 50 in each of his three seasons at Cambridge, including making a memorable 200 in the Varsity match of 1970.

The decline in the popularity of the match seriously began in the late 1950s and it has not recovered. In 1982 the University match was even scheduled to take place mid-week at Lord's while a Test match was going on at Manchester. Formerly, this would not only have been an unthinkable clash of great fixtures, but the MCC could never have staged the University match other than at the weekend. But that is how the market forces of the 1980s dictated and D. R. Pringle, the Cambridge captain, actually withdrew from his side for Lord's to play in the Test match against India.

However, the MCC has always proved itself pragmatic enough, though usually in the long run, to embrace change. To replace the old, established fixtures were new 'great' games, sponsored commercially and played over single limited-over innings. The first was a county knock-out competition, the Gillette Cup as it was when it started in 1963. The financial background of this 60-overs-per-side competition was so sketchy that the counties agreed that players should be accommodated privately at the

The first Gillette Cup limited-overs knockout competition in 1963.
Sussex have beaten Worcestershire, and Dexter is addressing the crowd.
(*Sport & General*)

homes of committee men and supporters should the match continue into the second day. Glamorgan, for example, believing the new-fangled game to be an irrelevance, left out five front-line players from their first match against Somerset at Cardiff, so that they could rest. Nowadays some county players would be resting from a three-day match in order to be fit for the one-day competition. In fact the competition so captured the public's imagination that 25,000 people turned up on a dull, miserable day to watch Sussex beat Worcestershire in the first final. Every year after that, the Cup Final day has been a sell-out.

Next, Hampshire's suggestion for a Sunday League took root and J. A. Bailey, the MCC assistant secretary, persuaded John Player and Sons to sponsor it for £75,000. The crowds again showed their faith in the new turn of enterprise. So successful was the formula of one-day cricket that, by 1972, two more competitions had been founded. Benson and Hedges put up £65,000 for their early season knock-out competition which would include a final at Lord's, and then Prudential Insurance offered £4,000 in prize-money and £26,000 to the Test and County Cricket Board, to sponsor three one-day matches against the visiting tourists. Each new venture was a success.

Sponsors have changed and the Test matches themselves are now played under sponsorship, that of Cornhill Insurance. The Gillette Cup has become the Natwest Trophy, and John Player and

345

Great enthusiasm is generated by the knockout competition.
This was the final of the Benson and Hedges, 1983.
But should cricket be dominated by market forces? (*Patrick Eagar*)

Sons are about to withdraw from the Sunday League. The county championship is funded by Britannic Assurance.

It is the commercial sponsors who are now cricket's great patrons, and every financial agreement is closely linked with anticipated television coverage. The National Village Cup Final is played at Lord's and so is the National Club final. The MCC, without easily forsaking their loyalty to established matches, in the end have to treat fixtures according to the attendance at the gates.

Not all of MCC's entrepreneurial ideas have worked out so well. I recall one effort in the mid-1960s to resurrect the single-wicket championship to find a latter-day Alfred Mynn. First Carling, then Bass-Charrington sponsored a county competition in which each individual was to have an innings of eight overs, all bowled by one opponent, and there would be ten fielders available. By an amazing miscarriage of justice in 1967, I won Glamorgan's domestic eliminator at Barry Cricket Club, not that it was fiercely contested, and so went off to Lord's for the final. In the dressing-room I met the winners from other counties; the competition was to last two days and there were plenty of young MCC ground-staff lads fit and ready for fielding. S. C. Griffith, the Secretary, was coming to make the draw for the first round. Suddenly the suggestion was made that we split the money before we start so that it did not matter financially who won or even got to the final: we would all leave with the same amount. This proposition did not upset me at all. I had taken only two first-class wickets in my life, and if the inner voice could have informed me, it would have indicated that I would only take four more in the next seven years before retirement. The chances of my winning were nil. Thus it was agreed that, on top of our match fee of £30, we would all take another £15 a head.

Billy Griffith arrived and made the draw. After a while he came out with – 'A. R. Lewis of Glamorgan will meet . . .' he shuffled the names in the bag, 'G. S. Sobers of Notts.' Not a bad all-rounder! I played Gary Sobers at midday on the first day, and scored 44 off his eight overs, having performed like W. R. Hammond reincarnate. Unfortunately, being undecided whether to bowl seam or leg-spin I attempted to bowl both, something only achieved before to my knowledge, by O'Reilly, Freddie Brown and Keith Miller. We walked off together after 3.5 of my overs. Sobers had completely ignored my field-placing, smashed 50, and condemned me to a day-and-a-half in London with £45 in my pocket. Officials of the MCC applauded me back to the dressing-room with several calls of 'Well played'. It would not have helped them if I had knocked out Sobers in the first round. Alas, it did not matter for from the first round to the last, no one turned up to watch.

The domestic scene is the first-class cricketer's bread and butter; but it has always been part of the MCC's role to foster cricket wherever it may flourish. Touring therefore is a vital part of the cricketer's life, as well as the jam on his bread.

The MCC touring colours are orange, yellow and navy blue; the George and Dragon on cap and blazer. For tours abroad the MCC took on the responsibility of arranging the playing programme, the financial agreement, and provided the management. The relationship between management and captain was always crucial, not least of course during the 'Bodyline' tour.

On the tour of 1972–73 to India, Pakistan and Ceylon, I was very fortunate in my own manager. Donald Carr had captained Derbyshire and England; and since 1962 he had been part of the administration at Lord's. Above all Donald Carr was a man of patience and humour. We disagreed only once, and he was right. I slowed down the England over-rate during the Test match in Calcutta in order to frustrate the Indians who were getting on top and scoring freely. Carr's argument was that the more balls we bowled the sooner we would get India out and, in any case, surely the 85,000 crowd deserved something better than the sight of an England team time-wasting?

Cricketers inevitably get too close to their pursuits. They need a tap on the shoulder every now and then and a word in the ear from someone who has been that way before. Slowing down over rates was not simply a cheat to paying spectators, it was not what people expected from the MCC. That became obvious in a later Test in Madras.

Long before I made any tours, the Marylebone Cricket Club had set standards of behaviour which the cricket world accepted. Even if MCC itself fell below those standards from time to time, everywhere the game had taken root they were there, as both guide and norm to live up to – the noblesse, the unspoken sportsmanship, the acceptance of honour, the understatement, the sense of mission, the fellowship.

In Madras, the Indian captain, Ajit Wadekar, snicked a ball which was caught at second slip by Tony Greig, about knee-high. Wadekar stayed at the crease waiting for the umpire to give him out. The umpire shook his head. Greig and a posse of others charged down the field towards him, demanding justice. I stood between my team and the umpire who by now was strolling across to consult his colleague at square leg. The discussion was brief, and Wadekar was given out. The umpires, Mr Mamsa and Mr Nagendra, then explained to me how the ground sloped sharply downwards away from the square and what was a knee-high catch seen from square leg appeared very close to the ground from the bowling end. There was mayhem in the crowd, booing, fire crackers going off, mirrors flashing, tins banging.

Donald Carr had missed the incident but that evening we still had an informal chat about it with the team, acknowledging how easy it was to get feverish in the humidity and dust, and in the frenzy of a tight Test match, but explaining also what reaction was expected from us and what restraint. At the ground next day, when we went out early for a fielding practice, we saw twin banners strung up in the stands on the far side of the field. Giant capital letters reminded us of exactly what was expected from representatives of the MCC: 'In defeat, defiance, W. Churchill'; the other said, 'MCC, win or lose, be sportive'.

The British had always stood for a rigidity of behaviour which the MCC represented. Playing for MCC therefore had an effect on the individual. That sense of mission and diplomatic purpose has now largely gone from cricket – since tours began to be treated by players strictly as work. Money is now the motivation in many cases: it is not cricket's fault, nor the cricketer's, it reflects society and the ease of travel. But there was a crossroads when England toured Australia in 1971. England was still called MCC on tour but in fact this was the first tour organised by the Cricket Council and the TCCB. Ray Illingworth was the captain. The manager was the former Kent captain and MCC committeeman, later Treasurer of the MCC, David Clark. It was an ill-advised marriage, unfortunately. Illingworth was a deeply knowledgeable leader on the field, but off it he seemed more concerned with leading his players to the financial rewards they thought they were due, and to a social life free from the usual confetti of invitations; in short to a matter-of-fact professional existence without lip-service to the extremes of diplomacy for which the MCC had become renowned and which David Clark believed still to be important. It was not long before captain and manager fell out. The traditionalist Clark was caught in the swirl of a players' revolution which began then and came to fruition some six years later when so many top Test players left the authorised version of cricket to join World Series Cricket. Illingworth can be defended because, by standing up for the rights of players in so many areas he was only anticipating what was certain to happen in times when money became paramount in cricket. Clark can be defended too. What he stood for were values, fast becoming nebulous and

Colin Cowdrey

shunned by modern players, of the privilege it is to be in someone else's country and of the duties of sportsmanship and politeness so required. The real error was made by those who paired Illingworth with Clark in the first place; just as their earlier error in giving S. C. Griffith as manager primacy over M. J. K. Smith as captain was 'corrected' by the good sense of and rapport between the two men.

Nor is it right to say that an England cricket team of the 1980s has no consideration for its hosts abroad. There are some extremely good sportsmen. However, when money and the earning of a living become the raison d'être of playing and touring, and when cricketers living in modern self-sufficient hotels do not need to meet the local people wherever they play, the professional game can become a cocoon of commerce, wholly out of touch with the game of cricket as it touches most people's lives.

Major tours have always created problems by their very complexity; so that often there have to be communications with the Foreign Office when the difficulties fall outside cricket's province. For example, the MCC tour of 1968–69 to Pakistan and Ceylon had to be abandoned because of political strife within Pakistan. The manager, Les Ames, and captain, Colin Cowdrey, carried on as long as they could with patience and understanding, but eventually the Pakistanis themselves had to recommend the team's withdrawal out of fears for their safety.

This tour was to have been to South Africa but the D'Oliveira affair had ended that; and it was the last major tour for which the MCC was responsible. It was fraught with difficulties. The revised plan had been to tour India, Pakistan and Ceylon (now, of course, Sri Lanka). In spite of two personal visits to India by Donald Carr however, and a promise of £20,000 from the Burmah Oil Company, the Indian government felt unable to release currency unless the tour to their country was extended to include more than two Tests. So the tour began with eleven days in Ceylon, where the side conceded a victory to their hosts in Colombo on scoring rate in a limited-innings match, and then they plunged into the civil disorders of Pakistan.

They managed to finish two Tests at Lahore and Dacca but the third, in Karachi, was abandoned because of rioting. At Lahore, Cowdrey scored his twenty-second Test hundred to equal the record held by W. R. Hammond; D'Oliveira, at Dacca, scored a superb 114 not out. Tom Graveney and Colin Milburn both made centuries in the partially finished match and the sadness, not appreciated at the time, was that this was Milburn's last Test innings. He was soon to lose an eye in a car crash. It was a tragedy for a popular cricketer, so young and so full of lusty strokes, to be so cheated of a full career. Unlike Pataudi, he was unable to repair his career after the accident.

As for the tours to the non-Test-playing countries, after the Cricket Council was reconstructed in 1983 it charged the MCC with the responsibility for organising these. It was a superfluous gesture because the MCC had always been sending sides abroad and it continues to do so. In the words of its secretary, Jack Bailey, it was 'to spread the gospel of how cricket should be played – a matter of spirit as well as technique – and to give those countries a bit of a fillip from Lord's, the headquarters of the game'.

My own first experience of such a tour was in 1964–65, a visit to South America – Brazil, Chile and Argentina – under the captaincy of A. C. Smith, now the secretary of the Test and County Cricket Board. There was, of course, the sheer excitement of travel, but there was more. Taking guard on a matting pitch, chalking your guard, seeing the ball slow up quickly as it ran over tropical, broad-leaf grass, looking down the pitch at the bowler through a torrent of sweat that was flowing down through the eye-brows, gulping cold drinks against advice, wringing out woollen socks after fielding – all these are unforgettable experiences for every first-time touring cricketer.

There are a multitude of touring possibilities these days, and I have played under many flags, but my last tour for MCC, to the United States, had the same priceless hallmark as my first. The MCC monogram, although mistaken for the motif of a band by one American, and despite my being called a 'cricketeer' by another, meant to our hosts the ultimate authority in cricket. In that expectation, they spent tremendous energy, hard-earned money, and willingly gave us their hospitality and their friendship, because they saw MCC not only as a power base but as a dispenser of good works.

On that first South American trip, in Vina del Mar in Chile, we were shown a faded photograph of an MCC side of 1926–27 led by 'Plum' Warner, which included Lord Dunglass, later Prime Minister as Sir Alec Douglas-Home. Then, down in Argentina, we met a man who, I believe, was representative of so many MCC members abroad who loyally kept in touch without being able to travel to Lord's. His name was McKay, and he had lived on a farm in central Argentina for twenty-five years. All his cricket news and information came from his MCC annual report, his *Wisden*, the airmail *Daily Telegraph* and *The Cricketer*.

It was January 1964. We had driven what felt like hundreds of miles from Buenos Aires for an afternoon match against the Northern Camps at Venado Tuerto. The more experienced among us knew that, wherever in the world cricket takes you, the old Empire is there somewhere, tucked away in some decorous corner. Where was this Empire? We found it in the British Club.

From behind the small corner bar came the smile and the handshake from a man with a handlebar moustache. 'Great, chaps, you've made it. We were worried. It's been ten years since the last lot came through. But it's worth waiting. What'll it be, G and Ts all round?'

The local expatriate cricket kit was lying in a corner. The pads were of faded yellow buckskin. The wicket-keeper's pads had the ancient flaps; Len Hutton's autograph was on the bats and the gloves. They were the old brown sausage-finger type – four fingers go in first and then you wind the thumb, which is attached by a length of elastic, around your wrist before putting it in position.

The game was played that afternoon in white heat on a polo field. There were deep hoof-marks all over the pitch. Fast bowlers could not bowl because it was dangerous. MCC scored 252 batting first. However, the big crowd arrived later on when the Camps were compiling a lively 172. Cowhands rode up on horseback, settled themselves around the boundary with gallons of local gin and treated themselves to a swig for every run.

For MCC, Ian Bedford, formerly captain of Middlesex, and the schoolmaster David Mordaunt, who had played for Sussex, both scored half-centuries. Alan Duff, our tricky little leg-spinner, took 7 wickets for 36.

We stayed overnight. But for my part nothing sticks in my mind as more astonishing than a conversation with my host. Alan Smith and I were dining with him of at his magnificent farm estate. Once the domestic staff retired, our talk drifted on into the early morning. We even teased our host, saying that the Second World War was over, that England had won back the Ashes in 1953 and had he heard of Peter May? Then, suddenly, McKay slammed his hand down on the table and turned his gaze to Alan Smith. 'It's nae good, Smith. I've got to come out with it. You, keeping wicket for Warwickshire. Why the hell do you stand back to a trifling medium-pacer like Cartwright?' Suddenly I got a feeling that he had forgotten more about cricket than we missionaries ever knew.

There are many other different places, and activities, to which working for cricket and for the Marylebone Club can take one, whether on the cricket field or in the Committee Room. In the name of MCC I have been bowled for nought by the Dulwich

College third seamer, have taken guard at Ipoh, and also in that gloriously freezing encounter which usually starts the club's season of out-matches each year, at Wisbech. On dark, rainy winter afternoons I have spoken my piece in sub-committee about the lbw law or the state of the pitch at wherever, and have helped to steer the club to the building of its Indoor Cricket School.

In addition to leading that one first-class tour to India, Pakistan and Ceylon in 1972–73, the MCC has asked me to take teams to Malaysia and the Far East, and on the first official tour to the United States of America. Also the club sends me each year, as a cricket writer and broadcaster, a press 'gold medallion' which reserves me a permanent seat in the press box at Lord's on the top deck of the Warner Stand: it also admits me to any first-class game in the country.

To·any one of its 18,000 members, however, and despite its public role, the MCC can still feel more like a private club than a public facility. Try getting in to Lord's if you have forgotten your member's card or pass!

For the few, the very fortunate few top cricketers who are selected to go on the major tours to the principal cricket-playing countries, there is the incomparable excitement of reporting at Lord's for a medical and then, on the next day, if all is well, collecting the famous kit – that sweater with the MCC orange, yellow and navy band, the blazer with the trim as worn by so many heroes on cigarette cards in the days when colours and middle partings counted – of M. S. Nichols, or handsome faces like that of E. W. Dawson (Eton, Cambridge and Leicestershire) or the modest smile of Jack Hobbs – all those heroes long ago. And here you are . . . yourself, at Lord's, treading in the footsteps of whoever it is you choose to dream about.

Those colours, to my generation, meant the British Empire. Not in any jingoistic sense, but because all the cricket I ever played abroad was where the British had been and left their mark – the railways of Argentina, the law courts of India, the commerce of Hong Kong; everywhere colonisation, with cricket as 'the hand-maiden of Empire'. The game of cricket itself, however, was a hard game. No room for sentimental claptrap. You were as good as your last innings or as your last over, or last catch. Arthur Shrewsbury would have approved.

A sense of patriotism, even jingoism perhaps, does no one any harm especially if, as Jack Hobbs pointed out during the Bodyline tour, it helps the players who are representing England abroad in MCC's colours; for even when earning a living is the primary consideration you need identity and purpose to keep a team together. Perhaps more so. When players' heads droop in the middle of a steaming afternoon in Perth they can still see the flag and feel glad to belong. It is then that MCC truly represents England: the old equation.

In truth, though, you are not playing for a club; you are playing for your country. That the Marylebone Club, originally formed by a group of gambling aristocrats to help pass their leisure time by playing a 'manly' game, has come to embody this idea as well, is surely one of the miracles of cricket's genesis, growth and development.

So, two hundred years after its founding the Marylebone Club moves healthily on, busying itself with the promulgation of cricket throughout the country and in any corner of the world where a new seed of the game needs nurturing or an old blossom looks to be withering, attending particularly to schools which, at this time, is the area most under threat in many geographical pockets of Britain.

There have been times when MCC has surprised and disappointed me: for example when I had been selected to captain the MCC tour to India, Pakistan and Ceylon in 1972–3, I attended a long, rambling selection meeting and, with the help of four selectors and MCC, chose 16 players for the eight Test matches to come.

Incredibly, however, only Don Kenyon among them had played Test cricket in the sub-continent at all and that in 1951. It seemed reasonable to me to include also in the selection discussion Ray Illingworth, the immediate past captain, and Mike Smith and Ted Dexter, who both had led tours to India in the 1960s. To me the failure to do this represented a lack of attention to the smallest detail of the sort that wins series.

More surprising and disappointing was the removal of Brian Close from the England captaincy in 1967. Close had been brought in to give his energetic approach to the job for the final Test against the West Indies in 1966. Next summer he led England to wins over India and Pakistan but he lost the leadership through an incident in a Yorkshire v. Wawickshire match at Edgbaston.

In damp conditions with Yorkshire fielding at the end of the match, Close embarked on a time-wasting exercise by frequent drying of the ball and non-stop field changes. At no time did Close instruct his bowlers to waste time, but they bowled only two overs in the final eleven minutes. The memory of it, even now, is appalling to Warwickshire players who were thwarted in their pursuit of victory on the day.

Close was called to Lord's to face a panel of former county

captains. They were unanimous – Yorkshire had used delaying tactics. Many heated, unofficial debates later, came the decision to appoint Colin Cowdrey as captain for the forthcoming trip to the West Indies. In his book *I Don't Bruise Easily* Brian Close recalls the moment with bitterness: 'It was all so bloody, horribly unfair. So Colin Cowdrey was recalled as captain and, in the West Indies, slowed down the bowling rate so ostentatiously that it is the only time I have ever seen Gary Sobers really angry! One law for Close . . .'

I do recall the whole playing fraternity at the time demanding a wigging for Close, some apology or concession that he had got emotionally carried away in the Edgbaston contest; but no one thought that his reduction to the ranks 'pour encourager les autres' was the punishment that fitted his crime. It was MCC demanding leadership that observed exclusively the amateur ethics of behaviour and fair play. There were indeed leaders like that, but Brian Close was not one of them; yet what he did have, more than most, was the personal quality to inspire others by his devotion to the game.

Especially in matters of discipline, MCC is still portrayed as establishment, reactionary, everlastingly public school and Oxbridge, and a power-centre for those who live in London and the home counties.

It is also true that people not fitting these descriptions when they first go to Lord's for committee work, often quickly acquire its establishment veneer. Gone is their club blazer, the strong point-of-view for which they were invited or put forward by their county; instead, they tend to become anonymously smart-suited and to sink their personality into the ambience of Lord's.

Presidents come into a different category of course. Sadly they are often ineffective, yet not through any fault of theirs. Originally an honorific appointment, the president's one-year tenancy is now too short. Initially a new president relies heavily on the judgement of the secretariat but by the time he himself has gained the knowledge and confidence to want to shape MCC's progress he has to make way for his successor. A two-year presidency might well create an office to which its distinguished incumbents can more productively give their talents.

Whatever accusations are made against the Marylebone Cricket Club, however, it is right to make three points in its favour.

First, any organisation which controls the organisation and running of cricket, albeit by the request of all, is bound to be criticised. The rule-makers in cricket cannot always be right or popular. The disciplinary board is certain to be unpopular; and the guiding principles of legislation are, of their nature, stiff and unbending.

Second, throughout MCC's life as cricket's government, its many committees that run first-class cricket were all composed of nominees from the first-class counties, the minor counties and the universities. A critic, say of Northamptonshire or Sussex, Yorkshire or Somerset, could be on his soap box one month, on his county committee the next, and soon on one of the many sub-committees at Lord's having his say in national cricket affairs. If he was blocked by his county, then that would not be the fault of MCC. The channels were always open for the widest possible discussion on any subject through the county system. MCC's governing process was far more democratic than many people believe.

Lastly, I must emphasise the immense responsibility which many men of Lord's have felt and feel towards cricket and cricketers. Imagine the number of times that long-serving committee men have boarded trains or cars in the dark on winter mornings and set out for Lord's – not half a dozen times, but hundreds. I have little sympathy with their detractors unless they themselves are prepared to devote the hours and match the conscience of such men, often former county players.

Of course there is also a domestic side to MCC, the private club, its development and its housekeeping; and this was mirrored in the bicentenary celebrations of 1987 as much as the Bicentenary Match itself reflected MCC's world-wide role, historical responsibilities, and present prestige in cricket.

The bicentenary began with an unpleasantness. The impasse between the Club's Secretary, Jack Bailey, and the Test and County Cricket Board finally became intolerable to the Club's committee and 1987 the birthday year began with the plain announcement that Mr Bailey would take early retirement. The Secretary's most conspicuous supporter, the Treasurer, David Clark, had resigned a month earlier.

On 13 January 1987, in falling snow at West Meon in Hampshire, the President, Colin Cowdrey, placed a commemorative wreath on the gravestone of Thomas Lord: it was as if a plea was being made to the old founder to revitalise the future and make Lord's a happy place again.

The Bicentenary Ball certainly returned revelry to the pavilion though by accident. Handsome marquees had no sooner been erected on the Nursery than equinoctial gales blew them down within hours of the party but with an entrepreneurial touch which Lord himself would have applauded, celebrations were switched to the pavilion. Dancing to the music of Joe Loss and his orchestra on the real tennis court was a master-stroke of improvisation. For the Acting Secretary, shortly to be confirmed in office, Lieutenant-Colonel John Stephenson, it was a day of trepidation and ultimate triumph.

The Club sold off artefacts from its reserve collection for £225,000; His Royal Highness Prince Philip opened the new Mound Stand, brave in its conception with a rooftop of white pavilion peaks, the work of Michael Hopkins and Partners. New gates were presented by the Duke of Westminster in memory of his uncle, Viscount Cobham, a past President and Treasurer of MCC.

At the 200th Anniversary dinner fine speeches were made by Prince Philip, J. J. Warr, the President Designate, and the bicentenary loving cup designed by Theo Fennell was on view for the first time.

However there had been a setback on that same day. At the Annual General Meeting the members refused to approve the Report and Accounts. Many argued for the fortress beliefs of Bailey and Clark, defending the rights, prestige and position in cricket of MCC and Lord's. The meeting, chaired by the President, ended in shambles with no one knowing quite what had been decided. In fact it took a Special General Meeting to get the Report and Accounts passed by a large majority who by that time had received fuller explanations of the Committee's opposition to the Secretary. MCC acknowledged blame for failing to communicate its domestic affairs in sufficient detail to its members.

The Bicentenary Match was held at Lord's on 20–26 August. There was unbroken sunshine for most of the time but the final day was washed out by rain. It scarcely mattered. It had been a magnificent match, fought hard and with much pride in performance by an MCC side chosen from cricketers playing currently in Britain and by an overseas based Rest of the World side.

The captains were chosen from the founder countries, England and Australia, Mike Gatting and Allan Border. Between the sides there were 1275 Test caps; Sunil Gavaskar had scored more Test centuries, 34, than anyone in the game's history; three bowlers had taken over 300 Test wickets, Imran Khan, Richard Hadlee and Kapil Dev. Dilip Vengsarkar was present, the only overseas player to have scored three hundreds at Lord's. It was an occasion given pomp and fun by the Band of the Coldstream Guards, and Royal Marine parachutists free-falling at lunchtime. On a flawless pitch four fine centuries were scored by Graham Gooch, Mike Gatting, Gordon Greenidge and Sunil Gavaskar.

The fielding was excellent and included an amazing run-out of Gooch by the West Indian off-spinner Roger Harper. Gooch blitzed the ball back down the pitch, Harper took a giant stride to combine an astonishing pick-up, leap and throw sending the ball screaming back past Gooch and shattering the stumps with the stunned batsman out of his crease.

Sir George 'Gubby' Allen chose the bowler of the match, Malcolm Marshall, and Denis Compton nominated Sunil Gavaskar as best batsman. The South African Clive Rice was jointly chosen by those former Middlesex cricketers as the outstanding fielder.

This match, played to full houses, was the perfect climax of the birthday year. The dinner on the eve of match was in Guildhall in the presence of the Lord Mayor of London where the speakers were Lord Home of The Hirsel, Hubert Doggart, the new Treasurer of MCC (standing in for the President who was recovering from open-heart surgery which sadly he had to undergo during his presidential year) and Clive Lloyd, the former West Indian captain. 700 guests attended, a distinguished array of players and administrators from all over the cricket world. The senior former player was W. H. Ponsford of Australia, and the youngest, Majid Khan of Pakistan.

Otherwise for MCC 1987 was business as usual. Plans were reaching conclusion for the redevelopment of the lower level of 'Q' stand; MCC toured Bermuda, and Pakistan played a winning series in England. William Bowyer, RA, painted the bicentenary match from the Nursery End. The introduction of squash leagues has encouraged the use of the courts but the Squash Club was still exhorting members to take part. Sadly Real Tennis and Squash lost D. J. Warburg, who died in November, aged 64. He was a leading player and administrator, elected to the Club in 1957. He won the MCC Gold Racquets seven times.

Four Life Members of the Club died: W. E. 'Bill' Bowes, aged 79, of Yorkshire and England whose cricketing experience stretched back to the Bodyline tour of Australia and further; John Goddard, who was 68 and captain of the triumphant 1950 West Indians in England; V. M. Merchant, 76, the prolific run-getter of wristy style who adorned Indian cricket and who will be remembered for his performances on the 1936 and 1946 tours; and J. G. Dunbar, a former Assistant Secretary of MCC and the first Secretary of the National Cricket Association.

The average club member does not appear to worry overmuch about MCC's relegation in cricket affairs now that its power has been transferred to the Test and County Cricket Board. As long as Lord's puts on the best cricket and they have their privileged entry and view, they are content. In fact, there is a chance that the original mood of a private gentleman's club, as it was at White Conduit in 1787, might in part return to Lord's. The first sign was the cosy member's bar and television lounge, furnished in 1986 at the top corner of the pavilion where the TCCB offices had been accommodated.

Membership of MCC offers active cricket, outdoors and in, real tennis, and a sight of some of the best cricket in the world: also participation in a fraternity which has the game as a common interest.

But if MCC is to be more than a private club, there seem to remain two tantalising possibilities. As the TCCB goes about the business of linking first-class cricket more permanently with commercial sponsorship and advertising, it is possible that the game of cricket itself might become distorted because it is forced to respond to market forces – more one-day cricket, shorter games, more constricting commercial hoops through which to jump. This would create a need to reinforce the old shape of the game, either by the creation of a stronger band of amateur competitive cricket which MCC could create nationwide or, perhaps, by the re-introduction of MCC into the professional game as a sort of Upper House of cricket's present parliament, filled by experienced people who are not submerged in the market place but who will judge every issue according to the old adage of what is good for cricket and cricketers.

There is another possibility too. The International Cricket Conference, whose secretary and chairman are the Secretary of MCC and its president of the year, is at present a toothless tiger of a council which talks much and achieves little because everything that is resolved by the delegates has to be approved by their home boards of control. International cricket and its administration urgently requires a more cogent executive, one that can be trusted, one that is divorced from its own country's day-to-day machinations. Now that MCC is freed from running English cricket, it has the experience to offer to become a world-unifying force. The chief executive, which world cricket seriously needs to speed up and bring order to decision-making, could well be the Secretary of MCC. The Chairman of ICC might well serve a three-year term and that too might fall to a MCC President such as Colin Cowdrey or whichever of these accomplished and talented men has the time and inclination. In other words, the Marylebone Cricket Club could find a new role: having lost control of England's cricket, it could run the world's cricket.

There is nothing in the club's history to suggest that its members have the instinct or the inclination to sit for long on the sidelines.

Appendixes

MCC Presidents

(from the earliest recorded times)

1825 C. J. Barnett
1826 Lord Frederick Beauclerk, D.D.
1827 H. Kingscote
1828 A. F. Greville
1829 J. Barnard
1830 Hon. G. Ponsonby
1831 W. Deedes
1832 H. Howard
1833 H. Jenner
1834 Hon. A. H. Ashley
1835 Lord Charles Russell
1836 Fourth Baron Suffield
1837 Fourth Viscount Grimston
1838 Second Marquess of Exeter
1839 Sixth Earl of Chesterfield
1840 First Earl of Verulam
1841 Second Earl of Craven
1842 Earl of March
1843 Second Earl of Ducie
1844 Sir John Bayley, second Bart.
1845 T. Chamberlayne
1846 Fourth Earl of Winterton
1847 Twelfth Earl of Strathmore
1848 Second Earl of Leicester
1849 Sixth Earl of Darnley
1850 Lord Guernsey
1851 Seventh Earl of Stamford
1852 Viscount Dupplin
1853 Marquess of Worcester
1854 Earl Vane
1855 Earl of Uxbridge
1856 Viscount Milton
1857 Sir F. H. Hervey-Bathurst, third Bart.
1858 Lord Garlies
1859 Ninth Earl of Coventry
1860 Second Baron Skelmersdale
1861 Fifth Earl Spencer
1862 Fourth Earl of Sefton
1863 Fifth Baron Suffield
1864 First Earl of Dudley
1865 First Baron Ebury
1866 Seventh Earl of Sandwich

1867 Second Earl of Verulam
1868 Second Baron Methuen
1869 Fifth Marquess of Lansdowne
1870 J. H. Scourfield
1871 Fifth Earl of Clarendon
1872 Eighth Viscount Downe
1873 Viscount Chelsea
1874 Marquess of Hamilton
1875 Sir Charles Legard, eleventh Bart
1876 Second Lord Londesborough
1877 Eighth Duke of Beaufort
1878 Second Lord Fitzhardinge
1879 W. Nicholson
1880 Sir William Hart-Dyke, seventh Bart.
1881 Lord George Hamilton
1882 Second Baron Belper
1883 Hon. Robert Grimston
1884 Fifth Earl Winterton
1885 Third Baron Wenlock
1886 Fifth Baron Lyttelton
1887 Hon. Edward Chandos Leigh
1888 Sixth Duke of Buccleuch
1889 Sir Henry James
1890 Twenty-second Baron Willoughby de Eresby
1891 V. E. Walker
1892 W. E. Denison
1893 Sixth Earl of Dartmouth
1894 Seventh Earl of Jersey
1895 Fourth Baron Harris
1896 Fourteenth Earl of Pembroke
1897 Third Earl of Lichfield
1898 Hon. Alfred Lyttelton
1899 Sir Archibald L. Smith
1900 Hon. Ivo Bligh
1901 Fourth Earl Howe
1902 A. G. Steel
1903 First Baron Alverstone
1904 Marquess of Granby
1905 C. E. Green
1906 W. H. Long
1907 First Baron Loreburn
1908 Third Earl Cawdor
1909 Tenth Earl of Chesterfield
1910 Second Earl of Londesborough
1911 First Baron Desborough
1912 Ninth Duke of Devonshire
1913 Earl of Dalkeith

1914–18 Seventh Baron Hawke
1919 First Lord Forster
1920 Fourth Earl of Ellesmere
1921 Hon. Sir Stanley Jackson
1922 First Viscount Chelmsford
1923 First Viscount Ullswater
1924 First Baron Ernle
1925 Admiral of the Fleet Sir John de Robeck, Bart.
1926 Third Viscount Hampden
1927 Third Baron Leconfield
1928 Fifth Earl of Lucan
1929 Field-Marshal Baron Plumer
1930 Sir Kynaston Studd, first Bart.
1931 First Viscount Bridgeman
1932 Viscount Lewisham
1933 First Viscount Hailsham
1934 Second Earl of Cromer
1935 Ninth Viscount Cobham
1936 Sixth Baron Somers
1937 Colonel Hon. J. J. Astor
1938 First Earl Baldwin of Bewdley
1939–45 S. Christopherson
1946 General Sir Ronald Adam
1947 Lord Cornwallis
1948 The Earl of Gowrie
1949 H.R.H. The Duke of Edinburgh
1950 Sir Pelham Warner
1951 W. Findlay*
1952 The Duke of Beaufort
1953 The Earl of Rosebery
1954 Viscount Cobham
1955 Field Marshal Earl Alexander of Tunis
1956 Viscount Monckton of Brenchley
1957 The Duke of Norfolk
1958 Marshal of the R.A.F. Viscount Portal of Hungerford
1959 H. S. Altham
1960 Sir Hubert Ashton
1961 Col. Sir William Worsley, Bart.
1962 Lt. Col. Lord Nugent
1963 G. O. Allen
1964 R. H. Twining
1965 Lt. Gen. Sir Oliver Leese
1966 Sir Alec Douglas-Home
1967 A. E. R. Gilligan
1968 R. Aird
1969 M. J. C. Allom

1970 Sir Cyril Hawker
1971 F. R. Brown
1972 A. M. Crawley
1973 Lord Caccia
1974 H.R.H. The Duke of Edinburgh
1975 C. G. A. Paris
1976 W. H. Webster
1977 D. G. Clark
1978 C. H. Palmer
1979 S. C. Griffith
1980 P. B. H. May
1981 G. H. G. Doggart
1982 Sir Anthony Tuke
1983 A. H. A. Dibbs
1984 F. G. Mann
1985 J. G. W. Davies
1986 M. C. Cowdrey*
1987 J. J. Warr

Treasurers of MCC

1866–1879 T. Burgoyne
1879–1915 Sir Spencer Ponsonby-Fane
1916–1932 Lord Harris
1932–1938 Lord Hawke
1938–1949 9th Viscount Cobham
1950–1963 H. S. Altham
1963–1964 10th Viscount Cobham
1965–1976 G. O. Allen
1976–1980 J. G. W. Davies
1980–1987 D. G. Clark
1987–1988 G. H. G Doggart

Secretaries of MCC

1822–1842 B. Aislabie
1842–1858 R. Kynaston
1858–1863 A. Baillie
1863–1876 R. A. FitzGerald
1876–1897 H. Perkins
1898–1926 Sir Francis Lacey
1926–1936 W. Findlay
1936–1952 Colonel R. S. Rait Kerr
1952–1962 R. Aird
1962–1974 S. C. Griffith
1974–1987 J. A. Bailey
1987– Colonel J. R. Stephenson

* From 1951 onwards the president's term of office begins on October 1st each year and he serves until September 30th the following year.

Note on Further Reading

The following are the principal books I have consulted in writing this book and I offer this list to readers who want to follow up aspects of the subject

Allen, David Rayvern (*Ed*) THE PUNCH BOOK OF CRICKET *Granada*

Arrowsmith, R. L. and B. J. W. Hill THE HISTORY OF I ZINGARI *Stanley Paul*

Altham, H. S. and Swanton, E. W. A HISTORY OF CRICKET *George Allen & Unwin*

Arlott, John FRED: PORTRAIT OF A FAST BOWLER *Methuen*

Arlott, John (*Ed*) JACK HOBBS *John Murray*
FROM HAMBLEDON TO LORD'S *Barry Shurlock*

Ashley-Cooper, F. S. CRICKET HIGHWAYS & BYEWAYS *George Allen & Unwin*

Bailey, Trevor SIR GARY *Collins*
WICKETS, CATCHES AND THE ODD RUN *Collins Willow*

Bailey, Thorn and Wynne-Thomas (*Eds*) WHO'S WHO OF CRICKETERS *Newnes Books*

Barker, Ralph THE CRICKETING FAMILY EDRICH *Pelham*

Benaud, Richie ON REFLECTION *Collins Willow*
THE NEW CHAMPIONS *Hodder & Stoughton*

Bolton, Geoffrey THE HISTORY OF THE OUCC *Hollywell Press, Oxford*

Bowen, Rowland CRICKET: A HISTORY OF ITS GROWTH AND DEVELOPMENT THROUGHOUT THE WORLD *Eyre & Spottiswoode*

Briggs, Asa A SOCIAL HISTORY OF ENGLAND *Penguin*

Brodribb, Gerald NEXT MAN IN *Pelham*

Brooke, Robert COLLINS WHO'S WHO OF ENGLISH FIRST CLASS CRICKET 1945–1984

Brookes, Christopher ENGLISH CRICKET *Weidenfeld & Nicolson*

Cardus, Neville CARDUS ON CRICKET *Souvenir Press*
AUTOBIOGRAPHY *Collins*
SECOND INNINGS *Collins*
FULL SCORE *Cassell*
CLOSE OF PLAY *Collins*

Cardus, Neville and Arlott John THE NOBLEST GAME *Harrap*

Cheetham, Jack 'I DECLARE' *Hodder & Stoughton*

Close, Brian I DON'T BRUISE EASILY *Macdonald & Jane's*

Compton, Denis COMPTON ON CRICKETERS – PAST & PRESENT *Cassell*

Constantine, Learie and Batchelor, Denzil	THE CHANGING FACE OF CRICKET *Eyre & Spottiswoode*
Cowdrey, Colin	MCC: THE AUTOBIOGRAPHY OF A CRICKETER *Hodder & Stoughton*
Dexter, Ted	TED DEXTER DECLARES *Stanley Paul* FROM BRADMAN TO BOYCOTT *Queen Anne Press*
D'Oliveira, Basil	TIME TO DECLARE *J. M. Dent*
Down, Michael	ARCHIE – A BIOGRAPHY OF A. C. MACLAREN *George Allen & Unwin*
Fairbrother, Jim	TESTING THE WICKET *Pelham*
Fingleton, Jack	THE IMMORTAL VICTOR TRUMPER *Collins* CRICKET CRISIS *Pavilion*
Frindall, Bill	*WISDEN* BOOK OF TEST CRICKET *Queen Anne Press*
Frith, David	THE GOLDEN AGE OF CRICKET 1890–1914 *Lutterworth Press* ENGLAND VERSUS AUSTRALIA – A PICTORIAL HISTORY *Collins Willow* THE FAST MEN *George Allen & Unwin* THE SLOW MEN *George Allen & Unwin*
Gibson, Alan	THE CRICKET CAPTAINS OF ENGLAND *Cassell* JACKSON'S YEAR *Cassell* GROWING UP WITH CRICKET *George Allen & Unwin*
Green, Benny (*Ed*)	*WISDEN* ANTHOLOGIES 1864–1900: 1900–1940: 1940–1963: *Queen Anne Press* *WISDEN* BOOK OF OBITUARIES *Queen Anne Press*
Harris, Lord and Ashley-Cooper, F. S.	LORD'S AND THE MCC *London & Counties Press Association*
Hill, Alan	HEDLEY VERITY: A PORTRAIT OF A CRICKETER *Kingswood Press*
Hobbs, Sir Jack	MY LIFE STORY *The Hambledon Press*
Hollowood, Bernard	CRICKET ON THE BRAIN *Eyre & Spottiswoode*
Insole, Douglas	CRICKET FROM THE MIDDLE *Heinemann*
James, C. L. R.	BEYOND A BOUNDARY *Hutchinson*
Knight, A. E.	THE COMPLETE CRICKETER *Methuen*
Laker, Jim	SPINNING ROUND THE WORLD *Frederick Muller* CRICKET CONTRASTS *Stanley Paul*
Lemmon, David	PERCY CHAPMAN *Queen Anne Press*
Le Quesne, Laurence	THE BODYLINE CONTROVERSY *Secker & Warburg*
Lucas, E. V. (*Ed*)	THE HAMBLEDON MEN *Henry Frowde*
Lyon, W. R.	THE ELEVENS OF THREE GREAT SCHOOLS 1805–1929 *Spottiswoode Ballantyne*
Marshall, John	THE DUKE WHO WAS CRICKET *Frederick Muller*
Martin-Jenkins, Christopher (*Ed*)	CRICKET: A WAY OF LIFE *Century* THE WHO'S WHO OF TEST CRICKETERS *Orbis*
Marwick, Arthur	BRITISH SOCIETY SINCE 1945 *Penguin*
Mason, Ronald	WALTER HAMMOND *Hollis & Carter*
May, Peter	A GAME ENJOYED *Stanley Paul*
Midwinter, Eric	W. G. GRACE: HIS LIFE AND TIMES *George Allen & Unwin*
Moorhouse, Geoffrey	LORD'S *Hodder & Stoughton*

Morrah, Patrick	ALFRED MYNN AND THE CRICKETERS OF HIS TIME *Constable*
	THE GOLDEN AGE OF CRICKET *Eyre & Spottiswoode*
O'Reilly, Bill	THE BRADMAN ERA *Collins Willow*
Parker, Eric	THE HISTORY OF CRICKET *The Lonsdale Library/Seeley Service*
Parker, Grahame	GLOUCESTERSHIRE ROAD *Pelham*
Porter, Roy	ENGLISH SOCIETY IN THE EIGHTEENTH CENTURY *Penguin*
Pawle, Gerald	R. E. S. WYATT *George Allen & Unwin*
Pollard, Jack	AUSTRALIAN CRICKET *Hodder & Stoughton*
Plumb, J. H.	ENGLAND IN THE EIGHTEENTH CENTURY (1714–1815) *Penguin*
Rait Kerr, Diana and Peebles, Ian	LORD'S 1946–70 *Harrap*
Robertson-Glasgow, R. C.	CRUSOE ON CRICKET *Alan Ross*
Robinson, Ray	ON TOP DOWN UNDER – AUSTRALIA'S CRICKET CAPTAINS *Cassell, Australia*
Rosenwater, Irving	SIR DONALD BRADMAN *Batsford*
Ross, Alan	RANJI *Collins*
Ross, Alan (*Ed*)	THE CRICKETER'S COMPANION *Eyre & Spottiswoode*
Sharpham, Peter	TRUMPER *Hodder & Stoughton*
Stevenson, John	BRITAIN 1914–45 *Penguin*
Streeton, Richard	P. G. H. FENDER *Faber*
Stollmeyer, Jeffrey	EVERYTHING UNDER THE SUN *Stanley Paul*
Swanton, E. W.	AS I SAID AT THE TIME *Collins Willow*
	CRICKET FROM ALL ANGLES *Michael Joseph*
	SORT OF A CRICKET PERSON *Collins*
	FOLLOW ON *Collins*
	GUBBY ALLEN – MAN OF CRICKET *Stanley Paul*
Swanton, E. W. (*Ed*)	BARCLAYS WORLD OF CRICKET – SECOND EDITION *Collins Willow*
Taylor, Alfred D.	ANNALS OF LORD'S AND HISTORY OF THE MCC *J. W. Arrowsmith*
Thomson, A. A.	HIRST AND RHODES *Pavilion*
Travers, Ben	94 DECLARED *Elm Tree*
Warner, Sir Pelham	GENTLEMEN V PLAYERS, 1806–1949 *Harrap*
	LORD'S 1787–1945 *Harrap*
Williams, Marcus	DOUBLE CENTURY – 200 YEARS OF CRICKET IN *THE TIMES* *Collins Willow*
	THE WAY TO LORDS: CRICKETING LETTERS TO *THE TIMES* *Collins Willow*
Wynne-Thomas, Peter	GIVE ME ARTHUR *Arthur Barker*

Index

(*Additional material for this edition on pages 356–8 has not been included.*)

O'Reilly, Bill (W. J.), 212–3, 220, 235, 347
Orwell, George, quoted, 253
Osbaldeston, Squire (George), 37, 46, *46*, 57, 58, 64, 66
Oscroft, W., 132
O'Shea, Jack, 246–7
Our Village (Mitford), 59
Oval, The (Kennington), 12, *67*, 73, 98, 108, 111, 112, 117, *134*, 141, 142, 147, 161, 186, 187, 201, 216, 222, 227, 238, 242, 262, 272, 280, 282, 293, 338, 343
Over-30s *v.* Under-30s, 121
Overs, length of, 99, 145–6
Overseas Players, 284, 286
Oxford University, 12, 14, 23, 57, 72, 84, 99, 118, 126, 158, 170, 173–4, 176, 183, 204, 210, 212, 214, 257, 276, 282, 308, 324, 342, 343
Oxford University v. Cambridge University, 14 (1957), 71–2 (1827, 1st at Lord's), 111, 126, 166, 174 (1893, 1896), 176 (1896), 189 (1913), 201, 210, 212 (1892), 214 (1920–23), 230 (1933), 239, 244, 257 (1947), 337 (1960–2), 343 (1931, 1957, 1959, 1960, 1982–3), 344 (1960, 1970, 1982)

Packer, Kerry, 318, 319, 322, 325
Pads, *see* Leg-guards
Page, M. L., 206
Paine, R. A., 178
Pakenham, Hon. W. L., 83
Pakistan, 12, 260, 273, 294, 312, 343, 348, 350, 354
Palairet, L. C. H., 166
Palairet, R. C. N., 221, 228
Palermo Park, Buenos Aires, 208
Palmer, C. H., 322, 323
Palmer, G. E., 145, 147
Parfitt, P. H., 340
Paris (city and club), 128, *128*, 137
Parker, C. W. L., 202
Parks, J. M., 296
Parr, George, *106*, 106, 107, 108, *109*, 130, 137, 144
Parsees, 144
Pataudi, Nawab of, snr, 217, 260, 343
Pataudi, Nawab of, jnr, 343, 344, 351
Patterson, W. H., 161
Paynter, E., 218, 235, 265
Peacock, Sir Kenneth, 274, 310
Pearce, Peter (Percy), 131, 136, 137
Pearce, T. N., 305
Peate, E., 144, 145, 166, 251
Peebles, Ian, 217, 254, *256*, 256, 306
Peel, R., 161, 166, 251
Pell, O. C., *106*
Pembrokeshire, 244
Penenden Heath, 73
Pepper, Cecil (C. G.), *247*, 303
Perkins, Henry, *128*, 133, *134*, 134, 135, 136, 143, 146, 151, 156, 157, 162
Perrin, P. A., 216, 275
Perth (W. A.), 305, 354
Philadelphia, 131, 144, 178, 203, 209
Phillipson, W. E., 248
Phoenix Park, Dublin, 100

Piccadilly Hotel, 227, 228
Pickering, W. P., 107
Pilch, Fuller, 48, 69, 71, 75, 82, 102, 104, *105*, *106*, 106, 120
Platts, J. T. B. D., 130
Player, John, and Sons, 202, 285, 345
Pocock, George, and 'Uncle', 114
Pollard, Dick, 248
Pollard, Jack, 294
Ponsford, W. H., 220
Ponsonby, Hon. F., later Lord Bessborough, 79, 98, 124, 128–9, 133, 136, 151
Ponsonby, Hon. Spencer, (later Sir Spencer Ponsonby-Fane), 98, 136, 143, *151*, 151, 154, 265
Ponsonby, Lord, 58
Pooley, Edward, 111
Pope, George (G. H.), 248
Porbandar, the Maharajah of, 206
Porritt, Arthur, 116
Porter, Roy, q. 19
Portman, George, 239, 263
Portman family, 25, 44
Port-of-Spain, Trinidad, 301
Pougher, A. D., 176
Presidents of MCC, 361–2
Price, Fred (W. F. F.), *266*, 304
Prichard, Matthew, 328
Prideaux, R. M., 313
Prince's Cricket Ground, 131, 135
Prince's ice-skating club, 116
Pringle, D. R., 344
Procter, Mike (M. J.), 286
Professionals, status of, 37, 39, 103–5, 109, 136, 183, 221, 232, 235, 240, 253–4, 264–5, 275, 282, 290, 305–8, 337, 342–3
Provis, Tom, 286
Prudential Insurance, 345
Pycroft, Rev. James, 72, 100

Queensland, 225, 299
Quidnuncs (Cambridge), 125, 235, 257

Rae, Allan (A. F.), 267, 268, 269, 319, 338
Rait Kerr, Colonel R. S., 243, *256*, 256, 265, 289
Rait Kerr, Diana, 27, 254, *256*, 256, 306, 308
Ramadhin, Sonny, 267, 269, 271
Ranjitsinhji, K. S., HH the Maharajah Jam Sahib of Nawanagar, 114, 117, 120, 122, 123, 156, 161, 166, 168–70, *169*, 178, 183, 190
Read, W. W., 162
Redgate, Samuel, 76–7, 83
Reed, Talbot Baines, 184
Regent's Canal, *45*, 45
Reid, John (J. R.), 259
Reynolds, Frederick, 40, 79
Reynolds, Sir Joshua, *21*
Rhoades, Cedric, 322–3
Rhodes, Harold (H. J.), 296, 298, 304
Rhodes, Wilfred, 166, 171, 172, 178, 251, 265
Rhodesia, 209

Richards, Barry (B. A.), 286
Richards, Frank, 184
Richardson, A. W., 305
Richardson, Peter (P. E.), 277, 278, 279, 288, 295
Richardson, Tom, 190
Richardson, Victor (V. Y.), 225
Riches, J. D. H., and N. V. H., 338
Richmond, 4th Duke of, *see* Lennox
Ring, Doug (D. T.), 12, 272
Ring, George and John, 37
Robertson, Dr Allen, 221
Robertson, Jack (J. D.), 243, 250, 254, 256
Robertson-Glasgow, R. C., 202, 251
Robins, R. W. V., 216, 243, 251, 256, 275, 305
Robinson, R., 43
R 101, airship, *211*
Root, Fred (C. F.), 227
Roper, A. W., 250
Rorke, Gordon (G. F.), 292, 294, 299–300, 301
Rosenwater, Irving, 218
Rowan, Lou (L. P.), 300
Royal Air Force v. Combined Services, 339
Royal Dutch Cricket Association, 286
Royal Engineers (team), 131
Royle, Rev. V. P. F. A., 140
Rules for Test Matches, 164
Russel, J. S., 157
Russell, A. C., 265
Russell, Lord Charles, 48, 104, 121
Russell, Lord John, 138
Rutherford, Harry, artist, 274
Rutter, Edward, 125, 146
Ryder, Jack, 298
Rylott, A., 131, 136

Sackville, John Frederick, *see* Dorset, 3rd Duke of
Sackville, Lord John, 39
Sadd of Cambridge, 99
Sandham, A., 265
Sandwich, 4th Earl of, 19, 20, 39
Saunders, D. W. (Canada), 150
Saunders, James, 48, 75
Schaw Park, Alloa, 100
Schools: Beaumont, 242, 338; Bell Lane, Hendon, 240; Charterhouse, 272; Cheltenham, 338; Cheltenham Grammar School, 176; Cirencester Grammar 258; Clergy Female Orphanage School, *150*, 151; Clifton, 189, 208, 338; Downside, 252; Dulwich, 352–3; Edinburgh Academy, 100; Eton, 23, 43, 57, 64, 65, 69, 84, 99, 107, 126, 128, 130, 136, *150*, 154, 158, 166, 179, 180, 209–10, 235, 244, 257, 328, 338, 339, 353; Haileybury, 338; Harrow, 43, 64, 65, 69, 99, 124, 126, 128, 130, 136, 143, *150*, 154, 166, 179, 181, 209–10, 244, 257, 328, 338, 339; Horris Hill, 211; Manchester Central Grammar, 271–2; Marlborough, 338; Old High, Edinburgh, 100; Oratory, 338;